A SPECTACULAR LEAP

A Spectacular Leap

Black Women Athletes in Twentieth-Century America

JENNIFER H. LANSBURY

The University of Arkansas Press
Fayetteville
2014

FOR JOHN

CONTENTS

ACKNOWLEDGMENTS

The only debts that are a joy to acknowledge are those one amasses during the writing of a book. That is a paraphrase of the beginning to Sarah Maza's acknowledgments in *Private Lives and Public Affairs*, which I read fifteen years ago in graduate school. It struck me then, as it does now, as a supremely appropriate way to approach acknowledging and thanking a long list of people and institutions without whom this particular book would have been a far lesser work.

The directors and staffs at the institutions I visited helped in ways that went beyond opening their facilities and retrieving materials. Before this project had even been fully conceived, the Tuskegee University Archives welcomed me, and director Cynthia Wilson arranged for me to meet and interview Alice Coachman (Davis). Gerald Parnell and the staff at Randall Library Special Collections and Archives of the University of North Carolina, Wilmington, put up with me for several days in the summer of 2005, retrieving materials, listening to the beginnings of a project, and making suggestions. I am particularly indebted to the Hubert A. Eaton family for granting me access to his papers, and many thanks to Mr. Parnell for suggesting and arranging an interview with Hubert Eaton Jr. A discussion with Mureil Dawson of the Southeastern Regional Black Archives at Florida A&M University in Tallahassee made my trip to that facility worthwhile despite the dearth of materials. Sharon Hull Smith and Loretta Divens of the Brown-Daniel Library Special Collections at Tennessee State University were a tremendous help as I pored through materials from the Ed Temple Collection during the summer of 2007. Ms. Smith arranged what turned out to be a valuable interview with Ed Temple. Christyne Douglas at the Franklin Library Special Collections at Fisk University in Nashville helped me with the Alice Coachman Davis papers. The staff at the Newspaper and Current Periodicals Reading Room at the Library of Congress assisted me for more days than I can tally. The staff at the National Archives II in College

Park, Maryland, and Mark Greek at the Martin Luther King Jr. branch of the D.C. Public Library were most helpful in helping me track down images of my athletes. Finally, the three people I interviewed—Alice Coachman Davis, Hubert Eaton Jr., and Ed Temple—tolerated my intrusion upon their lives, humored my questions, and gave me valuable hours of their time. Mrs. Davis even welcomed me into her home. I am grateful to them for sharing their stories.

At three different junctures, George Mason University provided valuable financial assistance. Twice, the McKinnon-Morton Dissertation Fellowship from the Department of History and Art History made it possible for me to travel to research facilities without dipping so deeply into my own pockets. At a later juncture, the College of Humanities and Social Sciences Fellowship allowed me to focus on my writing, which became the initial stage of this manuscript.

A number of people made important contributions in helping me arrive at the start of the project, as well as at significant points along the way. Many years ago, Dr. David Hewett fueled my interest in history, demonstrated the value of an interesting lecture (something I have never been able to emulate), and became the standard by which I measured subsequent undergraduate experiences. He is a scholar and a gentleman as well as one of the finest teachers I have ever known. In 2000, Rosie Zagarri thoughtfully asked if I had considered a course on African Americans and sport being taught by Suzy Smith in lieu of her own course on the early republic. That suggestion changed the direction of my research interest from early American child rearing and ultimately resulted in this project. Mack Holt continually recommended fellowship opportunities and suggested ways that others could best assist me. Jack Censer was there with job opportunities that enriched my experience, provided helpful income, and even encouraged me to finish. He also helped me consider the realities of the project I had chosen.

Many individuals made this a better monograph, by far. I am deeply indebted to Suzy Smith for her direction and continued support as I labored over the rewrite. She pushed me to consider and reconsider issues in both big and small ways and helped me navigate the difficult waters of constructive criticism. I appreciate her continued friendship more than I can say, and I count her recent conversion to an avid Washington Nationals fan as a major coup for the national pastime. David Wiggins has been part of this project from its inception, providing valued comments, suggestions, feedback, and support along the way. His own work in the field has challenged my thinking, and I have so appreciated his support at critical junctures. Several of my Ph.D. colleagues read and provided direction on early versions of chapters, particularly our "Murky Coffee group." My colleague Bill Carpenter has patiently listened to me ramble on more than one occasion, and reminded me that not everyone is as interested in sport as I am. We traveled the maze of grad school together, and he and his wife, Ellen, have become my good friends. Larry Levine, originally part of my committee, provided important insight on my dissertation prospectus, but passed away before I had produced a chapter for his review. His teaching and our conversations together always challenged me to think in new ways. I am grateful for the lunches and coffees we managed before he left us.

During the long transition from the conception of this project to the more expanded manuscript, my editor Larry Malley has provided experienced insight and encouragement, and regaled me with more stories than any one person should be able to remember. His patience and support during a particularly difficult time deftly guided me through to completion. I am deeply indebted to the insights of the anonymous readers that he chose to read an earlier version of the manuscript and for the ways they helped me crystallize what kind of book this would be. Chris Elzey stepped in toward the end to provide me with some excellent pointers about finding good images in the public domain; my checking account and I are indeed grateful. When my life took an unexpected turn a couple of years ago, my friend Carol Offutt told me, as good friends should do, that I had to complete this book before I could move on. My friend, neighbor, and walking buddy, Arlene Decina, was there for the day-to-day slog, listening to me rant at the process and celebrating with me over my own agonizingly slow progress. Myra Bridgeforth and Anne Mugler stepped in to rescue me from my own distress. On two separate occasions, their Poets, Writers and Artists Retreat provided the time and distance I needed to think and get to the other side of my own lethargy, as well as captive and welcoming audiences who did not fall asleep when I read sections aloud. I am especially grateful for their allowing me to crash their pre-retreat "party" in March 2013, which proved so important to the final push.

Finally, four others have been especially important to the development and completion of this book. More years ago than I wish to consider, my father instilled in me his own love of baseball as we watched games together and he taught me the ins and outs of the national pastime. Without his passing on to me the love of that sport, I do not think I would have found a home in a book involving African American women athletes. My mother, a lifelong learner, shared with me the gift and excitement of acquiring new knowledge and deep thinking. Her interest and encouragement in my education and this project never wavered. While ovarian cancer took her before she could see me usher the book manuscript through to completion, she is one of the few people who proudly read every word of my dissertation—and caught one grammatical mistake while doing so. My daughter, Anna, was nine years old when I wrote the first article that would become the impetus for this project. She is now a lovely young woman who has encouraged me through some very difficult times. My love and appreciation for her is deeper than I know how to express. Finally, it is because of my husband, John deJourno Lansbury, that this book exists at all. As I wrote, he read drafts for clarity and economy, listened to my musings, articulated ideas that were important, and lived with the project almost as deeply as I did. When he passed away from lung cancer in 2010, it was his deep desire that these athletes' stories be told and that his wife be the one to do it that, in the end, kept me going. While many things about this book have changed over the course of the last few years, I always knew it would be for him.

A SPECTACULAR LEAP

INTRODUCTION

A misty rain fell on the spectators gathered at Wembley Stadium in London, England, but the crowd was still strong at 60,000. It was the final day of track and field competition for the XIV Olympiad. Dusk was quickly approaching, but the women's high jump competition was still underway. Two athletes remained, an American by the name of Alice Coachman and the British, hometown favorite, Dorothy Tyler. With an Olympic gold medal on the line, both athletes seemed content to remain all night, if necessary, as they continued to match each other at height after height. But then at 5′6½″, neither one cleared the bar. The audience waited in the darkening drizzle while the judges conferred to determine who would be crowned the new Olympic champion. Finally, the judges ruled that one of the two athletes had indeed edged out the other through fewer missed attempts on previous heights. Alice Coachman had just become the first African American woman to win an Olympic gold medal. Her leap of 5′6⅛″ on that August evening in 1948 set new Olympic and American records for the women's high jump. The win culminated a virtually unparalleled ten-year career in which she amassed an athletic record of thirty-six track and field national championships—twenty-six individual and ten team titles. From 1939, when she first won the national championship for the high jump at the age of sixteen, she never surrendered it; a new champion came only after her retirement at the conclusion of the Olympics. While the high jump was her signature event—"a spectacular leap" that led to her 1941 victory just one of ten consecutive national titles—she also possessed speed.[1] For her prowess as a sprinter, the press dubbed Coachman, "the Tuskegee flash." For five consecutive years in the mid-1940s, her 50-meter sprint titles qualified her as the fastest woman in the United States. In 1943, she was named a member of the first All-American Women's Track and Field Team, continuing that yearly distinction until her retirement in 1948. When she returned from the Olympics to her hometown of Albany, Georgia, blacks and whites came together to celebrate her victory. And in the early 1950s, she became the first African American woman athlete to acquire a corporate endorsement when she appeared with fellow Olympic track star Jesse Owens in print advertisements for Coca-Cola.

But the glory of being an Olympic champion faded with the passing years and, in time, few people knew of her athletic feats, even in her hometown. Roughly twenty years after winning the gold medal, the extent to which history had been rewritten became shockingly clear. While teaching physical education in her hometown during the 1960s, she gave her students an assignment as they began their unit on the sport—read and report on the history of track and field. One of the students brought in a book that stated Wilma Rudolph was the first African American woman to win an Olympic gold medal. "But Mrs. Davis," her students remarked, "we thought you said you were the first." Coachman had spoken with them in the past about her Olympic experience. She informed them that the book was incorrect, but they remained skeptical. Reminiscing about the incident years later, she recalled that the only way to convince them was to bring her gold medal into class the following day.[2]

This is the story of African American women's relationship with competitive sport during the twentieth century. It is a relationship that allowed athletically talented black women, many of them from poor backgrounds, to attend college, travel, and experience life in ways that otherwise would have been unknown to them. It is a relationship that fostered widespread support and acclaim from members of the black community. And it is a relationship in which the athletes confronted and challenged contemporary perceptions of what it meant to be a woman and black in American society, and what it meant—both in white society and the black community—to be at the forefront of the struggle for civil rights.

When African American women began playing competitive sport in the 1920s, they did so through the support of their own, segregated communities. These communities often saw sport as a vehicle for both teamwork and competition, as well as individual and collective achievement in the face of a dominant white society. Coaches and mentors, neighbors, friends, entrepreneurs, and patrons collectively discovered young women who were athletically gifted and then developed a path for them to train and compete. Sometimes there was conflict about what was best for the athletes versus the community; nevertheless, high school girls received strong support from black communities whose goal was to help them succeed. And succeed they did, in track and field, tennis, and basketball. Black businesses sponsored industrial teams, establishing leagues for women to compete. Programs in high schools and historically black colleges and universities allowed for training and competition, enabling black women to explore their athletic talent. Black coaches scoured surrounding states for talented high school girls, and suddenly poor rural and working-class women found their route to college through competitive sport and work-study programs. College meant both advanced education and national and international travel as competition opportunities opened up at home and abroad. And as black women athletes competed against whites, they brought home national championships and Olympic medals. This pattern of community support and athletic success played out repeatedly over the decades of the twentieth century.

Black women's experience with sport was far from idyllic, however, often mirroring those of their white counterparts. Throughout the twentieth century, women athletes had to navigate stereotypes about their femininity, sexuality, and economic standing.[3] Sport was the playground for men, really always had been. As far back as the ancient Greek Olympics, women had been excluded from participating in, even watching, sporting events, and the modern world was not terribly different. When U.S. women did begin to play sports in the late nineteenth century, Americans questioned which sports they should participate in, how they should participate, what clothing they should wear, and whether competition, in a fashion similar to men, was appropriate for the "fair sex." Class identity combined with gender and prevailing notions of femininity to further label and constrain women's relationship with sport. When track and field and basketball became labeled as working-class sports, women who participated were characterized by disparaging gender stereotypes that questioned their femininity. As a sport of the elite, men and women who played tennis had to conform to its rigid social expectations. But for women, gender expectations were bound to class identity as well. Hitting the ball with too much power could result in masculine, working-class labels. In short, black and white women alike who participated in sport were often scrutinized, questioned, challenged, qualified, and even ridiculed by white society.

What African American women athletes had to contend with that white women did not were race and racism.[4] This may seem like an obvious statement, but it changed the dynamic of their relationship with sport in dramatic ways. These athletes had to deal both with how African Americans perceived them in terms of gender and class and how whites perceived them in terms of race, gender, and class. Race, then, became a defining element for these women among both African Americans and whites. In white society, they sometimes joined with white women athletes to combat common gender stereotypes that suggested that women who played sport were too masculine. In truth, however, race always made a difference. Black women had to contend with racial stereotypes that white women did not, such as the hypersexualized black female or the natural black athlete. Since race was a rallying cry within their own community, gender and class stereotypes persisted on a different level. The question for some within the black community became how to help black women athletes "overcome" their working-class backgrounds and combat gender stereotypes in white society. Excelling in athletic competition was, for many within the black community, significant for the race as a whole. As such, an important, though sometimes conflicted, relationship developed between black women athletes and their mentors, and those within the community who were connected to the broader civil rights campaign. Indeed, the way these women and their mentors navigated racism and racial relationships was one of the most compelling aspects of their careers.

While black women athletes competed, African Americans spent much of the twentieth century writing, marching, boycotting, and struggling to acquire equality under American law. While progress was slow, life in the United States looked very different for a woman of color competing in the 1920s, when black women first came on the African American sporting scene, than for one competing in the 1980s, when black women had been ruling the sport of national track and field for fifty years. Besides changes in the broader society, the world of sport had experienced its own transformation. In 1946, Kenny Washington and Woody Strode broke the thirteen-year exclusion of blacks in the NFL; four years later, Earl Lloyd broke the color barrier in the NBA. But no breakthrough during mid-century had the same impact on sport and society as the one Jackie Robinson made in the national pastime. When Robinson broke the color barrier in major league baseball in 1947, he became the standard against which other sports stories involving African

Americans were compared. His athletic performance, racial pride, and willingness to let racial slurs roll off his back affirmed African American athletic ability, challenged prevailing concepts of racial inferiority, and made at least some whites consider race relations in a new light. White ballplayers refused to play with him. Eventually they became his friends. Managers who had been raised in the South worried that they could not overcome their own prejudice. They did. Teammates, coaches, and managers came to defend him—both his abilities as a ballplayer and his value as an individual. Moreover, he stood as a symbol for African Americans against racial discrimination and prejudice throughout his life. He was a proud black man in a largely segregated, white America, whom whites and blacks alike came to admire and respect. His career and his position in America following his retirement provided a racial context for many within the black community to interpret other advances in sport, including those of African American women.

Throughout their athletic careers, then, black women athletes found themselves at the forefront of the racism that characterized much of the American twentieth century. When they were not pushing back against color barriers, stereotypes, and perceptions of white America, they were often being scrutinized and groomed by black communities that wanted to ensure they were acceptable race representatives. They did not always accept their place as race heroes. Some athletes fell into the role more willingly and naturally than others. Some vocally rejected it, wishing instead that their careers could be acknowledged on nonracial terms. Such rejection could lead the adulation, celebration, and support of black civil rights sport leaders to turn on a dime. Even so, the desire and sheer force of will of black women athletes to compete in a society that marginalized them made a difference over time. The advances were sometimes small. In the 1940s, it was a matter of whether they got noticed in the sports pages of the white newspapers. In another twenty years, however, black women track and field athletes were on their way to becoming "our girls" in the American press. And by the 1980s, they had become a dominant force in the world of U.S. sport, even as they continued to confront gender and racial stereotypes. Their story is one of hard work, resilience, and perseverance in the face of an American society that initially scorned and ignored them, and finally came to accept them, albeit sometimes still in racial terms.

The focus of each chapter in the narrative that follows is an individual athlete, a woman whose combination of dedication, training, athletic skills, and timing resulted in an exceptional career.[5] Ora Washington was a champion tennis player and basketball star in the black community beginning in the late 1920s. When white organizations erected color lines to bar black players, athletes like Washington found athletic opportunities within sporting teams and organizations that African Americans created for themselves. The 1940s and 1950s produced two important black women athletic champions in two very different sports. Track and field was one of the few sports in the country that permitted competition among and between African Americans and whites at the national level. Alice Coachman, the Olympic champion track and field athlete of the 1940s, and women like her, reveled in the opportunity to compete nationally. Althea Gibson was an amateur tennis player of the 1950s who became the first African American Wimbledon and U.S. national champion. She was a natural with a tennis racquet, but she was also a tough, tomboyish black woman from Harlem, a stark contradiction to white tennis society. Sprinter Wilma Rudolph, a track star of the late 1950s and early 1960s, overcame crippling childhood illnesses to become a triple Olympic gold-medal winner. During her time as America's sprint queen, black women track athletes became the United States' best hope to defeat the Russian women in track in a world locked in a bitter Cold War. The racial turbulence of the late 1960s and the rebirth of the women's movement in the 1970s is the backdrop for the story of Wyomia Tyus. A champion sprinter and Olympic gold medalist, her career occurred during a time of profound changes for women and blacks in America. By the 1980s, African Americans were the standard bearers of women's track and field. Raised in the wake of the Title IX legislation that opened up more sporting opportunities for women, Jackie Joyner-Kersee earned the title of "world's greatest female athlete" when she won six Olympic medals and set eight world records. She emerged from the ghetto into a world of international track and field that, with its million-dollar endorsement contracts, looked very different from the sport Alice Coachman, Wilma Rudolph, or Wyomia Tyus competed in.

These are not mini-biographies, nor are they meant to be. But most of the athletes are not well known today, and, therefore, some biographical context is necessary in each chapter. Their individual stories reveal interesting and complex individuals—their struggles and triumphs; what they accomplished and what they had to give up in the process; the important people and communities that helped them achieve athletic success; and the ways in which they were likable, and sometimes, not so likable. Their stories unveil striking similarities. All of the athletes came from poor beginnings. Many of their childhoods were mixed with pleasant memories and hard times. While their families were intact, the home lives for many of them were not always idyllic. All six were natural athletes and played multiple sports well, with basketball being a common denominator among them all. Strong male mentors often made their educations and athletic careers possible, and many of them received invitations to leave home as teenagers to train elsewhere. For all but one, sport was their vehicle to a college education that probably would have eluded them otherwise. After they retired from sports, most of them struggled with life to varying degrees; they often had a hard time finding steady work despite their athletic fame and college education. And those who had broken racial, gender, or sporting barriers questioned their place or, more accurately, lack of place in American popular culture.

Two of the similarities are particularly striking. First, all of these women used sport as a way to broaden the typical life that lay ahead of rural or working-class African American women of the period. Most poor black women of the first two-thirds of the twentieth century found work in agriculture, service, or industrial sectors.[6] While growing numbers of historically black colleges throughout the country were available to teach trades and provide higher education, many African American families could not afford tuition. Beginning in the 1930s, sport and work-study programs that black colleges like Tuskegee Institute and Tennessee State University extended to gifted athletes became their path to a skilled trade and/or higher education. By the late 1970s, white universities like UCLA were actively recruiting black women athletes and offering full athletic scholarships. Moreover, athletic competition provided travel experiences that many of these women would otherwise have been unable to afford. All the athletes traveled widely, first nationally, and by mid-century, internationally. Second, strong, influential, African American men made possible the athletic and college careers of these athletes. Most often the mentors were coaches, and they guided a number of other young African American women who excelled at sport through the same path. Most of them viewed sport as a way for their young athletic charges to better themselves, and they not only helped train the athletes but also encouraged them educationally and socially. The relationships between black women athletes and male coaches, mentors, and promoters, then, point to the community nature of betterment efforts within African American society, efforts that could easily cross gender barriers established by the dominant society. At a time when many in white America discouraged women from entering competitive sport, African American men were finding ways and developing programs to give young black women athletes a way to succeed in the sporting world and an opportunity at a better life.

Of course, using the stories of six athletes as a narrative for this history brings up the question of representation. Is it appropriate to think that these women could represent the many other black women athletes who competed throughout the decades of the twentieth century? There were other exceptional athletes over the years and many others who were very good. There were African American women who competed on white teams in the North that do not appear in depth in these pages. But the relationship that the athletes in this book had with sport clearly represents a path that many other African American women of their generations used to escape poor, rural, or working-class backgrounds; travel extensively; secure a college education; and reject the cultural stereotypes of African American women. Some additional names of athletes appear throughout the text as they intersect with the athlete in each chapter. Even so, many others are absent. I hope they, in some way, still see their story in these pages. In the end, it is a story of athletic women who faced and overcame a number of challenges as they strove for excellence, whose black communities gave them strong support, and who pushed back against stereotypes that attempted to define who they were as athletes and African American women. It is a story of champions whose talent, hard work, and determination to push back against racial and gender stereotypes resulted in a spectacular leap for black women athletes of the twentieth century.

ONE

Queen of the Courts

Ora Washington and the Emergence of America's First Black Female Sport Celebrity

In the summer of 1929, a twenty-eight-year-old African American woman by the name of Ora Washington stepped onto a tennis court in New Jersey. Across the net was Frances Gittens, and the two were competing for the top women's prize in black tennis. Washington had already made a name for herself in the African American community as a four-time consecutive national doubles champion. The national singles title, however, had eluded her. She was not an especially powerful player. But she was steady, intense, and determined. More than one opponent had been defeated by Washington's sense of superiority and competitiveness, feeling beaten almost before the first serve crossed the net. Washington lost the first set 4–6. But those who had seen her play before knew the game was far from over. She came back to take the second set 6–4, and to dominate the third, 6–2. The prize she had sought since entering the game in the fall of 1924 was finally hers. Washington was the women's champion of all of black tennis.[1]

Following that victory in the summer of 1929, she eventually went on to become a national sports star within the black community. As adept at basketball as she was tennis, she alternated the seasons between the two sports. She became the undisputed "queen" of African American tennis, winning the women's singles an unprecedented eight times. Her prowess on the basketball court was every bit as storied where, as a semiprofessional player, she led the Philadelphia Tribunes as captain for eleven consecutive years as they regularly dominated other white and African American teams. Black weeklies featured her in their sports pages. Sportswriters encouraged fans in cities lucky enough to host black tennis or Tribune basketball games not to miss the significant opportunity to watch the court queen play. She became, for a time, a celebrity within the black community, its first female sports star. While most of white America during the interwar years probably never heard of her, some whites in her hometown of Philadelphia would have known of her athletic exploits. And at least one white daily in the Jim Crow South, writing of the Tribunes' forthcoming visit to their city, referred to the "indomitable, internationally famed and stellar" Ora Washington.[2]

The most remarkable aspect of Washington's athletic career was that she rose to such heights as a working-class black female in an overwhelmingly white, male domain. American society often constrained black women of the interwar years in their athletic choices—the sports they had access to and the athletes they were allowed to compete against. An unofficial color line in white tennis that barred black players prevented Washington from testing herself against the white women champions of the day. Yet, African Americans began their own tennis association where tennis enthusiasts could compete and crown a champion. Coming from the black working-class Germantown neighborhood of Philadelphia, Washington did not really fit into the high-class image of tennis. But the elites who ran black tennis were more accepting of working-class entrants to the game than their white counterparts, and she made a name for herself on the black circuit. Not unlike the Negro baseball leagues, Washington had to content herself with being the champion of *black* tennis. It was, however, a vibrant black tennis. Even as her race limited her competition choices, contemporary perceptions of American womanhood should have limited the sports she played. By the 1930s, team sports like basketball were "off limits" to respectable white women. But within the black community, the status of women's basketball was not so clear-cut. While some African Americans insisted that black women withdraw from the sport, other black communities challenged this notion by continuing an exciting network of women's basketball.[3]

As the black community confronted entrenched segregation during the opening decades of the twentieth century, it provided an active sporting scene that helped make Washington's career possible. Yet African Americans did not always agree on the best ways to combat racism, and black women athletes like Washington could find themselves the target of a black community at odds with itself. Washington entered competitive basketball at the very time American society turned against respectable women playing a competitive form of the sport. Eschewing the trend, Washington, her teammates, and her competitors played the sport with abandon and played it to win in ways that contrasted with what it meant to be a "lady." Moreover, their manner off the court left them open to ridicule by those who were concerned by what they deemed "low-class" behavior. Even in tennis, Washington never worried about her image as a plain, working-class, relentless player, refusing to conform to the rigid social expectations of that game. When she rose to unprecedented heights within the black tennis world, some within that organization would have preferred a different type of tennis queen. In an era when African Americans often sought solid middle-class role models and intellectuals as representatives of their best and brightest, a working-class woman who happened to excel at basketball and played tennis her own way did not always seem to fit the mold.

As a black female athlete and sports star within the black community, Washington's life should have been conscripted by any number of limitations and conventions of the day. Basketball and tennis could be a dicey mix in interwar America, with one a sport on the decline for "respectable ladies" and the other largely a passion of the elite. Even as the black community facilitated her rise, some individuals and leaders within that community expected Washington to change her rough, outer exterior. Yet Washington defined what it meant to be the first female sport celebrity in the black community, pushing back against contemporary norms of respectability and African American expectations and playing the sports she could get access to on her own terms. Philadelphia ended up being an athletic "land of promise" for Washington; but like so many other African Americans of the early twentieth century, her life began in the South.

From Lynchburg to Philadelphia— Washington's Early Years

While we know a good bit about Ora Washington's impressive athletic career, much of her life off the tennis and basketball courts remains a mystery. Such obscurity in her story is fairly typical of a black woman of Washington's rural, then working-class, background coming of age during the early twentieth century. In contrast to African American intellectuals or even members of the middle class, precious few of the black community's poor left written accounts of their past. What have survived are largely family stories passed down through the generations. Although the bits and pieces of Washington's past make her story expansive when compared to the many athletes she played against and alongside whom we know almost nothing about, we long to know more about black America's first female sports celebrity.[4]

Still, Washington's story is similar to many African Americans of this era who were born in the South, but eventually made their way north to escape the blight and poverty that had come to define that region during the twentieth century's early decades. Born the fifth of nine children around the turn of the century on a family farm in Caroline County, Virginia, Washington's family was more fortunate than most.[5] Her parents—James Thomas (Tommy) Washington and Laura Young Washington—actually belonged to a small community of African Americans who owned their own farmland. Their good fortune likely dated back to the early years of Reconstruction when freed slaves in the area spent the money they earned through the laying of new rail lines on local land. One of the better-off families in a community of accomplished farmers, Tommy Washington was a good farmer. Tobacco was their biggest money crop. But the Washingtons also grew corn, wheat, and rye for sale after threshing and grinding it into flour, as well as the vegetables they needed for their own table. They also raised hogs and some occasional cows and sold the meat. Washington's father divided the work between the crops, outside, and the household, inside. He did not favor his girls working outside with the crops, so the boys helped in the fields while the girls worked in the house. For someone of the young Washington's athletic aptitude, her consignment to household duties was likely a frustration. Up until the difficulties with drought and boll weevil that drove many African Americans from the land, this is how the family made their living.[6]

Washington's father was known as a good farmer, a "church man," and a person dedicated to doing what he could for his children. By the end of her grade-school years, however, Tommy Washington, a widower from the time his wife died giving birth to their ninth child, was finding it increasingly difficult to support nine children. Washington became one of the first children to make the journey north, joining her Aunt Mattie in the Germantown section of Philadelphia at some point in the mid-1910s.[7]

The Washingtons were part of a tide of African Americans who relocated from the rural South to the urban North during the first decades of the twentieth century. The reasons for this mass migration stemmed both from problems with southern agriculture and opportunities in northern industry. In the South, increasing agricultural mechanization made it more and more difficult for African American laborers to find work. Pest infestation like the boll weevil coupled with flooding decimated southern crops, making sharecropping families and those like the Washingtons who owned their land especially vulnerable. Moreover, the lynching of black men and other sustained racial violence in the South also contributed to the lure of permanent relocation. The North, in contrast, held possibilities of industrial jobs, and such possibilities increased as the country moved closer to joining the allied cause in World War I. At the beginning of the century, around 90 percent of the nation's 8 million African Americans lived in the South. During the first decades of the twentieth century, roughly 2 million of this population moved to the country's northern and western cities. This Great Migration, as it is now known, transformed America's racial geography.[8]

The promise of a better life in the North—better jobs, education, the opportunity to vote—caused many southern blacks to flee the harsh conditions they were living under in the South's cities, towns, and rural areas. Those already in the North encouraged friends and family members to join them, thus facilitating the movement of the nation's African American population. Black newspapers also encouraged the migration, as northern newspapers began circulating more freely between those traveling back and forth to visit family members who had moved and those still living "back home." The first to resettle not only sent encouragement but also made it easier for those who would travel later, further fueling relocation. The steady stream of African American migrants relied on kinship networks comprised of extended families and friends already in place in the North and en route to their destination to help with housing and jobs. These networks reduced the burden and expense of moving as a family, parents sending children ahead to live with aunts, uncles, cousins, even close friends, until money could be saved or jobs secured. The result was the establishment of whole new black communities in enclaves of northern cities.

Life in these new enclaves brought with it familiar challenges, but also an unexpected benefit. On the one hand, blacks competed with native-born and immigrant whites for available work. White working-class men and women were resentful of the influx of blacks and eastern European immigrants looking to take existing jobs. While war industry brought new opportunities during the latter half of the 1910s, whiter-looking immigrants, even with their poor English skills, often won out in the labor market over African Americans. Blacks that could find work suffered in terms of wages, which were lower than their white counter-parts. This crowding and competition for jobs created significant labor strife, particularly with the conclusion of WWI when America's work-force swelled once again with returning servicemen. And while African Americans did not face the stringent Jim Crow humiliation of the South, northern racism could be virulent, making the promises of a better life seem, at times, like a pipe dream. On the other hand, the rise of black communities led to the flowering of black thought, artistry, and culture that came to be known as the Harlem Renaissance. Novelists, poets, and artists opened up black life, exposing the joys and stark sorrows of being African American. Intellectuals probed black thought, generating pow-erful discussions on the present and future of African Americans in the United States. Talented black musicians cemented a uniquely African American sound through new compositions, ushering in the "Jazz" age. New York is best known for this renaissance of black culture, but other cities with new sizable black populations, such as Chicago and Kansas City, experienced this expression as well.[9]

In this context of promised opportunity and a culture on the cusp of renewal, Washington's father sent her to Philadelphia to live with her aunt Mattie. There were other cultural developments that would spark Washington's interest, however—America was on the brink of a "golden age" of sport. For women especially, the early decades of the twentieth cen-tury were a sort of an athletic "coming of age." With a growing black com-munity and an increasing national obsession with athletics, Philadelphia was about to become a land of opportunity for black Americans interested in sports.

Becoming the Queen of Black Tennis

Although American women had been involved in sports since the latter part of the nineteenth century, their participation was initially restricted largely to the elite women's colleges of the East. American society's prevailing notions of middle-class white femininity at the time supported women's participation in exercise and, eventually, more active sports. In a culture that confined women to marriage and the home, women were encouraged toward physical activity in order to "fortify their constitutions" and further develop their beauty, thereby increasing their marriage prospects. Vassar College drilled its students in calisthenics, a forerunner to sports, from the school's earliest days. A portion of each school day was devoted to physical exercise, and students were required to participate as part of their "college duties."[10] By 1865, just four years after Vassar's founding, the college had constructed a gymnasium. Before the turn of the century, students at the school were enjoying a variety of sport activities and intramural competition, such as archery, baseball, basketball, rowing, tennis, and track. When Smith College was established ten years after Vassar, it also required calisthenics. By the 1890s, "Smithies" were playing both baseball and basketball, and intramural sports at Wellesley and Byrn Mawr followed before the close of the century.[11]

With athletics a regular part of women's college curriculums by the turn of the century, these young middle- and upper-class women were reluctant to leave sports behind upon graduation. Athletic clubs were popular among men, but most of them excluded women. Some women formed their own clubs, such as the Ladies Club for Outdoor Sports in Staten Island and the Crescent City Archery Club in New Orleans. The wealthiest of the graduates continued sports via the country club, where they could enjoy swimming, horseback riding, archery, croquet, tennis, and golf. This venue of exclusive clubs and resorts allowed women to pursue sports within an already established upper-class culture of leisure.[12]

By the last decade of the nineteenth century, many women were also caught up in the bicycling craze that swept the nation. The bicycle's acceptance in American popular culture constituted a significant change for women. Other forms of outdoor exercise and sport had been private, as in the case of walking, or separated into a distinct sphere, as with exercise and sport programs in women's colleges and clubs. Bicycling gave American women a form of sanctioned, public, outdoor exercise; with society's general approval, thousands of women took up cycling. The sport did attract some critics, though, who insisted that riding too much would cause physiological problems, including damage to the uterus and spine, and hardening of the facial muscles into a "bicycle face." These warnings did little to stave off the enthusiasm for bicycling, however, or to discourage these largely middle-class women to look for other sports to pursue. They took this newly discovered interest in sports with them to high schools and colleges, expanding the earlier movement begun at the nation's elite women's colleges. By the dawn of the twentieth century, a variety of sport opportunities were available to middle- and upper-class women.[13]

The reality for African American and working-class women, however, was far different. These women had little time, opportunity, or energy to journey into what surely much have seemed luxurious, leisure-time activities of the white upper classes. Yet a small and important opening into sport for working-class women that occurred in the first decade of the century eventually became the venue that would introduce Ora Washington to the world of black sport. This opening was part of a broad reforming impulse designed at curing societal problems that ran throughout segments of America's middle class and took on various forms, such as temperance, housing reform, and poverty. The "child-saving" reform was one such cause, focusing on issues such as child labor, education, and health. Part of this campaign involved finding a venue other than city streets for poorer children and teens to gather, and encouraging them in physical and moral instruction. Organizations like the Playground Association of America, Young Women's Christian Association (YWCA), settlement houses, and even public schools provided opportunities for young girls from working-class families to engage in various athletic activities and groups. African American versions of these organizations provided an outlet for black women. The one that did so for Washington was the black Germantown YWCA.[14]

African American women became associated with the YWCA as an outgrowth of their active club network of the late nineteenth century. When the first Y was founded in Dayton, Ohio, in the 1890s, others quickly sprang up in cities along the eastern seaboard. Members of the association worked to address the needs of women by creating a nurturing environment within the organization and offering programs to improve the lives and working conditions of young black women. The early organization also included a strong religious component, a means of bringing about the Kingdom of God among women, reflected in its regular offering of Bible study. After WWI, however, there was an increasing shift away from overtly religious programs toward an emphasis on the social gospel. Beyond Sunday School and athletics, YWCAs also provided training in trades applicable to young women—such as dress-making, office work, and hairdressing—as well as general development classes such as singing, English, and composition and letter writing. The Y also offered classes in citizenship, particularly following the ratification of the Nineteenth Amendment in 1920 that gave women the right to vote. These offerings, focused at assimilation to white standards, stood in contrast to the simultaneous importance of blackness reflected in the cultural outpouring of the Harlem Renaissance, exposing the duality experienced by black Americans.[15]

In addition to improving the lives of African American working-class women, members of the YWCA were also caught up in the "moral panic" of early twentieth-century American society, thought to stem from increasing numbers of young black women in America's northern cities. This panic led women members to adopt two opposite, though related, approaches. The black middle class sought both a safe environment for black women to gather and a haven to protect them from unfounded accusations of sexual misconduct. But working-class women were also thought to be a threat to the progress of the race in white society. This belief resulted in efforts to reform errant behavior in a private, structured environment and rescue the streets from vice. The "class-privileged" women who formed the core of the Y administration shared a belief that Christian sisterhood, and the transfer of values from the private realm to the public, was the path to building a better world. They made sure that the women who staffed the Y were "role models in the pursuit of excellence." But they were also participating in a middle-class project aimed at emphasizing class differences and bringing working-class women's conduct more closely in line with black Christian women.[16]

This impulse of black middle-class women to both help and reform the black working poor and the swelling African American population in the Philadelphia enclave of Germantown combined to produce the opening, in 1918, of the "colored" Germantown YWCA. Black women had been shut out of the Germantown YWCA run by white women of the community for thirty years. But a doubling of the Germantown black population during WWI prompted black women leaders of the community to petition the white-run organization in December 1917 for their own, separate association. The young women interested in a colored association cited the need for services specific to their needs, such as a day nursery, educational classes, boarding rooms for young girls and, in what may have seemed like wishful thinking at the time, a swimming pool. The women also proposed that, if the white YWCA would pay for a secretary to lead the project of developing the separate black facility, the black community would raise the money necessary to fund the remainder of the first year's budget. With funds raised and a facility located, the African American branch of the Germantown YWCA opened its doors on 17 November 1918. Celebrated poet and NCAAP field secretary James Weldon Johnson gave the main address on Friday evening, billed as "patriotic night" of the weeklong festivities celebrating the chapter's opening. By the end of the week, membership in the new organization totaled 803 women. The facility, with its classroom space, gymnasium, pool, and tennis courts, offered a variety of programs, classes, and activities for young women to advance themselves academically and occupationally; foster exercise and health; and, always important for this reforming organization, form clubs to develop healthy relationships and better their character. It also opened its doors for cultural events that celebrated black heritage and fostered race pride. By the early 1920s, the black Germantown YWCA was a center of activity and pride for the African American community in Philadelphia.[17]

Why or even exactly when in the early 1920s Washington began using the sport facilities of the Germantown YWCA is unclear. There is little evidence to suggest that her family was even particularly athletic, although most of the Washington men enjoyed participating in community baseball games. Yet what became clear rather quickly was that this particular Washington had natural athletic abilities, which she began displaying on the YWCA's tennis courts.[18]

At a time when organized black tennis was still in its infancy, the Germantown Y was deservedly proud of its courts. Barred from the clubs where whites played tennis, upper-class African Americans had been playing the sport on their own, mostly in northern cities, since the latter part of the nineteenth century.[19] It did not take long for some loose organization to occur, and players along the northeastern seaboard, from Washington, D.C., to the New England states, began participating in invitational matches hosted by the African American Ideal and Turf Tennis Clubs of New York. By 1898, such joint efforts had formalized themselves somewhat into the first African American Interstate Tournament, held at the Chautauqua Tennis Club in Philadelphia, another African American club. This interstate tournament rotated among various northern cities for the next several years. But without an organizing body there were few standards and little regulation. A meeting in November 1916 brought interested club representatives together to discuss the establishment of a national association. Organizers hoped that such an association would bring African American tennis enthusiasts and players into closer association, improve club standards, and provide for the formation of new clubs; establish an annual national championship tournament; regulate tournaments and generally promote a standardized form of the game among African Americans. Delegates from eleven tennis clubs scattered along the Atlantic seaboard attended the meeting to discuss the formation of such an organization. From that meeting, the American Tennis Association (ATA) began with an initial membership of twenty-three clubs. Indeed, the Germantown YWCA's formation just two years later and the historic connection of black tennis with the city of Philadelphia may explain the organization's desire to provide courts for their members.[20]

Washington's entry into sport and her ascendancy in black tennis coincided with a rapid growth in women's sports following the end of World War I and the dawn of the 1920s. This growth was part of a general trend in American society toward additional forms of entertainment and leisure. During the late nineteenth and early twentieth centuries, workers had fought and won the rights to eight-hour workdays, reduced workweeks, and, in some industries, even paid vacations. American workers now looked for ways to fill these new leisure hours. While local saloons had been the prominent after-work gathering places during the late nineteenth century, an increasing number of leisure activities now became available—amusement parks, dance halls, nickelodeons, and movie theaters, as well as a growing number of sporting events. Moreover, with commercial packaging and mass marketing on the rise, American businesses recognized new profit opportunities—in the mass marketing of leisure and recreation equipment, athletic and sporting wear, and public sporting events.

In this new era of expanded leisure, changes in communication and media helped fuel the trend. At first hesitant that radio would cut into attendance at games, baseball club owners soon discovered that live broadcasts expanded their fan base geographically, increasing ballpark attendance. As radio carried more sporting events into American homes across the country and newsreel coverage recapped sporting events in movie theaters, sport personalities became full-blown celebrities. Athletes like baseball star Babe Ruth, heavyweight-boxing champion Jack Dempsey, football halfback Red Grange, and golfer Bobby Jones captured the popular entertainment imagination of the period. Women athletes also enjoyed celebrityhood. In 1926, Gertrude Ederle became only the sixth person and the first woman to swim the English Channel, setting a new record by shaving two hours off the times of the men that had preceded her. A year later, Helen Wills captured the women's singles title at Wimbledon, the first of eight for the tennis star who came to be known as "our Helen." Americans were indeed in the midst of a "golden age of sports," and women wanted to participate. And participate they did, as scores of black and white working-class women now began entering the world of women's athletics. Ora Washington was no exception. In the midst of this sport explosion in the United States, she discovered, like black and working-class women throughout the United States, that her local YWCA provided a way for her to explore and develop her ability with a tennis racquet. In the wake of this development, it was time for Washington's path to intersect with the American Tennis Association.[21]

As is true of so much of Washington's story, we know little of what inspired her to begin pursuing championship tennis. Perhaps it was her intensely competitive drive. Or, as was the case with many African American sportswomen of the period, perhaps she encountered a mentor who encouraged her and helped pave the way. What does surface from the press accounts, however, is the picture of someone who did not labor for long in tournament play before she began winning ATA-sanctioned city and state championships. Her first victory of note came in 1924 when she won the city championship in Wilmington, Delaware, sweeping the women's singles, doubles, and mixed doubles titles. A year later, she upset the reigning, three-time ATA women's champion, Isadore

("Izzy") Channels, to take the New York City and state championships. That same summer, less than a year after she had started tournament play, she teamed with another Philadelphia native, Lula Ballard—who also got her start at the Germantown Y—to win the women's doubles title at the ATA nationals. By the time association ratings came out for 1925, Washington was ranked third, bested only by the new national champion Ballard and former champion Izzy Channels.[22]

For the next three years, Washington, Ballard, and Channels ruled the world of black women's tennis. Ballard and Channels exchanged the singles title, even as Washington and Ballard ruled the women's doubles. While Washington could not seem to best her two rivals at the national level, she beat them often enough at the state level to keep things interesting. In July 1927, she played an increasingly familiar style of play—a dominant net game with an ability to lure her opponent out of position—to defeat fellow Philadelphian Lula Ballard in what must have been a particularly satisfying win at the Pennsylvania Tennis Open. She retained the title in 1928, again defeating Ballard. And while Washington remained number three in the 1926 and 1927 rankings behind the two multiple-time national champions, the *Chicago Defender* still called her "a dangerous contender for championship honors." The *Defender* encapsulated the dominance of the three when they assessed the women's field at the beginning of 1928 national tournament play, suggesting that "the triumvirate of Miss Ballard, Miss Washington and Miss Channels, any one of whom might come through to the title," was virtually unbeatable.[23]

This women's triumvirate may have dominated black women's tennis of the late 1920s, but they were far from the first to vie for the championship. African American women were playing tennis before the founding of the ATA; organizers who met in November 1916 to form the association included a women's singles title in the first set of national championships played the following year. Lucy Slowe captured this first national ATA women's title held in Baltimore in 1917. By 1924, two more events that included women had been added—women's doubles and mixed doubles titles. Unfortunately, most of the women's singles champions that ruled the ATA in its early years come down to us merely as names on a page. We can learn where they were from, when they won and lost in the tournaments of black tennis and, sometimes, the techniques that marked their style of play, but the existing records provide little else. Isadore Channels was known for her uncanny ability to keep a ball in play. Edgar Brown, her contemporary in the men's division, longed to see her afforded the opportunity to take on French tennis sensation of the period, Suzanne Lenglen, suggesting that she would "hold her own with the best tournament players of the world." If Washington's story has holes, these other champions are almost completely illusive.[24]

Women had long found a comfortable sporting home within tennis for two reasons.[25] First, neither men nor women played the sport very strenuously in its early years, thereby making it suitable in the eyes of American society for the more fragile female body. Second, most of the major tournaments, including Wimbledon and the National AAU Women's Championships, were amateur events until the 1960s. Amateur athletics lent an air of suitability for females as opposed to the "shady" world of professional sports, where athletes played for money rather than the love of the sport. Acceptance in the amateur realm was not unqualified, however. The press commented on women who played the game with too much power, or in too "manly" of a way, as in the case of white stars Helen Wills or Alice Marble.[26]

Indeed, women had it even better in the ATA than in white tennis. In addition to playing in tournaments, black women also served in places of leadership within the organization. As early as 1924, ATA members had elected Laura Junior of Philadelphia first vice president of the association. Moreover, whereas white amateur tennis discouraged play by women that bordered on too aggressive, or "masculine," African American women were not criticized for displays of power on the tennis court. This difference stemmed, in part, from the dissimilarity in acceptable notions of middle-class white and African American femininity. While white women's femininity had traditionally been grounded in domestic and charitable pursuits, African American women seldom enjoyed such a luxury. Having to juggle multiple roles at home, work, and in the community, black women depended on strength. When such strength showed up in their tennis game, African American sportswriters praised it. "Smoking drives," "hard-hit, top-spin balls," or a "driving game" could as easily describe a woman's as a man's play.[27]

Washington, consistently ranked number three but unable to capture the women's national title, was no doubt frustrated with the situation of the late 1920s. Having broken rapidly into the organized black tennis scene with her national doubles championship, an expectation of capturing the singles title was, most likely, her ultimate goal. The fact that this prize continued to elude her when she routinely dominated her rivals at lesser tournaments must have consumed someone with such a competitive personality. Perhaps to shake things up a bit, Washington moved to Chicago during the spring of 1929, where she lived and worked as a hotel maid for a couple of years.[28] Regardless of why she made the move, Chicago had an active African American tennis culture that Washington would have been able to tap into. Far from moving west to get away from tennis, August 1929 found her "back in the East to settle her argument" with Ballard and Channels at the nationals. She played neither woman in the final match, however. That was the year she defeated Frances Gittens, taking the national title that had escaped her for four years. Undoubtedly her summer of promise, she swept the titles available to her, combining with able partners to capture the women's doubles and mixed doubles championships. Surely the women's singles meant the most to her, however.[29]

That 1929 victory was the first of what would become eight national titles, seven of them consecutive. She became a staple of the sports pages of the black press, sometimes capturing the headline over the male players. Such consistency would mark her style of play. Her hallmarks as a tennis champion were her steadiness and ability to cover the court, accurately returning seemingly unreachable shots. Her fiercely competitive nature also served her well. Once she became a champion, her intimidation of the contenders that attempted to unseat her became an additional advantage.[30]

Now a champion of African American tennis, Washington longed to try her skills against the reigning white women players of her era. She especially looked forward to a match-up with her counterpart in U.S. and international tennis, Helen Wills Moody. However, segregation was firmly in place throughout American society of the 1930s; the color line in tennis would remain undisturbed until 1948. Washington continued to dominate black tennis during the summer, but to fuel her competitive nature and keep herself active during its off-season she became more serious about the winter game of basketball. Once again, the vibrant black sports scene in Philadelphia served as the backdrop for Washington and other women interested in playing a sport that had become a staple of black women athletes throughout the country.

"Can't Stop Ora"—
Basketball and African American Women

In truth, only a small number of African Americans played tennis. It was predominately a sport for the upper classes, and the vast majority of black women, tired from working all day and shut out of many of the avenues open to white women, had neither the time nor the opportunity. In the midst of the sport explosion of the 1920s, however, working-class black women embraced a more easily accessible sport. Requiring virtually no equipment, basketball was relatively inexpensive to play; moreover, it was one of the few team sports acceptable to women.[31]

White women had been playing basketball since the late nineteenth century. Like most women's sports, it began predominately in the women's colleges of the northeast. After being introduced at Massachusetts's Smith College in the fall of 1892, it spread rapidly, traveling westward across the nation.[32] Once individual colleges established their own programs, intercollegiate contests in the West, where the concept of middle-class femininity was not as tradition bound, developed rapidly. The University of California at Berkeley and Stanford University played the first intercollegiate game for women in 1896, and other western colleges quickly followed suit. By the turn of the century, basketball was one of the most popular sports in American women's college athletics.[33]

One of the things women found most exciting about basketball was that it was a team sport. Other team sports like football and baseball were considered too rough and unladylike for women. Yet from the beginning it seemed as if basketball held promise. Rather than force the ball horizontally across a line as in football or hit it with a bat like baseball, players shot the ball upward. Moreover, players were not allowed to hold the ball close to the body or hit it with their fist. Other rules of the game prevented actions like holding, pushing, or striking any other player. In an era when most team sports were closed to women, basketball proved the rare exception.

Despite the intercollegiate competition that was taking place in the West, it did not take long for the women in charge of bringing basketball to women's colleges to develop a distinctly feminine version of the sport. The rules of the game, even for men, were in a state of transition during the first decade or so of its existence, and women educators decided to use this malleable situation to establish a set of rules for women's play. By dividing the court into sections and then limiting how many players could inhabit each, women leaders in the sport strove to develop attributes like quickness and agility while limiting rough play. By 1899, an official set of women's rules had been published by Spalding in its *Basket Ball for Women*.[34] Women educators also sought to rein in the competition that had developed in the West. They promoted their own play days in the East that involved intercampus visits and games, highlighting the distinctly feminine values of cooperation and teamwork by creating teams that purposely mixed players from the different schools. Finally, instructors developed forms of dress that stressed modesty so as to limit criticism from the public. Players were often required to cover their uniforms—the "bloomers" designed specifically for women's basketball—when walking to the gymnasium, and some educators even barred men from watching women's classes and games.

The excitement of playing a team sport would not long remain restricted to women's colleges as white working-class and African American women embraced the sport during the 1920s. Teams began springing up in the nation's high schools that gave women living in rural communities, working-class towns and cities, and African American communities an opportunity at a team sport most of them had never experienced. The game also provided a welcome relief from school and work that helped supplement the family income. Once out of high school, or in areas where schools limited participation, various organizations sponsored women's basketball, such as churches and ethnic and community organizations like the YWCA. But the most popular and successful development for working-class women's sports happened through the nation's businesses. Known as industrial-sport programs, businesses used a segment of their corporate profits for recreational facilities and activities, developing their own company-sponsored sports teams as a way of creating employee loyalty. These industrial teams played in intramural competition within the company or in local industrial leagues. A few engaged in national competition. Financial and insurance companies and business schools, all with their higher percentage of female employees, were the largest sponsors of women's basketball, bowl-ing, and even track and field teams.[35] Particularly after the Amateur Athletic Union (AAU) assumed organizational support of women's bas-ketball in 1926, many of the most talented and successful organizations were company teams.[36]

Within the African American community, women found two avenues to continue playing basketball after high school—a black industrial team, or college. Some African American businesses began teams, blurring the lines between industrial and African American ball. Moreover, the nation's black colleges had by this time developed a strong network of women's bas-ketball, testing their strength and skill against one another through inter-collegiate championships. Women's basketball in the African American community was so pervasive that, regardless of what other sports they com-peted in, most black women athletes of the era played basketball as well.[37]

As Washington stood on the brink of a new career in basketball, women's sport experienced a spasm of contentious growing pains. The spectacular growth of the 1920s gave way to critics who accused the women that participated in sport of excessiveness and unrestraint. In truth, these concerns in sport were closely allied to general societal con-cerns over the "new woman," embodied most familiarly in the flapper, whose shortened hair, flashy attire, and blatant sexuality reflected a strong and flagrant break with restrained Victorian womanhood of the previous century. Debates over the appropriateness of sport for women centered first on high school and college athletics, full of young women of the middle- and upper-middle class on the brink of full-fledged womanhood. Critics worried that the excitement of athletic competition would create a whole host of problems that often lay at opposite ends of the spectrum, from stripping women of their femininity and damaging their reproduc-tive organs to unleashing their strongly passionate sexual natures. Into this heightened atmosphere, an emerging profession of women physical educators began preaching and institutionalizing moderation. This pre-dominately middle-class cadre of instructors stressed athletics for the pur-pose of maintaining health, endorsing a concept of separate and unequal alternatives to competitive sport by offering "female" versions of games deemed too masculine for women to play without alteration. Women should refrain, they cautioned, from participating in meets and compet-itive games, since the frenzy of competition would make any semblance of moderation beyond young women's grasp. Competition was clearly only appropriate for men. For women, educators instituted the "play day" as a substitute. Play days provided the opportunity for different teams to "play" sports in a spirit of cooperation. This moderate alternative to the male world of competitive sports would allow women to enjoy the benefits of athletics without the associated risks that arose during competition. This sermon of moderation, however, did little to stem the popular tide of sport among young American women.[38]

The brand of basketball that African American and working-class women played in school and on industrial and community teams differed dramatically from the middle-class, "female" version fashioned by women educators. The guidelines of moderation held little appeal for working-class women whose lives differed sharply from those of the middle and upper classes, and workingwomen embraced competition with gusto. Many characteristics of their games dismayed physical education instructors. High school, industrial, and African American collegiate teams participated in competitions within their communities in ways similar to the male version of the sport.[39] A number of these teams had gravitated to playing in shorts with knees bared rather than the bloomers that educators insisted upon for their players. Some teams even chose to play with the boys' version of the game, refusing to adopt girls' rules. Moreover, participants played many of the games in front of excitable, raucous crowds that had been charged for admission, which educators felt was a clear exploitation of the women players. While female physical education instructors continued to promote their version of the sport for respectable women, the more "masculine" form of the sport blossomed in working-class, ethnic, and African American communities.[40] African American women like Ora Washington would not be denied the opportunity to play in those sports available to them and compete in the way they chose.

In the midst of this struggle over who would define women's athletics, Washington entered the realm of women's basketball in the winter of 1930–31. The Germantown Hornets were a community team sponsored by the same YWCA where Washington got her start on the tennis court. Coached by track coach at nearby Lincoln University Joe Rainey and led by captain Ora Washington, the Hornets quickly became an integral part of the active African American sports scene of Philadelphia. By mid-March of 1931, the team was 14–1, with Washington usually leading the squad as the high scorer. By that time, they had suffered their only defeat of the season, going on to finish with a record of 22–1. In early April, the Hornets traveled to Pittsburgh to play the cross-state rival Rankin Club for the national championship. Tied at halftime, Washington's teammates began feeding her the ball during the second half where she swerved and cut, passed, arched, and shot to put the Hornets ahead. "The triumph of the Hornets," observed the *Pittsburgh Courier*, could "almost be completely summed up in two words—Ora Washington," as she ranged all over the court, making the field goals that decided the game.[41] The season had been an exciting one for Washington and the Hornets. The real excitement for women's basketball and the city of Philadelphia, however, lay just ahead.

Encouraged by the Germantown squad's success of the previous year, two developments enriched women's basketball in the city. First, the Hornets broke with the YWCA and became a fully professional women's team. Second, the black newspaper of the city, the *Philadelphia Tribune*, decided to sponsor a rival women's team. To oversee this venture, they turned to their circulation director, Otto Briggs.[42] Before his career in the newspaper business, Briggs had made a name for himself in the black community as a Negro League baseball star. Playing for the well-known and successful Hilldale Club, sportswriters and fans often compared him to Ty Cobb for his prowess as a leadoff man. He also had strong defensive skills, earning the reputation as "one of the slickest outfielders of his day." Briggs was apparently determined to make the Tribunes a force in women's basketball from the outset. He was able to lure Washington's Hornet teammate and star forward Inez Patterson, who had assisted in the victory over Rankin the previous season, to play for the Tribunes. The stage was set for a brilliant season of women's basketball.[43]

The Hornets' 1931–32 season was an incredible one, and Washington, as center and captain, was the driving force. By mid-January, the squad had compiled a string of thirty-three consecutive victories. Washington was, as usual, the high-point scorer, even when two or three players from opposing teams were assigned to guard her. In addition to playing other African American teams, the Hornets also routinely played white women's teams and occasionally even African American men's teams. When they played the male Quicksteppers in January, it was an exciting contest. The Quicksteppers took a fast lead, but the Hornets pulled to within one point before halftime. The second half was close for the entire half. Just before the sound of the final buzzer, the Hornets' Evelyn Mann sank a basket to break the tie and secure a victory over the men. The Hornets, and their rivals, the Tribunes, offered such exciting games that they often outdrew the top male teams of the period. Moreover, the evenings promised more than sporting contests. Organizers often held dances after the games, making the events integral to both the sport and social scene of a vibrant black Philadelphia community. By the end of the season, the Hornets had not lost a game since early winter of 1931. The *Philadelphia Tribune*'s Randy Dixon argued that the season was the greatest to date for women's basketball in Philadelphia, in which both the Hornets and Tribune girls had developed "powerful teams and big followings."[44] What lay ahead for the spring, however, eclipsed even the regular season.

Over the course of two exciting months a five-game championship series to decide the African American women's champions engulfed not only the city of Philadelphia but also made news in the sports pages of the major black newspapers in the country. A full week before the first game, Dick Sun of the *Philadelphia Tribune* suggested the hype that consumed the city by writing "Here It Is at Last!" under the lead sports story of the day, "Hornets and Newsgirls Play for National Title." With "interest running at highest peak," the Tribunes were mapping out a special defense during their preparations for game one that would hopefully contain Ora Washington, generally recognized as "the greatest girl player of all time," and reign in the Hornets. When game one was played a week later, the two teams did not disappoint. Sports editor Randy Dixon called the game "the most fiercely played, interesting and thrilling basketball game" that he and the full house that was in attendance had ever seen:

> It was just like a storybook classic! From the opening 'til the closing whistle fans stood en masse and amid the rabid and demonstrative exhibition of partisanship, yelled themselves so hoarse that on one occasion, a halt had to be placed on hostilities to put a quietus on the pandemonious gathering.[45]

While initially it looked as if the Tribunes' special defensive strategy would be a success, Washington eventually turned the tide of the game when she contributed twelve points and won the game for the Hornets. The Tribune girls, however, had no intention of going down to defeat so easily. Two weeks later in game two, Coach "Shorty" Chappelle shifted

Inez Patterson to center. With the Hornets playing without two of their best guards, the strategy effectively shut down Washington and gave the Tribunes a decisive victory. The series stood tied at a game apiece.[46]

The last three games, which stretched over the month of March and into early April, were every bit as exciting. The Hornets took a healthy lead into halftime of game three. The Newsgirls, as the press often preferred to call the Lady Tribunes, edged back to within two points of the Hornets during the second half, but Washington's team held on to win. Helen Laws had been a vital force for the Hornets for most of the game. But it was again Washington who staved off the Tribune attack, twice executing shots under difficult circumstances in the final minutes to give the Hornets a 22–18 victory over their fierce rivals. With their backs to the wall, the "Tribune lassies" banded together to produce superior play, win game four, and force a deciding game, scheduled to be played Easter Monday on a neutral court. When illness struck five of the Hornets' players, Briggs and Rainey agreed to a postponement of game five to 2 April. For the first three-quarters of the game, it looked as if the Tribunes would completely dominate and easily win and take the series. Indeed, "had it not been for the masterful exhibition of Ora Washington the Hornets would have been slaughtered. The inimitable Ora added another of her copyrighted performances to her long list of luminous achievements." Yet, this time, Washington's final run was not enough. The Tribunes won the game and the series and captured the title formerly held by the Hornets. The scene at the New Broadway Athletic Club was one of sheer pandemonium:

> At the conclusion of the embroglio [*sic*] it was fully ten minutes before order could be restored. The cash customers fanned to fever heat by the ardor and closeness of combat gave outlet to all kinds of riotous impulses. They stood on chairs and hollered. Others hoisted members of the winning team upon their shoulders and paraded them around the hall. They jigged and danced, and readers, believe me, they were justified. It was just that kind of a game.[47]

At year-end when the *Baltimore Afro-American* featured their sports wrap-up for 1932, sportswriter Bill Gibson called the defeat of the Hornets by the Tribunes for the national title one of the big upsets in all of women's sports for the year.[48]

In the fall of 1932 with a new basketball season looming and the Tribunes starting practices, Otto Briggs reported that he planned some significant changes to the team. By early November, the official news was out. Briggs had lured "the peerless Ora Washington" to play for the new national champions. Briggs's coup to entice Washington to the Hornets' rival team cemented the Tribunes' dominance of the black women's basketball scene. On Thanksgiving night, the individual play of stars like Washington, Patterson, Helen Davis, and Evelyn Mann, coupled with the overall teamwork of the entire team, excited the overflow crowd on hand to watch the national champions easily win their season opener. In early January of 1933, the team had won eleven consecutive games. The reason for the Tribunes' success, according to the *Baltimore Afro-American*, was that opposing teams were discovering anew that they "can't stop Ora." It was, all in all, shaping up to be another exciting season, as fans were regularly treated to, even in the narrow defeats that occasionally happened, "another one of those exciting games that Otto Briggs' Philadelphia Tribune girls are famous for."[49]

As an all-around sportswoman, Washington's celebrated talent with a tennis racquet carried over onto the basketball court. Though only roughly 5′7″ tall, her basketball skills became legendary among African Americans in Philadelphia and throughout the black sporting world. She was considered an all-around player who displayed incredible stamina, the ability to pass or shoot with either hand and evade the elaborate defenses designed to limit her field goal success. As the years passed, Washington aged, and the Tribunes continued to strengthen their squad, basket totals would often be more evenly dispersed among players in contrast to Washington's early dominance. Yet she remained a powerful force, possessing the uncanny knack of scoring baskets at crucial moments in a game and displaying strong defensive skills, a "ball-stealing demon." When the Tribunes went on tour, sportswriters deemed their games "significant" sporting events. This was not only because it gave the local African American community an opportunity to see the well-known basketball team in action but also because fans could watch Washington, the most accomplished and famous of all black women athletes, take the court. Even as Washington was in command on the basketball court, the black press continued to remind the sporting public that she was the reigning queen in tennis as well, equally adept at shooting baskets as she was at placing "the white pill on the tennis court."[50] Mixing tennis and basketball was a good way to stay in shape and it broadened Washington's celebrity status. But even as Washington found herself atop the African American sport scene, an uneasiness about the sport of women's basketball surfaced within segments of the black community, questioning how women should play the sport.

Remaining Her Own Kind of Competitor

By the mid-1930s, Washington was the undisputable top black woman athlete in the country, the queen of two courts, as it were. She had arrived there by natural talent, hard work, and the aid of black Philadelphians who supported a vibrant sporting community. Black newspapers throughout the country lauded her. Crowds came out to watch her play. But African Americans did not live in a vacuum and some within the black community worried about how white Americans perceived black athletes.

This worry depicted an undercurrent of debate within the black community regarding the ability of sport to effect change within American race relations. On one side of the question were those who felt that excellence in competition could foster African American pride and eventual assimilation into white society. Others believed, however, that athletics was an inappropriate and ineffective way to achieve equality. The debate encompassed the role of both male and female athletes, but the question for women was influenced by the ongoing concern about women's sport in the broader society. Even African American leaders who favored sport as a pathway to eventual integration tended toward a masculine interpretation of that pathway. For example, while the administration at historically black Hampton Institute decided to pursue excellence in both the classroom and on the field, men engaged in competitive sport whereas women's athletics emphasized cooperation and social interaction rather than competition. Administrators at other historically black colleges, like Tuskegee Institute, eschewed such a gender divide and developed nationally recognized programs of competitive sport for women. At issue, in truth, was the conception of African American womanhood, and how closely that conception should align itself with white, middle-class femininity in an effort to facilitate integration.[51]

Far from playing out only in the nation's black colleges and universities, strands of the debate coursed throughout the black community as African American women played sport. Even in the excitement of the 1932 Tribunes/Hornets championship series, an undercurrent of unease with women's competitive sport arose in the black press. While women's competitive basketball lay at the heart of black Philadelphia sports, there was a limit, some reporters felt, as to how far women should go to win the game. Sportswriters generally praised the Tribune "lassies" in game four of the series, which the Tribunes dominated at least in part because of the absence of two key players from the Hornets' squad. Yet the article that appeared in the *Philadelphia Tribune* and in black newspapers around the country also reprimanded members of both teams for their roughness on the court. The play was considered "much too rough for girls," with some of the players resorting to "tactics too dirty and low to be worth recounting in detail." The women who participated in such play were not singled out. But "sooner or later," the article concluded, "these girls will wise up." Without the details, it is difficult to know how rough, dirty, and low the play actually became. Perhaps on the Hornets' side, at least, there was frustration that they could not clinch the series with this game, given that two of their starters were unable to play. Yet, the offending players were not chided for being too rough for basketball, or even for general sportsmanship. Their play was reproached as being too rough "for girls," suggesting that women's competitive basketball, even in the thriving sporting city of Philadelphia, should have some limits.[52] Sportswriters were not suggesting that women pull away from a competitive form of the sport. When the *Tribune*'s Randy Dixon made predictions for the 1932 All-Philly Girls' Basketball Team, he praised women's basketball in the city and the "tremendous strides" it had made over the previous few years: "While two seasons back a girls' game was considered more in the light of a feeble attempt by the weaker sex at playing a man's game, it is now, in several instances, quite different."[53] Quite different, indeed, often outdrawing the men's games. But it seemed that "tremendous strides" could only be taken so far before things got "too rough for girls."

Washington, however, along with Tribune players Inez Patterson and Mildred Perkins, were held up as exemplars of "real athletes" who never resorted to the types of low tactics that their teammates had engaged in. But two years later when the now Washington-led Tribunes took their brand of basketball on the road, the notion of what it meant for women to play competitively would once again come under the microscope. In March 1934, toward the end of their third successful season and with an institutional record of 97–12, Otto Briggs took his national champion Philadelphia Tribune squad on a three-city southern tour, where they played against college and local teams in North Carolina and Virginia. Major black newspapers in the East reported on the upcoming tour, and the *Pittsburgh Courier* announced that those teams playing "boys' rules" who wanted to test themselves against the national champions should write to Briggs in care of the *Tribune* offices. The first stop was Greensboro, North Carolina, where the Tribune women played a three-game series against the black women's college champions from Bennett College.[54]

As the debate about competitive sport widened within the black community, Bennett's prowess as a basketball powerhouse during the mid-1930s stood in stark contrast to the programs like those at Hampton. While individual college administrators grappled with issues of sport and black society, the National Association of College Women (NACW) discussed the issue of intercollegiate athletics at their 1929 conference. They concluded that intercollegiate "play" provided all of the benefits of athletics without its deleterious effects to the female body or the sociological problems stemming from competition. Two years later, sport columnist Ivora King seconded the NACW opinion with a column decidedly against mixing women and athletic competition. "The girl who is too athletic is on the wrong track to becoming a wife," she observed. Men were not interested in women who weren't *all* woman, and competitive sport often resulted in mannish "creatures" that were only half feminine and half something else. During the interwar years, administrators at Howard and Fisk joined with Hampton to rein in their competitive basketball programs for women. Bennett's administration and students saw little contradiction between femininity and sporting activities, however. "We were ladies, we just played basketball like boys," recalled Bennett alumnae Ruth Glover, as she looked back on her experience as part of the basketball team. Being a lady, cultivated inwardly and expressed in polite society, did not mean that one could not play competitive basketball.[55]

It was into this mix of divergent cultural backgrounds that the Bennett team hosted the Philadelphia Tribunes. Bennett entered the contest undefeated, but the Tribunes arrived in Greensboro led by "the indomitable, internationally famed and stellar performer Ora Washington."[56]

Unfortunately for Bennett, they would not stay undefeated after facing the Tribunes. Before a packed house of over 1,200 fans, the Tribunes easily defeated the Bennett team by a score of 31–22 in their first match-up. When the Tribune team came out to a slow first half, it looked as if Bennett would completely dominate the second game. But in the final three minutes, several "almost supernatural shots" by the national champions sealed victory number two. Before fans from a radius of one hundred miles and in a score reminiscent of their first contest, the Tribunes swept the series against Bennett with a 31–20 victory. "The strong Bennett college girls basketball team," observed the *Chicago Defender*, had "met its Waterloo."[57]

The Bennett players noticed more than the Tribunes' dominance on the court. Bennett was a historically black woman's college that insisted that its students maintain what they deemed a standard of upper-middle-class decorum. Its basketball team may have played boys' rules, but as Ruth Glover remembered, they were always "ladies." As the debate about women's competitive sport broadened into the black community, it became clear that perceptions of class difference were also very much a part of the conversation. With their cultural sensibility, then, Bennett's players observed the difference between their own style of playing boys' rules and that of the Tribunes. Lucille Townsend recalled Washington hitting her in the stomach every time she went for a jump shot. Indeed, Townsend and her teammates might have agreed with the description "Ora Runs Wild" that *Tribune* reporter Dick Sun used to describe the way Washington racked up field goals at crucial stages in game one. In short, the Tribunes played a brand of basketball that the Bennett team was unaccustomed to. It was not only the rough play that the Bennett teammates noticed, however. From their arrival on campus, Townsend's first glimpse of Washington made a lasting impression: "She looked like the worst ruffian you ever wanted to see. She looked like she'd been out pickin' cotton all day, shavin' hogs, and everything else." She and her Tribune teammates were "a different class of people."[58] To the Bennett players, there was a clear and important distinction between the way the Bennett "ladies" and the Tribune "lassies" played competitive basketball, and an even more important one between their conduct off the court. It was bad enough to play so aggressively but carrying such rough, unladylike characteristics into society was, in effect, "low" class. Other black colleges were already having trouble identifying the distinction and, eventually, Bennett would, too. The college succumbed to the trend in other women's collegiate athletic programs, supporting intercollegiate play days and withdrawing its support for competitive basketball during the late 1930s.[59]

In the midst of the ongoing conversation about the role of competitive sport in the black community, Ora Washington continued her reign as a national sports celebrity. Despite what the Bennett team saw in their opponents, the black press continued to rave about the "Tribgirls" and their captain. In February 1938, Briggs arranged for the team to head south once again. This tour was longer than the first, including stops in Orangeburg, South Carolina; Atlanta, Georgia; Biloxi, Mississippi; New Orleans, Louisiana; and at Tuskegee Institute in Alabama. Having been on top of the women's professional circuit for six years, such an extensive tour was an event for the black sporting public. Almost a month before the scheduled game in Atlanta, the *Atlanta Daily World* published the first of six articles in anticipation of the national champions' arrival. The upcoming game against an Atlanta all-star team was considered a "significant" event for the southern city. Black Atlantans would not only get the privilege of seeing the Tribune team take the court but also their first glimpse of the famous Ora Washington. In a distinct contrast from what Townsend had observed a few years before, Atlanta sportswriter Ric Roberts, in a full feature article on the net queen, praised her as a humble champion: "Miss Washington, unlike most females, effects the burden of national prominence with dignity and grace. She is wholly unaffected, has a most obliging and pleasing personality and is a favorite of all her associates."[60] What accounted for the vastly different descriptions of the court queen? In part, this could merely be a matter of two divergent experiences—one a coed at an elite women's college, the other a male sportswriter. Or perhaps it was an outgrowth of being on opposite sides of the court; surely most of Washington's "associates" were her teammates whereas Townsend had been an opponent. Regardless of the reason, it was clear that being a national black female sport champion was about more than sport itself as the language of gender and class surrounded discussions of women's basketball, even within the black community.

The compelling thing about Washington is how she was able to, in the midst of the debate in the black community, remain her own champion. This must have been particularly challenging given the longevity of her career and particularly frustrating when some of the concerns about class and gender in basketball bled over into the world of women's tennis that she had ruled for so long. In 1938, after over a decade of athletic competition and with eight national tennis singles titles to her credit, Washington announced her retirement from singles competition. She planned to continue competing in doubles play, which she did for close to a decade more. Then, unexpectedly, in 1939, Washington came out of retirement in order compete against up-and-coming star Flora Lomax. Lomax had been dubbed the "glamour girl of tennis" by the black press, and Washington was determined to put to rest rumors that she had retired rather than face a possible defeat to the new black tennis star. "Certain people said certain things last year," Washington told Harry Webber of the *Baltimore Afro-American*. "They said Ora was not so good any more. I had not planned to enter singles this year, but I just had to go up to Buffalo to prove somebody was wrong." Washington silenced the rumors by defeating Lomax and commenting, "I lost the second set to her but this was the first and only set she ever won from me."[61] Lomax had lain down the gauntlet and Washington, ever the competitor, could not resist the challenge. But the "Ora-Flora" feud was about more than women's tennis rivalry. In Washington's absence from the tennis scene, the black press had made quite a fuss over the new reigning women's singles champion. They wrote of Lomax's "modest personality," favorite color, and especially her "pretty white pleated tennis shorts." Washington, in contrast, had always been plain spoken and plain clothed. Put simply, the glamour embraced by tennis society was not her style. Not only did Washington's working-class background, dress, and demeanor suggest the opposite of society, but embracing the "working-class" sport of basketball in the off season indicated that she was not interested in trying to conform to the rigid social expectations of tennis.

Remaining at the top of two divergent sports for so long surely had its challenges. "It does not pay to be national champion too long," she remarked to Harry Webber of the *Baltimore Afro-American* after beating Lomax. "It's the struggle to be one that counts. Once arrived everybody wants to take it away from you and you are the object of many criticisms." On the one hand, sportswriters acknowledged that some competition in the women's tennis ranks would be good for the game. Even the general sporting public joined in on the desire to unseat the black tennis queen. As early as 1932, a former collegiate basketball player and tennis champion suggested that he expected to turn his newborn daughter into a "Negro

Helen Wills," predicting she would be "the nation's hope to dethrone Ora Washington." On the other hand, the press defended Washington's long reign as well deserved. Not only was she a "keen student of the game" but also a year-round sportswoman, keeping in shape in the fall and winter on the basketball court when she wasn't wielding a tennis racquet in the spring and summer.[62] In truth, it seemed that the criticisms laid at Washington's feet had more to do with her physical presence than her abilities as a sportswoman. Randy Dixon, now with the *Pittsburgh Courier*, observed in early 1939, the reason "the land at large has never bowed at Ora's shrine of accomplishment in the proper tempo" was because "she committed the unpardonable sin of being a plain person with no flair whatever for what folks love to call society." It was time, he argued, to give Washington her due before it was too late. Perhaps as the ATA matured it was less inclined to accept someone of Washington's background and style as a representative of black tennis. Or perhaps Dixon overstated the case a bit. In the absence of other evidence, it is impossible to know. Regardless, it is clear that Washington crafted her own way of being the nation's first African American woman sport celebrity.[63]

Conclusion

Following her defeat of Lomax, Washington initially announced that she intended to simply take a rest from singles competition. However, an injury on the basketball court in the final game of the 1940–41 season forced her to announce her final retirement from tennis singles competition. "What more can I get from playing tennis anyhow?" she asked a reporter with the *Baltimore Afro-American*. What more, indeed? She had won her 155th trophy the week before in Philadelphia, and was the only player to win national titles in the singles, doubles, and mixed doubles in the same year. There was also the issue of age, she argued. She was forty, and racing up and down the full court was not as easy as it used to be. In truth, her basketball career was over as well. She remained captain for the Tribunes' upcoming twelfth season, although she was expected to see very little, if any, time on the court. It was her eleventh consecutive year to serve as team captain. Except for their opening season when Washington was playing and leading the rival Hornet team, she was the only captain the Tribunes had ever known.[64]

Washington's retirement from tennis singles and her effective retirement from basketball did not mean her final exit from the African American sporting world. She continued to enter tournaments, paired with doubles' partners. In 1947, twenty-two years after winning that first national women's doubles title with Ballard, she paired with a rising African American tennis star, George Stewart, to compete in the mixed doubles competition at the ATA nationals. One of the players across the net was a young Althea Gibson, full of bravado, a blistering serve, and ready to take on the world of black and white tennis. First, however, "Queen Ora," so dubbed years before by the black press, served up a dose of humility to Gibson, when Washington and Stewart defended their doubles crown.[65] She was forty-six at the time. It would be her last national championship title.

Washington's years in the aftermath of her sports career were fairly quiet ones. In the mid-1940s, she and one of her younger sisters, Chris, bought a house in Philadelphia. Now that the athlete had settled down a bit from her travels as a professional basketball and amateur tennis player, she lived in the house with Chris and her husband and their brother Larry. She lived and worked in Philadelphia, and, although proud of her trophies, was not prone to much discussion of her athletic career and numerous victories. As the years progressed, "old-timers" were generally the only ones to recall her name and sports' prowess. But the civil rights advances of the mid-1960s caused Philadelphians to reflect on athletes of a previous generation that, due to segregation, had competed mostly within the confines of the black community. Washington was always among those remembered as one of the greats, a generation "born to soon" to achieve the recognition that athletes were becoming accustomed to. According to some she could have, while in her prime, easily bested any of the contemporary female athletes; to others, she had been better than many of the male athletes of her day. By 1967, "Doc" Young, sports columnist for the *Chicago Defender*, listed Washington's as a name that was never heard anymore. When she died in 1971 at the age of seventy-three, the *Philadelphia Tribune* obituary headline proclaimed her the "'Superwoman' of Tennis." And yet, many within the black community, particularly outside of Philadelphia, would have been hard pressed to recount her athletic conquests or comprehend the level of fame she had achieved almost fifty years earlier. She belonged to another era.[66]

It was an era teeming with male and white sport heroes, but one that, in the black community, embraced "Queen Ora." Her athletic talent, competitive drive, and work ethic were unquestionable. Her ability to remain at the top of both her games for so many years created a career for the record books. Shut out of some of the sport venues available to whites, she nonetheless acquired fame and adulation within the black community that was a first for African American women athletes. She benefited from opportunities created by an overall surge in women's athletics and a vibrant black sports community in Philadelphia that fostered athletic programs, a local YWCA tennis court, and an exciting rivalry of women's industrial basketball. Not all was praise and adulation, however. As the black community at large debated whether sport was an effective vehicle for race pride and assimilation into white society, women's competitive sport became an issue for those who wanted to align black womanhood with white middle-class femininity. No one could be more critical of Washington and her teammates than their Bennett opponents who found a way to play competitive ball and be ladies. Yet throughout her career, Washington refused to become something she was not. She was at once indomitable, stellar, and sensational and plain, rough, and aggressive. She was a black woman athletic star in a largely white, male sporting world, and she chose, rather incredibly, to remain the only kind of champion she knew how to be.

As Ora Washington dominated black tennis and led the Philadelphia Tribunes to basketball victory during the greater part of the 1930s, African American women in the South were just beginning to embrace a different sport. Their own experiences with track and field would be marked by unprecedented opportunity for black women athletes that they turned into national success. As African American women's relationship with sport expanded beyond the black community, the stakes related to their success and representation of black America became even higher. If Washington's experience were any indicator, these athletes would receive ample support from the black community as they traversed the new ground of competing against whites. But the perceptions and stereotypes that ruled the world of U.S. women's track and field coupled with the racial significance of national competition would also mean that the athletes could expect to confront what it meant to be a woman track athlete not only in white but also black America.

TWO

"The Tuskegee Flash"

Alice Coachman and the Challenges of 1940s U.S. Women's Track and Field

In 1939, when Alice Coachman was sixteen years old—or maybe seventeen or eighteen, depending on who you ask—the athletic director at Tuskegee Institute asked her to leave her home in Albany, Georgia, to travel with his women's track and field team to the national championships in Waterbury, Connecticut.[1] Except for her short time training that summer with the team in Tuskegee, Alabama, she had never been away from home. There were no planes or chartered buses to transport the team. They rode in cars and took their food with them. If they needed to stop to use the bathroom, they found a wooded area. There were no fancy hotels once they got to Connecticut but rather a network of Tuskegee alumni that put the athletes up in their homes. Despite the fact that this was the national championship meet for women's track and field, most white newspapers were not very interested in covering the story. When the Tigerettes brought home the national team championship for the third straight year, however, the story headlined many of the major black newspapers. Coachman, though still in high school, became the new national high jump champion. She didn't surrender the title until she retired from track and field ten years later. When she did retire, she did so as an Olympic champion. She was a race hero to African Americans nationwide, but there were no million-dollar endorsement contracts. Her picture did not appear on the Wheaties box. But her hometown, deep in the heart of southwest Georgia, did declare 1 September 1948, Alice Coachman Day. The *Albany Herald* placed the story on its front page. And a citywide reception, though segregated, was held in her honor. In truth, she did not really retire a celebrity, but for a young woman of twenty-six who used to sleep three or four to a bed and help supplement the family income by picking cotton, she had not done too badly.[2]

That Coachman has been forgotten—as the opening vignettes in this book illustrate—is regrettable but not unusual. In truth, the names of most Olympic gold medalists are fleeting, though why Coachman remains essentially forgotten in a black community that focuses heavily on historic "firsts" is puzzling.[3] Coachman's story is important not so much because she was "the first," but because she represented a defining moment in the history of black women athletes. Those before her, like Washington, competed within the black community, being barred from national competition and recognition. Those who followed would never again be confined solely to the African American community, although it would take Althea Gibson's ability with a tennis racquet to break down the color barrier in that sport. Coachman was the first African American female athlete of national and international fame to compete routinely against white women, and her athletic career was seminal for two different, though related reasons. On one hand, her career showed that a black woman track athlete celebrated by white American society was a distinct possibility. It also demonstrated, on the other, the ways that black women athletes would push back when confronted with the stereotypes of white society.

Coachman's experience with "fame" was both exhilarating and marginalizing. Emerging when a teenager from real poverty, her athleticism brought her to Tuskegee Institute where, for much of her career, she was part of a team of athletes that was ranked not only the best of their race but the best of the nation. The benefits that came with competing in the sport—a college education, travel opportunities, cultural enrichment, and personal fulfillment—were significant. At Tuskegee, Coachman discovered a community that encouraged and appreciated her talents, a coach willing to defy traditional race and gender stereotypes to develop his athletes' potential, and teammates who shared her competitive nature and love of the sport. Through the sports pages of the black press, she became nationally known in the black community even as she found herself marginalized by white society on three counts—as an African American, a woman, and a track and field athlete.

As Coachman confronted these categories, she not only had to contend with the stereotypes held by white society but also the ways in which African Americans responded to them. Black sportswriters in particular seemed concerned that black women track athletes develop a public identity to counter prevailing stereotypes. Proud to display the talents of African Americans virtually shut out of the white press, all the leading black weeklies featured Coachman's athletic victories in their sports pages. Her participation in track and field did not give her the national prominence of an Ora Washington. But her longevity and career success against whites and extensive coverage by the black press would have made her name and accomplishments well known in the black community. But middle-class women physical educators had convinced the broader society that the black and working-class women who chose to enter track and field were either unfeminine or in danger of quickly becoming so. Tuskegee Institute worked hard to refute such images, insisting that its athletes adhere to a concept of middle-class femininity and culture that permeated the school and surrounding community. Contrary to Washington's experience, there would be no references by competitors suggesting that Coachman or her teammates were low-class ruffians. Far from it, in fact, and they reveled in their experiences at the supportive Tuskegee community. But to counteract the racial, class, and gender stereotypes perpetrated in white America, the black press that carried the story of Coachman and the Tuskegee women's track team to its readership sometimes created images of its own that connoted not only femininity, but sexuality.

The masculinity connected with track and field had been one of the key issues preventing its acceptance in the broader society. So, too, was the working-class marker that middle-class educators pinned on it in the 1930s. Yet despite these labels, even white American society took notice when Coachman won an Olympic gold medal, applauding her athletic accomplishment in contrast to African American women athletes who had competed before her. She captured the acclaim of white Americans at a time when competing in track and field was considered inappropriate for an American woman of any color. And she captured it not only in northern cities but also in the unlikeliest of cultures—the American South of the late 1940s. She established herself as a nationally recognized black woman track and field champion not only with the help of the black community but also in spite of a segment of them. The trajectory of Coachman's career indicated that things just might be on the cusp of change for black women track athletes in the United States.

The Road to Tuskegee

Alice Coachman's path to Tuskegee Institute was not unlike many of the other women who became Tuskegee Tigerettes in the 1930s and 1940s. Raised in the rural outskirts of the southwest Georgia town of Albany, Coachman was the fifth of ten children born to Evelyn and Fred Coachman. Memories of growing up in the 1920s were punctuated with a firm and religious mother, a conservative father who was the unquestioned head of the household, and memories of picking cotton and sleeping three or four to a bed. Her athletic prowess revealed itself at an early age. When she could steal a moment, she could be found outside racing the boys since the girls offered little competition against her blazing speed. She could also jump higher than all of the girls and most of the boys she played with.[4]

Despite her natural track and field talents, she received little encouragement from her parents to pursue sports. There were several reasons for this. Coachman and her siblings supplemented the income brought in through their father's plasterwork by picking cotton, and her parents were not keen on anything that interfered with that or their schoolwork. Moreover, Evelyn Coachman worried that her daughter would seriously hurt herself, especially from jumping over bamboo fishing poles, rags tied together to fashion a rope or anything else that would serve as the bar. When a doctor collecting rents remarked to her that he thought her daughter would one day " jump over the moon," she replied that she would also probably break her neck. In truth, though, the Coachmans' strongest reservations regarding their daughter's interest in track and field probably stemmed from the fact that most Americans shunned the sport as too masculine. They feared that her pursuit of the sport would push her, as an African American woman, even further onto the margins of society. As a young girl immersed in sports, Coachman later recalled the stigma of being different: "It was a rough time in my life. It was a time when it wasn't fashionable for women to become athletes, and my life was wrapped up in sports."[5]

Despite her parents' hesitation, the young athlete eventually found adult support for her love of sport elsewhere. Her fifth-grade teacher, Cora Bailey, recognized that Coachman had a natural talent and encouraged her student to look for an opportunity to join a team. Such an opportunity came when she started Madison High School. Under the supervision of Coach Harry Lash, she discovered a sanctioned outlet for her talent on the Madison High women's track and field team.

It was not uncommon during the 1930s for African American high schools in southern towns and cities to sponsor women's track teams. Many of them had sprung up in the previous decade as women's sports had grown and spread into working-class, ethnic, and African American communities. Although competition was generally limited to other black high schools within close proximity, historically black colleges, like Tuskegee, hosted relay carnivals once a year. These meets provided opportunities for teams to test themselves against athletes and schools that were geographically out of their reach. Tuskegee Institute started their own relays in 1927, with the first of the women's events added in 1929. By 1933, the school was hosting a full complement of women's track and field events, and the U.S. Olympic Committee designated the 1936 meet a semifinal Olympic trial. The following year, Tuskegee divided competition into junior and senior categories with the high schools competing for the junior titles and the colleges competing for the senior. By this time, the relays were much more than just a local meet. The Tuskegee Relays drew high school and college track teams from Alabama, Georgia, Florida, Tennessee, Texas, and Ohio. In 1942, the *Chicago Defender* billed the annual Tuskegee event as a "national" meet.[6]

The relays also gave black colleges the opportunity to survey up-and-coming talent for their own teams. As Coachman's story illustrates, Tuskegee proved masterful at recruitment. In 1939, Coach Lash was preparing to take his Madison High women's track team to compete in the junior championships at Tuskegee's annual relay carnival. Lash had fast runners but needed points for field events, so he tapped Coachman for the high jump competition. Her jump of 5′4″ not only captured the junior title and points for Madison but also broke the meet record for both the junior and senior divisions.[7] Coachman's performance at the relay carnival caught the attention of Tuskegee Institute's athletic director, Cleve Abbott. Not long after Coachman returned to Albany, Abbott paid a visit to the young athlete and her parents, inviting her to attend his summer program for high school athletes at Tuskegee. Abbott also hoped that Coachman's parents would allow her to accompany the team to the Amateur Athletic Union (AAU) national championships in Waterbury, Connecticut, in September of that year to compete as a Tigerette for the high jump title. Years later, Coachman remembered her enthusiasm:

> I was tired of picking cotton, so I said to myself, if I'm going to spend the summer picking cotton, I can spend the summer learning. And then have a bed to sleep in by myself, and have three meals a day, and not have to do anything but work in the gym or out on the track. It was kind of fun, but it was hard work.[8]

Although hesitant at first, Evelyn and Fred Coachman eventually consented, and their daughter attended Abbott's program for the first time in the summer of 1939. She also joined the Tuskegee team for the trip to the nationals, where she won that first national high jump championship and the Tigerettes captured their third national team title. Coachman returned to Tuskegee's program the following summer, traveling with the Tigerettes to the outdoor nationals in Ocean City, New Jersey, where she defended her high jump title.[9]

The world of U.S. women's track and field that Coachman entered had followed an up-and-down trajectory that was similar, in many ways, to competitive basketball. Initially sanctioned as a healthy sport for women, it fell out of favor in American society during the first part of the twentieth century. Its origins for women lay not only in its male counterpart but also in the nineteenth-century exercise of walking. Whereas running was far too strenuous and unladylike for women of Victorian America, walking was both appropriate and good for women's health and physical appearance. Moreover, walking was easily accessible and required no equipment, no special clothing, no special instruction or coaching, and no gymnasium. By the latter third of the century, women had begun walking for competition. Women walkers competed for prize money in marathons, exhibitions, and "six-day" races, in which the entrant who walked the most quarter miles around the track over six days won the competition. In one such contest, the winner received both a championship belt and a purse of $1,000. Second- and third-place finishers also received monetary prizes, and any entrant walking at least 325 miles was awarded $200.[10]

During the transition from exercise to sports at women's colleges, track and field emerged as a clear favorite. Vassar, consistent with its leadership in women's sports, held the first women's track and field meet, in 1895. Their field day in November of that year began a forty-two-year history of the competitive sport at the college. By 1898, Vassar would be contesting eleven events that were more demanding than those of the first AAU women's meet some twenty-five years later. Before the turn of the century, Elmira, Mount Holyoke, Wellesley, and Randolph-Macon Women's College had all begun their own field days, comparing the results of their champions to those at Vassar. Intercollegiate competition was not long in coming, and by 1904, women's athletic records began appearing in the national publication *Spalding's Official Athletic Almanac.*[11]

Women's track and field grew fairly evenly through the class structures of white American society during its early growth at the turn of the century. From its beginnings at Vassar and other women's colleges, it spread in ways typical of other sports opening up to women—through industrial sport programs; school, park district, and athletic club programs; and track clubs sponsored by immigrant communities. When the AAU decided, in the mid-1920s, to provide organizational backing and support, popularity of the sport increased even further, particularly among its working-class participants who now had an association to provide organization for the disparate network of park, school, and athletic clubs.[12] Through these various avenues, increasing numbers of women began participating with enthusiasm.

During these early days, women's track and field enjoyed only limited male support. An important exception was Dr. Harry Eaton Stewart, one of the sport's most ardent backers during the 1910s and 1920s. Stewart was a medical doctor and served as the physical director at various girls' schools in Connecticut. He was a firm believer that the sport of track and field, including competition, was good for young women, and he worked tirelessly to promote its growth in the United States. He also performed medical research on the effects of training on women so he could refute the statements of those who condemned the sport for its damage to the female body—the jarring movement that some people thought hurt women's reproductive organs. A brilliant writer, he did not shy away from publishing his findings and support of the sport in the *American Physical Education Review.* In 1918, he was the only man named to the newly organized National Women's Track and Field Committee. His tireless work on behalf of the sport earned him appointment as chairman of the committee. This first national body to administrate United States women's track and field sanctioned American and collegiate records, established rules to govern the sport, and selected the standard events for competition.[13]

Women's track and field was growing internationally as well, and early in 1922, the International Federation of Women's Athletics in Paris announced their intention to hold an international women's meet in August. Under the direction of Stewart and the National Women's Track and Field Committee, the United States held its own qualifying meet in May to determine the athletes who would compete as part of an American team.[14] Fifteen athletes, all white, traveled to Europe to compete in what was known as the first Women's Olympics. In truth, the competition functioned more like a track meet than the Olympic games we know today, with the first several place finishes earning points for the country's team that the athlete represented. The athletes received an enthusiastic reception in Paris, and some 20,000 spectators gathered to watch the events. Back home, the *New York Times*, which had reported on the qualifying meet in May as well, followed the team of high school and college girls that earned thirty-one points and second place behind the British. It was, the *Times* continued, a competition "noteworthy for the number of new records set in the women's athletic world."[15]

While the athletes returned home to general acclaim and celebrations at their various schools and colleges, their accompanying sponsors returned home to a brewing controversy. At issue was whether women should be involved in the sport, and, if so, who should be in charge. On one side lay the all-male-led organizations like the International Olympic Committee (IOC) and the AAU. These organizations had previously been content to ignore women's track and field. Given the public's embrace of the Paris games, however, both experienced a change of heart. In 1923, the IOC decided to bring international competition of the sport under its control, revealing its plans to introduce five women's track and field events into the 1928 Olympics. The same year, the AAU announced its intention to begin supervising the sport in the United States and sponsoring an annual national championship meet for women the following year. In 1927, they added a women's indoor meet. Such change probably stemmed more from a desire to ensure that they would not be left out of decisions controlling the sport than from any altruism or strong interest in its growth. If there was to be women's track and field in the United States, the AAU leadership reasoned, they wanted organizational control. Regardless of its motive, the backing of the AAU lent credibility to the sport, further increasing its popularity. As more women began flocking to track and field, those who lay on the other side of the controversy, the women educators, became more vocal.[16]

The interest in women's track and field on the part of male coaches and male-led athletic organizations like the AAU struck women instructors as opportunistic and simply wrong. Men's intrusion into female athletics seemed both self-serving and a perversion of the more democratic alternative of play days that women educators had endorsed for their middle-class athletes. In particular, women instructors railed against the male coaches of women's teams who filled their athletes with competitive desires and perverted the terrain of women's sports these instructors had nurtured. Their response was to feed on society's obsession with and worry over the "mannish" athlete by linking women's participation with competitive track and field to the threat of masculinization. In part, the instructors were frustrated by their inability to wrest organizational control of the sport from the male-led AAU. Yet there were race, class, and gender issues at stake here as well. African American and working-class women overwhelmingly populated track and field, especially once the AAU lent its organizational backing, and physical education instructors upheld a particularly middle- and upper-class version of white femininity. Unable to control track and field and no longer successful in promoting a moderated alternative, the sport and its athletes became natural targets of middle-class instructors.[17]

The position of women educators did not eliminate women's participation in the sport. However, it did shape its perceptions in American society. As physical educators called for respectable, middle-class women to exit women's track and field, it became thoroughly marginalized by much of white society. Successful track athletes like Babe Didrickson, Helen Stephens, and Stella Walsh, who initially spurred interest in the sport, eventually did more harm than good for its image. With their working-class background, they epitomized the type of woman who was interested in competitive track and field. And their short haircuts, outspoken manner, and "mannish" mannerisms seemed to confirm the very concerns being voiced by female physical education leaders. Indeed, Vassar's experience with the sport mirrored its transition in the broader society. This pioneer in women's track and field continued to hold its field days, year after year, establishing records and comparing them to those of the other colleges holding competitions. In 1934, field day at Vassar became sports day. In 1936, it became a dual track meet. A year later, in 1937, the event became a "physical education classes track meet." And then it vanished. After forty-two years, the one-time leader of the sport surrendered to the pressure of the women physical educators and withdrew from hosting track and field competition.[18]

As a result of such concerted opposition and public negative attention, women's track experienced a significant reversal in popularity in the U.S. during the 1930s. In 1929, four thousand spectators had gathered at Soldier Field in Chicago to attend the women's outdoor nationals, where they enjoyed watching athletes set five new records. By 1935, a few hundred people gathered to watch the event at New York University and watch Helen Stephens set a new world record in the 100 meters. Due to the small number of competitors, the meet took only three hours to complete. By 1938, the AAU had stopped holding the indoor nationals on a regular basis due to limited interest in the sport. While the various park, school, and district club teams in the North continued to keep the sport going and produce remarkable athletes like Didrickson, Stephens, and Walsh, the sport lay at the margins of American society by the late 1930s.[19]

Into this depressed state of American women's track and field, African American women discovered and took advantage of an opportunity. Teams from the North had already produced a handful of individual black women track stars. Tidye Pickett, a hurdler and sprinter from the Chicago Park District team, and Louise Stokes of the Onteora Club out of Boston, a 50-meter sprint specialist, competed during the early and mid-1930s. Both earned reserve spots on the 1932 Olympic team; Stokes again served as a reserve member on the 1936 team, while Pickett earned a full berth. She became the first African American woman to represent the United States in Olympic competition when she competed in the 80-meter hurdles.[20] Nineteen thirty-six was also the first year that the Tuskegee Tigerettes participated in the national championships. They were quickly establishing themselves as one of the premier women's track clubs in the country.

The debates over women's competitive sport that were occurring among women educators also circulated within the African American community, though often within the context of larger questions regarding the role of sport in lifting up the race. As such, administrators and physical educators at historically black colleges and universities (HBCUs) often grappled with what role competitive sport should have within their institutions for both women and men. Concepts of black femininity and assimilation into white society influenced collegiate programs for women; even so, HBCUs developed attitudes and approaches that defied easy categorization. The women's sport programs at Hampton and Tuskegee differed dramatically, though both were industrial schools that emphasized an education in trades. Hampton tended to follow the pattern of middle-class white physical educators, defining women's sport through cooperation rather than competition. Tuskegee, however, had strong competitive programs for both their male and female students. And while the more intellectual Howard discouraged competition for women, the educationally elite Bennett College produced a fiercely competitive basketball program for years after Howard had withdrawn from the sport.[21]

At Tuskegee, Cleve Abbott was the man most responsible for developing the women's track and field program into a national powerhouse. Abbott, like Harry Stewart before him, was part of a third group that existed during the period that the AAU and women educators were locked in heated debate. Stewart was, unfortunately, a casualty of the controversy, having been virtually cut out of women's track and field upon his return from Paris. But there remained a group of male coaches and sponsors who, in contrast to both the AAU's recent about-face and the women educators' emerging distain for competition, supported women's competitive sport. Content merely to coach and sponsor women's teams, they were not interested in involving themselves in the existing controversy. High school coaches in many rural, ethnic, and African American communities who oversaw boys' teams realized that a significant portion of their school enrollments were being denied coaching opportunities and moved to form girls' teams.[22] Why Abbott waited until the mid-1930s to start the Tuskegee team in earnest in not clear. Perhaps he recognized that the timing was right to enter the sport. Maybe he recognized that this was one of the few opportunities that African American athletes had to enter head-to-head competition against whites and that success would be an important racial statement. Perhaps funding had been unavailable prior to that time. Rumor had it that he began the program at Tuskegee to give his daughter, Jessica, an opportunity to compete. Whatever the reason, we do know that he developed a series of women's teams that quickly began shutting down the competition. Constantly looking for new talent, he was interested in keeping things that way.

After two summers at Tuskegee in which she won consecutive national high jump championships, Abbott was eager to get Coachman under his constant tutelage and suggested a transfer to the institute. There, she could finish high school and become a regular member of the women's track and field team.[23] Abbott would get the benefit of Coachman's abilities for additional years, and Coachman would benefit from regular training and instruction from Abbott and his coaching staff. Since the Coachmans could not afford to send their daughter to Tuskegee, Abbott offered to have her attend on their work-study program. Her parents once again consented, and their daughter was more than ready to go. The two summers there had been hard work, but also fun, and she had met other young women whose athletic talents matched her own. At the age of seventeen, Coachman enthusiastically began a new chapter of her life.

Going National with the Tigerettes

When Coachman transferred to Tuskegee Institute, she entered a completely different world from the one she had left. She came further under the influence of Cleve Abbott, who became an important mentor. She became part of a nationally ranked track and field team and discovered acceptance both at Tuskegee and within the track and field world. As she matured as an athlete and reached her peak athletic years, she received expansive media exposure from the black press. And, she found herself surrounded by and absorbed into a culture that came with being part of the educational ideals and facilities of Tuskegee Institute. It was a culture that would make a profound difference in both her personal and athletic life.

When Booker T. Washington founded Tuskegee Institute in the late nineteenth century, he insisted on an emphasis on the skilled trades. Such an emphasis resulted from Washington's experience as an impressionable teenager during Reconstruction. He believed that Reconstruction had failed due to a misplaced emphasis on civil rights and political strategies over basic survival, and he carried this belief with him throughout his life. What he sought to do through Tuskegee was offer African Americans an education that would help them secure economic independence. "The opportunity to earn a dollar in a factory just now," he observed, "is worth infinitely more than the opportunity to spend a dollar in an opera house."[24] Under his leadership and influence, Tuskegee Institute became the largest and best-supported African American educational facility of his day. It was a completely African American school with an all-black leadership and faculty at a time when white missionaries ran most black schools. The emphasis was on practical education, or trades, that would enable a graduate to earn a decent living, and it permeated the school.[25]

The focus on trades and self-determination gave graduates a life beyond the rural, sharecrop agriculture that still dominated that part of the country, and transformed the surrounding area into a model black community in two ways. First, Tuskegee Institute introduced students to a middle-class lifestyle, insisting on a certain standard of dress and etiquette. Second, by buying up surrounding farmland and selling it to African Americans at low interest rates, the institute established a community of small landowners and homeowners that spread out from the school, extending its influence beyond the campus. Tuskegee was becoming much more than an educational facility. Eventually, graduates left the area and began establishing themselves in other parts of the country. In doing so, they created a nationwide network of farmers, artisans, teachers, and small businesspersons. What began as a small school known as Tuskegee Institute had developed into an established educational and cultural complex and a nationwide association of alumni known informally as "the Tuskegee Machine."[26]

The institute and surrounding community forged a middle-class culture that pervaded life at Tuskegee, and athletes like Coachman recognized it immediately upon being admitted to the school. Coachman's upbringing in southwest Georgia was fairly typical of her teammates'. Poor, rural, with sustenance coming from a combination of farming and unskilled labor, Coachman had, nonetheless, been raised with a fairly strict upbringing that encouraged faith, strength, and respect for others. Tuskegee began with and expanded on these concepts, stressing inward strength to foster self-reliance and emphasizing respect for others to include teachers, students, and especially visitors to the campus. Well versed in Tuskegee culture, Abbott brought the same commitment of inner strength, respect, and excellence to the women's track team. While the team had been competing locally and in Tuskegee Relays since 1929, Abbott began a program in the mid-1930s that brought these athletes national prominence. African American athletes like Pickett and Stokes participated on athletic club teams from the North, but the Tigerettes became the first all-black women's team to compete nationally. They placed second in their first trip to the AAU outdoor national championships in 1936. The team returned in 1937, and this time they came away as national champions. Thus began a string of indoor and outdoor team championship titles that ran through 1951, broken only once when they finished second in 1943.

While other colleges and athletic clubs had individual stars, Tuskegee had the depth needed to win team championships. At that time, team points were awarded for each of the first- through fourth-place finishes. More important than capturing a first place in each event was the ability to take multiple places throughout the meet events. By the time Coachman joined the team, Tuskegee already had a number of solid athletes whose second-, third-, and fourth-place finishes were doing just that, in addition to several athletes who were accumulating their own individual national titles.[27]

First among Tuskegee's early championship stars was Lula Hymes. Coming out of Booker T. Washington High School of Atlanta, Georgia, Hymes first won the 50-meter sprint at the Tuskegee relays for that school in 1933; by 1936, she was running for Tuskegee on a track scholarship. She was also a broad jumper, ran the 100 meter, and served as anchor on the 400-meter relay team. Described by the *Chicago Defender* as "the Jesse Owens of the fair sex of the cinderpath," she was often a multiple winner at meets, taking first place in the 50- and 100-meter sprints, the broad jump, and the 400-meter relay at the 1937 Tuskegee relay carnival. Competing as a Tigerette at the AAU outdoor national championships from 1937 through 1940, she won or placed in three events each year. She was, by Coachman's recollection, one of the best who ever competed for Tuskegee. Hymes and Coach Abbott's daughter, Jessie, joined to bring home the AAU 400-meter relay title from 1938 through 1940. While the names of the other two runners for the relay team changed, the combination of Abbott as the second leg, "a great runner when the chips are down," and Hymes in the anchor position, remained constant and became virtually unstoppable. The team also enjoyed the talents of broad jumper and sprinter Mabel Smith, hurdler and high jumper Cora Gaines, and Florence Wright, who handled the shot put and discus.[28]

By the early 1940s, other up-and-coming athletes were, along with Coachman, joining the older stars to continue what was beginning to look like a dynasty. So important was their success to members of African American society that black newspapers routinely reviewed the composition of the team and the various team members' strengths prior to meets, particularly the AAU nationals. This second group performed as well as, sometimes better than, the first, often capturing multiple finishes in an event: sprinters Hester Brown and Rowena Harrison, the latter who tied the world's record in the 100 meter; sprinter and broad jumper Lucy Newell, who succeeded Lula Hymes as the new national broad jump champion; Hattie Hall and Margaret Barnes, who handled the field throwing events; broad jumper and hurdler Lillie Purifoy; sprinter, high jumper, and hurdler Leila Perry, who had been a teammate of Hymes at their Atlanta high school; and, of course, Alice Coachman. So deep with speed was the 1940 team that enjoyed the talents of both this first and second group of athletes that the Tuskegee 400-meter relay team "B" of Brown, Hall, Perry, and Coachman came in second, but only to their teammates on the "A" team of Newell, Abbott, Harrison, and Hymes, who captured the title. In 1941, after Hymes, Abbott, and the other older athletes had graduated, the newer athletes continued to perform well both individually and as a team. Even as the black press was expressing concern over replacing Hymes and Abbott, assistant coach Christine Petty had enough confidence in the depth of her 1941 team to send fifteen members to the Prairie View relays in Texas while accompanying eight members to the AAU national indoor championships in Atlantic City. Her confidence was not misplaced; the Tigerettes won both meets, continuing their dominance of women's track and field.[29]

Tuskegee's years of women's track and field dominance occurred, then, through Abbott's ability to find, cultivate, and keep young athletic talent. Clearly, he knew what he was doing, and Coachman's story was a classic example of how Abbott operated. He discovered much of the up-and-coming talent in the area through black high schools' participation in the Tuskegee Relays that pulled track teams from as far west as Texas and north as Ohio. Once Abbott identified a young prospect, he often invited her to attend his summer program at Tuskegee where athletes conditioned, trained, and prepared for the AAU national outdoor championships held each summer. When talented and hard-working athletes graduated from high school, Tuskegee was already in the forefront of their minds as a way to continue their education. For those who could not afford to attend the school on their own, Abbott often arranged for them to attend as part of the work-study program, the only type of athletic scholarships available for Tuskegee's women athletes at the time. An occasional prospect caused the coach to suggest, as he did with Coachman, that the young athlete transfer to Tuskegee to finish high school so that he could have the benefit of her talent for more years.[30]

As important as finding athletic talent was Abbott's ability to cultivate it. For this, he initially relied on Christine Evans Petty, a former track and field and tennis star of the Tuskegee Relays. Petty coached the women's team from 1936 until 1942. Petite but tough, she took her job of preparing her athletes for nationals competition seriously. She understood how easy it was to become overconfident, particularly when these athletes generally overpowered their competition at the Tuskegee Relays. Coachman remembered Petty as being "real fiery," as someone who had no trouble taking any cockiness or laziness out of her athletes by abruptly upbraiding them: "You think you're good, but you're no damn good. You've got to wait 'till you get to the nationals and meet all them other folks." While Abbott remained closely involved with the team even during the years Petty oversaw their training, by 1939 the Tigerettes had become known by the black press as "the Christine Petty coached lassies."[31] When Petty died suddenly in July 1942, Abbott did not replace her, choosing instead to assume full coaching responsibilities for the team himself. Perhaps Abbott recognized that bringing in someone new would be difficult for the team, upsetting the camaraderie they had developed over the years. Coachman, in particular, appreciated the continuity. In truth, she had always related better to Abbott, who, even when Petty directed training, had been heavily involved with the team particularly in the lead-up to and during the AAU nationals. For Coachman, "Coach" was always Cleve Abbott.

The final key to Abbott's success was his ability to make sure that the athletes he recruited wanted to stay. This was, perhaps, the most important part of his approach. Once these young women became

Tigerettes, there was a family atmosphere to the team that drew them in, mentored them, and kept them there. When Coachman first started working with the team during the summer of 1939, most of the athletes were in college and raced for the senior titles. The few high schoolers there looked up to athletes like Lula Hymes and Jessie Abbott, who had been with the team since 1937. The older girls, in turn, took the "babies" under their wings, mentoring them, encouraging them in competition, and bringing them along in the Tuskegee way. Coachman remembered the relationship well:

> We had girls that were older that took care of us; they called us "babies." ... They were always behind us and rootin' for us. It was kind of like a little family. "Come on, come on, let's go, we need so and so points, come on, come on." It wasn't anything where somebody was over here talking about her, [saying], "She thinks she can run, she thinks she can jump." Everybody was just pulling for you—adding up points so we could win, you know. And that was what I liked about it.[32]

The mentoring and sense of family that the teammates fostered for one another was central to Abbott's success in sustaining the Tigerettes' powerhouse stature in the world of women's track and field during these years. By the time Hymes and Abbott had graduated, Coachman was a seasoned Tigerette who began mentoring the younger athletes that looked up to her.

During her Tigerette years, Coachman matured and came into her own as an athlete. The high jump earned her a regular spot on the team, but, soon, Abbott discovered she could run as well: "When Coach found out I could run, good God Almighty!" she remembered years later. Abbott began entering her in the 50-meter sprint and as the anchor on Team "B" of the 400-meter relay team. When some of her older, and at the time faster, teammates graduated, Coachman took their place on the "A" relay team. By 1942, "the Tuskegee flash" was capturing headlines in the black press for her multiple individual titles and her spot as anchor on the winning relay team. In 1943 she was named to her first AAU All-American team for the 50-meter sprint, high jump, and as a member of the 400-meter relay team. Moreover, Coachman was as talented in basketball as she was in track. She helped lead the Tuskegee women's basketball team to three Southern Intercollegiate Athletic Conference (SIAC) championships and was selected SIAC all-conference guard those three years for her individual contributions to the team.[33]

Coachman graduated from the high school at Tuskegee in 1943, entering the institute in the fall to pursue a trade degree in dressmaking. Incredibly, her most important years as a track and field athlete were still ahead of her. In 1945, she finally bested her perennial rival Stella Walsh for the 100-meter sprint, adding that title to the 50 meter, high jump, and 400-meter relay titles, and winning the individual high-point trophy for the championship. She was by now the unquestioned "queen" of American women's track and field. In 1946, she repeated the quadruple win. Coachman graduated from Tuskegee that year. In her eight years as a Tigerette, she had amassed a total of twenty-three national titles.[34]

As Coachman and her teammates ran, jumped, and threw their way into the record books, they felt uplifted by the Tuskegee community even as white, middle-class society found ways to "explain" the athletes' success. The battle between middle-class women educators and the AAU that had begun during the 1920s had left women's track and field completely marginalized in American society. Since "decent" white women did not participate in such a masculine, competitive sport, African American women's participation and success in track and field reinforced racial and sexual stereotypes long held by white society. In particular, the myth that African American women were better suited for hard labor, either within or outside the confines of slavery, helped explain both their suitability for and superiority in rigorous sport. The sporting world, in general, and track and field, in particular, became the natural playground of black women already masculinized by hard labor.[35] Yet African Americans generally rejected these views that white society held toward black women athletes. In so doing, they embraced and celebrated the victories of athletes like Coachman, Hymes, Abbott, and their teammates. The notion that anyone's individual victory or second-, third-, or fourth-place finish was also a victory for the team, the school, and even the race permeated the atmosphere at Tuskegee, where "they were proud of their athletes." The Tuskegee community reveled in their athletes' successes, particularly those on the national stage. "Everybody was proud of us," recalled one of Coachman's teammates, "because we were really outstanding."[36]

Beyond being encouraged and celebrated within the Tuskegee community, Coachman and her teammates also found acceptance from their white competitors. While white women track and field athletes could not understand the burden of race, they did understand what it meant to compete in a society that marginalized them. Commonly described as "muscle-bound" or referred to as "tomboys" and "muscle Molls," white women who participated in track faced derogatory gender stereotypes similar to their African American counterparts.[37] When the Tuskegee team traveled north to compete in the nationals, African American and ethnic white athletes respected, accepted, and genuinely tried to get to know one another in ways that overlooked the traditional racial barriers of the day. The Tigerettes and athletes from the other teams would spend time between the events talking with and getting to know one another. Coachman believed that talking during competition was robbing her of the energy and focus she needed to participate in, and win, the multiple events she was scheduled for, so she refused to talk to anyone—teammate or competitor—between events.[38] She enjoyed socializing with the other athletes after the competition, however. Years later, she remembered the camaraderie that the athletes shared: "All the white girls up above the Mason-Dixon line—we were just like a family as far as track was concerned. You know, we were there for the track meet and everybody was just friendly."[39] Overlooking the barrier of race and rejecting societal notions that refused to recognize them either as true athletes or "normal" women, they eschewed such thinking and found ways to affirm and acknowledge each other's talent and dedication to the sport.

Rejecting the stereotypes of white society was not the same thing as ignoring them, however, and back home the Tuskegee community worked to dispel such myths. In this regard, the emphasis on middle-class propriety and self-reliance at Tuskegee was particularly important to the athletes. The institute made certain their students knew rules of social etiquette that most of them had had limited exposure to. Champion hurdler Leila Perry, Coachman's teammate and member of the Tuskegee 400-meter relay team, remembered being taught proper table etiquette, such as "when you go out, which way you start with your fork and your knife and what have you. ... They always wanted us to look our best."[40] Tuskegee students were taught to pay attention to their appearance, conduct, and etiquette at all times, although the occasions when the Tigerettes traveled north to compete at the nationals and were thrust in the middle of white American society became especially important. Moreover, Tuskegee's program to instill in its students the accouterments of middle-class manners and etiquette helped the women track athletes representing Tuskegee dispute the negative class connotations associated with their sport.

At home, Tuskegee found additional ways to foster a middle-class lifestyle and enrich its students' lives. School administrators brought in a variety of arts and entertainment opportunities that many of the students would not have been exposed to otherwise. "They had all kinds of activities around the campus for you. And you just kind of grew as a person," Perry recalled. "You weren't just involved in athletics, you were involved in the happenings of the world. Because they brought the world to Tuskegee."[41] The campus, in short, was literally alive with cultural events. Moreover, Tuskegee's own programs and activities were of the highest quality. Coachman's particular focus outside of athletics was the Tuskegee Concert Choir. When she joined the choir in 1943 it was a renowned concert ensemble. Founded in 1931 by William L. Dawson, the choir was soon making appearances at the opening of Radio City Music Hall in New York and at the White House and Constitution Hall in Washington, D.C. Coachman remembered the famous Dawson as a man of strength, perfection, and dedication to his craft. He insisted on the same from his choir. Although Dawson was every bit as demanding as her athletic coaches, the experience with the choir was a healthy diversion for Coachman away from the world of athletics.[42]

In addition to the support and instruction the athletes received from Tuskegee, the black press worked to counteract the stereotypes black women track athletes encountered in dominant society. The phenomenal Tigerettes were no strangers to the sports pages of America's black weeklies as sportswriters celebrated the athletes, bringing the stories of their national championship bids to African American readers. "Tuskegee Girls Retain Nat'l Track Crown; Lula Hymes is Star of Meet," read the sports headlines of the *Pittsburgh Courier* in 1938. The following year sounded much the same in the *New York Age*: "Tuskegee Girls Successfully Defend National Track Title." Year after year the popular east coast black weeklies followed the "Tuskegee Lassies" as they first prepared to defend their national championship title and then handily defeated the other teams. By 1945, one headline captured what most African Americans, by that time, were proudly thinking, "Tuskegee Girls' Team Rules Women's Track World," as the Tigerettes captured their eighth title in nine years.[43]

Coachman's own emergence in the black sports news paralleled her rise in track and field. In 1941, while she was still known mostly for her high jumping capabilities, the *Pittsburgh Courier* captured an image of her performing the high jump at the AAU Women's Nationals, noting how she cleared the bar "with a spectacular leap." African American sportswriters noticed as Coachman began to emerge as the leader of the Tigerettes in 1942, reporting that the team took their sixth consecutive championship title "paced by Alice Coachman." The article featured several pictures, including one of Coachman, the "Tuskegee flash," crossing the finish line in the 400-meter relay. As Coachman reached her full potential in the mid-1940s, the black press celebrated her spectacular performances. "Alice Coachman Crowned National Sprint Queen," read the sport headlines for the *Baltimore Afro-American* in 1945 when Coachman finally bested Stella Walsh in the 100-meter sprint and captured the individual trophy for the meet. Walsh, "generally recognized as one of the all-time greats" in the running world, had already, by 1944, tagged Coachman as "the toughest opponent I have ever met," and "the finest runner I've ever raced against."[44]

Black sportswriters' extensive coverage of Coachman's achievements was necessary to balance the fact that white dailies downplayed or overlooked the contributions of African Americans. Moreover, because women's track and field had fallen into such disfavor in the United States, the white press had for years virtually ignored the sport. While national meets for men's track generally headlined the sports pages, complete with extensive articles and pictures from the meet, the white press granted the comparable women's meet a short one- to two-paragraph article or even ignored them completely. Accompanying photographs were a rarity. When a photograph occasionally appeared, white newspapers generally included a white athlete despite the fact that Coachman or one of her teammates had usually outperformed their white competitors.[45] In short, both their race and gender prevented Coachman and her teammates from appearing in the sports pages of the white press.

Cognizant, then, that women's track and field existed on the margins of both the sports world and American society, African American sportswriters did more than report the athletes' successes; they sometimes used their columns or articles to emphasize the femininity of African American women track athletes. In 1941, the *Baltimore Afro-American* ran a feature article on the stars of the Tuskegee team, discussing their plans after graduation: "I found the group of champions were practical and that they had made preparations to assure their future. These young women, while mixing athletics with studies, enjoy all the pleasures and indicated desires to become a nurse, modiste, teachers and social workers."[46] Coachman described her wish to be either a teacher or social worker, but also told the reporter that "being a good wife when she marries will probably be the fulfillment of her secret ambitions." These features gave the Tuskegee athletes more press, but their central design was to show that "our" female track and field athletes were all women. They were, in other words, not muscle-bound or masculine at all, but typical women with "normal" hopes and desires.[47]

Such efforts by the black press were designed to chip away at the masculine stereotype that plagued women track athletes; however, some articles actually undermined the athletes by conjuring up sensualized images. In a 1940 feature article entitled, "Tigerettes Owe Success to Dr. Carver's Peanut Oil," sportswriter Levi Jolley reported that he had uncovered the "secret" of the team's success. It is worth quoting at some length:

> Consistent use of Dr. George W. Carver's peanut oil is the secret behind the subtle muscular reactions of Tuskegee Institute's four-time women's national championship team. The peanut oil ... is used daily for rubbing members of the girl's track team, Mrs. Christine Evans Petty, coach of the Alabama team, revealed. Questioned regarding the unusual ease and muscular co-ordination of the girls after they set a new national record in the 400-meter relay on a slow track, Mrs. Petty made the secret disclosure. Mrs. Petty, who is easily mistaken for one of her pupils due to her attractiveness and youthful appearance, has coached the team for six years. ...
>
> The smooth velvet appearance of the girls' skin in addition to their rhythm in motion prompted the interrogation of the coach. Slightly evasive, Mrs. Petty spoke about the strict training rules and the fact that the girls frequently were matched against members of the boys' teams during practice sessions. Repeatedly asked what was used for rubbing the girls, Mrs. Petty finally admitted that it was the exclusive use of Dr. Carver's peanut oil. It has been used for more than four years by the athletic department and exclusively by the girls' team.[48]

The notion that a women's team would need a "secret," a magic bullet perhaps, to explain their string of annual championships suggests that the athletes also had to push back against stereotypes within the black community. Even as national champions, the meaning sportswriters sought to attach to black women athletes began to venture beyond their training, talent, and hard work. Phrases such as "the smooth velvet appearance of the girls' skin," and "what was used for rubbing the girls," and elsewhere in the article when Jolley reported that the girls "request rubdowns with the oil to obtain relaxation," evoked sexualized images—images that led to perceptions of athleticism conflated with sexuality. The fact that most sports journalists were men certainly dictated, at least in part, the type of coverage women athletes received, and indeed, African American male sportswriters often wrote glowingly about Coachman and her teammates. Yet in their efforts to counteract the racial and gender stereotype of white society depicting the naturally masculine, athletic black female, the black press created a different, though still gendered, sensual image of these athletes for the African American community.[49]

Even as the black press engaged in its dichotomous coverage of black women athletes, the athletes themselves found camaraderie and acceptance through their relationship with Tuskegee's male athletes. Both Coachman and Petty felt that the Tigerettes received some of their best training by racing against the men's team during practice. Doing so would increase their workout, hone their skills, and provide competition that was otherwise absent, since women's teams of a similar caliber did not exist in the area. Moreover, the camaraderie that the athletes felt toward one another crossed gender lines as well, particularly among the athletes that were there on work scholarships. Coachman recalled how working together really bonded the athletes into a family, like brothers and sisters. Indeed, she derived her greatest inspiration as an athlete not only from teammate Lula Hymes but also from fellow male track athlete Upshaw Sams. Women, as well as men, were athletes at Tuskegee where people overlooked gender stereotypes that persisted elsewhere within American society and the black community. To the public, women track and field athletes often found themselves constructed as some "other" that emphasized race, gender, class, or a combination of the three.[50] At Tuskegee and in the community of track and field athletes that existed there, Coachman and her teammates could be athletes.

Coachman's years at Tuskegee were important in laying the groundwork for the next chapter of her athletic career. When she graduated from Tuskegee in 1946, the Olympic games were just two years away.

Coachman was in an excellent position to qualify for the U.S. Olympic team in at least one event, perhaps more. The reality was, however, that she needed to find a team to train and compete with for the next two years in order to stay in peak condition. Track and field was providing a path and incentive for Alice Coachman to continue her education as she prepared to transition to international competition. Her Olympic experience would not only net her a gold medal but also earn her public praise and recognition beyond what women track and field athletes, black or white, could have imagined.

On the International Stage

While Coachman was anxious for an opportunity to test her skill in international competition, she also understood that track and field was not a solution to earning a living. She could turn to the dressmaking trade she had learned at Tuskegee. But her Olympic dream would most likely vanish without a way to continue her athletic training. Instead, she returned home to Albany to enroll in the historically black Albany State Teacher's College and pursue a college degree in teaching. She also joined the women's track and field team. When it was time for the women's nationals in 1947, Coachman was again competing, this time for a different team. She continued to dominate the 50-meter sprint and added another high jump championship to her unbroken string of national titles.

In 1948, Coachman began training seriously for the first Olympic games to be contested since 1936. Both the 1940 and 1944 games had been canceled due to World War II. Because Albany State's track at the time would not support the level of workout she needed to undertake an Olympic bid, Coachman returned to Tuskegee for a month of intensive training shortly before the Olympic trials, set for July 1948. There she worked with her Albany State track coach, Chris Roulhac, to prepare for that year's women's nationals and the U.S. Olympic trials that followed. At the national championships, she won her tenth straight high jump title, but was bested in the sprints by newer, younger talent, Mabel Walker of the Tuskegee team. At the Olympic trials the following week in Providence, Rhode Island, she bettered the old AAU record from 1933 to easily qualify as a member of the team in the high jump. Later that month, Coachman and the other eleven members of the U.S. Olympic women's track and field team set sail for London.[51]

When the team arrived in London, Coachman discovered that her picture appeared frequently in the press and that she was well known throughout the city. "Everyone seemed to know all about my track record. All those people were waiting to see the American girl run, and I gave them something to remember me by," she recalled years later. In fact, Coachman was not the first African American track athlete whose name and record had become known in Europe. In 1939, Coachman's former Tuskegee teammate and mentor, Lula Hymes, had her sights set on the Olympic games to be held in Finland the following year. In July, Hymes received a letter from a Finnish woman, resident of the town where the Olympic championship village was to be located, inviting the Tuskegee athlete to visit her during the games: "The papers are speaking of a young American girl from the Tuskegee institute in the state of Alabama who has made an outstanding record in athletics ... who may come to Finland in 1940 with the American team. I am writing to congratulate you on your wonderful success and to invite you to be my guest should you visit our country next year."[52] But when the games were canceled in April 1940 due to the global outbreak of war, Hymes never got the opportunity to test her speed against the other women track athletes of the world or take Miss Hildia Tarkiainen up on her offer to visit. Hymes and Coachman's reputations as champion track and field athletes, of little consequence in the dominant American culture of their day, made them important to a European society where women's track was more accepted.

As Coachman began her training in London, she started to feel some pressure to perform well.[53] In truth, the U.S. women's team was not faring especially well at this first postwar Olympics. Pre-competition expectations had been high in part because U.S. athletes had generally bested their counterparts in Canada for years. Yet international competition for women had been in its infancy at the outset of World War II, and the last two Olympic contests had been canceled due to the war. The strength of the various European teams was something of an unknown. As it turned out, they offered considerable competition. Dutch sprinter Fanny Blankers-Koen was the most impressive, winning four gold medals to dominate the sprints.[54] The one bright moment for the United States had been when Tennessee State sprinter Audrey Patterson had won a bronze medal in the 200 meter, making her the first African American woman to medal at the Olympics. But many of the American women track athletes failed to make it to the finals of their events, and those who did generally came up far short of a medal. "I just watched these fast girls out of Chicago, out of Tuskegee, out of Mississippi, out of Louisiana, everywhere all over the United States, just fade away," remembered Coachman.[55] Sitting in the stands and observing her teammates, she began to feel the weight of the team's hopes for her to take home a medal. Much to the frustration of the Olympic coaches, Coachman did not train the day before the competition. She had long made it a practice to rest the day before she competed. Her record seemed to bear out the wisdom of such a ritual, and this time was no different. Following the grueling standoff against Britain's Dorothy Tyler in a drizzling rain, the field judges proclaimed Coachman the new Olympic women's high jump champion for having the fewest overall misses in her jumps at all heights.[56]

Coachman's athletic career had been spectacular, but the press coverage she received in the United States often obscured that fact. On the one hand, the white press had overlooked her accomplishments predominantly because she was a woman competing in a "man's" sport. On the few occasions when white sportswriters had not completely ignored the sport, they had continued to disregard her because she was African American. The black press, on the other hand, had celebrated her achievements largely because she was African American. Because she was a woman who had chosen the most masculine of sports, they helped counteract the negative gender stereotype by focusing attention on her femininity. In doing so, however, they looked for a secret to explain her success and created an image that fused athleticism and sensuality. Coachman's response through the years had been to quietly yet decisively continue winning sprint and high jump titles. Now she stood atop the victory stand at the Olympic games, and the press responded. While the black press applauded Coachman as they had for years, it was the response of white sportswriters that indicated this victory would be handled differently.

The change in Coachman's treatment in the white press was not universal, but it was unmistakable. Indeed, some papers persisted in their habit of virtually ignoring women's track and field. The *New York Times* gave Coachman's win one line at the end of an article, despite the fact that she was the sole gold medalist on the American women's track and field team. Other papers provided more coverage but persisted in perpetuating racial stereotypes. The *Atlanta Constitution* granted an entire article to Coachman's victory, promoting her as a Georgia native.

However, the article concluded with an observation that left the reader with implicit references to two negative stereotypes: "An all-around athlete, Alice is an outstanding forward on the basketball team at college, but her instructors say confidentially that she's 'just a fair student' in home economics." Coachman was, they alluded, an African American who excelled athletically but was not terribly smart, and she was adept at "masculine" sports, in part, because she was not "feminine" enough to even do well in the clearly feminine terrain of home economics. With the Cold War already spreading into international sport by 1948, the *Chicago Tribune* chose to conclude their description of her gold medal performance as a decidedly American victory: "Thus the track meet started as begun eight days ago, with a victory for an American and the Star Spangled Banner of the United States providing the closing music." While the impact of the Cold War on women's track and field would be most clearly felt in the next two decades, the *Tribune*, rather than ignoring Coachman, lifted her up as an American hero who saved the U.S. women's team from a shutout.[57] Clearly, Coachman's determination and perseverance over the years combined with her athletic prowess had resulted in some subtle changes in the white press.

Yet a more marked and dramatic change was occurring in her hometown of Albany, Georgia. Coachman's hometown paper, the *Albany Herald*, had reported on her success as a track and field athlete since the mid-1940s. The coverage had been typical of the white press, consisting of short, one-column articles in the sports section.[58] With her qualification at the Olympic trials, however, Coachman jumped to the sports page headlines— "Alice Coachman, Albany Negro Star, Betters Record, Makes Olympic Team"—becoming the feature in an article that discussed the Olympic trials and the composition of the women's team. Still, while there were two photographs accompanying the feature, neither Coachman nor any of the other women track and field athletes to make the Olympic team were included in them.[59] A week and a half later, the white *Albany Herald* did something that was unprecedented. It devoted an entire article to Coachman's Olympic bid, lavishing praise on the Georgia native: "When the Olympics begin in London this week Albany and Georgia will be represented by one of the most outstanding stars on the American team, one that they may be justly proud to call a native Albanian and Georgian."[60] Such praise from the white press, while rare for a woman track and field athlete of the period, was not *completely* unknown to Coachman who had come to be known as "the Tuskegee flash" by black and white sportswriters alike for her sprinting prowess. What was unheard of was to have an entire article devoted to a woman track star. The article is even more exceptional for being written by the *Herald's* sports editor and for including a photograph of Coachman lined up for a training sprint. Moreover, it appeared two weeks before Coachman competed in the high jump rather than after she was a bona fide Olympic champion. When she won the medal, the *Herald* stepped up the coverage once again, responding with a front-page article. The white newspaper obviously had an interest in Coachman as a native Albanian. No one from the city and only one other Georgian had ever won an Olympic gold medal.[61] Coachman's win at the Olympics was huge. Yet, the *Herald's* location deep in the Jim Crow South of the 1940s makes this act of crossed gender and racial boundaries truly exceptional. Through her outstanding track career, Coachman had made her hometown stand up and take notice, and go on public record as doing so.

The recognition was not over, however. Following a tour to various continental European cities where Coachman and the other Olympic track and field athletes competed and the gold medalist continued her unbroken string of high jump victories, she returned to the United States to a round of celebrations. New York City had planned a reception and parade upon the Olympians' arrival back into the country, but the athletes asked that it be abandoned because they were anxious to return to their hometowns. Other celebrations went forward, however. Jazz musician Count Basie hosted a party in her honor, and she joined the other U.S. Olympic champions as President Truman welcomed them to the White House.[62] Once back in the South, another round of celebrations began. Upon her arrival in Georgia, seven towns on the 180-mile trip between Atlanta and Albany hosted receptions for her. In the city of Macon, in central Georgia, Coachman was greeted by a crowd of approximately two thousand people for a reception in front of the city auditorium. When she finally arrived back in her hometown of Albany, the city honored her with "Alice Coachman Day." The festivities, which city leaders of the black and white communities had joined in planning for a month, included a "mammoth" parade and a program at the City Auditorium featuring a welcome address by the mayor. The day concluded with a college reception at Albany State. *Life* and *Time* magazines covered the event and Movietone Newsreel attended to film the festivities. This was 1948 in the Deep South, however, and racism was entrenched. Coachman remembered how some city officials, despite their willingness to publicly celebrate the hometown Olympic champion, refused to shake her hand. Still, Coachman's hometown had clearly stepped over some rigid racial boundaries to celebrate their new Olympic champion.[63]

The culmination of Coachman's ten-year athletic career resulted not only in an Olympic gold medal but also in recognition beyond anything she might have imagined when her career began. White and black Albanians alike had come together to honor one of their own, a young African American woman who had achieved something significant on the international stage. And the white-run *Albany Herald*, far from burying Coachman's story in a paragraph or two in the sports pages, awarded her front-page status with six articles that reported her Olympic win and the planning and execution of "Alice Coachman Day."[64] Coachman's steady, ten-year career of running and jumping had challenged and pushed back the racial and gender stereotypes of American society that she and others had been facing since before she won her first high jump title in 1939.

Eventually the parades and receptions ended, and Coachman, now in her senior year at Albany State and retired from track and field, resumed her studies. She graduated with a degree in home economics and a minor in science in the spring of 1949. It looked as if the plans she had discussed in 1940 with *Baltimore Afro-American* sportswriter Levi Jolley—to teach and hopefully marry—would be the life that lay ahead of her. In the early 1950s, however, she was given another opportunity that would have seemed impossible just ten years earlier. Coca-Cola, in an effort to incorporate more African Americans in their advertising, approached her with an offer to promote their soft drink. In a company campaign that included several other well-known black athletes and musicians of the period, Coachman appeared in several print ads, both alone and with fellow Olympian Jesse Owens. The two former Olympians were among the first African American celebrities to be featured in company ads.[65] The advertising contract was short lived and the only one Coachman ever received. It paled in comparison to the million-dollar contracts that later sports champions would negotiate. However, the ads, by coupling her with Jesse Owens, equated her athletic significance with the famous Olympian whose four gold-medal performances at the 1936 Berlin Olympics had embarrassed Adolf Hitler. Given the marginal status of women track and field athletes when Coachman began her career in the late 1930s, the inclusion of an African American woman track athlete in an advertising campaign for a major American company marked a profound change.

Conclusion

After her contractual relationship with Coca-Cola ended, Coachman's life once again settled down. She married, had children, and put her degree to good use by teaching physical education in various elementary and high schools. She also stayed active in athletics, coaching women's track and basketball teams, including, for a time, at South Carolina State College and, her alma mater, which had by then become Albany State University. She gave back to the community, working for the Job Corps as a recreation supervisor. She also began the Alice Coachman Foundation to assist young athletes in pursuing their dreams and retired Olympians in preparing for post-Olympic careers.[66]

In the years since schoolteacher Alice Coachman resorted to bringing in her Olympic gold medal to convince her students that she had truly won it, the first African American woman to win Olympic gold has begun to receive some recognition and honors. She has been inducted into nine halls of fame, including the U.S. Olympic Hall of Fame and the National Track and Field Hall of Fame. She received special recognition during the Centennial Summer Games in Atlanta in 1996, being honored as one of the one hundred greatest Olympic athletes. She was also included in the top one hundred female athletes of the twentieth century as determined by *Sports Illustrated.*

Track and field had taken Coachman a long way from picking cotton and sleeping three or four to a bed. Along the way, she discovered a community that sanctioned her participation in track and field. At Tuskegee Institute, a middle-class culture of African Americans accepted her, teaching her the etiquette of a different world and equipping her with an education that would provide the economic means to sustain such a life. When Coachman, Hymes, Perry, and the others brought home national titles, Tuskegeeans throughout the country were proud to call these athletes and their championships their own. Moreover, in training and competing,

Coachman and her teammates pushed beyond the gender and racial boundaries of traditional society. At home, a male coach and mentor ignored American society's gender perceptions of track and field and gave African American women the opportunity to train and compete nationally at a time when few sports afforded them such an option. Beyond the confines of Tuskegee, the Tigerettes joined with white women track athletes to ignore the racism of the day. Understanding the difficulty that came with being a woman track and field athlete in the 1940s, they embraced one another as true athletes, admiring one another's abilities and competitive spirits. And while they were fierce rivals on the track and field, they nonetheless spent time getting to know one another while together.

To the dominant society of her own day, Coachman's position as an athlete and her sports accomplishments for almost ten years meant little. In short, American society had little use for women's track and field of the 1940s and its athletes. Society condemned the sport itself for masculinizing women and its supposed damage to their bodies, and stereotyped its participants as muscle Molls and black women long used to hard labor and therefore better suited to the rigors of the sport. Coachman and her Tuskegee Tigerette teammates understood that their decision toward this particular sport pushed them, as African American women, even further onto the margins of society. But they dismissed American culture's perceptions of themselves, choosing instead to embrace their athleticism and pursue their dreams of individual and team success.

Within the black community, Coachman and her teammates' athletic prowess had met with a different response. As the black press brought their stories to its African American readership, the community celebrated their championships and enjoyed their success on the national stage. Black sportswriters also sought ways to contradict the negative images that white society had created of women track athletes by using feature articles to stress how feminine the Tigerettes were. In doing so, however, they sometimes qualified the athletes' success by searching for magic potions that conjured images of the women's sexuality. The response from Coachman and her teammates was to continue to train hard and win championships, silently refuting the stereotypes and images of white society and black sportswriters.

Coachman's transition from poor, rural beginnings to the top of a medal stand in London, England, and the front page of the *Albany Herald* was a defining moment for black women athletes. Others, such as Lula Hymes and Jessie Abbott, had earned national titles before Coachman. There had been other black women track Olympians, although none of them had earned gold medals. Within black tennis, Ora Washington had even been something of a national sports celebrity to the black community. However, Coachman was the first black woman athlete that white Americans broadly recognized for her athletic accomplishment. Running faster and jumping higher than other American women of her era, persistently and determinedly for ten years, she forced even white Americans to take notice at a time when their general tendency was to ignore women's track and field altogether. Her goodwill and doggedness contributed to, if not the dismantling of the masculinity of track and field, then the beginning of changes in American society regarding the perception of women's participation in the sport. For those to follow, this distinction was an important one that spoke to the possibility of national and international competition that was routinely acknowledged, maybe one day even sanctioned, by the dominant culture.

The same summer that Coachman won her gold medal, a self-confident young Harlem woman named Althea Gibson was preparing to defend her women's title in the American Tennis Association. She and her mixed doubles partner had lost to Ora Washington and George Stewart the year before in 1947, but she had won the women's championship that year and now was looking forward to making it two in a row. It was the start of a tennis career that would rival Washington's for prestige and attention in the black community. When Gibson became the "one" who finally stepped over the color line in white tennis, African Americans celebrated the dismantling of another racial barrier. But along with the celebration came expectations of what it meant to be a race hero. As race, class, and gender commingled in Gibson's story, she discovered that trying to become the first black champion of white tennis meant she sometimes had to stand up to some of the very communities of African Americans that had supported her.

THREE

"A Nationwide Community Project"

Althea Gibson, Class, and the Racial Politics of 1950s Black Tennis

In the waning days of the summer of 1946, a tall, lanky, and tomboyish eighteen-year-old Althea Gibson stepped onto the tennis court at Wilberforce College in Ohio to face Roumania Peters. The women's singles championship in the American Tennis Association was at stake. Peters, a teacher from Tuskegee Institute, was two-time defending women's champion of the ATA, the black tennis association, separate from the United States Lawn Tennis Association (USLTA) that barred African Americans from membership. Gibson was already known for her power and blistering serve, but Peters was an experienced player. Possessing more finesse, and skilled in the nuance of tournament play, Peters overcame Gibson's raw power by pretending she was exhausted at the end of two sets with the score tied. Gibson got cocky and Peters surged back to take the third set, 6–3, as experience overcame youth with a classic psych-out ploy.[1]

Roumania Peters's victory that day was her third and final national title. That match also marked the final time that Althea Gibson lost an ATA national championship. The following year Gibson came back to face another opponent, and this time she walked away with it, retaining the title for ten straight years. By the time she retired in 1958, she had also managed to do what no other African American before her had done—become competitive in the USLTA. Her eight years in white amateur tennis resulted in eleven grand slam titles and back-to-back Wimbledon and U.S. Open singles and doubles titles in 1957 and 1958.[2]

And while she was hesitant to be known as a racial trailblazer, there is no doubt that her success made it easier for players who followed—Arthur Ashe, Zina Garrison, and Venus and Serena Williams—to enter the competitive ranks of lawn tennis.[3]

While it took someone with a competitive spirit, incredible athleticism, and independent personality to accomplish what Gibson did, her rise through first black and then white tennis was also aided by an African American community that stood behind her, helping to create a champion who could rival those of the white tennis establishment. Following Gibson's wins at Wimbledon and the U.S. Nationals in 1957, an African American journalist summarized the community nature of her accomplishment. "Here indeed was the culmination of a dream," observed Ted Poston, "the climax of a nationwide community project."[4] Nationwide in its scope, this community was varied in its composition—from the Harlem Police Athletic League to boxing champion Sugar Ray Robinson and his wife, Edna; from tennis coaches and school administrators at Florida A&M College to a cadre of sportswriters for the black press; and from an out-of-work, Harlem musician to a couple of African American, tennis-playing physicians. Althea Gibson was definitely a community project, but she was not the project of a single community.

Three specific communities largely provided Gibson with the help she needed—the upper-class black elites, represented by physicians Hubert Eaton and Robert Johnson; the American Tennis Association; and the black press. Eaton and Johnson, members of the black elite, not only helped their young protégée learn how to negotiate the elite world of tennis but also provided the financial support necessary to sustain a long-term tennis career in the 1950s. As the African American counterpart to white tennis, the ATA helped find additional financial sponsors, lobbied the USLTA on Gibson's behalf, and provided a proving ground for the young woman from Harlem to test her skills and practice court strategy and etiquette. Sportswriters with the black press brought Gibson's story to their African American readership—praising her triumphs, giving her advice, and providing encouragement during her career struggles. The varied and essential help that these communities provided involved transforming a rough-hewn, headstrong Harlem woman into someone who would be accepted by the tennis elite. In ways that would transcend Ora Washington's experience, class was a central part of Gibson's story. Her New York working-class neighborhood differed starkly from the high-class world of either black or white tennis. The black elites, the ATA, and black press sportswriters who helped her learn to navigate this new environment were willing to groom her for tennis despite what they perceived as the disadvantage of her class background. This grooming was essential, for unlike Washington it was crucial for Gibson to maintain the upper-class mores and dress that these communities helped her acquire.

Gibson and these communities did not always agree with one another over the direction of the project, however, and conflicts arose over what was best for Gibson vis-à-vis black tennis and African American society. Their help carried conditions, such as dictating which tournaments Gibson would play in or assuming she would become a spokesperson for the race. There was much at risk, here. As long as she remained a champion of black tennis, overcoming the obstacle of her working-class background was the primary concern. But as Gibson became the lone representative of the race in the elite, high-profile world of white tennis, the stakes became higher for the communities that had been extensively involved in the "Althea Gibson project." Her Wimbledon victory made her a valuable commodity, and the black press tried to insist that she accept the condition of race hero and civil rights advocate. Gibson chose to dictate the terms of her championship status, however, opting to downplay the racial aspects of her achievement. When she did, members of the black press retaliated, ignoring the obstacles Gibson faced as a women's tennis champion in American society and exposing hidden class prejudice.[5] Yet throughout her career, she negotiated what it meant to be "Althea Gibson," to both the white tennis establishment who finally let her in and African Americans struggling to secure civil rights.

The three communities that became important in Gibson's quest to become the champion of white amateur tennis provide an effective way to guide her intricate story. First, Hubert Eaton, and Robert Johnson, representing the black elite, became Gibson's supporters, sponsors and "family" shortly after seeing her play for the national women's title of black tennis in 1946. While theirs became a close, lifelong relationship, Gibson benefited most from the two physicians' support in these early years of her career. Second, from the time Gibson entered her first ATA tournament in 1942, the black tennis association provided a way for her to gain the experience she needed to eventually play in the white circuit. Yet the organization and its officials became most prominent to Gibson's story during the early 1950s when, as a regular player in the USLTA, her career became central to questions involving the future of black tennis. Finally, the black press followed Gibson's progress through the ATA and as she broke the color barrier on the USLTA and European circuits. But Gibson felt their influence most keenly during the middle–late 1950s when she finally emerged as a champion in white amateur tennis. Before even Eaton and Johnson entered the story, however, Althea Gibson learned to play a form of tennis, quite literally on the streets of Harlem.

Southern Born but Harlem Raised— Gibson's Early Years

In truth, the development of Althea Gibson into a world-renowned tennis champion reads like a modern-day Cinderella story. Born in rural South Carolina in 1927, she was the oldest of five children born to Annie and Daniel Gibson. The family income came from sharecropping corn and cotton on five acres of land. Similar to the Washington family's experience, three years of bad weather convinced the Gibsons to make plans to leave a life of farming and head north. In 1930, when Gibson was three, her parents took the opportunity to send her with her mother's sister when her aunt journeyed back home to New York following a visit to South Carolina. The agreement was that Gibson's father would follow in two months or so, secure a job, and then send for his wife when he had saved enough money. When Daniel Gibson arrived in New York, he found work quickly as a handyman in a garage, making $10 a week. This was an extravagant sum compared to the $75 he earned during his final year of farming cotton. Annie Gibson soon followed her husband and daughter, as the Gibsons became part of the two million African Americans who relocated as part of the Great Migration.[6]

Growing up in Harlem, Gibson was big and tough, and she knew how to take care of herself. Convinced that her father had been disappointed when she, his firstborn, had not been a boy, she recalled how he made up for it by treating her like one, even teaching her to box. "He would box with me for an hour at a time," remembered Gibson, "showing me how to punch, how to jab, how to block punches, and how to use footwork." Such training came in handy because Gibson spent most of her time in the streets, and she was not one to back down from a fight. She recalled Harlem as "a mean place to grow up," and establishing that she could take care of herself kept her from getting beaten up on more than one occasion. Her father's boxing lessons also toughened her up for the corporeal punishment she received from him. She had little use for formal education and would often receive fierce whippings from her father as incentive to go to school, although the beatings didn't dissuade her from regularly playing hooky.[7]

What she enjoyed most was playing ball. She could play any kind, but basketball was her favorite. There was little surprise that she immediately took to paddle tennis when she was introduced to it. Paddle tennis, a variation of tennis, was played on a "court" marked off much like a tennis court, with a wooden racket and either a tennis ball or a sponge rubber ball. The police would block off traffic on the Harlem streets during the day so that the children could use them as playgrounds, and the Police Athletic League arranged competition among children from the various street blocks. Paddle tennis was one of the games they played, and Gibson quickly became the paddle tennis champion of 143rd Street, where the Gibsons had moved after saving enough to afford the rent for their own apartment. Musician Buddy Walker was the first one to notice her athletic ability. During the summer months, Walker supplemented his income by working as a play street leader for the Police Athletic League. He saw her skill in paddle tennis and thought it might transfer over to the lawn game. He purchased a couple of used racquets and started her out by having her hit balls against the wall at some handball courts. Excited at how well she hit the ball, he suggested that the game would expose her to "a better class of people" and perhaps open up the opportunity for her to get off the streets and make something of herself. He was so impressed with the way she hit a tennis ball that he arranged for her to play a couple of sets with some of his friends at the Harlem River Tennis Courts.[8]

One of the men who saw Gibson during her first tennis outing, an African American schoolteacher by the name of Juan Serrell, suggested that they arrange for her to play a few sets with Fred Johnson, tennis pro at the elite, African American Cosmopolitan Tennis Club. The Cosmopolitan in New York City was one of the leading black tennis clubs in the nation. An

ATA affiliate, its members included prominent African American doctors, lawyers, college professors, and famous athletes. Gibson remembered it as "*the* ritzy tennis club in Harlem."[9] Serrell hoped that he could spark some interest among some of the other club members to join him in sponsoring a club membership and free lessons for the young Gibson. Again, her natural abilities impressed those who saw her play Johnson, and Serrell's plan worked. Gibson began taking lessons from Johnson, learning court strategy and why the ball was hit the way it was to achieve different outcomes. She was a fast learner. A year later, in the summer of 1942, Johnson entered his young protégée in her first tournament, the girls' singles division of the New York State Open, an ATA-sanctioned tournament. Gibson won that tournament, and, later that summer, made it to the finals in the girls' singles division at the ATA nationals.[10]

For the next several years, Gibson continued playing in ATA tournaments, moving up to the women's singles in 1946 when she turned eighteen, the year that she faced, and lost to, Roumania Peters. It was at this match that two African American physicians, Hubert A. Eaton and Robert W. Johnson—close friends, staunch tennis enthusiasts, and civil rights crusaders within their own communities—watched from the stands as Gibson and Peters battled each other for the title. Despite the young woman's loss to Peters, they liked what they saw and wanted to help her.

The black elite community, in particular, understood the kind of help and grooming Gibson needed if she were to advance in the world of amateur tennis. From financial support to tennis instruction, from a home environment to fatherly advice—Hubert Eaton and Robert Johnson became the patrons that gave the young athlete essential backing at a critical juncture. Gibson developed a close relationship with the two physicians. She always acknowledged the importance of their contribution to her success. They, in turn, made decisions and offered advice that usually weighed her personal interests ahead of advances for black tennis. Theirs was a good, solid, lifelong relationship. It was not, of course, perfect.

Gibson's "Two Doctors"—Hubert A. Eaton and Robert W. Johnson Represent the Black Elites

No individuals or organization did more to assist Gibson than "her two doctors."[11] Their assistance was varied and essential, and members of the black community, such as Thomas Young of the African American weekly the *Norfolk Journal and Guide*, recognized it:

> A year or so ago I had occasion to say to Whirlwind Johnson that it may take a great many years for history to put in its proper perspective the tremendous contribution that you and he have made to the cause of Negro tennis by developing such champions as Althea Gibson. … I think a great many people already realize that the race would not have a Wimbledon champion today had you not taken her into your home and given her the benefit of your knowledge and experience and the use of your courts for constant practice and training. And when you weren't providing this opportunity, Whirlwind was.[12]

Providing financial support; refining her tennis; making it possible for her to finish high school and secure a college degree; demonstrating the importance of adopting on-court and off-court etiquette and offering a stable, family atmosphere, surrogate parenting, and friendship—these two members of the black elites helped Gibson overcome the immense obstacles that her working-class background presented when faced with trying to break into the sport of tennis.[13]

Black patronage was important within African American society. It often involved black elites working outside their own social circle to help others find ways to become more independent economically. Johnson spent years bringing young tennis talent from various socioeconomic backgrounds into his home during the summers to work with them and see that they had an opportunity to play the ATA circuit. But working-class African Americans also used what they had to help others. Gibson's play street leader for the Police Athletic League in Harlem, Buddy Walker, bought her first tennis racquet though he was an out-of-work musician during most of that time. One of Walker's neighbors, writing to thank Eaton for his involvement in Gibson's life, was also trying to make a difference in the black community: "In a small measure I have been helping youngsters too, only I have so little with which to offer. … May God bless you and your dear family and all others responsible for our step upward as a people among all people."[14] Gibson's experience was a classic example of black patronage by members of the black elite, writ large.

As physician-surgeons living in the South, Eaton and Johnson had similar lifestyles. They each had thriving clinics that provided needed medical care to the African American populations where they lived—Eaton in Wilmington, North Carolina, and Johnson in Lynchburg, Virginia. Both were involved in civil rights issues within their communities. And they both had a passion for the game of tennis.[15] Eaton had won the ATA national junior title in 1933 and played the black intercollegiate circuit while in college. Johnson, a football star at Lincoln University in Pennsylvania, had picked up tennis while there. Both doctors were active in the ATA throughout their lives—playing the circuit, winning nationals doubles titles, and serving as officers, Eaton as president during the 1960s. They even met through the game. When in the 1940s Johnson joined a group of professionals from North Carolina who spent the weekends at one another's houses playing tennis, their lifelong friendship was born.[16]

Though Eaton and Johnson were close friends with much in common, their personalities were colorful opposites. "They're quite different, the two doctors," Gibson remembered in her autobiography. Eaton was tall and slim, while Johnson was short and stocky. Eaton, a graduate of the predominately white University of Michigan, was quiet and his pursuits of tennis, golf, and photography reflected it. "Whirlwind" Johnson was a more active sportsman as reflected in his younger days as a football star at the historically black Lincoln University. Gibson described him as someone who liked to hunt and fish and thought nothing of "driving a couple of hundred miles to see a good football game."[17] Eaton's life was ordered and stable, and he lived it with a sense of duty and conviction. Johnson was more outwardly passionate, his nickname Whirlwind an accurate assessment of his personality both on and off the football field.[18] Through their similarities and differences, they had forged a deep friendship. Together, they used their material wealth, different personalities, passions for tennis and civil rights, and sense of responsibility for the black community to reach out to a young woman who they thought could use their help.

Their joint proposal to help Gibson involved a mutual assessment of two factors—she demonstrated enough raw tennis talent to warrant special attention, and she needed additional formal and informal education to overcome the class barriers of the sport. Indeed, the various accounts of the match in 1946 in which Gibson battled Peters for the ATA women's title have, over time, been colored by the events of later years. They do not agree on specific details, but the points they do agree on are meaningful. As the two doctors watched Gibson play, they both remember Johnson remarking to Eaton that he wished they could find a way to help her. Eaton agreed, and sitting in the stands they began to discuss what shape their assistance might take. Their thoughts ran along two equally important lines. Gibson was a natural talent but needed more formal training in tennis than she had received to be competitive; and she needed instruction in etiquette and personal grooming—wardrobe and hairstyles—as well as additional general education to fit in with the upper-class society that populated the world of tennis. The plan they offered the promising young tennis player was based on these two points.[19] Meeting Gibson after her loss to Peters, they proposed that she live with the Eatons during the school year so she could finish high school and Eaton could help her refine her tennis game on his backyard court. Gibson had graduated from junior high school several years before but then gone irregularly to her first year of high school until she finally dropped out. Under their plan, she would spend her summers with Johnson in Lynchburg, Virginia, concentrating on improving her tennis and traveling the ATA tennis circuit to continue getting tournament experience.

Only one obstacle remained; Gibson had to buy into the proposal. A decade later, she remembered that the decision was not so clear-cut: "How did I know what it would be like for me to live in a small town, especially in the South?" She described the South as "a strange country," where whites did terrible things to African Americans, just because they were African American. "I wasn't at all sure going into something like that was a good idea," she remembered thinking. "Harlem wasn't heaven but at least I knew I could take care of myself there." She might have skipped the whole adventure had it not been for her friendship with the welterweight and middleweight boxing champion Sugar Ray Robinson and his wife, Edna, whom she had met a few years earlier through a mutual friend. Gibson went to the Robinsons for advice, and they insisted that she go. "You'll never amount to anything just bangin' around from one job to another like you been doin'," the champion boxer told the future tennis great.[20] They assured her that no matter what she chose to do with her life, she would be more successful at it if she completed her education. So Gibson wrote Dr. Eaton to say she was coming, and, less than a week later, she found herself stepping into a new world—a world that would teach this Harlem tomboy how to be a "lady," turn the high school dropout into a college graduate, and result in tennis fame on both sides of the Atlantic.

Gibson's move back to the South required considerable adjustment. She may have been born in South Carolina, but she was, by this time, a true Harlemite. The Jim Crow South was unfamiliar to her, and segregation took some getting used to. Years later, she recalled her first shopping trip into downtown Wilmington and being confronted with the "White in front, Colored in rear" sign on the bus. "It disgusted me," she remembered, "and it made me feel ashamed in a way I'd never been ashamed back in New York."[21] Gibson never adapted well to life in the South during the Jim Crow era, but she learned to accept segregation as part of the price she had to pay to succeed in tennis.

The two doctors did not possess Gibson's raw talent on the court, but they were equipped athletically and financially to help her. First, whereas Gibson had come to the game through paddle tennis, both men had been instructed in regular tennis from the start and had played for years. Therefore, they could help her with court strategy and learning to play to her strengths and her opponents' weaknesses. Second, they began teaching her the importance of controlling her emotions during play. If Gibson fell behind in a set, she would often become so angry and agitated that she would end up defeating herself. Although it took her years to learn the art of mastering her emotions on the court, the process began with her two doctors. Third, with courts in their backyards, both men could ensure that their young protégée received regular court time. During the school year, Eaton and Gibson would get in a few games after school before the family sat down to their late afternoon dinner. In Lynchburg, she and Johnson would spend concentrated time on his court before they started playing the summer ATA circuit. As such, they provided Gibson with something that was hard to come by in the world of tennis—plenty of instruction and court time, at no cost to her. Finally, each in turn also paid her living expenses, Eaton during the school year and Johnson during the summer.

Indeed, finances were the bane of a tennis player's existence. In addition to the cost of equipment, dress, and club fees, competition required additional expenses for entry fees, good coaching, and travel associated with participating in the summer tournament circuit. Unfortunately, winning tournaments produced no income since all of the major championships at the time were amateur rather than professional. Champions received considerable prestige and a nice trophy but no money to offset the expense of competition. Amateurism fit the refined, genteel, elitist contours of tennis. It also kept the game more open toward women's participation since professional sport was considered unladylike. However, women who did not have husbands, family, or friends to support them or were not wealthy enough to sustain themselves financially found it necessary to quit the circuit in order to find a career that would bring in money. While there was a professional circuit, this was not necessarily the answer, either. There were very few opportunities for women, and players were barred from amateur tournaments once they turned professional. It was not until the major tournaments went professional in the closing years of the 1960s that tennis players found they could make tennis a career.[22]

Eaton and Johnson did more than provide financial support and help Gibson improve her game. They knew that if she was to succeed in the world of championship tennis, black or white, they also had to help her refine her manners. Fred Johnson, the black tennis pro at the Cosmopolitan Tennis Club that Gibson first worked with, had already tried to help her in this area. He had taught her some footwork and court strategy, and had also talked with her about changing what Gibson had referred to as "her personal ways," such as her arrogant attitude. Unfortunately, Johnson met with little success. Her independent streak was not ready to listen to what anyone had to say about how she conducted herself off the court. She was not, as she remembered, "ready to start studying how to be a fine lady" just yet.[23]

By Gibson's own admission, trying to change her was not an easy task. "I didn't like people telling me what to do," she wrote in her autobiography. She was extremely competitive and confident, even cocky, and the combination could be difficult to take. "The Gibson gal is being accused of giving herself airs since her recent phenomenal successes in contests throughout the world," observed Fay Young of the *Chicago Defender* later in her career. Young thought the accusations by other women players on the tour unfair, but those who knew her had little trouble believing that they *could* be true. Even as the lone black in the USLTA and European tournaments, she had no qualms about telling former champions that bested her that she was really the superior player and would "get them" next time. While Gibson routinely won doubles titles, her success generally came from sheer power and athleticism as opposed to working well with her doubles partners. Only her friend and partner for their 1956 Wimbledon ladies' doubles victory, Angela Buxton, ever managed to work on the court with Gibson the way doubles partners were meant to. Yet the beginning of their partnership had been far from idyllic when Gibson became visibly annoyed with Buxton's poor showing at the Queen's Club championship earlier in the year.[24] Gibson was always convinced that she was the best player on the court, and those who played with, and against, her learned quickly that she felt this way.

Both doctors confronted this part of Gibson's personality as they worked with her on court etiquette. These lessons centered mostly on helping her learn to be a gracious winner *and* loser. Eaton's son and oldest child, Hubert Jr., remembered that the few times his dad would beat Gibson in a set, she would storm into the house and slam the door to her bedroom.[25] In short, she hated to lose. Such behavior was completely unacceptable in black or white tennis of the period. If Gibson expected to advance in the sport, improving her behavior during play was essential. Slowly, the tennis lifestyle began to appeal to her, and she started conforming to the rigid social rules of the game. She also began to learn that "acting like a lady" did not have to adversely affect her game on the court: "After a while I began to understand that you could walk out on the court like a lady, all dressed up in immaculate white, be polite to everybody, and still play like a tiger and beat the liver and lights out of the ball."[26]

Gibson needed help off the court as well, and Eaton's wife was instrumental in working with her on grooming and social etiquette. In her first autobiography, Gibson reminisced about first meeting Celeste Eaton:

> I must have given Mrs. Eaton a turn when I got out of the car and walked through the kitchen door. I was wearing a tired old skirt that I had picked out because I figured it wouldn't matter if it got beat up on the train ride. I hated to wear anything except slacks, anyway, so I probably looked every bit as uncomfortable as I felt. I'd never owned a real dress since I'd been a little girl; a sweater and a skirt combination was as far as I was willing to go in the direction of looking feminine. But Mrs. Eaton didn't bat an eye. I'd never met her before but she hugged me and kissed me as though I were her favorite niece.[27]

Under Mrs. Eaton's watchful eye, Gibson began to pay attention to her personal grooming, presenting herself as a young lady rather than a tomboy. Mrs. Eaton helped her new "daughter" experiment with a new wardrobe, makeup, and hairdos, perhaps for the first time. She also learned that the Eatons expected good manners, honesty, and respect, and that a stop at the neighborhood pool hall was unacceptable behavior for a young woman of the upper class. "Althea was kind of rough around the edges, and my mama tried to do what she could to make a lady out of her," remembered Eaton Jr.[28]

It was not enough, however, for Gibson to take on the outside trappings of an upper-middle-class socialite and remain a high school dropout. Her move to live with the Eatons in Wilmington was also a reintroduction to high school. At the age of eighteen, she entered Williston Industrial High School as a sophomore. Gibson handled school far differently than she had as a teenager in Harlem. She attended regularly, studied hard, joined the women's basketball team, and played saxophone for the school band. Shortly before her graduation from high school in the spring of 1949, Eaton helped Gibson investigate colleges so that she could continue playing tennis and further her education. They visited several campuses of historically black colleges and wrote letters to college administrators. Florida A&M in Tallahassee responded with the best offer—a full athletic scholarship—and Eaton accepted on Gibson's behalf. Two days after graduation, Gibson was college bound.[29]

In three years, she had made significant changes in her personal presentation, had finished high school, and was continuing her education. She was, in short, acquiring the lifestyle of a member of the tennis elite. She was also making important advances in the world of black tennis. Indeed, the doctors' help started paying dividends right away. The first summer Gibson spent with Johnson she won the singles championship in nine tournaments, including the ATA national, and she and Johnson won eight mixed doubles championships. Gibson was on a path to becoming the unquestioned women's champion of the ATA.

Johnson and the Eaton family did more for Gibson than become her tennis patrons, however; they became another family for her. Eaton and Johnson became surrogate fathers to Gibson, and she became particularly close to the Eaton family the three years she lived with them. Eaton and his wife treated her as if she were one of their own children.

She received an allowance just like the Eaton children and was given the responsibility to drop off and pick up young Hubert Jr. at the elementary school on her way to and from school each day. "It was the first real family life I had ever known," she later reflected. After her transition to college, Gibson began a correspondence with Eaton that lasted until he died in the early 1990s. Their letters are replete with his offer of fatherly advice and Gibson's request for it, covering a whole range of topics—her tennis career, education, health concerns, even marriage. They also reflect the Eatons' position as family to Gibson.[30]

Her relationship with her own family at this point remains something of a mystery. The Eatons never communicated directly with Annie and Daniel Gibson after their initial agreement to allow Althea to live in Wilmington. There is evidence, however, that Gibson remained in contact with her parents and occasionally spent breaks back in New York. They saw relatively few, if any, of her tennis matches, but she bought a house for them when she began making a little money after retiring from amateur tennis. What is clear is that once in college, Gibson thought of the Eaton family as home. She would generally go "home," as she called it, to Wilmington during Christmas and at the beginning of the summer before beginning the tennis circuit. "By then," Eaton Jr. remembered, "she was calling my mama, 'mom,' and my dad, 'dad.'"[31]

The two doctors welcomed Gibson into their homes and accepted her as family, but there was also an element of paternalism to the relationship. Eaton and Johnson represented a community of black elites that valued working for the common good of the race. The character of this working for the common good—this racial uplift—could differ across time and community, however. For some African Americans, racial uplift was grounded largely in the economic independence that Booker T. Washington espoused. Others believed that economic independence, though necessary, must be accompanied by a middle-class identity rooted in the patriarchal family. Both of these approaches spoke to uplift as a group struggle that also addressed some very individual needs, as both Coachman and Gibson could attest to. Despite the genuine desire to help individuals, these efforts could also be accompanied by a sense that educated African Americans knew what was best for those less fortunate, as well as for the race as a whole. For Johnson and Eaton, then, bringing Gibson into the upper-middle-class Eaton family grounded her in an identity that helped achieve such uplift and prepare her for the world of white tennis. The paternalism that characterized their efforts to help Gibson was clear from the start. "Knowing that the Jim Crow signs on the tennis courts of the world had to come down sooner or later and that a strong black contender should be waiting in the wings, Dr. Johnson and I began to plan Althea's future," Eaton remembered about the day he met Gibson. Eaton and Johnson's actions in the years to come reflected that they genuinely wanted what was best for their young protégée. But the notion that they "began to plan Althea's future" that day at Wilberforce College reflected a certain arrogance that they knew even better than Gibson what was in her best interest.[32]

Nonetheless, it would have been difficult, perhaps insurmountable, for Gibson to scale the class barriers that stood between her and a Wimbledon or Forest Hills championship without the help of her two doctors. Moreover, as patrons who were well connected to the ATA, they served as advocates for her as she continued to advance in the world of amateur tennis. As Gibson rose to the pinnacle of black tennis, the American Tennis Association emerged as the second community to help her. Similar to her black elite patrons, the ATA wanted Gibson to succeed. The two communities were not always harmonious in their approaches, however. Eaton and Johnson were influential members and officers of the ATA, but they weighed issues involving Gibson's future from a different perspective than others within the black tennis association. The two physicians were concerned predominately with their young charge's welfare, whereas the ATA often made its decisions based on what it thought was good for black tennis. Yet the ATA was not always unanimous in determining what "good for black tennis" meant, and its internal conflicts surfaced as Gibson came to represent African American tennis to a white world.

Gibson and the American Tennis Association

By the time Gibson played her first ATA tournament in 1942, the African American counterpart to the USLTA was celebrating its twenty-fifth year. After the ATA's formation in the decade before Ora Washington began playing at the black Germantown YMCA, the ATA had grown quickly. By 1927, eleven years after the organizing meeting, membership had grown from 23 to 113 clubs. The association had grown in geographical terms, as well, expanding beyond its northeastern beginnings to include representation as far west as California, south to New Orleans, to the midwestern states of Ohio and Illinois, and from Massachusetts to North Carolina along the eastern seaboard. The ATA was flourishing, but only within a particular segment of the black community. There were two reasons for this—expense and limited playing opportunities. Black tennis, like its white counterpart, was predominately pursued by the upper class and occupied an elitist space within African American society.[33]

In the sporting world, tennis had always been expensive to play. Tennis in African American society was no different. In addition to the expense of owning a racquet, players had to be dressed in white with regulation tennis shoes. Most tennis enthusiasts also wanted a club membership in order to obtain regular court time. Yet the expense of recreational tennis was nothing compared to the cost of competition, as was evident in Gibson's case. Financing tournaments was, as the *Chicago Defender* observed in 1940, "the major problem of most tennis players."[34]

A second reason tennis stayed within the upper echelons of African American society involved its setting. As with white society, tennis developed within the network of private clubs.[35] Only a small percentage of African Americans had disposable income to spend on such an extravagant expense. Other venues existed outside the club network, but these posed problems as well. Private courts were small and only accommodated the family and friends of the upper class who built the courts. Parks and playgrounds provided another option, but these were limited and often overcrowded.[36] In short, comparing the expense and opportunity of a sport like tennis with team sports such as baseball, football, or basketball it is easy to understand why the latter spread more evenly throughout African American society. Not only were courts and fields for these sports easier to come by, team sports fostered community and provided opportunities for more people to play at one time.

A 1947 clash among ATA officials clearly reflects the elitist nature that existed in black tennis. This public dissension among top officers pitted officials Maceo Hill and Richard Hudlin against executive secretary Arthur Chippey. Hill was concerned that tennis had fallen behind other sports, like football, basketball, and baseball, in terms of popularity and professional advancement among African Americans. He was convinced that the problem was largely a lack of funds to promote the sport. Along with Hudlin, he proposed moving ATA tournaments off college campuses and into the nation's cities, hoping to generate income to filter into the organization. Chippey flatly disagreed, however, insisting that it would be many years "before the masses can be sold the game, which they do not understand. Tennis will continue … to be a sport played for the love of game and not for the coining of money." Clearly, there was a class prejudice inherent in the culture of tennis. Not only did a word like "masses" and the sentiment that such masses did not understand tennis connote condescension, the amateur nature of the sport also reflected its status as a pastime of the elite. Professionals played for money; amateurs played as part of a superior calling, "for the love of the game." Only those individuals who had the status and money from other sources, however, could afford to hold such high ideals and thus remain in the game. Chippey may also have objected to the cities as a less desirable environment than the college atmosphere that no doubt attracted a more professional and moneyed crowd. While Hill and Hudlin may have been two of the more open-minded officials, the general sentiment of the ATA apparently lay with Chippey; the tournaments remained on the campuses of historically black colleges.[37]

In truth, the nation's network of historically black colleges and universities had provided another avenue for the spread of African American tennis. Upon seeing tennis played in the North, members of Tuskegee Institute's faculty introduced the game to students at the Alabama college as early as 1890. Others followed suit, and by the early part of the twentieth century, many of the nation's black colleges had tennis teams that afforded young men and women a chance to play and compete. Eventually, schools like Tuskegee, Xavier, Prairie View, Florida A&M, and West Virginia State College came together to form various intercollegiate championships. So established was this collegiate network that by the early 1930s, black colleges were contesting the Southern Intercollegiate and Southwestern Intercollegiate Championships, in addition to a National Intercollegiate Championship. At the same time, many of the larger, more established colleges, such as Tuskegee, Prairie View, and Xavier sponsored relay carnivals in which area high schools and colleges would compete in annual tournaments.[38]

Black collegiate tennis helped both sustain and contribute to the growth of African American tennis. Black colleges often had better, more numerous courts, and some of the better coaches. Moreover, collegiate players enlarged the ranks of the summer ATA circuit. Many of the best tournament players, even champions, came to the ATA from some of the nation's top historically black colleges with established tennis programs. Such results had a reciprocal effect. College students that represented their schools well at ATA tournaments often earned recognition for the school, resulting in increased funding for their institution and general support for school athletics. Moreover, black colleges were an important venue for women's athletics, and tennis was no exception. In 1938, Hampton Institute's third annual "Women's Day"—designed to bring together women students and inform the campus community of their abilities and accomplishments—included the finals of the intercollegiate tennis tournament. However, the growth and success of tennis within the nation's black colleges also served to keep the sport circulating predominately among professional African Americans.[39]

Even with its drawbacks and elitist character, the American Tennis Association was an important part of African American society. It connected African American tennis enthusiasts to one another and gave them a means to develop their potential, offering a summer tennis circuit that included an annual national tournament complete with rankings and championship titles. Barred from participation in the white ULSTA, the ATA became the African American equivalent. The organization included a group of committed officers; an organized, sanctioned tournament circuit; and regular publications. The ATA *was* the face of black tennis, and it was becoming an important force in Gibson's life as she became a college freshman.

Gibson's transition from the Eaton household to a dorm room at Florida A&M in Tallahassee in the spring of 1949 was swift. A&M tennis coach Walter Austin wanted Gibson for the team's summer tour that began in July; her arrival in early June allowed practice time with the team before departure. She also enrolled in classes for the summer semester in order to get a head start on her college credits. In addition to participating on the intercollegiate circuit as a member of the Florida A&M team, Gibson also continued playing the ATA circuit. She retained the women's national title, winning it for the third straight year. In truth, she really did not face any serious competition within the ATA, and she longed to see how she would fare against the top women players in the USLTA.[40]

ATA officials had been working steadily for several years to break into their all-white counterpart, lobbying with USLTA officials and looking for the appropriate talent within black tennis.[41] In 1948, they managed to secure an invitation to the National Indoor Championships in New York for Dr. Reginald Weir. A five-time ATA national men's champion in the 1930s, Weir was past his prime and did not advance far in tournament play. As Gibson came to dominate black women's tennis, however, the ATA felt they had someone who could be competitive in the USLTA. In the summer of 1949, they secured invitations for her to two New York tournaments, the Eastern Indoor Championships and the National Indoor Championship tournament that Weir had played in the year before. She represented herself and African American tennis well, lasting until the quarterfinals in both tournaments.[42]

As Gibson was finishing her freshman year at Florida A&M in the spring of 1950, Bertram Baker, executive secretary of the ATA, and Arthur Francis, assistant executive secretary, began seriously working toward invitations to various USLTA tournaments, including the U.S. National Championships at Forest Hills.[43] Invitational tournaments allowed white officials to easily exclude blacks since inclusion in the tournament was through invitation only. The Nationals, coming at the conclusion of the season, could most conveniently exclude African Americans. They refused to issue an invitation to Gibson, as they had African American players in the past, on the grounds that she did not have enough lawn tournament experience. Yet getting such experience meant playing and making a strong showing in some of the major eastern USLTA tournaments earlier in the season, many of which were also invitational. As Alice Marble, white tennis great of the 1930s and 1940s, noted, USLTA officials had Gibson over a "cunningly-wrought barrel."

Marble was perhaps the most important, though not the only, white retired champion who helped Gibson secure the invitations she needed.[44] She was revered by the tennis world, having won the U.S. women's singles championship at Forest Hills in 1936 and 1938–1940. Between Forest Hills and Wimbledon alone, she held eighteen singles and doubles titles. Gibson's style of tennis, her penchant for strong, powerful—what the press referred to as "mannish"—strokes, would later be compared to

Marble's.[45] In terms of personality, she and Gibson were cut out of similar cloth, both being outspoken and confident.

Marble could not understand denying Gibson a place at Forest Hills based only on the color of her skin and was not hesitant to say so. In the July 1950 issue of *American Lawn Tennis*, the former champion wrote an editorial regarding the current position of the Forest Hills committee, publicly taking on the power structure of white tennis. "If tennis is a game for ladies and gentlemen," Marble wrote, "it's also time we acted a little more like gentlepeople and less like sanctimonious hypocrites." She called for the opportunity for Gibson to challenge the current field of women players on the court in the game of tennis, as opposed to the "inner sanctum" of the committee, where a different kind of game was being played. Moreover, she likened Gibson's treatment based on color to the absurdity of denying Marble entrance based on the heavy tan she acquired during the summer, or the bridge of freckles that Margaret duPont collected across her nose. It was, Marble insisted, just as "ridiculous" to snub Gibson for her dark skin as it would be to reject white players for changes to their own pigmentation. Finally, she called the entrance of blacks into tennis "inevitable," as inevitable as it had been in the team sports of baseball and football, and the individual sport of boxing. While the committee may have the power to turn away Gibson, eventually there would be other African Americans who would follow her that could not be denied. "Eventually," she wrote adamantly, "the tennis world will rise up en masse to protest the injustices perpetrated by our policy-makers." While Gibson may or may not have "the stuff of which champions are made," the time to find out should be now, she concluded, not eventually.[46]

Marble's editorial, accompanied by the endorsement of *American Lawn Tennis* magazine, publicly shamed tennis officials for their blatant racism.[47] In fairly short order, tournament officials of the Eastern Grass Court Championships in New Jersey extended Gibson an invitation to play. Her showing there and at subsequent USLTA tournaments were respectable enough that the committee at Forest Hills finally succumbed to the inevitable and issued Gibson an invitation to play at the Nationals that August. Indeed, Marble's almost unbelievable success in securing Gibson an invitation provides important insights into the culture of tennis. USLTA officials had repeatedly denied or even ignored ATA officials' requests to issue Gibson tournament invitations. Yet they responded rapidly to Marble when she exposed their prejudice, suggesting that public embarrassment by one of their own was a more effective tactic than years of patient requests by outsiders. Moreover, Marble's willingness to intercede for another woman coupled with the help Gibson received from other prominent women players like Sarah Palfrey Cooke illuminates the way in which women could stand together in the culture of 1950s white amateur tennis.

Gibson's debut at Forest Hills could not have been more dramatic even if it were crafted by one of the literary world's greatest fiction writers. She won her first match, advancing easily to the second round of play. There she found herself up against Louise Brough, experienced USLTA player and Wimbledon champion. There was little expectation that Gibson would give Brough much competition, particularly after obvious nerves caused the newcomer to drop the first set, 1–6. But during the second set, Gibson settled into her game and came back to win 7–6. The young African American sensation led the third set and was on the verge of one of sports' greatest upsets when lightning, thunder, and a deluge of rain halted play. Gibson had all night to let her nerves remind her she was the rookie and Brough the champion, while the seasoned champ had the night to remember the same. Gibson came back the following day and battled hard, but the match, near completion anyway, was over in eleven minutes with Brough the victor. However, Gibson had made it to the hallowed grounds of Forest Hills, and she had been a more than able representative of African American tennis. It would not be long before she played her first tournament across the Atlantic. The following year, in the summer of 1951, Gibson broke the color barrier at Wimbledon where she made it to the third round before being eliminated by Beverly Baker.

The ATA heralded Gibson's dramatic breakthrough into white amateur tennis, but her advance also exposed tensions that lay just under the surface of its official ranks. At issue was the future of black tennis, and Gibson's advance laid it bare. What would the future of the ATA look like if its players began routinely deserting it for the USLTA? How should the ATA develop young tennis talent that was good enough to compete against white players in the American and international tennis scene? Would the development of talent to such levels backfire on the organization, causing African American tennis players to leave the ATA circuit? How, in short, should African Americans integrate into the dominant white society and continue to sustain racial organizations and retain an ethnic identity? These questions that faced the ATA—the same ones that were facing baseball's Negro Leagues and other parallel organizations within African American society as integration proceeded—became increasingly important as Gibson broke the color barrier and attempted to win a major championship during the 1950s. In the process, the ATA, Gibson's black elite patrons, and Gibson herself struggled and disagreed over the young tennis player's own interests versus those of black tennis.

The ATA believed that helping Gibson was good for black tennis. They just did not always agree on whether "good for black tennis" meant making headway in the USLTA or supporting the ATA tennis circuit that had given Gibson her start. "It is rumored," reported the *Baltimore Afro-American* just prior to her first U.S. Nationals tournament, "that an ATA executive threatened to keep Miss Gibson out of the Forest Hills tourney if she failed to appear at the ATA nationals." The difficult choice between whether to play in white or black tournaments peppered her career. While the decision was ultimately Gibson's, the ATA continued to make it clear that her choice had consequences. Even Eaton's entry into the discussion did little to persuade other ATA officials that, by the mid-1950s, Gibson faced virtually no competition in the ATA and was better off playing the women's doubles at Forest Hills.[48]

These were hard choices, and the tension of what was best for Gibson versus African American tennis could play out differently depending upon the situation. In the fall of 1950 and into the spring of 1951, the decision was to come down as a choice between the white tennis circuit and black education. This time, the same ATA officials who had stood against the black elites and white tennis on other occasions felt that Gibson's entry into European tournaments would now advance the cause of black tennis.

While she was in New York debuting at Forest Hills, Baker and Francis of the ATA had met with Gibson to discuss the possibility of a European tour prior to the 1951 Wimbledon tournament. The plan involved leaving school early in the spring in order to spend a few weeks in Detroit. While there, she was to work with renowned tennis instructor Jean Hoxie before departing the country to participate in ranking European tournaments in preparation for Wimbledon. Johnson and Eaton, as well as administrators from Florida A&M, were not invited to the New York meeting.[49] When they learned of the proposal, they opposed it on the grounds that Gibson would potentially lose that semester of college. Baker and those within the ATA that sided with him accused Johnson and Eaton of "doing the race a great injustice."[50] In part, these conflicts were the result of struggles for power over who would determine what was best for African American tennis. Also at stake, however, was the future of Althea Gibson.

Eaton and Johnson both hoped Gibson would continue to advance in the USLTA and world tennis, but not at the expense of her education. "I told her [Gibson] that I did not approve of any tennis that would interfere with her scholastic work to such an extent that she would lose time out of school. That explains my attitude towards her future," Johnson wrote to Baker in his typically forthright way.[51] Eaton concurred with Johnson and went on to advise Gibson against listening to officials and factions that may not have her best interest as their primary motive. Writing to her while in school at Florida A&M, he assured her that, in weighing the alternatives of this or any decision, he would always try to let what he thought was in her best interest be his guide. In this case, he concurred with Johnson, thinking it was best that she not do anything that would jeopardize completing her education. While he, Johnson, and others could advise, he noted, the final decision was up to her. His final recommendation, however, was that she should be "very skeptical in going against the advice and decisions of those whom you must know are personally interested in you and your welfare." Both doctors understood that Gibson would one day leave tennis competition and need something to sustain her financially. They hoped a college education would help provide that something.[52]

Moreover, Eaton's comment to Gibson that it was up to her to make the final decision addressed the main actor in the entire drama—Althea Gibson. At the beginning of their relationship, the three had come up with an arrangement for making decisions if there were disagreements—they would each get a vote on the issue, with the majority deciding. This was an agreement in principle only, however, and Eaton understood perfectly that, in the end, their protégée was an independent young woman more than capable of making her own decisions. Eaton suggested that Gibson might consider checking with her professors about taking her semester exams early, cutting down her time in Detroit with Hoxie, and/or shortening the length of the tour, thereby making the trip without jeopardizing her college semester. Gibson took Eaton's advice and rearranged the plan somewhat so as not to lose her semester.[53]

In 1954, while Gibson continued to dominate the ATA and attempted to win a major tournament in the USLTA, ATA officials once again publicly quarreled over issues brought on in part by Gibson's transition to the white tennis circuit. At the center of this controversy was one of Gibson's black elite patrons, "Whirlwind" Johnson. Johnson was committed to expanding the small junior development efforts he had started from his home, convinced that only through a solid program could the ATA ever hope to continually see its top players compete against the best in the USLTA. Yet, there was a downside to accomplishing such a goal. Just as the Negro Leagues were in decline as more opportunities opened up for African Americans in the Major Leagues, executive secretary Bertram Baker represented those within the ATA who feared black tennis would suffer a similar fate from an exodus of its best players to the USLTA. While African Americans longed for an end to segregation, in truth the prospect of integration also generated concerns over the fate of black institutions and anxiety over a loss of identity and community. What would become of the black press and other black businesses, as well as the livelihoods of African American doctors, dentists, hairdressers, funeral directors—the list seemed to go on—when blacks were allowed access to white institutions? These were real concerns that plagued the black community even as they struggled hard toward full integration and civil rights.

In the midst of such anxiety, African Americans could have very different approaches to moving forward. Johnson and those who sided with him, already recognizing a decline in the ATA, were looking for ways to develop the black circuit while continuing to make inroads in white tennis. Johnson wanted to pattern the ATA junior events and a development program after those in the USLTA, which he considered superior. He lobbied for support to separate the junior from the senior tournaments, to introduce teaching and demonstration clinics, and to establish competition by age group. These efforts, he hoped, would infuse new life into the organization. The subject of the junior development program deteriorated from a discussion to a verbal brawl in which Johnson accused Baker of "running the ATA" and wanting to "kill our program," while Baker shot back that Johnson's words were those of "a childish and irresponsible mind."[54] There was more involved here than a difference of opinion over cultivating young talent, as Baker made clear in a letter to Johnson. Noting that the ATA cultivated black tennis when there was no other avenue open to African Americans, he went on to contrast Gibson's dedication to the ATA—she had "never deserted an A.T.A. Tournament, although some tried to influence her to do so," a direct dig at Johnson—with Reginald Weir's "desertion." Weir had been the black men's champion that had been invited to play at the USLTA National Indoor Championships in 1948. According to Baker, he had deserted the ATA and was now unknown to the junior players and his value within the USLTA was nonexistent. In truth, Weir was a champion in the 1930s, and his "desertion" was in reality more akin to retirement. Baker's final comment to Johnson exposed the true underlying tension, however. "We welcome integration," wrote Baker, "but believe me, the Negro will always have to make good on his own and with his own people thus demonstrating racial pride, self respect and integrity. These qualities are the passport to integration." On the one hand, Baker was clearly concerned that rapid integration into the USLTA would eventually lead to the demise of the ATA. Johnson, on the other, felt that integration was the only path to enriching and spreading tennis within the African American community, regardless of what the ATA itself came to look like in future years. At issue, in reality, was not only the future of black tennis, but how best to move forward as a race in the sport while retaining an ethnic identity.[55]

Conflict between the ATA and the black elites placed Gibson at the center of controversies involving the future of the ATA. In the disagreements that developed, officials and patrons sparred over how best to advance her career, ensure her continued education, and continue to make inroads into the integration of white tennis. While Gibson was far from a passive participant in the ATA conflicts, these controversies seemed to play out around her.[56]

As Gibson edged closer to becoming the first black champion of U.S. amateur tennis, the third community that aided her became increasingly important. Initially, the black press guided, nurtured, and advised the emerging tennis star. But when Gibson established herself in opposition to black sportswriters, the relationship between the two became strongly contested. The direction of Gibson's career and how it could best serve black tennis was a central concern of the ATA. Black sportswriters, however, sought to determine how Gibson could best serve the African American community as a whole. With the welfare of the race now at stake, "winning" the disagreement became pivotal. As a result, the ensuing exchange between Gibson and the black press became more heated than those within the ATA or between ATA officials and the black elites. More important, still, was the *nature* of the exchange, the manner in which black sportswriters chose to attack Gibson. By resurrecting the young tennis player's working-class beginnings, the black press exposed the rawness of class within African American society of the 1950s and the way it could become an issue when someone like Gibson tried to negotiate her place as an important sports figure in the burgeoning civil rights movement.

From "The Slender Harlem Stroker" to "The Daughter of a Garageman"— Gibson and the Black Press

By the time Gibson was becoming a force in amateur tennis, black newspapers had been in existence for some 120 years, having gone in that time from pleading the cause of abolition to calling for an end to racial segregation. Through their columns, they sought to provide counsel, education, and guidance to the black community; assist people in trouble; and work toward the eradication of injustices. Shut out of most white newspapers, black weeklies also featured the newsworthy accomplishments of African Americans in the arts, sports, and politics.[57] It was common for someone of Gibson's athletic abilities and accomplishments to be featured in the black press, just as Washington and Coachman were in decades before her. As they brought her story to the African American public, sportswriters not only lauded her successes but also gave her advice and encouragement.

Excited by her rapid progress, the black press began seriously covering Gibson's tennis exploits as she started winning ATA tournaments in the late 1940s. "She is a prohibitive favorite to once more clean up the opponents who gather at Orangeburg this week," reported the *Pittsburgh Courier* as Gibson prepared to defend her national title in 1948. Sam Lacy of the *Baltimore Afro-American* was already surmising in 1947 that the "youthful femme sensation" was being groomed for the U.S. Nationals in the USLTA. Following her spectacular match against Louise Brough at Forest Hills in 1950, Jackie Reemes of the *New York Amsterdam News* captured the sentiment of the sporting news community that there was "little doubt that more will be heard from Althea in future competition." The black press did more than report Gibson's accomplishments and predict future success; it addressed her weaknesses as well. As sportswriters assessed Gibson's readiness for her 1950 debut at Forest Hills, they noted that she played a "good attacking game," but it was one they also described as erratic. Fay Young of the *Chicago Defender*, a perennial advice giver throughout Gibson's career, predicted great things for her as early as 1947, "but only if she keeps both feet on the ground and doesn't 'lose' her head." The black press considered the young woman from Harlem a work in progress, worth helping. Clearly, they were poised for her continued advancement in the world of white tennis.[58]

But the years that followed the historic firsts of 1950 Forest Hills and 1951 Wimbledon were disappointing for Gibson, perhaps due to the pressure of balancing school, finances, and tennis, coupled with her own immaturity. In terms of tennis, she managed to win everything in the ATA and nothing in the USLTA. She had been only a point away from beating a U.S. national champion in the late summer of 1950, but since then could not even make it to the finals. During these barren years, black sportswriters reported her victories in the ATA but remained graciously silent over her struggles in the USLTA. They praised, advised, and encouraged, but they did not give up on her.

Outside of tennis, Gibson graduated from Florida A&M in the spring of 1953 and accepted a job in the physical education department at historically black Lincoln University. But having lived mostly in cities, she was unaccustomed to life in the small town of Jefferson City, Missouri, where Lincoln was located. By the fall of 1955, she was tired of Jefferson City, frustrated with her tennis career, and ready for a change. While at Lincoln, she had begun dating an army captain. The idea of joining the Women's Army Corps (WACS) sounded like a more sensible and exciting thing to do than continue the downward spiral she was on with tennis. She completed an application for the WACS, easily passed the physical, and awaited a phone call from the army to give up her life of amateur tennis and accept a commission as a second lieutenant. Before the phone call came, however, a conversation at that year's Forest Hills tournament with Renville McMann of the USLTA made Gibson think that the change she was seeking might come within the world of amateur tennis. The U.S.

State Department was sponsoring four tennis players on a goodwill exhibition tour of Southeast Asia, and they wanted Gibson as one of the two women players. The United States used these goodwill tours of athletes or entertainers during the Cold War to strengthen their image abroad, and it often selected African Americans to participate to dispel "rumors" of poor American race relations.[59] Gibson accepted the offer to accompany Karol Fageros, Ham Richardson, and Bob Perry, and the four left in January 1956.

The 1956 tour was not only a memorable experience for Gibson but it also turned around her sagging game of tennis. Ham Richardson, the captain of the foursome, was a seasoned player at the international level. He and Gibson developed a friendship on the tour, and he began teaching her how to use her formidable athletic skills to win matches. He taught her which points in a game were most important, when it made sense to try an ambitious shot, and when to try to gain control back from her opponent. Such instruction was exactly what Gibson needed. She learned quickly, and the improvement in her game was palpable. While on tour and in its aftermath in the European season, she won sixteen of eighteen tournaments, including the French Open. The black press noticed the change, commenting on the improvement in her legwork and praising her hard work through the years to overcome her mistakes.[60] Although she arrived at Wimbledon on top of her game and favored to win the women's singles title, she also arrived exhausted. The Wimbledon victory would have to wait a year. But she had finally matured as a tennis player, learning court strategy, how to capitalize on an opponent's weaknesses, and how to control her emotions on the court so that a rough patch of play didn't completely undo the match for her. As such, Gibson never became a second lieutenant in the WACS but returned to the States and continued a rejuvenated tennis career. The following two years became the reign of Althea Gibson with back-to-back wins at both Wimbledon and the U.S. Nationals at Forest Hills, the highest prizes in the world of white amateur tennis.

Gibson's success was important in and of itself, but it and her relationship to the black press were also heavily influenced by a huge sports news story of the late 1940s—Jackie Robinson's breakthrough in major league baseball. Sportswriters like Wendell Smith of the *Pittsburgh Courier* and Sam Lacy of the *Baltimore Afro-American* had worked steadily since the 1930s toward ending the unofficial ban of African Americans that had existed in baseball since before the turn of the century.[61] Through their sports columns, Smith and Lacy questioned the economic "sense" of African Americans attending games and supporting major league teams, debunked the myth that black ballplayers were not talented enough to play with white professional ballplayers, and blasted white team owners who refused to hire black players. They also arranged meetings with white major league officials to try to make inroads. Finally, when Brooklyn Dodgers' general manager Branch Rickey began looking for a black ballplayer who could make it in the major leagues, both Smith and Lacy recommended Jackie Robinson.[62] Rickey liked Robinson, and in 1947, after a year with the top Dodger farm team in Montreal, the Brooklyn Dodgers introduced American society to the first black major league baseball player of the twentieth century. To say that the eyes of African American society were fixed on Robinson and that he did not disappoint is to make an understatement of huge proportions. "To black America," observed historian Jules Tygiel, "Jackie Robinson appeared as a savior, a Moses leading his people out of the wilderness."[63]

It was the same summer that Robinson donned a Brooklyn Dodger uniform that Gibson began her ten-year reign as the women's champion of the ATA. African American sportswriters, encouraged by the breakthrough in baseball, turned to Gibson and tennis looking for another victory. The young woman from Harlem quickly made the predictions of black sportswriters come true. But having witnessed Gibson break the color barrier in tennis in 1950 and 1951, African American journalists then waited six years for a major tournament victory. As they waited, the black press was not alone in considering Gibson's career in terms of what it meant for the race. The black elites and the ATA also thought in these terms, particularly as they contemplated an African American Wimbledon or Forest Hills champion. ATA officials Baker and Francis thought advances in white tennis should, at times, take priority over Gibson's college education. And the spring before her first Forest Hills berth, Eaton reminded his young protégée of her responsibility to the African American community: "You need to constantly remember that the eyes of the tennis world are on you and what you do this summer can make or break the immediate future of negro tennis."[64] Indeed, many of the participants in the Althea Gibson project saw her as the "Jackie Robinson" of amateur tennis.

When Gibson ascended to the top of white tennis in the late 1950s, the tenor of African American civil rights within American society had changed significantly in the ten years since Robinson had broken the color barrier in baseball and Coachman had won her gold medal. In 1948, President Truman signed the order to desegregate the military. Six years later, the Supreme Court dealt segregation its first mortal blow, ruling in *Brown v. Board of Education* that school segregation was inherently unequal, and therefore, unconstitutional. In the wake of the *Brown* decision, the civil rights movement began to gain increasing momentum. When Rosa Parks refused to give up her seat to a white patron on a Montgomery, Alabama, city bus in December 1955, a young Martin Luther King Jr. mobilized the African American population of that city to boycott city buses for over a year and win the end to segregation in that arena. And Gibson's own electric summer of 1957 when she won both Wimbledon and Forest Hills occurred at the same time as the *Brown* decision was being tested in Arkansas. When Arkansas governor Orval Faubus called out the National Guard to prevent nine African American children from entering a white public school, President Eisenhower sent in federal troops and federalized the Arkansas Guard troops to protect the children—now known as the "Little Rock Nine"—and carry out integration of the school. While important federal legislation like the Civil Rights and Voting Rights Acts were still a decade away, the 1950s were a period when African Americans began to expect changes and look to those who were living out the changes as race heroes.

Given this backdrop, then, black sportswriters wanted more than to frame Gibson's career in racial terms; they insisted on another race hero. Perhaps they even felt that Gibson owed them for their patience during her barren years of the early 1950s. During that time they had encouraged and advised. They had touted her victories in the ATA but remained patiently silent regarding her mediocre play in the USLTA. They worked with her to soften the abrasiveness of her personality. Fay Young had "chided" her at one of the ATA championships when she chose not to mix freely with other players. The exchange, apparently, was pleasant and the advice accepted because the reporter later complimented Gibson on her "improvement," at which she laughed, understanding what he meant. Sportswriters even convinced themselves that the tennis star viewed things similarly to the way they did. "You can take it from me," Young wrote during the 1956 Wimbledon tournament, "she [Gibson] looks upon herself as an evangelist whose skill with the tennis racquet, and her sincerity, is breaking colour barriers."[65] Black sportswriters were hungry for Gibson to prove that their trust in her abilities had not been misplaced. When success finally came, they assumed she would be willing to use her position as tennis champion to push back against Jim Crow injustices of American society.

The Robinson legacy and the "future of Negro tennis" was, no doubt, a heavy load, and Gibson was not interested in carrying it. "I have never set myself up as a champion of the Negro race," she reflected in her autobiography. Those who really knew Gibson understood that, whereas Robinson seemed to thrive on his role as a civil rights hero, she shied away from it. She freely acknowledged the debt she owed to Robinson, that his success in the major leagues most likely made hers in tennis possible. Although realizing the importance of her own breakthrough to other African Americans who wanted to compete against whites, she was not interested in "flaunting" it as a racial success. Others may choose to stress that aspect of her career, "but I have to do it my way," she insisted.[66] She was willing to allow others to "make a fuss" over her role in breaking down color barriers, but wanted none of it herself. Perhaps Gibson was a bit naïve to think that her success in white tennis could be completely divorced from its racial significance. Or perhaps she understood her limitations in being a public face for integration. Regardless of the reason, as sportswriters reached back to her humble beginnings to try to "shame" her into becoming the kind of champion they wanted, Gibson stood her ground to remain the kind of champion she had crafted for herself.

Following her Wimbledon victory in 1957, Gibson traveled to Chicago for the National Clay Courts Tournament. While there, an elite hotel and restaurant refused her reservations. When the Wimbledon champion chose not to "make a fuss" over the incident, it seemed as if she became a target of black sportswriters overnight. In truth, such a rupture had probably been brewing for a while. Not afraid to speak her mind, Gibson was not always savvy with the press. But rather than mention the hotel and restaurant situation or her refusal to be a civil rights' crusader, the black press chose to attack Gibson's personality, specifically her independence and self-confidence. It appeared as though they were upset with the tennis star's treatment of them in Chicago. Stories circulated through several of the black weeklies about Gibson "brushing off" the press while in town, postponing or refusing to grant interviews, and being, in general, a prima dona. This, in turn, led to accusations of stubbornness, arrogance, and impudence.[67] "The most arrogant person I've ever seen," "ungracious as a stubborn jackass," and "obsessed with herself and her court skill," read the descriptions. Yet Gibson had always been brash, temperamental, and over-confident. In the past, the black press's response to this difficult yet brilliant athlete had been to advise and sometimes chide, but never attack. Fay Young had even called her "misunderstood." As a newly crowned tennis champion, however, she now possessed the stature to speak out for the race. When she refused to be molded into a civil rights advocate, the black press turned Gibson's difficult personality against her.[68]

But the attacks did not stop at her personality; sportswriters raised Gibson's working-class background as well. Formally known by the press as the "slender Harlem stroker," she now became "the lanky daughter of a garageman." Russ Cowans of the *Chicago Defender* questioned whether Gibson's transformation to the genteel, gracious, high-class world of tennis had really taken: "I admire Althea's ability on the court," noted Cowans, "but you can't make a silk purse out of a sow's ear, and you can't make a gracious person out of Althea." Another reporter suggested that Eaton and Johnson had enabled Gibson to "skip" through college "under the pretense of being a student and scholar," a subtle reference to her pre-Wilmington days as a high school dropout.[69] Clearly the substance and viciousness of the attacks were out of proportion to the episode and point to something beyond Gibson's difficult personality. At issue here was her inability to completely transcend her working-class roots. Such class prejudice remained buried while she was a champion of African American tennis. But her championship status in white tennis, in American society, was so important an achievement for the race that the black press would not tolerate Gibson's rejection of their condition that she serve as a race hero. When she did, the subject of her working-class background became attached to her public image.

In truth, the stakes were now so high—Gibson's willingness to advocate on behalf of the entire race—that anything short of Gibson's full acceptance and participation would probably have been problematic for the black press. The Chicago episode became so important and charged an exchange as to make it difficult to determine how much of it was attributable to Gibson's brash manner versus the black press's desire for a race hero. References to the incident varied widely in what they chose to address, and, of course, where they placed the blame.[70] When Gibson's cocky personality got the best of her, she could be an obstinate and complicated individual who was difficult to relate to. However, the *nature* of the press attacks by black sportswriters is what is at issue here as well as the decision to return so clearly and directly to an athlete's working-class upbringing. Moreover, the class prejudice and desire to reshape Gibson's public identity after her Wimbledon victory extended beyond the black press. Nana Davis, who had beaten Gibson for the 1942 ATA junior girls title, gave an interview and spoke about her former competitor in the aftermath of the 1957 Wimbledon tournament: "Althea was a very crude creature. She had the idea she was better than anybody. I can remember her saying, 'Who's this Nana Davis? Let me at her.' And after I beat her, she headed straight for the grandstand without bothering to shake hands. Some kid had been laughing at her and she was going to throw him out." Davis's recollection of Gibson some fifteen years earlier as "a very crude creature" was probably motivated largely by jealousy. But as with the black press, it was the nature of Davis's comments that is telling. Despite the intervening years and her efforts to present herself differently, Gibson's working-class background was pulled out, dusted off, and attached to her in a public, powerful way.

In truth, however, the attacks on Gibson were more complicated than an intersection of the community's desire for race heroism and latent class prejudice resurfacing, for 1950s womanhood further proscribed her place in American society. The class requirements of tennis made demands on Gibson from the start, but race expectations and class prejudice lay dormant as long as she remained in the confines of black tennis and African American society. As she emerged as a champion in American society, there were those in the black community who expected her to serve as a public advocate for the race. Yet middle-class femininity made it virtually impossible for her to live up to such expectations and assume the hero-like status of a Jackie Robinson. In the culture of 1950s America, it would have been inappropriate for a woman, particularly a woman of the elite, white amateur tennis world, to "make a fuss" in a public setting. Perhaps Gibson understood such limitations when she made it clear that she preferred to make civil rights advances through her individual accomplishments. Or perhaps she was just being her typical independent self. Perhaps the black community would have been willing to overlook such a breach of etiquette in exchange for her willingness to become a civil rights advocate, but would white America? When Gibson refused to be a race hero but instead acted in accordance with the class and gender rules dictated by her emergence as the "queen of women's tennis" in American society, it was almost inevitable that her public image became as complicated as it did. Being a black woman tennis champion in a white world was difficult indeed. It was to Gibson's credit that she chose to do it on her own terms.

Conclusion

Gibson's climb to the pinnacle of white amateur tennis had clearly been "a nationwide community project." From her early days playing paddle tennis on the Harlem streets, members of the black elites, the ATA, and the black press noticed Gibson's natural athleticism. They understood that such talent, if nurtured, might be her ticket to a better life and African Americans' ticket to entering white tennis. After sixteen years, "a Harlem urchin discovered by Negroes, nurtured by Negroes, trained by Negroes, educated by Negroes, was now the best in the world in 'the game of ladies and gentlemen.'"[71] The "project of Althea Gibson" had reached a successful conclusion. It was time for the queen of women's tennis to begin shaping the rest of her life.

While Gibson had experienced a dream come true as the Wimbledon and U.S. national women's champion in 1957, she was finding it increasingly difficult financially to remain in competition. She recognized that she was at a crossroads in her life, that her days on the tennis circuit were drawing to a close. "All of my problems weren't, of course, solved because I was the champion tennis player of the world," she reflected in her autobiography. "I had to think about making enough money to support myself, about fitting myself, a Negro girl, into the larger world that I had come to know and to enjoy."[72] Gibson spent most of the rest of her life trying to find her place in that larger world. If in her first thirty years she achieved her dream "to be somebody," the remainder of her life proved a stark opposite.

After defending her titles in 1958, Gibson surprised the sporting world by announcing her retirement from tennis. While she had not made a decision about what she would do next, she expressed optimism regarding what she thought were some viable options for the future. Initially, she hoped to launch a singing career. She cut one album, entitled *Althea Gibson Sings*, and appeared twice on *The Ed Sullivan Show*, but her singing voice, while pleasant, was not exceptional. She also accepted a bit part in a John Wayne western and hoped for more calls from Hollywood, but they never came. For a year she tried cashing in on her tennis fame by joining the Harlem Globetrotters on tour. She and her friend Karol Fageros from their State Department tour days played tennis exhibition matches before the Globetrotters' games. This arrangement earned her some money but not enough to compensate for the difficulty of spending a year barnstorming the country. Next, she decided to try funding her own exhibition tour. However, she underestimated the risks involved and ended up losing money when she had to cancel the tour halfway through its schedule. She was able to earn a bit of steady income through her celebrity status by becoming the spokesperson for Ward Baking Company. She eventually let this relationship go in order to spend more time on her next adventure—professional golf. She broke the color barrier in this sport as well and earned a little money but never a major tournament. While launching her golf career, she and William Darben, the brother of her close friend Rosemary Darben, renewed a twelve-year on-again, off-again relationship. In 1963, she married him in a quiet ceremony in Las Vegas.[73]

By the 1970s, Gibson was truly struggling. She continued to dabble in various arenas, trying to cash in on her tennis fame. She spent some time as the commissioner of the New Jersey Athletic Association. But this was a figurehead position as opposed to real employment, paying only a small stipend. She attempted a run for political office in New Jersey, but was unsuccessful. Living apart much of the year due to her continued attempts to become successful in golf, she and Will Darben divorced in 1976. She married again in the early 1980s, to former coach Sydney Llewellyn, but this marriage lasted less than three years.[74] Eventually, Gibson was living virtually destitute in a small apartment. Unable to pay her bills, feeling as if the sporting world had forgotten her and contemplating suicide, she placed a call in 1993 to her friend and former doubles partner Angela Buxton to say goodbye. Buxton rallied the tennis world to Gibson's cause, raising money and awareness to her friend's plight.[75] Gibson lived another ten years. When she died in 2003, her contribution to women's tennis and African American civil rights once again became news as her obituary populated the Internet and newspapers throughout the country. Clearly Gibson had had a rough transition from her tennis fame and lifestyle to ordinary life.

What accounts for Gibson's fall from the pinnacle of amateur tennis to a poverty that she had not even known as a toddler in a sharecropping family? It seems clear that Gibson, like many successful athletes, had some trouble finding an identity outside of the one she was accustomed to within the world of sport. Clinging, perhaps, to the "rush" of competitive tennis, the bold, stubborn, independent nature that served her so well on the court seemed to betray her off of it. Yet, the answer also can be found in the fact that Gibson herself accepted the notions of class that had been such a part of her life as a tennis star. As she looked ahead to life after tennis, she reflected on the ways that her experiences had molded her:

> I had education, thanks to the magnificent kindness of Dr. Eaton and Dr. Johnson. I had the other kind of education, too, a little experience in the world as a result of my extensive traveling. ... In my travels around the world, I had had a chance to observe the comfortable way that many decent people lived. This exposure had touched me not with envy but certainly with a modest ambition to live as comfortably. I didn't aspire to luxury, but I did believe there was no reason why I, too, shouldn't have some of the good things that make life pleasant.[76]

Eaton and Johnson knew that education would not only help Gibson meet the expectations of the tennis elite but also help sustain her in the aftermath of her career. Unfortunately, the two doctors underestimated the way in which the class of white amateur tennis and the status of being a Wimbledon and Forest Hills champion played against their protégée. Eaton's son understood the problem when he reflected, years later, on the situation: "You don't win Wimbledon and then go back and try to teach physical education. ... It was too much of a come down."[77] Women's tennis provided a path for Gibson to leave the streets of Harlem and secure a college education. Yet it also exposed her to a status and lifestyle that was unattainable and that made a solid, middle-class living seem like a step down, snubbing its nose at the idea of a humble P.E. teacher in the sport's aftermath. In short, Gibson herself had trouble negotiating the different class cultures she encountered as she transitioned from the streets of Harlem to the courts of Wimbledon and Forest Hills.

From the start, it was clear that Althea Gibson possessed talent with a tennis racket and learned quickly. But it was equally clear that she needed help throwing off her sharp manner and the aura of her working-class origins. The Althea Gibson who wanted to throw the person out of the stands for making fun of her at her first ATA national tournament would not make it in white tennis. She might be tolerated in black tennis, but she simply would not fit into the culture at Forest Hills or Wimbledon. And so the black elites, the ATA, and the black press came together to work on this "nationwide community project," to give her advice, teach her how to play championship tennis, fund her amateur tennis career, and help her gain acceptance into the worlds of both black and white tennis.

However, the different visions of what Gibson's success meant to her personally versus black tennis or, ultimately, the black community proved a complicated piece of the project to manage, resulting in conflicts both within and between the communities. Johnson and Eaton clashed with other ATA members and officials over questions of Gibson's education versus her tennis career as she tried to become competitive within the USLTA. Within the circle of upper-class blacks that ran the ATA, officials jockeyed for positions of power concerning how best to grow the association and how young talent should be developed. Moreover, Gibson's entry into white tennis exposed tensions within the ATA over the future of black tennis as some members worried it would follow the path of decline experienced by the Negro Baseball Leagues. Finally, sportswriters with the black press attempted to mold her into a race hero and champion for civil rights after she became the first African American champion at Wimbledon. When Gibson pushed back and refused to accept such a mantle, conflict erupted between the newly crowned tennis champion and the black press. Indeed, the objective of each community that stepped forward to help Gibson became increasingly expansive—from Gibson's welfare, to the future of black tennis, to the good of African American society. As the stakes rose, winning the differences and conflicts that emerged also assumed increasing importance, and the parties who "lost" became increasingly vituperative in the aftermath.

"If I've made it, it's half because I was game to take a wicked amount of punishment along the way and half because there were an awful lot of people who cared enough to help me out," Gibson reflected in 1958.[78] She clearly understood and appreciated that a tremendous amount of help from within the black community led to her path-breaking success. In the end, however, Gibson's emergence to a place of prominence in white society occurred through a contested relationship with the black "nationwide community" that helped produce her. The three constituencies that were the most instrumental in helping her could not keep their own expectations out of the equation leading at times to the "wicked amount of punishment" she received along the way. Before the project was finished, producing a civil rights crusader in addition to an African American tennis champion in white amateur tennis became a priority. But even as Gibson accepted copious help, she stood her ground with the communities that helped her, and negotiated her place within a civil rights movement that hoped to dictate the kind of tennis champion she would be. It was not the kind of champion she wanted, nor probably the kind that 1950s America would have tolerated from a black woman athlete. Defined not only by race but also class and gender, she chose to abide by the model of upper-class femininity that opened up the world of white tennis, rather than overtly champion the cause of her race. Navigating between two worlds—one the world of upper-class white tennis and the other an expansive black community—Gibson used her own grit, determination, and independence to decide how to be the first black female champion in a white sporting arena eventually willing to accept her.

Gibson's career, though historic, did not result in a rush of black tennis stars into the USLTA. There was still the issue of training young African Americans tennis players that Whirlwind Johnson had tried so hard to address. Besides Arthur Ashe's time at the top of amateur and professional tennis during the late 1960s through the mid-1970s and Zina Garrison's unsuccessful bid to become the second black woman to win Wimbledon, there were few black prospects until Venus and Serena Williams literally burst onto the grand slam circuit in the late 1990s.[79] Even as black women athletes struggled to make a name for themselves in tennis, they continued to rule the world of U.S. women's track and field. During the mid-1950s while Gibson was having her share of troubles in the USLTA, Tuskegee unwillingly passed their powerhouse status in track and field to another historically black college, Tennessee State University. There, another African American coach would develop a program to rival the one Cleve Abbott had built in Alabama. While Ed Temple coached many Olympians during his forty-plus career at Tennessee State, none of these athletes captured the popular imagination of the American public like Wilma Rudolph. During her career, American women's track and field would find new legitimacy as Temple, Rudolph, and the Tennessee State Tigerbelles pushed back against existing perceptions of women track athletes in the United States.

Ora Washington poses behind some of her trophies in 1939, near the end of her fifteen-year career as a singles player in the American Tennis Association. *John W. Moseley Photograph Collection, Charles L. Blockson Afro-American Collection, Temple University Libraries.*

Washington, *second from left*, teamed with George Stewart, *far left*, to take the mixed doubles title at the 1947 American Tennis Association championships. Also pictured is the pair they defeated, Whirlwind Johnson and a young and cocky Althea Gibson. *Courtesy Tuskegee University Archives.*

Alice Coachman leaps over the bar to take her first national high jump title at the 1939 AAU Nationals in Waterbury, Connecticut. © *Bettmann/CORBIS.*

Coachman with the national champion Tuskegee Tigerettes, ca. 1940–41. Coachman is kneeling on the far right in the first row; coach Christine Petty is holding the trophy. *Courtesy Tuskegee University Archives.*

A young Althea Gibson displays her backhand form at the 1950 U.S. Women's Indoor Tennis Championships. *Courtesy National Archives, Still Photographs.*

Gibson, reigning Wimbledon and U.S. Nationals women's champion, demonstrates her powerful forehand on tour in 1959 following her retirement from amateur tennis. *Courtesy National Archives, Still Photographs.*

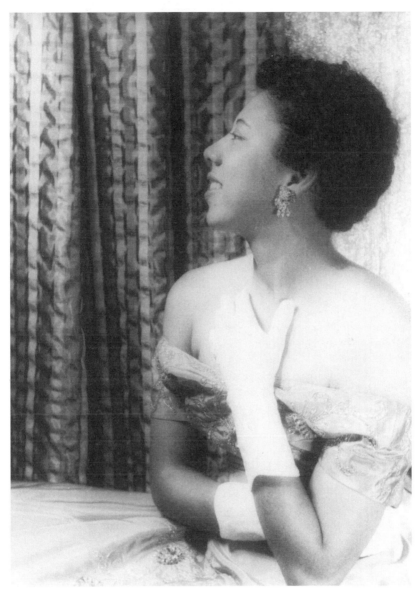

A 1958 photograph by Carl Van Vechten shows the way Gibson came to embody white middle-class femininity by the end of her career. *Carl Van Vechten Photograph Collection, Library of Congress Prints and Photographs Division.*

Wilma Rudolph shows off what became her famous smile after winning the 100-meter sprint at the 1959 AAU Nationals. *Courtesy National Archives, Still Photographs.*

Rudolph in science class at Tennessee State University, 1960. *Courtesy National Archives, Still Photographs.*

Wilma Rudolph, with her signature stride, breasting the tape at the 1960 Olympic games in Rome. *Courtesy National Archives, Still Photographs.*

Rudolph in 1979, almost twenty years after becoming a national sensation at the 1960 Rome Olympics. *Courtesy DC Public Library, Washingtoniana Division.*

Wyomia Tyus, in her famous "Tyus lean," breasts the tape in Mexico City at the 1964 Olympics to win her first of two consecutive 100-meter Olympic sprint titles. *Courtesy AP Images.*

Tyus maintained her same great form during her professional career in the mid-1970s. *Courtesy DC Public Library, Washingtoniana Division.*

Jackie Joyner-Kersee competing in the 100-meter hurdles event of the women's heptathlon competition at the 1993 World Championships in Stuttgart, Germany. © *BERND WEISSBROD/epa/CORBIS.*

The off-the-field image of Joyner-Kersee is on display in
Essence Magazine in 1995. © *Matthew Jordan Smith/CORBIS.*

Florence Griffith Joyner prepares for a race in one of her one-legged track outfits at the 1988 Olympic trials. © *Duomo/CORBIS*.

Griffith Joyner competing at the1988 Olympic games in Seoul. © *Duomo/CORBIS.*

Gail Devers, *center,* and Gwen Torrence, *right,* along with teammate Inger Miller celebrate their gold medal in the 4x100 meter relay at the 1996 Olympic games in Atlanta. © *Giansanti-Langevin-Orban/Sygma/CORBIS.*

Marion Jones during happier days is flag draped after winning the gold medal in the 100-meter sprint at the 2000 Olympic games in Sydney. She was stripped of her medals after admitting, in 2009, to performance-enhancing drug use during Olympic competition. © *Duomo/CORBIS.*

Venus and Serena Williams, in an example of their colorful tennis outfits, take the court for a doubles match at the 2000 U.S. Open. © *Reuters/CORBIS.*

"Foxes, Not Oxes"

Wilma Rudolph and the De-Marginalization of American Women's Track and Field

She had already won two gold medals that Olympics. The year was 1960, the city was Rome, Italy, and the remaining event was the women's 400-meter relay. The athlete was Wilma Rudolph, and she was the anchor of the U.S. women's relay team. She had run with the rest of the relay team before, at Tennessee State University, where the four of them were Tigerbelles, the U.S. national women's track and field champions. Pee Wee, B. J., Lady Dancer, and Skeeter—their Tennessee State Coach had nicknames for all of them—were ready to show the world their blistering speed.[1] When Rudolph broke the tape 44.4 seconds later, she had her third gold medal and the four Tigerbelles had set a new world record. Newspaper reports started pouring in to introduce this Tennessee native and three-time Olympic champion, now the "darling" of the Rome Olympics, to the world: "This queen of the 1960 Olympics is a slender beauty whose eyes carry a perpetual twinkle, as if she were amused, and a little puzzled, at what is going on around her. Miss Rudolph is five feet, 11 inches and weighs 132 pounds. Vital statistics: 34–24–36. [And] she has the legs of a showgirl," so reported one background piece.[2] Tall and slender, and with no trouble securing a date, she represented a new type of American woman track and field athlete. And that was exactly what most people connected with the sport wanted Americans to think.

This new generation of track and field athletes that Rudolph belonged to rose to prominence in the wake of Coachman and the Tuskegee Tigerettes' historic run as national champions. As the Tuskegee women's team started to fade in the early 1950s, the Tennessee Tigerbelles were just a few years from taking their place as the national women's track and field powerhouse. As part of that group, Rudolph had competed in the 1956 Melbourne games and won a bronze medal as a member of the 400-meter relay team. Yet it was her performance in the Rome Olympics that made her famous throughout the United States and Europe. She was not, of course, the first African American woman to win Olympic gold, as many Americans eventually came to believe. But by winning three gold medals in the same Olympics she seemed to capture America's attention. In the span of her seven-year track career, she was responsible for four world records, one Olympic record, and five American records. She was the first African American woman and the first female track and field athlete to win the prestigious Sullivan Award, awarded annually by the AAU to the best U.S. amateur athlete.[3] She was twice voted Female Athlete of the Year, in 1960 and 1961. When she hung up her spikes in 1963, she had become an international celebrity. And all of the records, medals, and honors occurred following a series of childhood illnesses that prevented her from walking without the use of aids until she was ten.

Rudolph's career occurred during an especially dynamic and vibrant period in women's track and field. Since the 1920s, a "tomboy" image had dogged women track and field athletes. This image suggested that "real" women did not compete in the sport. Those who did either debased the "real," masculine sport of track and field, or were masculinized freaks themselves. This was the image that the black press had worked so hard to refute during the 1940s through feature articles that stressed the femininity of Coachman and her teammates. The first decade and a half of the Cold War, however, had a strong impact on the way Americans viewed women's participation in competitive track and field. Competing internationally in the late 1950s and early 1960s, sports developed into a Cold War battlefield between the United States and the Soviet Union. As such, the sports pages of white newspapers began granting more space to women's track and field, particularly when American women went head to head with the Russians. Moreover, the fine, yet definite distinction between black and white women track athletes that had existed when Coachman competed all but disappeared. Women track athletes became accepted as "our girls" as they competed for the United States in its quest to win this aspect of the Cold

War. Overnight, it seemed, competitive track and field had become an acceptable activity for American women.

Of course, the de-marginalization of women's track and field did not happen overnight. It also did not happen solely through the advent of the Cold War. Supporters of women's track and field, particularly Rudolph's coach, worked hard to refute the tomboy image that had marginalized women track athletes for so long. Coach Temple insisted that Rudolph and her teammates show the world that they were young ladies first, track girls second, and they became determined to demonstrate that women track athletes could be competitive and still put on their lipstick like "normal" women. This new image, combined with the political importance of sport during the Cold War, helped legitimize women's track and field in the United States. Following her success in the Rome Olympics and with acceptance of her sport now on the rise, Rudolph's popularity swelled to celebrity proportions. As it did, she broke open the door of male-only invitational track meets, making gains for women's track and field. All the time, Rudolph continued to show the country that she was first and foremost a young lady who happened to run fast. Enthralled with this new national sensation, however, the press sexualized this new, feminine image. Similar to how sensual language had surrounded the peanut oil story in Coachman's day, sportswriters imbued Rudolph's invitational track appearances with sexual meaning, turning them into spectacle events where largely male promoters and crowds came to see Rudolph's "long gams" and "sizzling speed."[4] Yet throughout her career, Rudolph clung to the carefully scripted image that Ed Temple had crafted for her, turning the tomboy stereotype on its head and using white 1950s femininity to help legitimize her sport in the eyes of the American public. Before becoming the sensation of the track world, however, Rudolph spent her early years battling childhood illnesses, discovering sports, and meeting the mentor who would develop her athletic potential to help shape the person and athlete she was to become.

Overcoming Illness to Become a Tennessee State Tigerbelle

Throughout her career, the story of Rudolph's childhood was told so often and was so steeped in legend that it is impossible to discern which version yielded the "real" story. From the nature of her crippling childhood illnesses to the first summer she participated in the summer track program at Tennessee State,[5] differences in the various accounts abound.[6] In truth, however, much of her basic story echoes that of Alice Coachman and Althea Gibson—a poor background, an intact family, and an influential male mentor who gave her the opportunity to earn a college education through sport.

Born and raised just about forty miles east of Nashville, Tennessee, in the small town of Clarksville, Rudolph was the twentieth of twenty-two children born to Blanche and Ed Rudolph. Her father worked as a railroad porter and picked up odd jobs around town to supplement the family income. Like most African American women of that period, Blanche Rudolph found work cleaning the homes of Clarkesville's white families. Similar to Coachman, Rudolph remembers her father as a strict disciplinarian—"he ruled with an iron hand"—and her mother as a person of strong faith.[7]

As a child, Rudolph endured a host of illnesses. When she was not suffering from scarlet fever, pneumonia, or whooping cough, a common cold would keep her ill for weeks. Moreover, she had a twisted leg with a foot that turned inward, a condition her mother attributed to being born with polio. Regardless of the specifics, it is clear that Rudolph spent most of her early years in the house ill rather than running and playing with the other children. Due to her poor health, she did not begin attending school until she was seven. By that time, she had been wearing a brace on her crooked leg for two years to help keep the leg straight during the day and to facilitate walking.

That crooked leg and the associated treatments to straighten it defined Rudolph's childhood, and the brace marked her as different from the other children. "Psychologically, wearing that brace was devastating," she recalled in her autobiography.[8] By the time she was six, Rudolph was traveling twice a week by bus with her mother to Meharry Medical School in Nashville for additional treatments designed to strengthen and straighten the leg. For four hours each visit, she would endure the same regimen as doctors would poke, prod, and examine the leg; string it up in traction; place her in a steaming hot whirlpool bath; and, finally, massage the twisted leg. When she returned home following the hour bus ride, Rudolph would race to her bedroom to examine the leg in the mirror, hoping to see some visible improvement. In between the hospital visits her mother would perform exercises and apply heat, thought to be one of the key treatments for healing. Although the treatments were difficult, Rudolph recalled that the bus rides to Nashville opened her eyes to a bigger world, giving her a thirst for something beyond the small town of Clarkesville. Moreover, she credited the struggles she underwent with her leg and her other childhood illnesses with creating the competitive spirit within her that paid off years later when she entered athletics.

The trips to Nashville lasted four years, until Rudolph was ten. She continued wearing the brace on and off for two more years, generally when her leg ached or she needed the extra support. Finally, when she was twelve, her mother packed up the brace and sent it back to the Nashville hospital. In Rudolph's words, she was "free at last." A new chapter of her life was about to begin.

Confined to the house as a young child and limited by a leg brace through adolescence, Rudolph now longed to become involved in the childhood activities that she had missed. Basketball, in particular, captured her attention. At the start of seventh grade, she entered the newly completed Burt High School, a secondary school for African American children covering grades seven through twelve. The girls' basketball team was open to students in all grades, and Rudolph's older sister Yvonne was already a member of the team. This was a definite advantage, not only with Coach Clinton Gray but also with Ed Rudolph, who liked his children doing things together. "He had this thing about family togetherness," Rudolph remembered about her father, "so he told my sister, 'Yvonne, you take Wilma along with you to play basketball, you understand?'"[9] Basketball worked well for the younger Rudolph who was still trying to strengthen her weakened leg. She could limit her running, playing a game where she pivoted, passed, and waited for shots. She tried out for and made the team but, as a seventh grader, spent the year on the bench. She used her time wisely, however, learning the rules of the game, observing how effective rebounders positioned themselves, and studying how players drew fouls while shooting.

Rudolph made the basketball team the following year but again experienced only limited playing time. She thought she might get some playing time as an eighth-grader but it was not to be, and she still felt that the coach only accepted her onto the team because of her sister. Coach Gray did put her in a few times during the season, but only for a minute or two at the end of games that the team was winning by large margins. The most important thing that year happened at the end of the basketball season. Coach Gray announced that he was planning to resurrect the girls' track team, and he invited the basketball players to try out for it. Rudolph did, more to have something to do in the spring and to stay in shape for basketball than for any love of track. While it was not clear at the time, she had found her athletic calling.

Her love was still basketball, but it quickly became clear that Rudolph had a natural talent for running. Coach Gray knew virtually nothing about the sport. The competitions the team participated in for the first two years functioned more like field days with area high schools than like track meets. But the young basketball player turned sprinter won every race she ran during her first two seasons. Both her awakening and comeuppance came during the track season of her sophomore year. By that time, life had never been better for Rudolph. After three years of warming the bench, she played first string the entire season for a team that won their conference title to advance to the state championships. She also continued her unbeaten streak in track, having by this time developed a real love of the sport. During the season, the track team traveled to Alabama to participate in the Tuskegee Relay Carnival. The Burt High School girls' track team, having been exposed thus far only to "field day" meets, experienced a true track competition for the first time. It was a humbling experience for Rudolph. She lost every race she ran, failing to qualify for any of the finals. She felt crushed. But she came away from the experience having learned two important lessons. First, she realized that the measure of a true champion would be determined by how she responded to defeat. Second, she understood her natural talent, while important, would only carry her so far. Training was essential if she wanted to run competitively. For that, she needed to get help somewhere besides Burt High School and Coach Clinton Gray. That help was forty miles west at Tennessee State University in Nashville—in the person of Coach Ed Temple.

It is impossible to separate Rudolph's story from this important, influential man in her life who taught her how to use her natural talent and speed to win races. Temple had been offered the job to coach the women's track team upon his own graduation from Tennessee State in 1950, the same year Rudolph finished making her trips to Meharry Hospital for treatments on her leg. He was a friend of Tuskegee coach and athletic director

Cleve Abbott, and the older, seasoned coach's work with the Tigerettes helped shape the approach of the younger, Tennessee State coach. Influenced by Abbott's success, Temple created a summer program for the women athletes, patterning it after the one Abbott used to lure athletes like Alice Coachman. Temple would scout the surrounding area states for promising talent and bring in ten girls during the summer to live in the dorms, train with the college athletes, and make the trip to compete as Tigerbelles at the AAU outdoor national championships. The families of the high school girls were responsible for paying their transportation to Tennessee State, but the university took over expenses once they were there for the summer. Temple followed a rigorous training regimen for his athletes, practicing three times a day. He also had strict rules for them during their free time, such as a 9:00 p.m. curfew, no riding in cars, and no outings to nightclubs or other unsuitable establishments. The athletes enjoyed the camaraderie that came with being part of a team, learned the fundamentals of track, and improved their times. They also discovered that track and field could be their ticket to a college education. Generally, after several years at Ed Temple's summer program, Tennessee State was their natural first choice to continue their education.[10]

Through the years, Temple enjoyed incredible success with the Tennessee State women's track program, producing championship athletes and instilling in them the importance of finishing their college education. The Tigerbelles won their first national championship in 1955; by 1967, they had captured eleven more. Temple also had a gift for locating talented sprinters and turning them into Olympic champions. From 1956 through 1976, thirteen of his Tigerbelles won a combined twenty Olympic medals: eleven gold, five silver, and four bronze. But looking back on his coaching experiences, the three-time coach of U.S. Olympic women's track and field teams remembered with most satisfaction instilling the importance of education into his Tigerbelles: "I always told them, you can't run and jump up forever. You're here to get the education." Giving his athletes the opportunity to earn a college education over the years was as important to Temple as producing Olympians: "When we [Tennessee State] put 40 people on the United States Olympic team, 40 had graduated with their degree. And I think just as much of that as I do the gold, silver and bronze medals."[11] Just as Coachman had found her mentor in Cleve Abbott, Wilma Rudolph was on the verge of finding her own "Coach."

Temple had already had two opportunities to see Rudolph in action. One was on the basketball court. Rudolph noticed him serving as referee during the basketball season of her sophomore year. Working the games of area high schools allowed him to scout for talent in the rural areas around Nashville. She remembered him for two things—he was fair and he always called by her last name, not by her number. She also remembered when, after one game, he called her lazy, too lazy to really jump. He suggested that Coach Gray mark a target on the wall and have Rudolph jump twenty or thirty times each day at practice until she could routinely hit the target. "I didn't realize it at the time," she reflected in her autobiography, "but Ed Temple was taking an interest in me back then because he had his eye on me for his own track program."[12] The second time Temple noticed Rudolph, she was competing, and losing, at the Tuskegee Relays. While she felt certain no one would be interested in her after her performance there, nothing was further from the truth. Temple had taken his own team to the relays that year. But he also used it as an opportunity to scout for young talent, not only from Tennessee but also from the neighboring southern states. When the track season was over later that spring, Coach Gray told Rudolph that Ed Temple planned to pay a visit to her parents to ask permission for their daughter to join him that summer at his track program in Nashville. While her parents, particularly her father, were as hesitant as Coachman's parents had been some fifteen years earlier, Temple's rules helped put them at ease and they finally relented. Rudolph was about to embark on a course that would change her life dramatically.[13]

Similar to Coachman's experience at Tuskegee, Rudolph learned the fundamentals of running and encountered a community of track athletes that summer. Temple started his summer program with two weeks of pure cross-country training that would build endurance and help establish the athletes' natural breathing patterns for the shorter races. Next, they ran different competitive distances and learned the various techniques to improve their times. "I can remember learning some of the basics of running right there, how to smooth out, how to stop fighting yourself, keeping the fists loose," she recalled, and how to lean into the race as opposed to leaning backward. The competition among the athletes helped as well, as some of the fastest young women from the southeast pushed each other to faster times. The friendly competition and camaraderie they built over those summers, and later as Tigerbelles running for Tennessee State, were strong indeed. Rudolph remembered it well: "Always, Coach Temple kept things on a team basis; we were a team, not just a bunch of individuals. He kept the motivation high because under the team concept all of us became very competitive. In fact, the competition among us that summer was about as intense as any competition I can ever remember. Still, we all stayed friends."[14]

Clearly, Temple's techniques paid off. By the time Rudolph became part of his summer program, the Tennessee State Tigerbelles were making a name for themselves in the world of women's track and field. In 1955, they won the AAU national outdoor championships in Ponca City, Oklahoma, winning six of eleven events and outscoring the second-place team by fifty-seven points. They retained the title in 1956, and by 1959, they had captured five national championships in a row. Just as Tuskegee's program began fading in the early part of the decade, Tennessee State emerged as the new preeminent force in U.S. women's track and field.[15]

By this time, the AAU had separated junior- and senior-level competition into the "girls'" and "women's" divisions at their national championship meets.[16] As a result, Rudolph and the other high school athletes participating in Temple's summer program competed in the girls' division, rather than in the women's division, or the senior level, as Coachman had. Occasionally, Temple would bump up his high schoolers to compete in the older division if he needed them for the team. Generally, however, he preferred to have them compete in the younger age group while in high school in order to get the experience they would need to compete at the higher level when in college.[17]

Following the 1956 AAU outdoor nationals in Philadelphia, Temple took six of his athletes to the Olympic trials in Washington, D.C. Rudolph, who had placed second to her teammate Mae Faggs in the 200-meter sprint at the nationals, was among the six. Faggs was a veteran of the Olympics, having, as a young girl, been a teammate of Coachman's at the 1948 London games. She had also won a gold medal as part of the U.S. women's 400-meter relay team in Helsinki in 1952. Rudolph was a sixteen-year-old high school student. Going into the last event, the 200-meter final, all of the Tigerbelles had made the Olympic team except for Rudolph. But Faggs was intent on making sure that her young teammate would be "on the boat" to the Olympics with the rest of them. Faggs planned on winning the race. She instructed Rudolph to stay on her shoulder, assuring her that she should be able to take second or third to her own first, good enough to qualify for the team in that event. They were a study in contrasts—Faggs, short, with quick steps and a short stride, and Rudolph tall, with long legs and an expansive stride. Temple remembered watching the race; as they came around the curve, Rudolph's long legs were stretching out, and she was right on Faggs's shoulder. At about the 175-meter mark, the teenager pulled up right beside the veteran, he recalled, as if to say, "Come on, Faggs, pick it up." True to the seasoned Olympian's prediction, she took first place in the race and Rudolph, right on her shoulder, placed second. All six of Temple's Tigerbelles had qualified for the 1956 U.S. Olympic team. Moreover, Temple saw something important in Rudolph at that meet. "It looked like, if Wilma wanted to she could have just moved on out in front. But she just pulled and stayed right on her [Faggs's] shoulder. Well, right then, we knew that she [Rudolph] was, you know, that she had something."[18]

Similar to Coachman's experience in London, the American women sprinters at the 1956 Olympics in Melbourne, Australia, struggled to overcome the speed of individual stars in other parts of the world. This time, the star of the women's track and field competition was Australia's own Betty Cuthbert. Like Fanny Blankers-Koen in the 1948 London games, Cuthbert won gold in the 100 and 200 meters, and as part of the 400-meter relay team.[19] U.S. sprinter Isabelle Daniels, another Ed Temple product from Tennessee State, just missed a medal in the 100 meters, but she was the sole U.S. track athlete to qualify for a final in the sprints.[20] The 400-meter relay was another opportunity, however, and this time, the Tennessee State women would be running as a team. Faggs, the seasoned veteran and the backbone of the still young Tennessee State program, encouraged her teammates as they prepared to compete. Rudolph remembered how vital her teammate's enthusiasm had been: "On the day of the relay, Mae Faggs was at her best. She was the motivator for us. … She really psyched us up that day; she went around telling us, 'Let's go get 'em, let's give it all we've got, let's make it into the top three and win ourselves a medal.'" Despite their inability to win individual medals, the four sprinters, carrying with them the team focus instilled by Temple, finished third and earned a bronze medal. At the age of sixteen and as a rising high school junior, Wilma Rudolph was an Olympic medalist.[21]

FOXES, NOT OXES

Rudolph finished the Melbourne games proud of her relay medal but determined to continue her training, make the 1960 Olympic team, and win at least one gold medal. Her plan was to finish her remaining two years of high school and then attend Tennessee State and run track for Ed Temple. She had a memorable junior year in basketball—the team went undefeated and won the state championship—and continued her unbeaten track record in the local high school meets. In the summer, she returned to Nashville to participate in Temple's summer track program and travel to the nationals with the Tigerbelles. Once again, the Tennessee State team came away as national champions.

At the beginning of Rudolph's senior year, she was ready to repeat the athletic success she had enjoyed as a junior. However, when she went for her preseason physical before the start of the basketball season, the team doctor discovered she was pregnant. Still quite early in the pregnancy, she had not suspected anything and was completely overwhelmed to discover the news. Rudolph and the father of the child, Robert Eldridge, had known each other since seventh grade. He had become the star of the high school football and basketball teams, and by their sophomore year, he was her steady boyfriend. During those days, Rudolph recalled, "abortions were un-heard of." Moreover, unlike middle-class whites, young African American women who became pregnant out of wedlock were not sent away to live with a relative for several months while they were "showing" and had the baby. Young women who were still in high school simply continued to attend school while pregnant. After the birth, relatives generally helped the new mother care for the baby. Moreover, the African American community itself often came together to support and help the young woman. This was particularly true when the young woman had dreams and talent, as in college and an important track career. So while Rudolph's pregnancy meant an abrupt end to the basketball and track seasons of her senior year, the bigger concern for her was whether she would still be welcome at Tennessee State. Temple's rules were strict, and she had heard that he did not permit young women with babies on the team. However, either the rule was a rumor or Temple bent it for Rudolph.[22] The Tigerbelle coach stood by the young athlete, assuring her that he wanted her to start her freshman year at Tennessee State in the fall after the baby was born.

In June 1958, Rudolph gave birth to a daughter, Yolanda. The price for her family's support, however, was that Rudolph and Eldridge were not allowed to remain a couple. Eldridge, by order of Rudolph's father, was banned from the Rudolph home. Before the start of the fall term, the young mother and her family had developed an arrangement where her parents and older sister would take care of the baby while the young track athlete attended college. In September, Rudolph left Clarkesville to become a freshman at Tennessee State and a full-fledged Tigerbelle, running track for Ed Temple in the women's division.

"Young Ladies First, Track Girls Second"— The Emergence of the "Feminine" Image of Women Track Athletes

By the end of Rudolph's sophomore year in college, she had matured into a fine athlete and was an important part of the Tennessee State Tigerbelle team. It was a team that continued to dominate the AAU national indoor and outdoor championships. Following the outdoor nationals in Corpus Christi, Texas, in the summer of 1960, Rudolph found herself once again slated to participate in the Olympic trials. She was no longer the baby, being coached and helped along by an older, seasoned Mae Faggs. She easily qualified for the U.S. Olympic team in the 100 and 200 meters, even setting a new world record with her time in the 200 meters.

As Rudolph prepared to compete in her second Olympics, she was in good shape physically. Moreover, her coach and mentor of five years, Ed Temple, had been named as head coach for the U.S. Olympic women's track and field team. Having Temple direct her training for the Olympics was a decided benefit. "He knew his runners like a book," Rudolph recalled, knowing when to step up practice and when to scale it back. The thought of having her own coach in Rome with her was a huge psychological boost for Rudolph, and she felt it would make all the difference in the world for her mental preparation. "I knew I would be ready mentally no matter what, simply because he was the coach," she recalled.[23] It was, for her, the icing on the cake, like bringing her "second father" along to keep her prepped and psyched up.

Once in Rome, Rudolph felt relaxed and ready for the upcoming races. The day before she was to begin the preliminary heats for the 100-

meter competition, however, she fell and hurt her ankle. Thankfully, it turned out to be sprained rather than broken. Running the 100 meters first helped tremendously since the short distance was run on a straight track; the curve required in the 200 would have been difficult with an injured ankle. Temple reminded her that her times made her the fastest woman there, helping to reassure her. She quickly advanced to the 100-meter final. With a good start in the final—she had always been slow coming out of the blocks, finding it difficult to uncurl her 5'11" frame—Wilma Rudolph had her first Olympic gold medal in just eleven seconds. It was the fastest any woman had run the 100 meters, but an aiding wind prevented it from becoming a world record. By the time she ran the final for the 200 meters the next day, she felt supremely confident. The 200 meters was where she felt most at ease because the longer distance allowed her to overcome her slow start and put her long stride to work. A light rain the day of the race did nothing to diminish her optimism, and she quickly added a second gold medal to her performance in the 100 meter. Her last opportunity to medal came in the 400-meter relay. Although there was stiff competition from the teams from Russia, West Germany, and Great Britain, there was a lot of experience and familiarity on the U.S. team. The other three members of the relay squad were all Rudolph's teammates from Tennessee State—Martha Hudson, Barbara Jones, and Lucinda Williams—and they routinely ran this relay together in the States. Not only did they "wipe out" the other teams, as Rudolph remembered, but they also set a new world record in the process. As she had planned and dreamed since leaving Melbourne, Rudolph had returned to the Olympics and followed in Betty Cuthbert's footsteps. In doing so, she became the first American woman track and field athlete to win three gold medals in the same Olympics.

As Rudolph was wining three gold medals in Rome, it was clear that the tomboy image, the "muscle Moll" myth that marginalized women's track and field when Coachman competed, was still a part of American culture. "Although women are accepted freely now in tennis and golf," observed reporter Sid Ziff in the early 1960s, "the track girls have struggled unsuccessfully to shake the Muscle Moll concept." Indeed, this image of women track and field athletes had been around since the 1920s, when women physical educators and the male-led AAU had battled over who would be in charge of the sport. As Alice Coachman had heard repeatedly, respectable women did not participate in track and field. Women who did compete were not "real" women, but tomboys—masculinized freaks. Some writers equated the image with all women athletes, not only those who competed in track and field: "Girls and athletics are certainly not to be considered synonymous and the combination of the two usually brings to mind an overgrown tomboy with overgrown muscles to match." Moreover, if "real" women made the mistake of entering track and field competition, some thought the sport would probably injure their more delicate female bodies. "Too many people feel girls will be hurt in sports," Ed Temple told a reporter in 1960. As he made clear in the interview, Temple did not subscribe to this idea. But he understood that some, perhaps many, still did.[24]

While this image was not as prevalent in the press as it had been when Coachman competed, where it did surface, it was deeply held. Sometimes the thinking came out in reverse. Women did not belong in track and field because they were so feminine, and their presence in the sport debased it. Moreover, some sportswriters went past sexism to misogyny in their writing about women's presence in the sport. Arthur Daley of the *New York Times* wrote a particularly scathing commentary at the conclusion of the Rome games. The ancient Greeks, he observed, had the correct idea when they chose to exclude women from watching, let alone competing in, the games. Furthermore, the Greeks had a solution for violators: "Women who became too curious—if you'll forgive the redundancy—and sneaked into the Olympics were gently tossed off a near-by cliff on to the rocks below. It taught them a lesson too. None ever repeated the offense." It was unfortunate, Daley continued, that modern man's nature was so weak as to trump his good sense and allow women to first observe and, now, even compete. "Now they clutter up the joint and feminine frills have begun to debase this temple of masculinity." His particular concern was the use of stuffed animal mascots by the women swimmers and track and field athletes. It was bad enough that the swimmers carried their mascots around with them, but some of the high jumpers used theirs to mark where they needed to begin their approach to the bar.[25]

In truth, Daley contended, the Russian women were the real problem. They kept pushing for more and more women's events because the Russian women were masculine whereas American women were dainty. If the Soviets had their way, he suggested, it would eventually be hard to tell men and women's Olympic track and field competition apart given how similar they were becoming. "And how would you like to see your son marry a lady marathon runner," Daley asked. "Back home," American women were so feminine they wouldn't even rush to catch a cab. And what about the "dream boats" that did participate in track and field? The two the reporter noticed competing in the high jump really belonged more appropriately in the Miss Universe contest. "It just doesn't seem right to watch a female leap clumsily over the bars, throw the weights awkwardly or scamper over a track in unladylike fashion," he concluded. The end result was that they lost their allure. And track suits, even the "skimpy ones," did not enhance women's figures like Paris designers could.[26]

Daley's column was replete with variations of the muscle Moll image, sometimes employing a misogynistic twist while other times relying on unadulterated sexism. The field of sports, particularly track and field, was a male domain. Women's participation was not only out of place, but demeaning to both the sport and the women who crossed the barrier. The Greeks had the right idea when women's curiosity got the better of them— simply throw them over the cliff. Of course, "real" American women wouldn't be interested in the sport because, unlike the Russians, they were feminine and dainty. The best competition for these "dream boats" was a beauty contest. Moreover, patently stark contradictions were imbedded in Daley's article. With masculine contempt, he wrote of how the female track and field athletes—whom he considered more masculinized than the swimmers—were in reality more feminine than the women swimmers. These "damsels" shunned the traditional wooden pegs, choosing to mark their approach with very feminine stuffed animal mascots—a stuffed rabbit that was "simply precious" or a "most divine stuffed poodle dog."[27] The particular argument one chose to perpetuate this stereotype did not especially matter. The *New York Times* columnist's message was clear—women did not belong in the masculine sport of track and field.

Even as Daley maligned women track athletes, some sportswriters acknowledged the strength of the Tigerbelle team. Yet they did so by conjuring the image of women's nature as inherently at odds with the discipline required to become a champion athlete. Perhaps, suggested columnist Melvin Durslag, Temple's techniques for producing the top female athletes in the country—his incredible success with the "ladies"—could be applied to strengthening their domestic endeavors:

> Certainly, he [Temple] is the best coach of ladies. He has turned out
> some remarkable female athletes down there, which makes one won-
> der about his secret. Women are rebellious by nature. How does he
> whip them into line? And will the same principles for encouraging
> them to run apply to getting them to push a vacuum?[28]

Durslag's sexist comments—they possess a rebellious nature, require whipping into shape, and are naturally well suited for domestic chores such as
vacuuming—tempered the compliment the columnist paid these talented
athletes. Moreover, the sportswriter complimented not the athletes but
their coach for his work in turning the women into remarkable athletes.
Similar to Petty, the Tigerettes' coach in the early years of Coachman's
career, even Temple's success was suspect. It must involve a secret. Such
remarkable results, particularly given the natural rebelliousness of women,
could not stem from talent, hard work, dedication, and know-how.

This was the general atmosphere, then, in which Rudolph began her
career and entered the Rome Olympics. Some journalists, and many
Americans, still held women's track and field and its athletes in contempt.
Some, such as Daley, even used that framework to interpret Rudolph's
unprecedented three gold medals. However, the Cold War made those
within women's track and field think now was an especially good time
to work on that image. Both Coachman and Gibson had benefited, to
varying degrees, from changing attitudes about women's sport brought
on by the Cold War. The *Chicago Tribune* had depicted Coachman's 1948
Olympic win as an "American" victory. It was a small, yet palpable,
change since most other white newspapers continued to either ignore
women's track and field or perpetuate racial stereotypes. Seven years later,
the Cold War had given Gibson's career a significant boost when the
American State Department, looking to enhance its image in Southeast
Asia, chose her to participate in one of its goodwill tours.[29]

By the late 1950s, it appeared this momentum might even contribute to the sanctioning of women's track and field in the United States,
at least as an arena where Americans hoped to claim victory over the
Russians. Since Coachman's 1948 victory, the United States' ideological
conflict with the Soviet Union had gained in intensity as each country
strove to prove that it had the superior form of government and society.
The difference in approaches led to formal and informal contests in tech-
nological advances, the space program, the arts, and sports. The ultimate

contest to test the strength of the two superpowers' sports programs was the Olympics. Yet it occurred only once every four years, and both countries looked with hope toward more frequent contests and how they might cement their image as the preeminent superpower.

In 1958, the United States and Soviet Union reached an agreement to hold a dual track and field meet in July of that year in Moscow. The agreement provided for competition in the thirty-two standard events for men and women, with two athletes from each country competing in each event.[30] These competitions were part of a joint agreement reached by the American and Soviet governments that involved not only sports but also technical visits and cultural exchanges. The biggest difficulty regarding track and field involved agreement on how the meet would be scored. The United States insisted that the men and women's competitions be scored separately. The Soviet Union wanted to follow the standard system used in European and international competition of a combined total for the meet. In truth, each power had a strong desire to win these sporting events and each preferred the scoring methodology that played to their strengths. The United States was confident it would at least win the men's competition with separate scoring. The Soviet Union anticipated that its stronger women's score over the American women would more than compensate for a lower score by their men, giving them a combined victory. Russia finally conceded to tally separate totals although, in their own country, they reported the meet totals both ways, giving preference to the combined score. Despite the typical propaganda spin that the two superpowers attempted, the dual meets became an annual event, with each country alternating as host.[31]

So critical were these annual contests to the period that they became important in altering the perception of black women track athletes in American society, particularly among the cadre of sportswriters that covered the meets. Specifically, the Cold War helped to make the world of women's track and field less race conscious than it had been in Alice Coachman's day. Especially when compared to Coachman's coverage in the white press, it becomes clear that race was considerably more disassociated from the press accounts of black women track athletes beginning in the late 1950s. With the onset of the dual meets with the Soviet Union and Rudolph's historic win, white sportswriters were less and less prone to discuss race or invoke racial stereotypes in their reports. Moreover, the white press stopped favoring white women track athletes over African Americans as they had in the 1940s. And in 1959, Lucinda Williams, an African American sprinter and teammate of Rudolph's, served as the captain of the U.S. women's track team that met the Russian team in Philadelphia. This is not to say that Rudolph and her teammates were free from dealing with racism in the broader society. But within the context of reporting on women's track and field, they received the same treatment as their white counterparts.[32]

The Cold War also began to have an effect on the way women's track and field was viewed in the United States. As the sport became a setting for Americans to prove the superiority of their way of life, general coverage of women's track and field events began to blossom within the sports pages of the white press. The type of coverage that the *Albany Herald* gave Coachman during her Olympic bid had been virtually unheard of. By Rudolph's generation, however, articles leading up to and reporting women's meets, complete with pictures of the athletes in action, became more and more commonplace. Gone were the days of ignoring women's track and field altogether. Coverage of the sport began to more closely resemble that of its male counterpart.

In the midst of changes brought on by the Cold War, those within the world of women's track and field moved to fashion a new, "feminine" image of women track and field athletes. Supporters of the sport began to publicly insist that the femininity of women track athletes was as pervasive as any woman. In fact, they continued, track and field was good physical exercise that kept women trim and in good shape, further enhancing their appeal and good looks. No one worked harder during the late 1950s and 1960s to construct this new image of women's track and field athletes than Ed Temple.[33] He was persistent and repetitive in his refrain, and he told anyone who would listen. "I'm afraid too many schools frown on girl athletes. And that's ridiculous. Our girls are just as feminine as any. We teach them to be young ladies first and track girls second. They work hard out on the field but after practice they put on their powder and lipstick just like everyone else." Temple insisted that his Tigerbelles become the example of feminine track athletes. He set strict codes of personal conduct for his athletes and also made sure that they looked nice in public, especially after winning a race. Not only did "his girls" put on their powder and lipstick like any other woman, Temple insisted on it. "I had a motto," Temple recalled of the period. "I said, I don't want oxes; I want foxes. I want nice-looking girls." Once his Tigerbelles started winning, he had strict instructions for them to follow after they finished a race—"I want you to wipe your face," he told his athletes, "comb your hair and put some lipstick on so you look presentable when somebody interviews you."[34] The image of women's track and field was exactly what was at stake, and Temple decided that the best way to strengthen it was to work on the image of its athletes.

The Tennessee State coach used every opportunity he could to address that image, and he employed the press masterfully. He routinely held up the Tennessee State Tigerbelles to the press as examples of women athletes who were attractive and feminine despite being competitive, champion track and field athletes. Near the close of the 1950s, the press ran a feature article on Barbara Jones, one of Rudolph's TSU teammates and a member of the gold medal 400-meter relay team at the 1960 Olympics: "Twenty-one-year-old Barbara, now a senior at Tennessee State college, is an attractive, charming and effervescent female." While women and athletics generally brought to mind a tomboy with bulging muscles, the article opened, getting to know Barbara Jones was all that was needed to clear such a stereotype from the mind. "A sneaky visit where you may catch her 'playing it cool' around the house in a pair of fetching red toreadors is highly recommended as a means of developing new points of view concerning girl athletes," suggested the reporter.[35] Similar to the ways in which the black press had used articles to feminize Coachman and her teammates for its readers, the press began buying in to the feminine image of Temple's athletes that he worked so hard to fashion.

In addition to the fact that women track athletes were completely feminine, its advocates continued, the sport had decided benefits for women. "Temple advocates track for women because 'it keeps them slim, and trim and in good physical condition,'" noted a 1959 interview of the Tigerbelle coach. Reporter Frances Lewine wasn't disagreeing: "Nobody jumping the hurdles or running the 440 was having any weight problems. Exercise takes care of their waistlines."[36] As opposed to masculinizing women, track and field helped keep them in shape so that they would be *more* feminine.

This new image, while different than the muscle Moll, continued to be grounded in the athletes' femininity. A pragmatist, however, Temple understood how long women's track and field had been tagged with the idea of the masculine track athlete. He knew he needed to offer an alternate concept solidly in the feminine gender image that contemporary American society accepted as the ideal. "I was working on this image," Temple clearly recalled years later. "First, when you start winning, [people say] oh well, she's so ugly she's supposed to win. ... I wanted to break that image up." Champion track athletes were, as Temple said over and over, "young ladies first, track girls second." Despite the fact that Temple and other advocates thought of this perception of their athletes as new, it was, in reality, grounded in the same image that the black press had promoted for the Tuskegee Tigerettes. Those who promoted it during the late 1950s and early 1960s carried it to new lengths, however, showing the world a purposefully stark contrast to the muscle-bound tomboy image they were fighting. Using the stereotype of 1950s white middle-class femininity for their own purposes and aided by the Cold War, Temple and the Tigerbelles began pulling women's track and field back from the margins of society.[37]

Several aspects of the competition with the Russians helped cement this new image of women track and field athletes. First, the dual meets with the Soviet Union served to emphasize the fact that the United States was losing this particular Cold War battle. Losses to the Russians were difficult to tolerate, casting a dark pall over the United States' track program. Newspaper headlines followed the preparation—"Track Stars Train Here to Meet Reds"—and then lamented the outcome—"Red Gals Too Much." As the 1959 match-up with the Russians loomed and then passed, the results were no better than they had been the previous year: "All week long, Ed Temple gloomily told everyone he could collar that the American girls were overmatched against the Russians. All week long he kept hoping it wasn't true. But the Russians, led by lumpy-muscled Tamara Press, thumped our drenched damsels, 67–40, widening last year's 63–44 margin." The American men were generally competitive against the Russian men, but the women often fell short. Once again, Temple made a pitch for more help, explained the problem and defended his athletes "We need all the help we can get. ... Sure our track officials are embarrassed by the showing of our women, but our source of material is limited to only five colleges. In view of this I think our women have made a tremendous showing." By 1962, Temple voiced what Americans well understood: "It's all part of the cold war."[38]

Second, Russian women gave Americans a convenient "other" on which to place their muscle Moll image.[39] Whenever possible, coaches and officials emphasized the femininity of American women track athletes by contrasting them to the heavy, muscle-laden, Russian women. "Lumpy-muscled Tamara Press" led the 1959 Russian women's team that crushed the American "damsels." Indeed, "none of my girls have any trouble getting boy friends," Temple told the *Detroit News*. In a now-familiar refrain, he continued: "I tell them that they are young ladies first, track girls second. I want them well-groomed all the time, even when they run. And nobody takes their picture unless their hair is combed and their face is fixed. We don't want Amazons," he concluded, implicitly contrasting American track athletes to the large, "lumpy-muscled" Russians.[40]

Finally, the Cold War focused attention on women's track and field itself, as more and more sportswriters turned their attention to why the United States could not win this contest. These articles allowed advocates of the sport to suggest the central problem. American women were every bit as talented and capable as the Russian women, but they lacked sufficient opportunities to compete at home. Once again, Temple was one of the central architects of this message, and he drove it home at every possible opportunity. "We need more meets, more emphasis, more support," Temple told reporter Stan Hochman in the aftermath of the 1959 contest. "They can't ask our girls to go into international competition with one meet a year while the Russians have 20 or 30." Speaking just after the AAU championships that same year, Temple lamented having only two meets every year with Tuskegee in addition to the indoor and outdoor national championships: "That's just not enough. If they want our girls to be as good as the European and Russian women, they'll have to give us more meets to compete in." In yet another interview, Temple noted, the male track athletes, by comparison, had ten to twenty indoor meets to the women's one. This stood in stark contrast to the Soviet Union and European countries, where the women competed at every track meet that the men did.[41]

Over time, this new image of women track athletes took hold in the United States. Women could be "ladies first, track girls second," as Temple had described it. In fact, it had taken hold so well that, while none of the Tigerbelles had any trouble getting boyfriends, young men were being asked to back off for another reason: "If your girl friend can run faster, jump higher, or throw farther than you—it's your patriotic duty not to date her," counseled one article in the white press as the time drew near for the 1964 U.S. Olympic team qualifying trials. The goal was to keep women interested in track for four additional years to yield a strong team for the 1968 Olympics. If men interfered, putting themselves above the needs of the country, they would, in fact, be hurting America's Olympic effort. But the four-year Olympiad was a long time and boys' interest in female track athletes could upset the best intentions of continued competition. "Boy likes girl. Boy dates girl, and blooey goes the training schedule," concluded the article. Coaches like Temple and Percy Franklin in Chicago tried to keep them interested and in training longer but found it hard. Suggesting that the two superpowers had different social systems, Franklin commiserated the way the difference played against the United States: "This is where Russia and the European nations have it all over the United States. Their women athletes compete longer."[42] In contrast to being called into question, the femininity of American women track athletes was accepted as a downside to preparing the United States for competition against the Russian women. Indeed, American women track stars were so feminine that they would often rather pursue a relationship with their boyfriend than remain in track competition. Ed Temple's constant hammering that none of his women had any trouble getting boyfriends had finally become part of popular thinking. American men were being called on to do their civic duty to let these talented, feminine, athletic women compete for their country rather than "steal" them away from track and field.

It was into this period of a new image of American women track and field athletes and Cold War sports battles that Wilma Rudolph won an unprecedented three Olympic gold medals. Here was someone who not only satisfied the requirement to be feminine and attractive but also raced hard and could easily beat the Russians. As women's track and field continued to be more popular in Europe than the United States, Rudolph immediately found herself engulfed by adoring Italian fans and an unrelenting barrage of reporters. "She is the darling of the Rome games," reported the *Philadelphia Inquirer*, "surrounded by admiring fans and autograph-seekers at every turn." Initially, she found such attention difficult to handle. "I'm afraid to go out in the morning," she confessed to one reporter. "They recognize me everywhere, whether I'm wearing a dress or my sweat shirt. If I'm walking through the Olympic Village, if

I'm going to eat, even if I'm just sitting in a group at the men's quarters, people want autographs and pictures." Her popularity continued to swell when the U.S. Olympic Committee arranged for the winning 400-meter relay team and some of the medalists from the men's team to stay in Europe following the close of the games. They were scheduled to participate in the British Empire games in London and an exhibition tour in other European cities. All of the athletes were tired, most of them having been away from home since June for the U.S. nationals, the Olympic trials and two weeks of training prior to departing for Rome. It was difficult for them to watch their other teammates return to the United States. Temple recalled years later how all of the coaches and athletes who had to stay in Europe were frustrated and simply wanted to go home. Yet the foreign press and the crowds that came to see the exhibition meets adored Rudolph, increasing her popularity and adding to her image as the "darling of the games."[43]

As the "darling of the games," Rudolph came to completely embody the new feminine image that Temple had crafted. Having been a part of Temple's program for five years, the young Tigerbelle was well versed in her coach's rules for projecting this image. She was always careful to attend to her hair and put on lipstick after a race and before she granted any press interviews. Even the press picked up on the ritual. After she broke the record in a heat of the 200 meter in Rome, the white *Nashville Banner* observed how "teammate Barbara Jones arrived with comb and brush." Clearly, Rudolph was not "masculine" in any way, and the press noted it repeatedly. As one headline so appropriately summed things up in the aftermath of the games: "Wilma Proves They're Not All 'Muscle Molls.'" Whereas women athletes were often pegged as masculine, the reporter observed, that description was "entirely unsuitable for Wilma." Indeed, "they may have been Muscle Molls in [sportswriter Paul] Gallico's time but they're pretty feminine today," he concluded. The black press also picked up the refrain, describing how Rudolph was "pursued by the press and adored by an Italian populace which has equal fascination for a good athlete and a striking woman."[44]

As more reporters shared this newest celebrity with the American public, Rudolph's femininity often became a central part of the story. Moreover, she was more than simply *not* a tomboy. She was completely feminine, preferring pretty dresses, high heels, and real jewelry. When reporters interviewed her, she easily portrayed this carefully crafted image. She may admit to enjoying the "occasional" game of basketball with her brothers, but followed that comment up with the qualification that "it doesn't mean I'm a tomboy." For emphasis, reporters noticed, she let her hands fall gracefully over her feminine attire—her brightly plaid skirt, purple bodice, and gold buttons. She was also apologetic for her new black shoes, which were flat rather than high heels. "I prefer high heels," she told the reporter, "but my legs get too tired if I wear them before a race." But she was especially fond of jewelry, not the costume variety, but good gold jewelry, showing off an attractive bracelet. "No one in looking and listening distance was arguing," suggested sportswriter Robert Teague, "for the Tigerbelle looked more like a homecoming queen than a woman athlete."[45] Stories like this, the opening excerpt revealing Rudolph's "vital statistics" and the "comb, brush and lipstick" rules circulated freely in the days and months following the Olympic games. Even as Arthur Daley's *New York Times* piece proved that the old image of the masculine woman athlete was still around, this new image gave the American public an alternate way in which to experience Rudolph's success. In the celebrations and news press that followed her victories, Rudolph had become the "poster child" of the feminine woman track athlete.[46]

While Rudolph was the one in the spotlight that most clearly came to embody this new, feminine image, all of Ed Temple's Tigerbelles represented it. In doing so, their adherence to this image suggests how they used notions of white middle-class femininity for their own purposes to gain acceptance into 1960s American culture. A period when women's public apparel included not only a nice dress but also hat and gloves, Temple made sure that all of his athletes followed this dress code. Even if they had only one dress, they were required to keep it clean and ready for whenever they traveled or appeared in public. His greatest success, he remembered, was one occasion when the team was dining and mistaken for a women's choir. Moreover, before the popularity of the 1970s "afro" hairstyle, the late 1950s and early 1960s was a time when many African American women used hot rollers to "tame" their hair, styling it in ways more comparable to white middle-class women. When the Tigerbelles traveled internationally, their luggage always weighed far less on return trips because they had, while abroad, used most of the canned heat they brought with them to heat their curlers, which had so weighted them down on the trip over.[47]

But Rudolph's ultimate representation of the feminine woman track athlete—both as a black woman and one with a "past"—also indicates the diminishing importance of race in the world of women's track and field. The press seemed to take special care in their portrayal of Rudolph. Even her high school pregnancy did not derail her popularity. Certainly if white sportswriters were interested in bringing race to the forefront, casting her teen pregnancy through the stereotype of the hypersexualized black female could have done it. But they never mentioned it. When reporters began featuring Rudolph's life story, they focused predominantly on the childhood illnesses she had overcome. If they said anything at all about her missing the track season during her senior year in high school, they attributed it to illness.[48] Indeed, American sportswriters rarely referred to Rudolph's race at all. In contrast, Europeans' embrace of the new female track sensation celebrated her blackness. Italian sportswriters used the pet name *la gazzella nera*, "the black gazelle," when referring to her, whereas French writers preferred *la perle noire*, or "the black pearl." Yet the American press rarely used these nicknames without tying them to their European roots. Perhaps this was an avoidance strategy as opposed to outright acceptance. Perhaps Rudolph's light skin and embrace of white femininity helped white sportswriters and the American public ignore her blackness. Regardless, it was clear that Americans had taken to the Tennessee State Tigerbelle in a way that seemed to downplay her race, in stark contrast to black women athletes of the past.[49]

As Rudolph prepared to return to America, the reception she had experienced in Europe would be replicated in a way that was completely unfamiliar to her, Temple, or her Tigerbelle teammates. Awaiting her in the United States was a welcome and homecoming beyond what she might have imagined. Also awaiting her was sensationalism and celebrityhood well beyond what any African American woman track athlete had experienced before. As Rudolph returned home and began accepting the congratulations and applause of the American public, she also began receiving invitations to run at track meets that had, up to that point, traditionally excluded women. The last vestiges of exclusivity in this very masculine of sports were beginning to crumble. As the American public came out in droves to see her in person, Rudolph clung to the feminine image that Temple had crafted to refute charges of masculinity even as the press focused on the sexualized spectacle of watching Wilma run.

"Wilma's Coming to Town": The Sexualized Spectacle of Rudolph's Post-Olympic Career

When Rudolph finally returned to her hometown of Clarksville, she was honored with a celebration every bit as grand as the one Albany, Georgia, had given Alice Coachman twelve years earlier. The parade celebrating her victory began two miles outside of town where the Clarksville police met the Olympian to escort her into town. In Rudolph's eyes, the crowd was so large it was as if the entire town of 40,000 people was in attendance. Following the parade, the military officers at Fort Campbell, Kentucky, the army base near Clarksville, welcomed the entourage. There they enjoyed a parachute demonstration and reception. The celebrations concluded that evening with a banquet in her honor at the Clarksville Armory. Rudolph remembered the racial significance of the celebrations, it being the first time African Americans and whites of the town had come together to plan and participate in a citywide event. The parade included representatives of the traditionally white and black organizations in town, and the Olympic star recalled that it was the first time the armory had been filled with both races.[50]

While Rudolph was anxious for a period of quiet and relaxation at her parents' home, the house was filled for the next several days with friends, family members, and other well-wishers who wanted to give her their personal congratulations. Next, she, Coach Temple, and a chaperone that was usually her mother, launched on something akin to a homecoming tour in various U.S. cities: Chicago, Detroit, Atlanta, New York, Washington, D.C., Philadelphia. Tennessee State Alumni who wanted to honor one of their own sponsored most of these events. There were nice hotels and fancy restaurants, banquets and awards, and a never-ending line of people to meet—foreign ambassadors, Roy Wilkins of the NAACP, entertainers Harry Belafonte and Lena Horne, and eventually, even President Kennedy.

When life looked like it was going to settle down for Rudolph, the indoor track season was looming, and it was time for the sprint star to get in shape to run again. The women's indoor season normally would have seemed like a break to Rudolph's hectic schedule. Women had only one indoor meet—the AAU nationals. However, something happened that changed the young Olympian's schedule, altered women's track and field for the future, and forever cemented Rudolph's place in the sport. Invitational track and field meets, long the sole preserve of men, began inviting Wilma Rudolph to participate.

Track and field invitationals and meets like the Drake and Penn Relays were scattered throughout the country as part of the men's indoor and outdoor track seasons. Some meets, like the Los Angeles Invitational Indoor meet, only in its second year, were relatively new events. But many, such as the Millrose Games in New York with its famous Wanamaker Mile, and big outdoor events like the Drake Relays at Drake University in Des Moines and the Penn Relays at the University of Pennsylvania, were well established, having begun around the turn of the century.[51] Some of these institutions, as they had now become, had at one time included women. New York's Millrose Games, the traditional start of the big-time indoor track season on the East Coast, included women's events in the late 1920s up through 1931. Coachman's rival Stella Walsh had participated in 1930 and 1931, breaking the indoor record for the 50-yard dash in 1930 and earning the distinction of the Millrose Games' Outstanding Performer for the year. But as women's track and field fell out of favor in the United States in the early 1930s, meet officials stopped inviting women to participate and the games had become, as *Time* magazine put it, "stag night for the competitors." The only track "queens" that were likely to appear at these meets were local actresses or beauty queens so designated, such as Columbia Pictures actress Vicki Trickett, who served as the queen of the 1961 L.A. Invitational. As Temple had repeatedly told reporters, taking into consideration both the indoor and outdoor season, the men competed twenty to thirty times a year—the women, twice.[52]

It was into this stronghold of men's track and field, in the winter and spring of 1961, that meet officials throughout the country began inviting Rudolph to participate. Local women sprinters or her own teammates would be invited to race against the triple gold medalist. The anticipation that built around Rudolph's appearance at these meets was clearly about one thing—seeing Wilma run. "'Skeeter' is comin' to town!" wrote Sam Balter of the *Los Angeles Mirror* in January 1961 in advance of Rudolph's scheduled appearance in the second annual Los Angles Invitational Track and Field meet. "'Skeeter' is the queen of the world of track and field— Wilma Rudolph, the Tennessee State Tigerbelle and toast of Rome. She is coming to Los Angeles to do what she does best—run." As the date approached, it became clear that this was shaping up to be the premier event of the Los Angeles track and field season: "Full House Looms for Wilma," observed the *Mirror*'s Harley Tinkham, who predicted that Rudolph would run before a packed house at the Sports Arena. When the Olympian finally arrived to run before the sellout crowd, she did not disappoint. "Running with a graceful stride and sizzling speed," Rudolph set a new American record for the women's indoor 60-yard dash, thrilling the "runaway" crowd in attendance. Male track athletes Ralph Boston and Parry O'Brien appeared with the Tennessee State Tigerbelle to make this invitational "the most spectacular ever run on the boards out west." And a reporter with the black press described how the crowd became so excited that it "tried to tear down the sports arena" when the meet announcer introduced Rudolph. Clearly, it was "wonderful Wilma Rudolph" that most people were coming to see.[53]

The following month, the situation was the same back on the East Coast. A week or so before the 1961 Millrose Games in February, officials scheduled a special women's 60-yard dash for one purpose—"to give the New York track crowd its first look at Tennessee State's willowy Wilma ('Skeeter') Rudolph." Similar to Los Angeles, sportswriters anticipated that the New York crowd would be a large one, lamenting that the new Madison Square Garden that could seat 25,000 and provided a clear view of the entire track wouldn't be ready until the following year. The Millrose Athletic Association definitely thought it could fill it.[54] On the night of the event, the former Olympian entered the existing stadium, packed with 16,000 track enthusiasts, signing autographs for a throng of kids and even "a number of shy male track stars." In this bastion of masculinity on the East Coast, the initial applause was more reserved than in Los Angeles. But "then Wilma began to run with her long, floating stride, and suddenly the cigar-chewing track buffs—the men who had seen them all—began to cheer like schoolboys." The Los Angeles and New York meets were just the beginning, however. "Where There's a Wilma ... 9,295 Desert Home and TV Set for Track" at the Mason-Dixon Games in Louisville, Kentucky; "Sellout Crowd Will See Cal Relays" in Modesto, California; "Admirers Storm Wilma Rudolph" in Boston—in meet after meet, crowds came to be amazed by Rudolph's blazing speed.[55]

Why the extreme hype that surrounded Rudolph's immediate post-Olympic career? Of course, no other female American track star had won three gold medals at one Olympics before. Yet the level of attention crowds bestowed on Rudolph and the frenzy surrounding her appearances in different cities was out of proportion to this achievement alone. No doubt, the advent of television played a role in her popularity. Small portions of the Winter Olympics in Squaw Valley in February 1960 were the first games shown live on American television, with CBS providing the broadcast. The Rome games were the first to be broadcast live in Europe. CBS again had the broadcast rights for the United States, which they televised on a delayed basis, establishing a precedent for the way networks would handle broadcasting the games when there was a significant time difference involved.[56] Certainly television coverage contributed both to the general excitement and Rudolph's celebrity status as more Americans, having seen her run on television, wanted the privilege of seeing her run in person and perhaps even set a new world record. She may have also become a sentimental favorite to the public due to her early childhood illnesses, her ability to overcome extreme physical adversity to meet some of sports' great physical challenges. There was in her story, in other words, a sort of physical "rags to riches" tale.

Ed Temple believed that Rudolph's personality was the key to her popularity. Years later, he remembered her as unlike any of the other successful Olympians he coached:

> Wilma was different. Of all my girls I ever had, she had the different personality than any of them. I mean, outgoing all the time … friendly with everybody, everybody. The rest of them—they were more business. They were nice people, but they were quiet, very quiet. She wasn't loud and boisterous, now. Wilma was a lady, wasn't no doubt about that. But when she walked into a room, you could see the room light up.[57]

Indeed, the press seemed to concur with Temple's assessment. The reporter for *Time* observed how she began charming New Yorkers as soon as she arrived for the Millrose Games "with one of the most relaxed personalities in all sport," happily signing autographs, patiently answering the same questions posed by different reporters, and letting foul-ups and changes in schedules roll off her back. After an initial shaky start with the press in Europe following her gold medal haul, Rudolph found a way to relate to the press in a manner that Althea Gibson never captured.[58]

The key to understanding the spectacle nature surrounding Rudolph's participation in these meets lies in American society's obsession with the femininity of women track and field athletes for the previous three decades. Alice Coachman and her teammates had to contend with a societal concern regarding the "masculinizing" effects of the sport on its women athletes. To counter this, the black community engaged in its own version of feminizing, even sexualizing, the athletes. The Cold War had helped reshape society's perceptions of women's participation in track, and the sport's advocates had fashioned a new image highlighting how feminine women track athletes really were. Black women athletes used this new image to help once again legitimize the sport in American society, and the fastest of them all had become a national celebrity. It was, at last, acceptable for a largely male crowd to gather to watch women run. However, such a spectacle was more of an art than a sport, the beauty of the woman in motion. In city after city, they deserted home and TV sets. They sold out the arenas. They came out in snowstorms. And far from being worried about Rudolph thinking herself good enough to race men, the crowds gathered to see Wilma run. And as Americans came to witness it, sportswriters altered the feminine image into one of the fully sexualized American woman on display. Here was a woman who was not only feminine but also attractive enough to be a beauty queen, with long, beautiful legs and blazing speed. And here was a chance to see her in person. In Los Angeles, they sold out the arena to see her run with that "graceful stride and sizzling speed." By the time the evening was over, "she had all the sports people eating out of her hand and drooling as she passed by." They came to a packed Madison Square Garden in New York to see those "long gams" that produced that "long, floating stride." This crowd had initially been quieter than in Los Angeles, but when they saw Wilma run, they "began to cheer like schoolboys." By the time she ran the final, the schoolboy cheers had turned into "an appreciative hoarse male bellow" that swept through the crowd as Rudolph turned on the speed with just thirty yards left and "won as she pleased." And at the Drake Relays in Des Moines, they produced a record crowd to see her "display her form" during an exhibition dash.[59]

Rudolph was not the only runner the press applied this sexualized image to. As other women track athletes eventually became part of the invitational track circuit, there were now other sprinters to look at: "Glancing down the long, lean line of women contestants at Saturday night's Mason-Dixon Games the only bulges we saw were male eyeballs. The wows and whistles that greeted Germany's Jutta Heine answered one of the questions we were about to ask … What makes Jutta run? With that figure, she has to." In choosing the word "contestants," however, sportswriters tended to conflate women track athletes with beauty pageants rather than track meets. In fact, competitive sport was now being touted as the way to enhance women's figures. Even as Rudolph readied herself to compete at the Los Angeles Invitational in the early 1960s, sportswriters suggested that American women could achieve "Hollywood worthy" figures through sport and exercise: "If many American girls and women started to really exercise and compete in sports, it would bring such a flood of beautiful figures that the Hollywood directors would go from one nervous breakdown to another." It was, at last, acceptable for a woman—white or black—to compete in sports, even track and field. But along with that acceptance often came the requirement that the athletes accept that the press would now refer to them as hyper-feminine, even sexy, spectacles in the art of performing. In New York, officials put Rudolph's picture on the cover of their souvenir program. It was the first time in Millrose history, they noted, that "we've ever had a cover girl."[60]

As Rudolph entered the male domain of invitational track meets, however, she adhered to the feminine image that Ed Temple had crafted, essentially ignoring the sexualized spectacle that the press created. The *Los Angeles Times* ran a feature article on Rudolph prior to the Los Angeles meet entitled, "Speedy Wilma Rudolph Not Interested in Racing Men." Understanding that the position of women's track and field in the United States remained fragile, she strove to make one thing clear. Although her unofficial time of 11.0 seconds for the 100 meter in Rome was competitive with the men decathletes and she might occasionally practice against men, she was not interested in participating in even exhibitions against male sprinters. "I'm a young lady," she told reporter Jeane Hoffman. Indeed, the reporter wasn't disagreeing: "She [Rudolph] showed up in Los Angeles in a cool, feathered chapeau, and a stylish grey suit, which accented her slender legs and made her look like a page out of *Vogue*." Later in New York, the refrain was similar. Photographers gathered to take her picture following her equaling of her own 60-yard American record: "The girl who had just successfully stormed the male citadel of the Millrose Games turned around to a nearby friend," reported *Time* magazine. "'Quick, do you have a mirror?' Wilma Rudolph asked. 'Quick, do you have a comb?'" And Temple, recognizing the importance of the invitations, echoed Rudolph's comments in Los Angeles about racing against men: "Skeeter never makes the common mistake of trying to prove she's as good as a man," he told *Time*. "She's a woman." The Tennessee State women's track coach had been instrumental in making sure that no one would mistake his runners for otherwise, always seeing them as young ladies who exuded graciousness and respect.[61]

The invitations came in succeeding years as well, but the hype surrounding the spectacle of seeing Wilma Rudolph run had dissipated. The door for women track and field athletes to participate in more than two meets a year had been opened, and more male-only meets began adding women's events. Following in the wake of the Drake Relays' exhibition dash in 1961, the Penn Relays, the old stalwart on the East Coast, added an official dash for women in 1962.[62] By the mid-1960s, the Tennessee State coach felt that the sport had finally gained acceptance in the United States, as a piece in *Sports Illustrated* made clear:

> Ed Temple is the coach of the U.S. women's Olympic track and field team. He is also a man with a mission, and it was therefore with a certain amount of emotion that he heard one little word last month while listening to a TV playback of the Russian-American track meet. The word was "our," and to Temple it meant that girls in short shorts and spikes were no longer a subject to be avoided in gracious conversation. "I've heard those television people before," said Temple. "It was always '*the* girls.' But when they started beating the Russians in Los Angeles, you know what that announcer called them? He called them '*our* girls.'"[63]

"Our" girls seemed to have finally shaken the muscle Moll image. Their coach had crafted an image for them that exploited the stereotype of 1950s white middle-class femininity, and they became experts at employing such an image to the world. And even as the press turned Rudolph's celebrity appearances into sexualized spectacle, the fastest woman on earth at the time stayed on script as a young lady first, track girl second.

Conclusion

Wilma Rudolph continued to run track as a Tennessee State Tigerbelle during her junior and senior years of college. She also began considering whether to remain in the sport long enough to try to make the 1964 U.S. Olympic team. She eventually decided that to return to the Olympics and earn anything less than another three gold medals would cast a shadow over her career. So she looked for an opportunity to retire while she was still on top. In 1962, with the dual meet against the Soviet Union in Palo Alto, California, approaching later that summer, she stepped up her training with a view to making this her final competition. During the meet, she easily won the 100 meter and was the anchor, as usual, on the relay team. The Russians were better relay runners than sprinters and had a considerable lead by the time Rudolph got the baton. She remembered the exhilaration of coming from behind by close to forty yards. When she crossed the finish line in front of the Russian sprinter giving the United States the relay victory, she decided it was time to retire.

She graduated from Tennessee State in the spring of 1963 with a degree in elementary education. She had again begun dating Robert Eldridge, the father of her child, and they married following graduation.[64] The young family settled down for a time in their hometown of Clarkesville. Rudolph taught second grade at her old elementary school and took over the coaching job from her former high school coach, Clinton Gray, who had been killed recently in an automobile accident. Life seemed good. She taught there two years, giving birth to two more children in the summers following each year of teaching.[65] Yet administrators at the small-town elementary school were not interested in the new methods and ideas that Rudolph had been exposed to at Tennessee State, and the former Olympian turned schoolteacher became frustrated at being stymied. When a job offer came her way to become director of a community center in Evanston, the Eldridges left Tennessee for Illinois.

Thus began a roughly ten-year succession of short-lived jobs in cities throughout the country that either did not work out or failed to live up to Rudolph's expectations. In many situations, she felt used and exploited. It seemed to her that several of her bosses offered her the job only to be able to point to having the triple gold medalist Wilma Rudolph on board. Even when she found something that she enjoyed and was worthwhile, it wasn't enough. In her autobiography, she fondly recalled a teaching job at a junior high in Detroit. While there, she also worked after school with the students in track. She enjoyed the experience of coaching every bit as much as her athletes did being coached by the famous Olympian. But she only stayed a year and a half because she felt she wanted more out of life—

both for herself and her family. "Eight years had gone by since I won the three gold medals in the Olympics," she reflected on that time, "and I still hadn't found the fulfillment outside track that I had found in it." Clearly, she had a difficult time adjusting to life outside of athletic competition. Moreover, like Gibson, she struggled with the transition from being a celebrity and the lifestyle that goes with it to the inability to sustain such a lifestyle. "I was besieged with money problems," she reflected in her autobiography. "People were always expecting me to be a star, but I wasn't making the money to live like one."[66]

The remaining years of Rudolph's life became a little more settled, although she continued to have periods of difficulty, struggle, and even depression. Similar to Gibson, it appears as if she never quite found the identity outside of competitive sport that she had found within it. She was periodically honored for her sports accomplishments as additional accolades came her way. She was elected to numerous halls of fame, including the U.S. Olympic Hall of Fame and the National Track and Field Hall of Fame—as part of its first class of inductees in 1974. Her autobiography was published; when NBC turned it into a television movie, she served as a consultant. Similar to Coachman and Gibson, she established a nonprofit organization, the Wilma Rudolph Foundation, to help train young athletes. In July 1994, she was diagnosed with brain cancer. On good days, she could be found walking the old track that she had trained on with her friend and mentor, Coach Temple. She died in November of that year.

Women's track and field had undergone distinct changes during the years Rudolph competed. At the beginning of her career, the tomboy image continued, for a time, to haunt women track athletes. Even as Rudolph finished competing in Rome, the *New York Times* concluded that women absolutely did not belong in track and field. The Cold War, though, became responsible, in part, for moving the sport from its place at the margins of American society back to one of acceptability. As American track women went head-to-head with the Russians each year, Americans embraced them, worrying more about whether the United States could beat the "reds" than whether "our girls" were black or white. But the Cold War was responsible only in part. Black women track athletes made measurable gains for themselves by employing a gender image Americans could relate to. For his athletes, Ed Temple fashioned a new image, the feminine track woman. This idea of "young ladies first, track girls second" was based on the premise that "real" women could participate in track—women who were good looking, liked dresses and high heels, put on lipstick, paid attention to their hair, and easily captured boyfriends. The Tigerbelles followed the script closely, and as Rudolph competed in her second Olympic games and won three gold medals, many Americans came to think of this attractive African American athlete that exuded white middle-class femininity, with her affable personality and charming smile, using that image. Many sportswriters even cast her as the "original" feminine track athlete as she went skyrocketing toward celebrity-hood. During her post-Olympic career, she broke through the last gender barrier in American track and field that had kept women athletes confined to two track meets a year, accepting invitations to compete in meets that had traditionally been closed to women. In the process, the press sexualized this feminine image, developing it into one that captured the "privilege" of watching a beautiful woman in motion. Sell-out crowds and media frenzy waited with anticipation for her to come to town and then gathered to see Wilma run—her "long gams" churning up the track with that long, graceful stride. Even years later people remembered the sexualized spectacle of "seeing Wilma run": "Those who saw her in action claimed that Wilma Rudolph was the most beautiful thing that ever ran. ... It was the sheer beauty of the girl herself, and her style of running, which caught the fancy of the entire world. Five feet eleven, weighing 132 pounds, Wilma was willowy, streamlined and shaped like a girl. She ran with the grace and speed of a wild thing."[67] Yet Rudolph continued to ground her own image in the femininity of being a young lady, laying waste to the muscle Moll and staunchly refusing to acknowledge or be transformed by the sexualized showcase sportswriters tried to create for her instead. She may have been "the black gazelle" in Europe or create "hoarse male bellows" when running back in the States, but her reputation as a young lady made it once again acceptable for women to step up to the blocks and compete in track and field.

Tennessee State's status as the place to be for women's track and field training did not fade with Rudolph's graduation and retirement from the sport. Temple's program of scouting and recruiting from the surrounding high schools continued to pay off throughout the 1960s. The Tennessee State coach, patterning himself after predecessor Cleve Abbott, traveled to neighboring states to check out talent that he had seen at the Tuskegee

Relays or that had impressed him in the junior division at the nationals. In particular, several of his "superstars," as he called them, came from Georgia.[68] One of those Georgia superstars was a sprinter from Griffin, Georgia, up near Atlanta. When Temple recruited Wyomia Tyus to join the Tennessee State tradition, he found someone with the gift of speed akin to Wilma Rudolph. Moreover, entering the university as a freshman in the fall of 1963 meant that, if she stayed healthy, Temple might be able to prepare her for two Olympic games. Though Tyus missed participating on a Tennessee State team with Rudolph by only one year, it might have, in retrospect, seemed more like twenty given the radical changes that were occurring in American society. As Tyus and her teammates attempted to maintain the high standard that the Tennessee State Tigerbelles and Tuskegee Tigerettes had set before them, it remained to be seen how they would alter the sport during the troubled racial times that came to characterize the 1960s.

FIVE

"The Swiftie from Tennessee State"

Wyomia Tyus and the Racial Reality of Black Women Track Athletes in the 1960s and 1970s

No one had ever done it before. In seventy years of modern Olympic history, no track sprinter, man or woman, had ever repeated as 100-meter champion at the Olympic games. Not Jesse Owens. Not Wilma Rudolph. Not an American, a Russian, or an Aussie. There was good reason. As amateur athletes, Olympians who hoped to compete in multiple games needed not only staying power but also money. For track and field athletes, it was the latter that was most often in short supply. But in 1968, one athlete stood poised to capture the elusive prize. Her win in 1964 at the Tokyo games had been somewhat unexpected. She had been barely nineteen and regularly taken the silver medal in competitive meets just behind her Tigerbelle teammate, Edith McGuire. But Wyomia Tyus eclipsed McGuire in Tokyo. Now here she was four years later in Mexico City, just seconds away from what could be Olympic track and field history. When she crossed the finish line eleven seconds later, she had not only won her second consecutive gold medal but also set her seventh world record. The quiet, twenty-three-year-old "swiftie from Tennessee State" had just raced her way into the record books as the first Olympic sprint champion to repeat. She would enjoy her next Olympics, she told reporters, as a spectator.[1]

True to her word, Tyus retired from amateur competition after the Mexico City games. During her amateur career, she had held world records eight different times, and, at twenty-three, she undoubtedly still had some good years of speed in her.[2] With her college days at an end and no professional track circuit available, however, her future in the sport looked bleak. But her retirement was short lived, for a pro track circuit emerged in 1973. Its promoters encouraged Tyus out of retirement to compete, this time for profit. Her athletic success as a professional was every bit as complete as it had been as an amateur. She continued to set records, this time in indoor track, and finished the 1974 season unbeaten in the 60-yard dash. By the time she retired from the sport for good, she had set eleven world records. And it would be twenty years before another sprinter would duplicate her most significant amateur achievement—consecutive 100-meter Olympic victories.[3]

These victories—in reality Tyus's entire career—played out during a time of radical social change in American society. It was change that, as both African American and women, deeply affected Tyus, her teammates, and competitors. Frustrated by the slow pace of the civil rights movement, a younger generation of African Americans began challenging Martin Luther King's adherence to nonviolent resistance, and splinter groups of black activists began to look and sound more militant in their activism. It was natural that some of this radicalism spilled over into the world of sport where black athletes became inspired to do more than compete. They chose to speak out on racial injustices that they continued to experience, looking more like the radical activists on the outside of sport than black sport stars of earlier decades. For eight months, America's black athletes had contemplated boycotting the 1968 Olympics to protest the continued oppression they experienced both inside and outside the world of sport. In the end, most of them decided to compete, choosing instead to win their medals and make whatever statements or protests each felt individually appropriate. When two male sprinters, in a cry for freedom from racial oppression, raised black-gloved fists on the Olympic victory stand, Mexico City forever became the Olympics of racial, political protest and the capstone of 1968, an athletic "year of awakening" for African American athletes.[4] As the 1960s gave way to a new decade, the birth of the women's movement, inspired in part by African Americans, reawakened a feminism that had seemed to languish since the 1920s. Women began agitating for reproductive rights, equal pay, and general recognition of equality in a society that had long been grounded in patriarchy. The women's movement also spilled over into the world of sport, and women athletes became more vocal about the ways in which their competitive opportunities and earnings lagged their male counterparts. Wyomia Tyus and other black women athletes of the period raced at the intersection of these two social movements.

But Tyus was also part of Ed Temple's program of track athletes, and he brought her up, like Rudolph, to adhere to his "young ladies first, track girls second" ethic. Less than ten years since the start of Temple's program, American women's track and field was only in the beginning years of its newly legitimized status. What would be the proper response to a stridently changing world that had only recently begun to accept women track and field athletes as "our girls?" If they joined black male track athletes in their efforts to make a racial statement in Mexico City, black women track athletes might quickly find themselves and their sport marginalized once again. And if they spoke up too loudly along with white women athletes who advocated for a more equal standing in the world of sport, might they not also risk the same? It would have been, in effect, understandable and safe for Tyus to keep a low profile during her amateur and professional careers, particularly given her quiet personality. However, as she navigated a rapidly changing America, she chose to forge a middle ground that recognized her place in all these worlds— women's track and field, the radicalized civil rights movement, and the women's movement. Choosing neither to remain quiet nor to speak out too stridently, Tyus became an able, balanced, and respected spokesperson for women's track and field and black women athletes of the period. Like African American athletes of the past, she spoke out on the track with her speed. But by speaking out off the track as well, she acknowledged her place as a black woman in American society in ways that differed dramatically from those who came before her. Before being thrust into such a role, however, she had to learn how to follow in the footsteps of Wilma Rudolph as a Tennessee State Tigerbelle.

Georgia Born but Temple Trained

Ed Temple once remarked that a number of his superstars at Tennessee State came from Georgia—Lucinda Williams and Martha Hudson, both on the gold-medal Olympic relay team at the 1960 Olympic games in Rome; Edith McGuire, who won the gold medal for the 200-meter sprint at Tokyo in 1964 and two silvers to go along with it; and Wyomia

Tyus. Of the top five athletes on Temple's "Most Outstanding Twenty-Five Tigerbelles" list, four of them grew up in track and basketball programs in Georgia high schools. When Temple went looking for young talent, the state of Georgia was generally at the top of the list.[5]

Growing up in Griffin, Georgia, just outside of Atlanta, Wyomia Tyus remembered years later the advice her father gave her and her brothers—"You'll have to work twice as hard to get what you want." Born in 1945 in this rural section of the state just south of Atlanta, there seemed to be little doubt that he was referring to the difficulty of being African American in the Jim Crow South. Willie Tyus was a dairy farmer, his wife, Marie, a laundress. Their daughter was the youngest and only girl of the four children born to them. While the family couldn't afford treats like cookies and candy, there were always eggs, cheese and milk, and plenty of fresh vegetables. Those good eating habits, Tyus thought, helped give her the strength and stamina, as well as that late burst of energy, needed to cross the finish line first when she started running track.[6]

Tyus played sports not only because she liked to but also because her father insisted that her brothers not exclude her from their outdoor activities. Since they ran and played football and basketball, she did as well, and her early athletic prowess showed. But not all the boys were accepting of having a girl join in their pick-up games, she remembered, especially when they were picking teams for football. Remembering their father's instructions, one of her brothers would say, "Oh, we'll just take her." But the Tyus brothers also had an ulterior motive. During play, they would have their sister go out for a pass. She would catch it, and then outsprint everyone else. By the time she was thirteen, most of her friends were involved in the school band or some other school activity. But none of these captured her interest the same way that sports did, so in junior high, she began playing on the school basketball team. Track was the only other sport open to girls at the time. Tyus liked running and obviously had some natural speed. Plus, the boy she liked ran track, so shortly after she began playing basketball she decided to run track as well. When she went to high school, she tried out and made both the basketball and track teams, and the track meets began.[7]

Even as Tyus received encouragement from her father and brothers, the 1950s, as Rudolph and others had discovered, were a time when women who participated in track or basketball still labored under the "tomboy" image. The young Georgia athlete remembered her mother, as well as other friends and relatives, being "confused" about her desire to participate in sports. "They were reluctant to encourage my new avocation because it seemed a threat to my femininity," she recalled years later. The myths that had prevailed throughout most of the century that were connected with this image continued to persist—girls who became athletes would have difficulty bearing children and become masculine-looking due to their interest in such male-oriented activities. Despite her mother's concerns, she continued to run track and play basketball competitively, although her serious days of competition lay just ahead.[8]

Constantly on the lookout for young talent, Ed Temple first saw Tyus compete at the 1961 Georgia High School State Track Championships. For U.S. women's track and field, the historically black Tennessee college was still the place to be. "If you can beat the girls at Tennessee State," Temple told recruits, "you can beat anyone." His comment was not mere bragging. Since 1955, Tennessee State had won the team championship at the women's nationals every year.[9] The seasoned coach noticed that Tyus had natural speed but that she was inexperienced and needed to be coached in proper sprint technique. He also discovered over the years that she was extremely quiet, so quiet she would hardly string two sentences together. She was a woman of few words who kept her thoughts to herself, even with her family. After returning from an overseas trip with Temple some years later, Tyus's mother pressed her for details about the exciting experience. In her typical, efficient reply, she said, "It was alright." Through the years, he also realized that she had an incredible amount of courage on the track. There was hardly anyone better to have out there when things got tough in competition because she would find a way to come through. But those things came later. What he saw at the Georgia Championships besides her natural speed was passion and resolve. Impressed with these, he invited her to attend his summer program for high school athletes. As a rising high school junior in the summer of 1961, then, Tyus began training at Tennessee State.[10]

When Temple entered the picture, he not only provided Tyus needed training but also allayed the fears of those who had worried about her passion for sport. Temple had a particular gift in bringing out the best in sprinters, as runners like Barbara Jones, Mae Faggs, and Wilma Rudolph had shown. But just as Alice Coachman and Wilma Rudolph before her,

Tyus discovered that running track the right way was hard work. She remembered that first summer at Tennessee State as "horrible." She had never really trained before, and Temple had them out running three times a day—at 5:00 and 9:00 in the morning and again at 1:00 in the afternoon. "We had to be at the track at five, and you could never be late," she reminisced years later. "All you did was brush your teeth, put your clothes on, and when you got there the coach was waiting." Tyus was convinced that one of the reasons he made them train so hard was so they would be too exhausted to go out and get themselves in trouble. That way, Temple could, fairly easily, keep the promise he made to parents that his runners would adhere to strict rules. It did not take long in this setting for Tyus to show that she was championship material. In the girls' division of the AAU national championships that July, she took second place in the 75-yard dash and third place in the 100-yard. A year later, she swept the 50-yard, 75-yard, and 100-yard dashes at the same championships, setting an American junior record in both the 50- and 100-yard. After attending the rigorous summer program for two years, Temple offered Tyus a work-study athletic scholarship—still the only type of scholarship available for women—to attend Tennessee State, get a college education, and run track. Her mother and others who had been skeptical of her interest in the sport suddenly began to see certain benefits to her talent and hard work.[11]

Once at Tennessee State full time, Tyus blossomed under Temple's tutelage. In July 1963, the summer before her freshman year, Temple moved her up to the women's division. She placed fourth in the 100 meters and was part of the winning 4x100-meter relay team in the dual meet with the Soviet Union, held in Moscow that July. Later that summer in a meet in Germany, she placed third in the 100 meters. In February of the following year, still just a freshman, she set her first world record when she finished the 70-yard dash in 7.5 seconds at the Mason-Dixon Games. By the lead-up to the Olympic games in Tokyo, the black press, and Ed Temple, were suggesting that Tyus was being groomed to "fill the track shoes" of Tennessee State alumna and triple Olympic gold medalist Wilma Rudolph. She was, according to Temple, something of "an athletic time bomb" that he expected to go off at the Mexico City games in 1968. It seemed, however, that everyone was so focused on four years in the future that they virtually forgot that Tyus, along with her teammate Edith McGuire, was competing in the 1964 Olympics.[12]

The 100-meter sprint at the Tokyo games was set to be an interesting race. Edith McGuire was the current "golden girl" of track, the one expected to take up the mantle of Wilma Rudolph, at least in the near term. She was a year older than Tyus, and with an additional year of training from Temple, a little more seasoned. While both runners competed in the 100 and 200 meters, McGuire tended to dominate in the 200. During the months before the Olympics, however, she had also been dominant in the 100 meters. She placed first in the 100 meters at both the dual meet with the Soviet Union that summer and at the Olympic trials in early August. Tyus came in third in the 100 meters to make the team. It seemed that the stage was set for McGuire to repeat Rudolph's 1960 performance. In a feature article on McGuire, the *New York Times* predicted that she was the only woman on the team with the potential to come home from Tokyo an Olympic champion. However, the *Times* underestimated the talent and determination of the young Wyomia Tyus, whom the black press was describing as a runner that could "dig out like a Mexican roadrunner." McGuire won her gold medal in the 200, but it was her younger teammate who took home gold in the 100, scoring an upset against the slightly older and more seasoned McGuire. Tyus returned to Tennessee from Tokyo an Olympic gold track medalist at the age of nineteen.[13]

Tyus and McGuire may have returned home Olympic champions, but women's track and field in the United States was only beginning, as Ed Temple put it, to no longer be a topic most people avoided in drawing-room conversation. Thanks to Temple's program to highlight women track athletes' femininity coupled with some decisive victories over the Russian women in the sprints, U.S. track women had finally become "our" girls among television sports reporters. While this was music to Temple's ears, the reality was that such a status was new. No one dedicated to sustaining the sport over the long term was interested in disturbing this change in attitude among American sportscasters and the broader society. In the turbulent racial days that lay ahead, it remained to be seen whether African American women athletes, whose race had become less of an issue during the Cold War, would risk wanting to be perceived as *black* women athletes.[14]

World Records and Civil Rights

There had been dramatic advances for African Americans in the ten years since Althea Gibson was struggling in the USLTA and Rosa Parks had refused to give up her seat on a Montgomery bus. Martin Luther King Jr. had emerged from the 1955–56 Montgomery bus boycott as the young leader of a burgeoning movement. The subsequent formation of the Southern Christian Leadership Conference (SCLC) helped provide organization and structure for the struggle. King's belief in nonviolent activism to fight racism and achieve parity in civil rights led to approaches that built upon the success of the Montgomery boycott. In February 1960, the same year Wilma Rudolph would have the Olympics of a lifetime, young black college students in cities such as Greensboro, North Carolina; Nashville, Tennessee; and Atlanta, Georgia, began a series of sit-ins. This form of protest involved sitting at lunch counters and restaurants despite statutes allowing local establishments the right to refuse service to blacks, its purpose to push for the desegregation of local restaurants and lunch counters at nationwide chains. The local African American community in these locations joined with the students to picket the stores, encouraging a boycott until desegregation became a reality. As in Montgomery, an economic approach proved successful and stores and restaurants throughout the South capitulated to the demands of local African American communities that they serve blacks as well as whites.

Even as Rudolph approached retirement and a young Tyus began attending Temple's summer programs, African Americans continued to use these nonviolent tactics, such as boycotts, sit-ins, and freedom rides, to further the dismantling of segregation throughout the South. In August 1963, nearly 250,000 activists marched on Washington, gathering before the Lincoln Memorial to sing songs of freedom, hear speeches, and show their support for the Civil Rights Act and the movement at large. In the afternoon, King delivered what would become known as his "I Have a Dream" speech, outlining his hope for the future. While the speech inspired the crowd of protesters and became a clarion call for freedom, it did not dissuade a violent faction of the opposition from continuing their own tactics. In mid-September, just a few weeks after the March on Washington, white racists bombed the 16th Street Baptist Church in Birmingham, killing four young girls that were attending Sunday School. These years of protest, jailings, beatings, and deaths finally resulted in legislative action. The Civil Rights Act of 1964 was the legislative death sentence to Jim Crow, banning segregation in public facilities and prohibiting racial discrimination in employment practices.

Not only did the act provide strong enforcement of its provisions, it also permitted government agencies to withhold public funds to programs that violated the law, a provision that had important ramifications for public schools and colleges.

Though segregation was now illegal, voting rights remained a critical issue. Only approximately one-third of the eligible African Americans were registered to vote in the South, in contrast to 60–70 percent living in the North. Individual states in the Deep South had even lower percentages, such as Alabama, with just 22 percent, and Mississippi, where under 7 percent of eligible blacks were registered.[15] Without the vote, leaders of the movement understood that they would never be able to turn white racists out of office, put an end to police brutality, and get a fair hearing in a court of law. In the summer of 1964, civil rights organizations mobilized to pan out through Mississippi to register black voters. Known as the Mississippi Freedom Summer, Klansmen and other white racists retaliated with beatings, bombings, and the murder of volunteers like white New Yorkers Michael Schwerner and Andrew Goodman and black Mississippian James Chaney.

The following year the battle over voting rights turned to Alabama where Selma sheriff James Clark was blocking voter registration. With King's support, the SCLC planned a march from Selma to the state capital of Montgomery. But as the marchers crossed the Edmund Pettus Bridge in Selma, Alabama, state troopers, along with Sheriff Clark's men, threw teargas and beat the marchers, forcing them back across the bridge and trampling over those retreating with their horses. This "Bloody Sunday" spurred the activists to march again. The protest, coupled with continued pockets of violence even in the North, prompted a national outcry that resulted in President Johnson sending voter registration legislation to Congress. In his speech to the nation, Johnson outlined the discrimination that blacks faced when attempting to register, such as being told that they had come too late in the day, on the wrong day, or when the proper official was not in his office. When African Americans did get through to the registrar, Johnson continued, they might be disqualified for having not spelled out their middle name or for abbreviating a word on the application. If they managed to successfully pass the application process, blacks might be given a test that involved explaining certain provisions of state laws or reciting the entire U.S. constitution. "And even a college degree cannot be used to prove that he can read or write," the president lamented. "For the fact is that the only way to pass these barriers is to show a white skin."[16] The protests at Selma coupled with a considerable white outcry led Congress to pass the Voting Rights Act of 1965 in the summer of that year, striking down the numerous ways that had been used to deny African Americans the vote.

The same summer that Congress passed the Voting Rights Act, Wyomia Tyus was coming into her own in U.S. women's track and field. While Edith McGuire retained her place as the country's 200-meter specialist, Tyus took over as the top 100-meter sprinter and the Tennessee State Tigerbelles continued to dominate the sport. In July 1965, Tyus tied the world record for the 100-meter sprint, sharing with two European athletes the distinction of being the three fastest women in the world. At the same meet, she also staged a come-from-behind win to salvage a win over the Russians in the 4x100-meter relay.[17] Thanks to the popularity and celebrity-hood of Wilma Rudolph, women's track and field had made great strides since the days that Alice Coachman and the Tuskegee Tigerettes ruled the sport. Women track athletes now routinely competed at the invitational meets that Rudolph had opened the door to. And as the U.S./ U.S.S.R. dual track meets continued yearly, women track athletes' position as important players in the cultural Cold War helped further legitimize their improved status.

The contrast with the Soviet Union women's track program served to highlight both the physical differences of the two superpowers' athletes and the apparent disadvantage American women faced against the Soviets. In truth, American track women continued to gain popularity in part because the "big-boned, muscular" athletes of the Soviet Union served as a convenient "other" for American society to transfer lingering concerns over the masculinizing effects of sport on women's bodies. To U.S. sportswriters, the Soviet women could run and certainly master field events, but they simply were not attractive. Polish sprinter Irena Kirszenstein, co-holder of the 100-meter world record in 1966, was pleasant and possessed a nice smile. But her face was too narrow and sharp, and she had much too large of a nose. In short, "she wouldn't turn a head if she took a stroll up Fifth Avenue," observed the *Los Angeles Times*. American women track athletes, however, were beauties—slender, shapely beauties that had no trouble securing a date. The Soviet women, particularly the bulk and muscularity of those who competed in the field events, led sportswriters to question not only their womanhood but also the legitimacy of the contest between the two nations. Pitting stars from the Soviet Union against American runners was, in the words of a *New York Times* reporter, like "a man running against a girl." Irina and Tamara Press, Russian sisters who dominated their track and field events during the mid-1960s, were considered women "only incidentally." And there was some doubt whether the Romanian high jumper that held the record in 1967 even qualified incidentally. The ultimate "proof" came in February 1968 when Eva Klobukovska, the Polish sprinter who shared the 100-meter world record with Kirszenstein and Tyus, failed a chromosome test to determine her sex. The International Amateur Athletic Foundation (IAAF), the governing body of international track and field, had mandated random testing beginning in 1966. Klobukovska became a random victim before the 1968 European Nations Athletic Cup when the test to determine her gender was inconclusive. The IAAF withdrew ratification of her victories and records; the IOC would make their decision regarding past Olympic medals when they met before the games in Mexico City later in the year. In short, the outward physical differences and now the chromosomal evidence seemed to indicate to sportswriters that American women were competing against the Soviets at a decided disadvantage.[18]

The Soviet bloc track women could lay claim to something that their counterparts in the United States could not, however—a kind of superstar status in their own countries. In August 1965, as Tyus prepared to go up against the two Polish runners who shared the 100-meter world record with her, fans in Warsaw flocked to get photographs and autographs of the Polish sprinters. Questions and information about the upcoming race dominated news conferences. "Were there a local Wheaties," observed the *New York Times*, "they would be endorsing it." Tyus, however, reigning world, Olympic, and national champion, did not receive anywhere near comparable attention in the States. At this point, there was a sense that at least American women's track and field and its athletes were substantially ahead of where they used to be.[19]

In the midst of the stark differences between women's track and field in the two superpowers, Tyus continued her dominance of the shorter sprints in the United States. Her 1965 victories and world record were recognized when she was named a Sullivan Award finalist and the 1965

Woman Athlete of the Year. But it was 1966 that she was virtually unbeatable. In January, the "Tennessee A&I flash" set a new world record for the 60-yard dash at the Motor City Invitational, "shattering" the former record by shaving one-tenth of a second off the old time. Two months later at the indoor nationals, she lowered the mark yet again, this time by two-tenths of a second. She also set a new American record of 5.6 seconds for the 50-yard dash at the Maple Leaf Track Games in February. And later that summer, she captured headlines in the *Chicago Tribune* when she won the 100-yard and 220-yard dashes and anchored the winning, Tigerbelle relay team at the AAU outdoor national championships. She clearly seemed to be on her way to becoming the new queen of U.S. women's track and field. In the midst of her dominance, the racial climate in American society continued to undergo profound changes.[20]

Though the first half of the 1960s had been an active and fruitful period of the civil rights movement, white violence and the seemingly slow pace of change frustrated some African Americans. Moreover, there were those who questioned what seemed like an exclusive use of King's nonviolent methods, particularly younger activists like the students involved in the sit-ins of 1960 and 1961. The organization they formed during that early activity, the Student Nonviolent Coordinating Committee (SNCC), followed the code of nonviolence set forth by the older leadership. Yet they also acknowledged that there might come a point in the struggle when a more militant approach would be necessary. By the middle part of the decade, this student group had become influenced by the radicalism of Malcolm X, who dismissed King's approach as passive and infective. "Revolutions," he wrote, "are based on bloodshed."[21] Malcolm X also spurned integration, espousing a separatist philosophy based upon black nationalism. When Stokely Carmichael became chairman of SNCC in 1966, his desire to move the organization toward black nationalism became clear when he purged the group of the few whites who had been on staff. Suggesting that freedom had still not come after six long years of intensive efforts and bloodshed, Carmichael articulated the need for "Black Power," which became a rallying cry for this younger generation of activists. It would be this more radical strain of the civil rights movement that would awaken a younger generation of black athletes and their supporters.

If there was a corresponding figure to Stokely Carmichael within the realm of athletics, it was Harry Edwards. While Edwards was not responsible for the spate of athletic protests that erupted during 1968, the "year of awakening" for the black athlete, he served as the most visible face and voice of the black athletic revolt. A former field athlete for Bud Winter's track program at San Jose State, Edwards left athletics to teach sociology. He eventually moved from San Jose State to pursue his doctorate in sociology at Cornell. His status as one of Coach Winter's former athletes coupled with his time in the classroom provided him with the opportunity to meet and discuss his thoughts on the plight of the black athlete with members of Winter's track team, the famed Speed City. Among these athletes was a man by the name of Tommie Smith.[22]

Smith's discussions and meetings with Edwards and other athletes, along with his own reading and intellectualism, awoke in him a desire to use his athletic talents as a platform to expose racial discrimination within collegiate sport. This tall, quiet sprinter was part of a growing number of African American athletes who were beginning to believe that winning races and medals was no longer enough. Activism meant doing something beyond taking the victory. Encouraged by the confident position of the Black Power movement, the increasing number of student protests, and the rigid stance heavyweight champion Muhammad Ali was taking on the Vietnam War, black athletes participated in disturbances throughout the country, generally against white coaches and players. From Princeton University in the East to the University of California at Berkeley in the West, thirty-seven forms of protest took place during 1968. Black collegiate athletes spoke out against the discrimination they faced—housing, the quality of education, social exclusion, interracial dating, and unemployment—and used sit-ins and their own athletic power in the form of the boycott to highlight their grievances.[23]

During this year of awakening, the *Negro* athlete fell into the shadows and the *black* athlete was born. There were important distinctions between the two. The *Negro* athlete was a hero of the Jim Crow era, the one that had broken through entrenched segregation to prove African Americans could compete and win championships against white competitors. Their voice against racial discrimination was most often heard through their athletic victories on the field rather than activism off it. At times, the *Negro* athlete had even won the momentary adulation of white America. When Jesse Owens and Joe Louis had defeated Hitler's German "supermen" and Wilma Rudolph routinely beat her Russian adversaries, they became brief symbols of American athletic dominance that confirmed for many the superiority of the American political system. But after decades of the *Negro* athlete's success, little had truly changed. Student athletes had trouble finding housing due to the color of their skin. Travel, particularly in the Deep South, exposed the sluggish speed at which segregation was being dismantled. And athletes returned from Olympic glory or retired as champions only to find that their victories made little difference when it came time to look for a job. The *black* athlete was fed up with these injustices. Feeling like a pawn in a political chess match in the Cold War era rather than an athletic hero making racial breakthroughs, the *black* athlete was no longer content to remain silent off the playing field. In the view of the *black* athlete, the *Negro* athlete was an "Uncle Tom" not wishing to too strongly rock the boat of racial polarity. African American athletes had become radicalized, and it displayed itself even in the way the athletes referred to themselves. Admonishing the *Negro* label assigned them by whites, their designation as *black* athletes reflected a pride in their racial heritage, a pride in being black. In short, the black athlete had been awakened, and he was in revolt. The most memorable protest of the year, however, and the one most directly related to Wyomia Tyus was almost a year in the making.[24]

"It Was Their Moment"— The Dynamics of Olympic Protest

The 1967 track year was a tough one for Tyus. She began the year on a positive note when she eclipsed young Barbara Ferrell—an up-and-coming African American athlete from the rival L.A. Mercurettes track club—in the 60-yard dash at the AAU Indoor Nationals to hang on to that title. But the Outdoor Nationals were a different story. She lost the 100-meter sprint to Ferrell, actually placing third behind her own teammate Diana Wilson. Ferrell and Wilson switched places in the 200 meters, leaving Tyus with another third-place finish. Things would get worse before they got better. At the United States-British Commonwealth track meet in early July, she dropped to a fourth-place finish in the 100 meters and fifth place in the 200, and she failed to make the team in the 100 meter for the Pan-American games when she again came in fourth. She managed to turn things around in the 200 meters, however, when she placed second to

Ferrell at the trials and beat her by one-tenth of a second to take first at the games. In August, she finally looked like she was beginning to recapture some of her old form when she bested her Polish rival Irina Kirszenstein to win the 100-meter sprint in a track meet between the Americas and Europe. While she had ended things on a high note, it had been a very long track season for Wyomia Tyus.[25]

As Tyus, Ed Temple, and athletes and coaches throughout the country began to turn their attention to preparing for the upcoming Olympic year, the roots of what became Olympic protest were forming on the campus of San Jose State University. Other black athletes joined with Tommie Smith and Harry Edwards to discuss the injustices they faced. With the Mexico City games a year away, Edwards, San Jose State football player Ken Noel, and many Olympic hopefuls organized themselves into the Olympic Project for Human Rights (OPHR) in October 1967. As their spokesperson, Edwards announced that black athletes planned to boycott the 1968 Olympics in Mexico City unless certain changes were made to secure better treatment of African American athletes. These demands included the ouster of Avery Brundage as president of the International Olympic Committee (IOC); the immediate reinstatement of Muhammad Ali as heavyweight champion; the elimination of the exclusion of blacks and Jews to the New York Athletic Club; the appointment of an African American to the United States Olympic Committee and an additional black coach to the U.S. Olympic track and field team; and the expulsion of South Africa and Rhodesia from the Olympic games due to apartheid policies.[26] Clearly, the athletes had found their voice and were using the possibility of withholding their athletic abilities as a means of power to secure the demands of their platform.

Despite wide belief in the principles of the OPHR among young African American athletes, a number of them refused to back the boycott that the organization proposed. The reasons for their refusal differed. Long jumpers Ralph Boston, competing in his third and final Olympics, and Bob Beamon, on the verge of breaking the world record, were both adamant about their unwillingness to "stay home." Free-style wrestler Bobby Douglas had placed fourth in 1964, and the three athletes who had medaled in Tokyo were no longer competing. He was hungry for a medal and felt he could do more to interest other African Americans in his still white-dominated sport by competing rather than "sitting on the sidelines and yelling black power." Charlie Scott felt constrained by geography. He was the first and only African American basketball player on the squad at the University of North Carolina where Jim Crow, though illegal with the Civil Rights Act of 1964, was still deeply entrenched. These athletes acknowledged ongoing discrimination in sports and many believed in the basic tenets of the OPHR, but they were not going to participate in a boycott of the Olympics.[27]

As the OPHR got underway, black women athletes seemed to be strangely absent from the boycott conversation. The written record on Tyus and other black women Olympic hopefuls concerning their lack of involvement in the OPHR is sketchy and conflicting and does not always shore up with their absence from the discussion. During the Olympic games, Ed Temple told a reporter for the *Nashville Banner* that his Tigerbelles had been approached in December 1967 about the effort. Three black male athletes—one of whom Temple named as Lee Evans, 400-meter specialist and a teammate of Tommie Smith's at San Jose State—talked with members of the Tigerbelle team in an effort to convince them to support the boycott effort. At the time, Temple was attending the AAU convention in New Orleans. Apparently, Tyus and the other Tigerbelles were giving some consideration to what Evans and the others were proposing. "Once they got an emotion built on one side of this situation," Temple remembered, "it was hard to present the other side so my girls could make up their own minds."[28] Moreover, both Tyus and Temple questioned, in the months following the Olympics, whether it would have been better for her to be more involved in the effort. Many years later, however, Tyus, Smith, and John Carlos, another athlete involved in the project, remembered things differently. Tyus felt like most of the energy for the movement was on the West Coast and that the men simply took the women for granted. "It appalled me," Tyus told sportswriter and former teammate Kenny Moore. "They [the men] assumed we had no minds of our own and that we'd do whatever we were told." In response, Smith acknowledged the lack of relationship that OPHR had with the women athletes: "They should have been involved. … It was not meant to be denigrating. So many things were happening, and there was so little time. It was an inadvertent oversight." Carlos remembered thinking at the time that the women should have been involved as well. But he absolved himself of responsibility by indicating that the pattern of exclusion had been established in the OPHR before he came on board.[29]

That the women athletes remained silent and separated from the boy-cott discussions is beyond dispute; what is less clear is the reason for their separation. Scholars have seen the intersection of the male-dominated black power movement and masculine sports world as integral to what they term the women's exclusion from the OPHR. Certainly the language of the proj-ect was almost exclusively masculine. "Now that so many brothers have awakened," remarked Harry Edwards at the Olympic trials in Los Angeles during the summer of 1968, "there's nothing we can't accomplish."[30] Indeed, Edwards referred to athletic *brothers* repeatedly throughout the boycott deliberations. Moreover, the black power movement that so influ-enced the OPHR was strongly masculine. The more important issue, it argued, was to first place black men on an equal footing with white men before worrying about the gender discrimination faced by black women. In short, black women would "stand by their men" for the good of the race.[31] However, this masculine-oriented reading of the OPHR does not seem to square with the fact that Lee Evans and others involved with the boycott approached the Tigerbelles early on, and their coach was worried that they might choose to participate in the effort.

In part, the women athletes' silence reflects the influence of their coach and his position on the importance of Olympic participation. Temple wanted his athletes focused on one thing when competing—doing their best. "Politics and competition are too much for our athletes to become involved in—you can't mix the two without cutting down on some of the athletes' performances," he told reporter Al Stilley. The con-summate coach, he wanted his athletes' minds focused on competition. Temple's views on Olympic competition also reflected the often disparate and contradictory approaches within the African American community toward civil rights and moving the race forward. Such conflicting approaches had already come to the surface with Althea Gibson as various communities suggested different ways to advance her career and empha-size her racial role. Now here they were being exposed again. Temple felt that success at the Olympics could be life altering for a black athlete, and he wanted to present that side of things before his athletes made up their minds about whether to become involved in the boycott discussions. "When an athlete wins a gold medal, it helps them. It will help Tyus to get a better job and to be in a better position to help Negroes," he told reporters in the wake of her win in Mexico City. In short, he believed in the power of a college education and world-class competitive sport to change individual lives. Perhaps Temple's opposing approach to civil rights could be chalked up to generational differences. However, the fact that young black male athletes across the country could not agree on the boycott issue exposes how conflicted the black community could be when it came to deciding how best to move the race forward.[32]

Yet certainly Temple and his athletes were also considering the long road black women athletes had endured to reach their present position in American society. Temple had conducted a virtual one-man crusade to rescue women's track and field from the margins. They had spent far fewer years as *our* girls than they had as *those* girls. Mixing themselves up in racial politics—particularly in the Jim Crow South—just as they were becoming accepted by American society would be something to consider strongly. The Tigerbelles were stuck in the middle of a bold and persuasive argument by some of the male athletes to include them in the movement, and a no doubt equally persuasive appeal by their coach to remain uninvolved and focused on competition. The masculine-oriented black power movement undoubtedly influenced the OPHR. Harry Edwards, in particular, promoted the connection. Nonetheless, some male athletes prominently associated with the OPHR invited Tyus and others to join the movement. In the end, it was the women athletes' decision to make, and they chose not to become involved in the boycott effort. This cautious choice was based, at least in part, on a realization that their place in American society was still a tenuous one.

In truth, other forces—within the world of U.S. track and field—conspired to exclude the women athletes from the boycott discussions. By June 1968, support for the boycott had concentrated itself into a group of the black track and field athletes.[33] Toward the end of the month, Edwards met with the athletes who had passed the first round of Olympic trials in Los Angeles and were scheduled to go onto high-altitude training at Lake Tahoe in September. The plan for the meeting was to take a vote regarding the boycott. If 75 percent of the affected athletes voted in favor of boycotting, Edwards would proceed on their behalf.[34] On 1 July, he announced to the press that the athletes involved had decided to keep their plans a secret, possibly even waiting until after the games started or the athletes were in the starting blocks to announce their decision. Edwards's decision not to announce the outcome of the meeting merely raised speculation that he really did not have the support he needed among the athletes to stage a successful boycott. He certainly did not have the votes of the women athletes. Tyus and the other black women track athletes were not at this meeting because up until 1976, Olympic trials for men and women track and field athletes were held separately. In 1968, the initial stage of the men's track and field trials were in Los Angeles around the end of June. The first stage of the women's trials, however, would not be held until the end of August, a week following their own national outdoor championships that were also held separately from the men until 1976.[35] While women's track and field had come a long way since the days of Alice Coachman, keeping their national championships separate from the men's spoke to the continued "inferior" status of the sport.

At the women's Olympic trials, Tyus faced stiff competition from Barbara Ferrell, a sprinter with the L.A. Mercurettes who had tied the world record at the AAU outdoor championships in 1967. But another young sprinter, seventeen-year-old Margaret Bailes with the Oregon Track Club, had also tied the world record at the AAU outdoor nationals that summer. There was speculation that Bailes—a "complete" runner who could both explode out of the blocks like Ferrell and hold off Tyus's scorching finish with the now famous "Tyus lean"—may be the one to run eleven seconds flat and break the record. But Tyus had a competitive edge that could be unsettling to the younger sprinters. Bailes, in particular, told reporters as much. "That Tyus bugs me," she remarked to sportswriters, explaining how she got "psyched out" when the older sprinter was competing. Possessing the experience that the other two lacked, Tyus always seemed to come through in the clutch. Getting off to her best start all year, her lunge at the tape was still there, this time with enough force to send her sprawling across the finish line in first place. Bailes was able to hold on to win the 200 meter, but Tyus and Ferrell were just behind her in second and third, solidifying places for the three sprinters on the Olympic team in both sprints.[36]

As the women athletes competed for berths on the Olympic track and field team, it became clear that the new, feminine image that Temple had worked so hard to create during Rudolph's reign was by now fairly entrenched in American society. This team, "more mobile, stronger, deeper and faster" than any before it, also possessed something else: "There was a youthful touch of femininity in the air, perhaps a faint breath of hairspray, a mysterious new something nobody could quite define but which one coach called 'a great influx of pretty young things coming into the sport.'" At the trials with his Tigerbelles, Temple of course continued to promote the image. Contrasting them with women swimmers, he argued that track athletes didn't have the muscles that the swimmers did, some of whom looked like weight lifters. "Our girls are definitely more feminine," he told *Sports Illustrated's* Bob Ottum. "There it was," Ottum continued, "track can be beautiful." Why all this new, young talent? The key, it appeared, was to get women to start the sport early. The incentives for an early start were clear. Not only did girls get to meet boys—lots of them—but they also got a lot of attention from participating in the sport. And it was attention from the right places, as the boys got to watch them. Moreover, girls were starting to understand that there was a certain glamour to the sport, a glamour also appreciated by the men, no doubt, since running helped make women's legs "shapelier." In short, Ottum observed, "these pussycats are ready to call the future theirs."[37] Even as black women track athletes struggled with their stance on racial issues such as the Olympic boycott, they understood that the key to remaining accepted in American society meant continuing to promote and accept a feminine image.

By the end of August, it became clear that sportswriters' July speculation that the boycott effort was crumbling was indeed correct when Edwards told those assembled at a Black Power Conference in Philadelphia that the boycott was off due to lack of support. Other forms of protest, such as wearing black armbands or refusing to participate in victory stand ceremonies, were not out of the question. In truth, however, the final decision regarding a boycott was still pending. While Edwards continued to be the "face" and "voice" of the OPHR through the remainder of the summer and into the fall, there were broader influences at work that lay just beneath the surface of his announcements to the press. Support for the boycott *had* seriously dwindled, but the final decision by the athletes themselves was yet to be made.[38]

Following their Olympic trials in California, the women set off for high-altitude training in Los Alamos, New Mexico, in order to simulate the conditions they would face in Mexico City. The men, meanwhile, were undergoing their own high-altitude training and their final trials at a separate facility, carved out of the woods of Echo Summit at Lake Tahoe, Nevada. Despite the fact that there was, by that point, little support for an

all-out boycott, the time at Lake Tahoe was extremely important in bringing black male track athletes together as a group. Here they were able to
train together, meet socially, and exchange ideas. The athletes who had
been wary of the movement and those who stood behind it could see that
men like Tommie Smith and Lee Evans were not of the militant strain that
Edwards had been projecting. The movement that Edwards had begun
had, in reality, taken on a life of its own, and the athletes themselves were
determining what the next step would be. In fact, it was not until a meeting
in Denver after the men's Lake Tahoe trials and women's Los Alamos
training—as the Olympic athletes were being fitted for their uniforms—
that the athletes reached their final decision on whether or not to boycott.
Edwards was not at that meeting. And while Smith, Evans, and Carlos
were, they did not lead it, but simply participated along with the others
who attended. Ralph Boston moderated "a very organized and very well
run" meeting where those in attendance discussed the OPHR, what it
stood for, and what had taken place over the past year and half. During
the discussion, it became clear that a consensus about a boycott or any specific protest was unattainable. Some, such as those in the military, felt they
had too much on the line, while others were struggling to determine their
stance. "This is when we decided that we would not boycott as a group,"
Smith remembered, "but that each athlete would do what he individually
felt was necessary in the fight."[39] The athletes had reached a final position
in the days leading up to their departure for Mexico City.

Despite almost a year of unrest surrounding the Olympic games, a
colorful and festive atmosphere met the women's track and field team as
they deplaned on 3 October. Tyus had not, thus far, been at the forefront
of any discussions with the press concerning the now-defunct boycott or
possible protests. But she was a seasoned competitor who was returning
to defend her 100-meter Olympic sprint title. Considered an "old-timer"
in Mexico City, reporters surrounded her with questions concerning
what might occur if African American athletes took the victory stand.
Nothing had been decided, she told reporters, despite Edwards's public
suggestions that black athletes might refuse to stand at attention or wear
black armbands as a sign of mourning over strained race relations back
home. Without referring to the Denver meeting or its outcome, Tyus
was, in essence, silently affirming that, although no group action had
been agreed upon, individual forms of protest were not off the table.[40]

First, however, there were medals to win. Tyus had not been expected to take the gold in Tokyo, but now she was a champion defending her title. Temple had said all along that 1968 would be her year. Sportswriters were even predicting that she might duplicate Wilma Rudolph's three-gold triumph of eight years before. She was convinced that she wasn't putting any pressure on herself to win a gold medal, feeling that she could be content as long as she ran her best in each race. But as she was getting ready to settle into the blocks on 15 October for the final in the 100 meter, she started sensing signs of nervousness and looked for a way to stay loose. Remembering that she was the defending champion, she told herself that she would leave the nervousness to her competitors who should be scared of her. At the sound of the gun, Ed Temple recalled that she "came out [of the blocks] like a hydrogen bomb—just one explosive push. ... She was out front after 40 meters, and at the Olympic level you don't catch anyone who's leading after that." She was the new world record holder at eleven seconds flat, and she was a two-time, consecutive Olympic gold medalist in the 100-meter sprint. She was, as the *Baltimore Afro-American* put it, in a special class. In truth, she was in a class of her own, and would be for the next twenty years. Placing sixth in the 200-meter race, Tyus did not duplicate Rudolph's 1960 gold-medal haul. Her teammate Barbara Ferrell was the top U.S. finisher, coming in fourth, just behind bronze medalist Jennifer Lamy of Australia. But Tyus and Ferrell would combine with teammates Margaret Bailes and Mildrette Netter to win gold and set a new world record in the 4x100-meter women's relay.[41] There would be no protest on the victory stand by black women athletes, however—no black socks or black armbands or refusing to stand at attention. Any protest, as Tommie Smith had remembered, would be an individual decision, and Tyus and her teammates chose to accept their medals without one.

As Tyus was capturing her second consecutive Olympic gold medal in the women's 100 meter, Tommie Smith was advancing through the preliminaries of the men's 200 meter. Just a day after her world record performance in the 100 meter, Tommie Smith turned in his own world-record, gold-medal performance in the men's 200 meter. Teammate John Carlos took the bronze when Australian Peter Norman edged him out at the tape for the silver. Smith had been heavily involved in the OPHR from the beginning, although he had not become militant like Edwards.

He was quiet, intent more on listening than talking. But he was a determined individual, and he was convinced that black athletes, in the fight
for racial justice, needed to do more than go out and win. The world
barely had time to digest his Olympic victory before the image of Smith
and Carlos on the victory stand took hold of the news media. With their
shoes in hand and their black socks exposed, they mounted the victory
podium—Smith with the military precision of his ROTC training—and
received their medals. All three athletes, including Australian silver
medalist Norman, were wearing buttons declaring their support for the
Olympic Project for Human Rights. A black glove on Smith's right hand
and its pair on Carlos's left, the two black athletes bowed their heads and
raised their gloved fists into the air with the first strains of "The Star-
Spangled Banner." And there they remained throughout the national
anthem, silent and, in Smith's view, reverent. The stadium erupted into
a chorus of "boos." Smith prayed he would live to come down off the
stand, convinced that someone in the crowd would shoot him for his
"silent gesture." They did survive the victory stand, and their protest
became *the* iconic image of a generation of young blacks.[42]

Then, as now, the world associated their victory stand protest with
black power.[43] Smith, who developed the idea for the protest, insisted
that it was not. "This was not the Black Power movement," he recalled
in his memoir. "To this very day, the gesture made on the victory stand
is described as a Black Power salute," he wrote; "it was not." As Smith
told Howard Cosell in an interview following the medal ceremony, there
was symbolism and meaning in the protest:

> My raised right hand stood for the power in black America. Carlos's
> left hand stood for the unity of black America. Together, they
> formed an arch of unity and power. The black scarf around my neck
> stood for black pride. The black socks with no shoes stood for black
> poverty in racist America. The totality of our effort was the regain-
> ing of black dignity.[44]

This act was what two individuals, both members of the OPHR, felt was
necessary in the fight for human rights.

The response and repercussions that followed Smith and Carlos's
protest were swift and strident. The press erupted with a firestorm of
reports, interviews, and commentary. As the USOC remained silent for

a day a two—perhaps in hopes that the firestorm would blow over—IOC president Avery Brundage was enraged, and the IOC demanded that severe and decisive action be taken. Apparently, there had been some sentiment on the part of the U.S. body not to take any action against the two athletes. But when USOC president Douglas Roby asked the international body what would happen if they took no action, the IOC responded that "they might be forced to pull the entire United States team out of the Olympics." In response to the threat, Roby told the press, the USOC chose to act. Expressing its "profound regrets" to the IOC, the Mexican Olympic Organizing Committee, and the Mexican people, the USOC suspended Smith and Carlos from the U.S Olympic track and field team, banished them from the Olympic village, and ordered them to leave Mexico and return to the United States within forty-eight hours. The committee felt that the two athletes' "immature behavior" was an isolated event but assured other athletes that any additional incidents would be deemed "a willful disregard of Olympic principles that would warrant the imposition of the severest penalties at the disposal of the United States Olympic Committee." So complete was the USOC's turnaround following the threat by the IOC that Roby read the committee's statement—with its caution to other athletes—just before Lee Evans, Larry James, and Ron Freeman, the U.S. triple threat in the 400 meter, took their marks for the final.[45]

As the USOC took action on Smith and Carlos's protest, the black sports community responded, once again laying bare conflicting voices within the black community over civil rights. This time the responses were more along generational lines. Sam Lacy, sports editor for the *Baltimore Afro-American*, was profoundly embarrassed and disturbed by the incident. Although Lacy had supported Smith, Carlos, Evans, and the other black athletes during the long months they discussed boycotting the Olympics, he called their victory stand protest "childish and in extremely poor taste." Once reaching the decision to accompany the team to Mexico and participate on the U.S. squad, Lacy felt it was best to leave the racial difficulties they all encountered behind within American borders. If their demonstration "was meant to embarrass the United States," he wrote, "it had a dual effect. It embarrassed me more." The USOC asked Jessie Owens, premier athlete of a previous generation, to talk to the athletes as an "athlete's representative" to find out if they planned any more protests. But he was truly of a different generation, a *Negro* athlete that this younger generation of *black* athletes could not identify with. He left their meeting without any information. Ed Temple struck a middle ground. While he could not throw his whole-hearted support behind what Smith and Carlos had done, he thought that the Olympic committee should have waited until after the conclusion of the Mexico City games to suspend the two athletes from future competition. He also suggested that having an African American on the USOC would go a long way toward airing some of the issues that black athletes were raising.[46]

While an older generation of African Americans in the sports community spoke out against the protest, the suspension and banishment of Smith and Carlos united young black track and field athletes in a way that the OPHR activity over the long months leading up to the Olympics never could. Comments in support of their teammates were widespread. Triple jumper Art Walker remarked on the "silliness" of banishing the athletes over a protest while the United States had, since the early 1900s, protested the act of dipping its flag to the Olympic banner during opening ceremonies by refusing to follow the practice. Vincent Matthews, member of the 4x400-meter relay team, told the press that he was in "open opposition" to the USOC's action, and Ron Freeman thought that a lot of the black athletes would choose to go home in support of the banished pair. Support took other forms as well. Despite the personal warning that Roby issued to them at the start of their 400-meter final, Evans, James, and Freeman chose a protest of their own following their sweep of the event. As they stepped up on the podium to accept their medals, they wore black berets and gave clenched-fist salutes before and after the playing of the national anthem. But the three removed their berets and stood at attention, facing the flag while "The Star-Spangled Banner" played.[47] The most significant sign that the USOC's action had united black track athletes was the response of long jumpers Bob Beamon and Ralph Boston. Neither athlete had supported the boycott. But as they mounted the victory stand to receive their gold and bronze medals, both did so without shoes, exposing their black socks. Beamon had his sweat pants rolled up so that his knee-length black socks would be more visible. Moreover, neither athlete remained silent on their actions. Beamon told reporters that he was also "protesting what's happening in the U.S.A." Boston, the level-headed leader of the Denver meeting, seemed to issue a direct challenge to Roby and Brundage with his comments: "They are going to have to send me home, too, because I protested on the victory stand." However, no one else was sent home. All the other protesters had avoided what seemed to be Smith and Carlos's biggest sin, their action that had raised the most ire—what many people thought was a conscious and conspicuous disrespect of the American flag.[48]

Not only did the Smith and Carlos's ouster unite the black track men; it also induced the black track women to speak up in support of their teammates. "Negro girls on the U.S. Olympic team have been less outspoken on racial matters than their male counterparts," observed a *Los Angeles Times* reporter. "But sprinter Wyomia Tyus spoke out the other day." Speaking on behalf of her teammates on the gold-medal 400-meter relay team, she told reporters that they were dedicating their win to Smith and Carlos, who had already been suspended from further competition and sent home. Indeed, Tyus had found her voice on racial matters. During another interview in which the Cuban women and men's track relay teams announced they would dedicate their silver medals to support the African American quest for freedom, a Cuban reporter asked Tyus whether "deep down" she thought she experienced freedom in the United States. "Deep down," she replied, "I believe I enjoy freedom to a certain extent." The consecutive Olympic gold medalist seemed to understand the limits to acceptable comments on racial matters, striking a measured but important balance. Like her predecessor Rudolph, Tyus made sure she grabbed a comb and lipstick before speaking to the press. But when she spoke, she gave voice to the changing racial environment in which she competed.[49]

When she arrived back in Griffin, Georgia, Tyus did not return home to anonymity. As the press sought her out, she once again spoke up for Smith and Carlos, this time indicating that it was their prerogative to protest on the victory stand. "It was their moment," Tyus told reporter Kathleen Light of the *Atlanta Constitution*. "They had won the medals, and they had a right to make a protest." Winning a medal was an individual achievement that an athlete did first for herself and secondarily for his country, Tyus felt, and she was not alone in that sentiment. White sports columnist Shirley Povich of the *Washington Post* argued that, by placing first and third in the race, Smith and Carlos had not only won their medals but also the opportunity to protest racial conditions in their country. It was, after all, a country whose passage of the Civil Rights Act had confirmed both that right and the centuries of injustice the athletes were protesting. "Worldwide television cameras and news services do not tune in on losers. Even those who would deplore the time and the place of their demonstration will concede that a right of protest was theirs," observed Povich. Much had changed since Coachman's day, a time when a black woman competing in track would not have been interviewed by the white press. Even just eight years earlier, Rudolph had stayed on message in keeping with Temple's plan to promote the femininity of his women track athletes. But in 1968, the black female track star and the white male sportswriter both spoke out and spoke with similar voices.[50]

Tyus was not finished, having more to say on the subject of politics and the Olympics. The games were supposed to present an occasion for individuals—not countries—to come together in athletic competition. The reality, Tyus told the reporter, was far different. Whereas the Olympics, at one time, put forth the concept of the world's people coming together in peace for an athletic event, the three-time gold medalist felt that this was no longer the case. "They say there aren't supposed to be any politics, but there's a lot of it," she asserted. Though Tyus was not prone to cynicism, she saw a stark disparity between the image captured on television and the reality behind the event. "Behind the veneer of thousands of athletes meeting to test their physical prowess," wrote Light, "Wyomia sees the grim picture of the United States and Russia flagrantly trying to outmatch each other, with the athletes becoming pawns in the two countries' bids for publicity." In truth, politics had long been intertwined in the Olympic games but the ideal of individual athletes coming together to compete stood in particularly stark contrast to superpowers that kept track of their respective medal hauls in a cultural Cold War.[51]

In the aftermath of her historic Olympic victory, Tyus became "Griffin's best-known citizen." Her state senator, Robert Smalley, presented her to the Georgia Legislature, who, along with Governor Lester Maddox—a man that had, a few years earlier, driven blacks out of his restaurant with an axe handle—declared 25 January 1969, "Wyomia Tyus Day."[52] She was a celebrity and a retired world-class athlete, at least for the time being. Tyus chose retirement because there was no other route for a track and field athlete who had completed college unless they could finance their own training and competition travel. With no professional track circuit available and celebrity endorsements in their infancy, most track athletes did not have the independent means to sustain careers once out of college. But opportunities for professional track were just on the horizon, and Tyus would be at the forefront of the effort for women.

Running for Money— Professional Track and the Women's Movement

The first several years following the 1968 Olympic games were ones of discovery for Tyus. The biggest realization was one that had confronted other retired gold-medal Olympians and champion black athletes. She thought she had done everything right. Yet despite her gold medals, world records, *and* college degree, Wyomia Tyus could not find a job that paid her a respectable salary. She began to think she would have been better off if she had participated in the OPHR and had made a more visible protest in Mexico City. Even Ed Temple, the man who had made such a difference to the status of women's track and field in the United States, began to wonder if he would have been wiser to encourage his Tigerbelles to be active in the movement. Feeling like she had outgrown Griffin, Georgia, thinking she would be successful in landing a job out on the West Coast, and wishing to stay connected to her steady boyfriend, Art Simburg, Tyus moved to California. Several months passed as she pursued jobs that friends and contacts promised would be the "perfect" one. Finally, she secured a position as a research assistant at UCLA's Afro-American Studies Center, where she found herself working alongside the former star Tigerbelle, Wilma Rudolph. She experienced changes in her personal life as well. She and Simburg married in April 1969, and in January 1972, Tyus gave birth to their daughter, Simone. By that time, she was teaching physical education at a junior high school in Los Angeles and she felt certain that she would never run competitively again.[53]

Yet even before the year was out, a new venture had Tyus reassessing her retirement. In March 1973, the newly formed International Track Association (ITA) started a new professional track circuit. Retired amateur track and field athletes embraced the idea, and several important names came on board quickly—miler Jim Ryun; Olympic gold-medal sprinter turned football star "Bullet" Bob Hayes; and 400-meter specialist

Lee Evans and long jumper Bob Beamon, both of whom had won gold medals and set world records in Mexico City. Tyus decided to come out of retirement as well, and her former Olympic teammate Barbara Ferrell joined her.[54] True to form, Tyus became a dominant force on the circuit for the next four years. During the first season, she shared victories with Ferrell and Lacey O'Neal. But in 1974, the circuit's second season, Tyus was unbeatable—literally. She won every race she competed in, and set a new world record for the 70-meter sprint in February. In May, she capped off her unbeaten year by tying her own world mark in the 60 meter. That string of unbroken victories lasted through the 1975 season and into 1976 when in March, Ferrell scored "the major upset of the evening" when she nipped her former teammate at the wire, ending Tyus's string of twenty-nine consecutive victories.[55]

Tyus found herself at the top of the first viable professional track venture, but it was one that operated far differently from what she had been accustomed to when she ran for medals as opposed to money. Amateur track had been about running fast enough to not only win but also break records. However, the *business* of breaking records was a difficult one to be in since they didn't happen often enough to satisfy any but the most ardent fans. Moreover, track stars that participated in the pro circuit leaned on the practical side—unless there were athletes on the circuit to push each other to faster times, the incentive was just not there. "Running for money doesn't make you run fast," noted successful pro track athlete Ben Jipcho of Kenya, "it makes you run first."[56] What good was it to watch professional track and field athletes compete against one another if the performances were often below the standard set by amateur athletes competing in college? Staunch track enthusiasts, then, tended to dismiss the ITA first and foremost because of the unwritten rule that required professional athletes to be better than amateurs. As such, the association searched for ways to promote fan interest outside of the small cadre of die-hard enthusiasts.

Hoping to attract a broader fan base, the ITA turned to entertainment. There was little to indicate that track and field, even in its pure form, would ever be as popular in the United States as baseball, football, or basketball; it had to sell more than just track and field. "We want to make every meet a happening," observed association president Michael O'Hara in 1975. To do so, it added "innovations" that the amateur sport did not have like electronic starting blocks and pacer lights. The association also added what it termed "entertainment events," which included one of the women sprinters racing shot-putter Brian Oldfield, and Bob Hayes racing other pro footballers in a 40-yard dash. Track purists decried these events as gimmicks. Tyus agreed that these gimmicks resulted in the circuit becoming more of a circus than a professional track venture. Years later, she remembered how the athletes would just travel to different cities and "put on a show." However, O'Hara and the association found that other fans loved these special events. The professional track circuit was, he noted, in the entertainment business as well as the business of breaking records.[57]

The ITA's decision to emphasize entertainment over performance arose not only from the dearth of records but also from the influence of the burgeoning television industry on sporting events. While pro track never secured the breadth of television coverage it hoped for, the prospect of a lucrative contract with ABC, NBC, or CBS—the three networks in existence at the time—would mean a wider fan base and the infusion of much-needed cash for the fledgling track organization. Major league baseball, the NFL, and the IOC had already discovered just how lucrative these contracts could be, as the three networks engaged in bidding wars to acquire broadcast rights to televise sporting events that had become profitable business for them. Television was still in its relative infancy but the contract numbers were growing exponentially. When CBS televised the Olympic games in Rome during the summer of 1960, they had paid the IOC close to $395,000 for the rights to do so; the Munich games, just twelve years later, cost ABC $13.5 million. *Chicago Tribune* television critic Gary Deeb suggested that the gimmicks were there to stay because they were popular with the mass TV audience, attracting sports fans and even non-fans. Market share, in other words, had become paramount in the business. If there had ever been any question about how closely sport and entertainment were wedded, the introduction of television into the mix was bringing them ever closer together.[58]

Even as Tyus found herself in the midst of what she later deemed a circus, there were broader cultural forces at play during the decade. The growth of the civil rights movement in the 1960s and the development of a counterculture that questioned traditional gender roles and sparked a sexual revolution led to a rebirth of feminism. Betty Friedan's *The*

Feminine Mystique gave women a language to express their discontent with traditional roles and also endorsed their quest for education, work, and other activities outside the home. Dissatisfied with the lack of protection and advancement they were receiving with coverage under the Civil Rights Act of 1964, women united in 1966 to form their own civil rights association, the National Organization for Women (NOW). By the early 1970s, women's public lives had expanded markedly, and their increasing presence in the political sphere helped bring women's rights more visibility and support. When Congress passed the Educational Amendments Act of 1972, which expanded the Civil Rights Act to include educational institutions, a paragraph known as Title IX became an important victory for women. Addressing the issue of sex discrimination, the paragraph stated: "No person in the United States shall, on the basis of sex, be excluded from participation in, be denied the benefits of, or be subjected to discrimination under any educational programs or activities receiving federal financial assistance." Colleges and universities that received federal funding could no longer discriminate against women in any of their programs. Other legislative and judicial advances occurred during this timeframe, as when Congress expanded affirmative action to include women and the Supreme Court passed *Roe v. Wade*, granting women abortion rights. However, without ever mentioning the word *sport*, no one paragraph would have as much impact on women athletes in educational settings. While women had been involved in sport and sports competition since the early part of the century, this legislation would eventually expand programs in high schools, colleges, and universities, making it possible for more women to have the access to sport programs that their male counterparts had enjoyed for years.[59]

Despite these advances, the women's movement as delineated by NOW spoke to only part of who African American women were and, before long, black women became dissatisfied with their place in the movement. Several factors contributed to their discontent. First, white middle-class women comprised the group that exerted the most power in the organization. For many black women, these were the very employers who had, for decades, exerted power over them in the workplace and they had no desire to experience it anew in the movement. Second, the women's movement became most visible at the very time that the civil rights movement appeared to be disintegrating. It seemed, then, that white women stood poised to sweep in and enjoy the benefits of the years of strife and hard work of African Americans. Moreover, black women felt that white women could not relate to the years of oppression they had experienced due to racism. Whereas women had received the vote in 1920, it took forty-five more years of violence, segregation, and nonviolent resistance for the Voting Rights Act to ensure that African American women could enjoy the fruits of the Nineteen Amendment. Finally, black women objected to the harsh manner in which white women referred to men. Inherent in the difference was the fact that whites understood sexism to be the culprit while black women often continued to feel the oppression of racism more forcefully.[60]

Even with this dissension, however, the women's movement influenced the world of black women athletes in two distinct ways as it reverberated throughout American society. First, the movement's convergence with the growth of television transformed a previously unacceptable event—men and women athletes competing against one another—into the basis for sport entertainment. But such head-to-head competition, what the athletes referred to as "fun and games," also exposed the important discrepancy between the earnings of professional male and female athletes. Second, as the women's movement expanded the public debate on motherhood and the workplace, women athletes became part of the conversation in ways that were dramatically different from their predecessors. In the process, Tyus found herself at the forefront of a new movement that became instrumental in further altering the position of women track athletes in American society.

While women agitated for gender equality throughout the 1970s, television networks waged a battle for market share; the confluence of these two forces resulted in the rise in popularity of televised male/female sport battles. On the surface, these were pure entertainment events, such as when Tyus raced the forty-seven-year-old George Rhoden, a former Olympic sprinter, in a match race on the tour and beat him by a stride. Outside of the pro track circuit, the networks jumped on the bandwagon. In the mid-1970s, CBS launched its series, "The Challenge of the Sexes," which pitted a number of male and female athletes against one another, each pair competing against one another in their own sport. Tyus and the other athletes who participated in the contests considered them merely "fun and games." However, these gender battles also reflected women's rapidly changing roles in American society and the attendant anxiety that accompanied such changes. In a show of speed *and* strength, ITA organizers had Brian Oldfield, the shotputter who regularly raced the women track sprinters on the professional tour, carry Lacey O'Neal around the track on his shoulders after his victory.[61]

In no other contest was the anxiety about women's roles more transparent than in the September 1973 "Battle of the Sexes," in which former tennis star Bobby Riggs challenged top-seeded tennis player Billie Jean King. The hype that surrounded the lead-up to the event was unlike any of the other man/woman sport contests of the period. It was a match some felt had been devised merely as entertainment, a "money-making gimmick." However, it was also one that served to highlight the gender debates that circulated freely during the decade. Women claimed that they were the equals of men, yet could they prove it on the playing field? Or should women even be involved in sport at the competitive level? These were issues that had plagued Americans for decades, and now they were going to be played out before a television audience. Riggs spent the months before the match telling reporters that he liked his women in the bedroom and the kitchen—in that order. While some of this was merely pre-match publicity, his comments also spoke to a sexism that women were fighting and some men still clung to. King beat the former tennis great in three straight sets. Some people were certain that the age difference between the two players was the real deciding factor. King was twenty-six years younger than the fifty-five-year-old Riggs. It was not so much a battle of the sexes, they felt, as a generational match-up. But women, and many men, were thrilled that King had triumphed and finally quieted Riggs. These challenges between men and women athletes, so popular during the decade, highlighted the important political, social, and cultural debates taking place during the 1970s. They also reflected a stark contrast to the previous decade. Just twelve years earlier, Rudolph and her coach had insisted that she did not race against men. Now the "network boys" were using such match-ups to increase market share because they were popular with the American viewing audience—both men *and* women who tuned in to watch one of their own hopefully best the opposite sex.[62]

Despite the entertainment atmosphere of it all, women athletes had made strides culturally as Americans began to accept head-to-head competition with men; however, female athletes continued to lag far behind their male counterparts in earning power. Throughout the 1970s, "equal pay for equal work" became a rallying cry for American women throughout society agitating against discrimination in the workplace. In tennis, Billie Jean King had worked tirelessly to promote a more viable and profitable professional women's tennis tour, but, in general, there was a wide disparity between what men and women could earn in sport.[63] Whereas top woman golfer Kathy Whitworth earned close to $83,000 in 1973, Jack Nicklaus won in excess of $300,000, three and a half times as much. In bowling, the discrepancy was even starker, with the top male bowler earning almost ten times his female counterpart. But nowhere was the earnings gap more glaring than with black women athletes. Despite winning all fourteen of her races in 1974, Tyus ended the year with half of what the top male runner made. Moreover, the next top four male money-earners beat her out as well. Part of the problem stemmed, of course, from the fact that, of the twelve races contested on the tour, the women competed in just two of them. Tyus lobbied for more events every opportunity she had, and though the ITA promised "next year," the additional events never materialized. Beyond the situation that existed in the young professional track and field circuit, there was the larger issue of the sports that black women athletes had access to. The sluggishness of dismantling "separate but equal" education and enforcing the still nascent Title IX requirements meant that black girls continued to find basketball and track the offerings of their junior high and high school experiences. Few could afford to pursue the better-paying sports of golf or tennis, which remained out of reach due to the expense of their club setting. So while white women athletes were earning far less than men, black women athletes lagged even farther behind. Top pro track athlete Wyomia Tyus's 1974 earnings of $8,225 was a meager tenth of golfer Kathy Whitworth's 1973 golf earnings of $82,864. Even bowler Paula Sperber earned three times more than Tyus during their respective 1974 seasons.[64] And while black men were almost as scarce in golf and tennis as black women, their access to higher-paying team sports like baseball and football meant their earnings power outranked black women as well. Similar to the pay of African American women in non-sports jobs, black women athletes found themselves on the bottom rung of the pay scale. There seemed to be little to suggest that their situation would change any time soon.

As women athletes continued struggling to catch up to men financially, the women's movement affected them in a different way, ushering in a stark reversal in the cultural perception of competition and motherhood. As increasing numbers of women entered the workforce in the 1970s, the option to combine motherhood with a job or career became a priority for many middle-class women. At the same time, the entry of women into the workforce raised concerns within society over their capability to do both—have a career and manage the family. Surely one would suffer, Americans on one side of the debate thought, and they worried about the breakdown of the American family as women "forsook" their responsibilities as mothers to work outside the home. Those on the other side of the debate, however, thought women *could* do both and believed the time had come to allow them the opportunity. Of course, these debates seemed far removed from most African American women who, having been working mothers for centuries, had long before had to find a way to balance the two.

When track and field turned professional, however, black women track athletes faced new possibilities and questions about their own role as working mothers. The concern that had so dominated Alice Coachman's track career—that women's foray into athletics would affect their ability to bear children—was giving way to an emphasis on the ability of women athletes to blend motherhood and sport. Tyus exemplified this new prerogative. "Fleet Ex-Olympian Wyomia Likes Motherhood and Track," observed a 1975 headline in the *Baltimore Afro-American*. "Mrs. Wyomia Tyus Simburg has one child and wants another," wrote reporter Jim Cour, "but the two-time Olympic gold medal winner isn't ready to quit running yet." And in the 1970s, it had become clear that she did not have to. A month later, a *Los Angeles Times* Mother's Day article focused on athletes who had found a way to incorporate the dual roles of sport and motherhood, observing that "pregnancy, for some, is but a pause in an athletic career." Tyus was again hailed as a success story, one who had come back to track and field when the professional opportunity opened: "Now at 29, she's still running and winning and wants another child." In an about-face from the stereotype of previous decades, experts spoke out on the ways that sport and motherhood actually reinforced each other. Dr. Joan Ullyot, exercise physiologist at the University of California in San Francisco, articulated the benefits of the athletic body— improved cardiovascular system, muscle control, and abdominal muscle tone—that aided women in childbirth.

When it came to mothering, psychologist Bruce Ogilvie maintained that a woman had the capacity to be both "tough and aggressive as an athlete and loving and attentive as a mother." Mother-athletes, he suggested, made better mothers, perhaps because they were fulfilled. But the reverse was also true, argued surgeon Allan J. Ryan. Motherhood made athletes better at their jobs: "If they were good competitors before, they become better. I don't think anybody could say why, but it's an observed fact." Far from the myth of previous decades—that the sport of track and field made women unable to bear children—women track athletes were now being held up as exemplars of motherhood.[65]

Tyus had become the "face" of women's track and field, showing modern women how women athletes could combine a professional career and motherhood. In her position, she spoke to the issues that continued to plague the sport. On the amateur side, she was encouraged by the increasing number of college sports programs for women, but insisted that there remained room for improvement. Rudolph had opened the door to track invitationals, but the number of women who received invitations and those who could afford to go still lagged male athletes considerably. From her days on athletic scholarship at Tennessee State, Tyus recalled how "it just wasn't economically feasible to invite women track people places," and she wanted today's athletes to "have it better" than she did. Professionally, she and the other black women track athletes on the tour, especially Lacey O'Neal, lobbied for more women's events. Two years into the circuit, however, they still only competed in two events compared to the men's ten. And Tyus even had some thoughts on open competition—allowing both amateurs and professionals to compete— at the Olympics. "We're generating interest in the sport," she told a reporter with the *Christian Science Monitor*, referring to professional track and field, and she felt the pro track athletes could help the Olympics. Since professional and amateur athletes competed together in other individual sports like tennis and golf, she suggested, "why not in the Olympics?" In truth, many of these issues were variants of the ones that Ed Temple had begun to address in the previous decade. He continued to "preach" on them when he got the chance in the mid-1970s.[66] The difference was that, in the wake of the women's movement, Wyomia Tyus and other black women track athletes now joined him.

Conclusion

The ITA approached the end of its 1976 season just barely in the black. Hoping that by attracting Olympic stars from the upcoming Montreal games they could breathe new life and fan interest into the circuit, organizers rescheduled some of the televised tour stops from May to August. They also received a renewal of their contract with Dairy Queen, one of the corporate sponsors helping augment sagging ticket sales and television revenue. But the life of the amateur athlete had changed since the birth of pro track four years earlier. In 1972, Olympic track stars had no way to continue competing once their college careers were over unless they could finance themselves. Pro track had addressed this problem. By 1976, however, amateur athletes had begun to receive substantial endorsement contracts that enabled them to continue their amateur careers. The meager compensation that the ITA offered simply could not entice the 1976 Olympic medalists to give up their amateur status and turn professional. When O'Hara approached the stars of the Montreal games about turning pro, they told him to talk to their agents. The agents, it turned out, were looking for three-year contracts for their athletes in the ballpark of $400,000. This was a far cry from the $10,000 signing bonus some of the stars of the Mexico City games had received just four years earlier. The inability to attract new stars proved to be the death knell for a pro track circuit already needing more television and advertising revenue as they sought to please an audience continually hungry for world records, often just as easily found in amateur competition. Following its meet in Gresham, Oregon, on 25 August 1976, the ITA canceled the remaining three stops on the tour. Professional track and field had come to an end.[67]

Tyus found life after pro track in a number of ways, staying involved tangentially in sport, particularly issues related to women and sport. At the 1976 summer Olympic games in Montreal, she joined ABC in the broadcast booth as the expert commentator for women's track and field. She was, noted television critic Gary Deeb, one of the "real stars" in the TV booth. Later that year, she teamed up with other women athletes to support Billie Jean King's brainchild, the Women's Sports Foundation. Established in 1974, the foundation promoted equal opportunities in sport and encouraged women and girls to participate in sport for their health, enjoyment, and personal development. By the time Tyus became involved in November 1976, the organization had become a clearing-house for information on women's sports, locating colleges with scholarships, citing good sports magazines, and finding sport camps for girls. In April 1978, Tyus participated in a symposium on sports and society at California State University that included topics on racism and sexism in sport and the threat of over-commercialization. In 1982, she joined two other former women Olympians to tour the country, encouraging women to train for the 1984 Los Angeles Olympic games, particularly the ten new women's events being added. By the early 1980s, she began to receive honors for her stellar track and field and Olympic career. She was inducted into both the National Track and Field Hall of Fame and the Women's Sports Hall of Fame. She also received the honor, along with seven other former Olympic medalists, of carrying the Olympic flag into the Los Angeles Memorial Coliseum for the opening ceremonies of the 1984 Los Angeles games. And in 1985, she was finally inducted into the Olympic Hall of Fame after being passed over as part of the first two classes of inductees.[68]

There was also life outside the connections to her Olympic past. Having learned so much about sprinting from Ed Temple, she passed along some of that wisdom by coaching track at Beverly Hills High School in California. She also had another child, a son, with her second husband, Duane Tillman. Then, in 1994, she found the "dream job" that united her passion for the outdoors with her love of education. She began working as a naturalist for the Los Angeles Unified School District, conducting hikes through the San Gabriel Mountains and teaching the children about the natural flora and fauna. She had, it seemed, broken the cycle of struggle and even poverty that had beset her predecessors.[69]

In her track and field career, Tyus accomplished something that no track athlete had done before her. Yet she never received the acclaim that Wilma Rudolph had. There were at least two reasons for this. The protest that Smith and Carlos made during the Mexico City Olympics was certainly one, thrusting the world of sport onto the center stage of a civil rights movement many felt was rapidly spinning out of control. Mere records and historic firsts tended to fade quickly as sportswriters and reporters became caught up in covering this important social change.

But Temple felt it was also Tyus's introversion. "Of all my girls," he remarked years later, "Tyus was the quietest." She was, he thought, the exact opposite of the effusive, extroverted Wilma Rudolph, and she never really "got her due."[70]

In truth, however, it was Tyus's quiet personality that made her an able representative for black women athletes during the latter 1960s and 1970s. Caught in the intersection between two important social movements, she was a part of both, yet not wholly a part of either. As an African American, she identified with the injustices that blacks experienced during the turbulent and violent years of the 1960s and 1970s. How included she and other black women athletes felt in the Olympic Project for Human Rights remains at issue. Whether they could relate to the platform of the OPHR does not. But the movement was undeniably slanted, particularly in its language, toward black men, leaving Tyus and her teammates feeling, at least in retrospect, like their opinions were unimportant and their participation assumed. As a woman, she identified with the political and social inequality that the women's movement spoke to during the 1970s as issues of unequal pay and status arose even within the professional track circuit. Yet legislative and judicial advances for women could not erase the racism that black women athletes experienced. Both of these movements worked against a social order that had been in place in the United States since before its founding. Tyus not only found her voice in Mexico City; she found the right voice. She was confident and assured but also self-effacing and measured. And while she continued to wholly embrace the feminine approach to track and field that had helped American society embrace women track athletes, sportswriters began asking her questions that revolved around more than her latest hat or new shoes. In order for black women athletes to continue to push back against the stereotypes that had defined them, it was important that they not take on new ones during this period of radical changes. It would have not helped their own cause for Tyus or any of her teammates to be labeled as either a radical black activist or strident feminist. On some level, it seemed, Tyus understood this and became the spokesperson for black women athletes that they needed at the time.

In 1972, the year that the ITA called Tyus out of retirement, a ten-year-old African American girl signed up to join a girls' track team at her local community center. Jackie Joyner would be part of the first generation of women athletes that grew up with the benefits of Title IX. Her experience as a long jumper and heptathlete would be marked by incredible change to track and field, making it, in some ways, a sport that her predecessors would hardly recognize. By the time she began competing nationally, men and women's Olympic trials and national championships were no longer separated, the AAU had surrendered control of track and field to a new national governing body, and black women athletes were being recruited by white universities and participating in NCAA championships. And as the IOC loosened its definition of "amateur," even women track athletes were finding it possible to remain in the sport far longer and make considerably more money than ever before. With this continued movement forward in the world of women's track and field, black women athletes in America found new ways to reject stereotypes that had defined them for decades.

"A Jackie of All Trades"

Jackie Joyner-Kersee and the Challenges of Being the World's Greatest Female Athlete

She had waited four years for the opportunity to prove she had overcome her mental demons. In 1984 in Los Angeles, with the East German women boycotting the Olympic games, Jackie Joyner stood as good a chance as any other heptathlete at winning the seven-event competition. But the solid performance of competitor Glynis Nunn of Australia along with Joyner's obsession over the fitness of her recently healed hamstring had left the United States' best heptathlete with silver, just five points shy of a gold medal. Now here she was in Seoul, South Korea, four years later, the world champion and holder of the last three world records in the event. The gold medal didn't seem quite enough anymore. Everyone, including Joyner-Kersee and her husband-coach, Bob Kersee, wanted another world record. She was comfortably ahead of her nearest competitor after the first day of competition. But she had aggravated a tendon in her knee during the high jump and was 103 points off of her own world-record pace. Had she learned anything about fighting off her own injury worries from her experience in Los Angeles? The following morning she started the second and final day of competition by setting a new heptathlon long jump record, but then followed it up with a disappointing score in the javelin throw. At this point, the gold medal was hers. But as usual, something—in this case the world record—would come down to the last event, the grueling 800-meter run. She needed just a little over two minutes, a time of 2:13:67, to overtake her own record. At the 400-

meter mark, she was off the goal she had set with her trainer, and three German athletes were passing her. This was the Olympic games; the other medals and records meant little if she could not win this. When she crossed the finish line in fifth place, she was overjoyed. The clock read 2:08:51. She had just won her first Olympic gold medal, and set her fourth world record in the span of two years. She was, according to the press, "the world's greatest female athlete."[1]

Joyner-Kersee's athletic coming of age occurred during a time of bold changes to women's track and field. Title IX had been passed while Tyus was competing on the pro track circuit in the early 1970s, and Joyner-Kersee's generation was the first to benefit from the legislation that provided women equal access to sports in federally funded educational settings. Despite the legislation, progress had been slow. However, by the time she approached high school graduation in the late 1970s, white universities were attracting women athletes throughout the country with recruiting budgets and athletic scholarships. Moreover, women's track and field championships were now being held jointly with men's. The days of the sport's separate and unequal treatment, of casting it as an inferior stepchild to the real, masculine version, were solidly in the past. The most sweeping change to the sport, however, was in the loosening of amateur rules. While Olympic competition was still closed to professional athletes, the rigid rules prohibiting amateur athletes from making any income from sport belonged to an earlier era. Athletes could accept payments from sponsors as long as the money was used for athletic training. In truth, amateur track and field athletes had been paid to wear athletic shoes since the early 1960s, but the payments had been under the table. Overnight, it seemed, track and field athletes became openly tied to athletic shoe and apparel companies, entering contracts that provided valuable training income in exchange for agreeing to exclusively wear the company's products. It was not long before U.S. corporations were snatching up Olympic champions, the stars of the athletic world, to advertise a whole host of products that ran the gamut from McDonald hamburgers to Primatene asthma spray. Would "the world's greatest female athlete" be able to keep her attention focused on competition with all these changes and the attendant advertising hype now focused on the sport? How many years would this new source of income add to the careers of track and field athletes? Less than a decade earlier, they had faced retirement at the end of their college athletic careers or struggled to make a few thousand dollars on the pro track circuit. How would these far-reaching changes to sport affect black women track and field athletes, who remained the backbone of the sport?

In the two years leading up to the Seoul games where she won her first gold medal, Joyner-Kersee proved that she could focus on competition regardless of what changes were going on in the sporting world. In 1986, she became the first athlete to break the 7,000-point mark in the heptathlon; she went on to do it five more times. Since that time, only two other hepathletes have broken 7,000 points, but they still rest comfortably behind Joyner-Kersee's Seoul performance.[2] Her world record of 7,291 points from those games still stands. Moreover, she was not only a generalist when it came to track and field. Her favorite had always been the long jump, so she routinely competed in that solo event as well. After the heptathlon competition in Seoul, she competed in the long jump to win her second Olympic gold medal. Four years later, Joyner-Kersee competed in her third Olympics, becoming the first heptathlete to win back-to-back gold medals; she also added a bronze in the long jump. If there was a woman track and field athlete bent on answering the question of how long the infusion of cash from endorsement contracts could extend careers, Joyner-Kersee seemed the one to do it. Before her long, remarkable athletic career was over, she had competed in yet a fourth Olympics. An injury forced her out of the heptathlon competition, but she came from behind in the long jump to win another bronze, her fifth Olympic medal. Bruce Jenner, decathlete champion from the 1976 Olympic games, called her the best athlete, man or woman, in the world.[3]

By the 1980s and 1990s, Americans had generally come to accept women's track and field as legitimate. The sport of Joyner-Kersee's day hardly resembled that of Alice Coachman's. It even looked vastly different from the one Wyomia Tyus competed in. However, one thing persisted. While Bruce Jenner was busy hailing Joyner-Kersee as the best athlete in the world, the press noted that she was also a woman "with a figure that could make a chorus line."[4] Despite sportswriters' proclivity to continue to ground women track and field athletes in images of the past, however, black women athletes used a variety of approaches to push against these lingering stereotypes. Joyner-Kersee did so by separating her on- and off-the-field personalities. On the field, she was all athlete with little care for how she looked after finishing all or part of a competition. In a distinct contrast to Rudolph, Tyus, and other Temple-trained athletes, Joyner-Kersee had little use for comb or lipstick during competition. Off the field, however, she embraced her femininity, showing the public that she enjoyed the fashion and style that, for her, went with being a woman. Interestingly, the more successful she became in competition, the more Americans wanted to see her feminine side—the "Jackie" off the track and field. Joyner-Kersee's sister-in-law, world-class sprinter Florence Griffith Joyner, employed a different approach. Griffith Joyner embraced her femininity on the track, embodying both glamour and speed. With long hair, talon-like fingernails, and exotic running attire, she flaunted her sexuality while running the sprints in world-record time. Comfortable with her own style, she threw the stereotype right back into the faces of those that had employed it against black women athletes for generations. In the process, the sisters-in-law not only ruled the track world but also the world of public opinion and endorsement contracts. Americans could not get enough of the athletes they referred to as "Jackie" and "FloJo."

More difficult to answer were the racial slurs that accompanied the era of performance-enhancing drugs. In the late 1980s, clear evidence surfaced that track athletes were doping as top athletes tested positive and lost their medals, even on the world stage of the Olympic games. Neither Joyner-Kersee nor her sprinter sister-in-law, Florence Griffith Joyner, ever tested positive for the use of steroids. But innuendo and accusation swirled at the Seoul games, where the illusion of "natural" speed, strength, and hard work flew apart when the world's top male sprinter failed his drug test following a world-record performance in the 100-meter sprint. Everyone, it seemed, was under suspicion, especially athletes who had enjoyed sudden bursts of speed and accomplishment like Griffith Joyner. The comments leveled at the Joyner sisters-in-law were more than drug accusations, however. In a society that had long been obsessed with how black women athletes looked, "before" and "after" comparisons of Joyner-Kersee and Griffith Joyner's bodies became the proof Americans often used to level their accusations. One need only look at them, argued a fellow Olympian who accompanied his comments with a racial stereotype, to be convinced that they were "using." As Joyner-Kersee and Griffith Joyner spoke out to clear their names, they found it difficult to "prove" that they were not doping and to fight back against stereotypes so thoroughly grounded in their race and gender. Before the world records, gold medals, and drug accusations, however, the first step for Joyner-Kersee was finding a way to emerge from the ghetto.

Out of the Ghetto

Much had changed in American society in the fifty years that black women had been competing in sport, but during the 1960s and 1970s many African American families were still living on the margins. The Joyner family was surviving but making do with very little. Joyner's parents, Mary Ruth and Alfred, were teenagers when they married and had her older brother Al. Two years later, in March 1962, Mary Ruth Joyner gave birth to a girl. Her grandmother insisted that she be called Jacqueline after First Lady Jacqueline Kennedy. She was, after all, the first Joyner girl, and grandmother Evelyn was sure Jackie would one day be the "first lady" of something. By summer of 1964, two more girls had followed. Mary Joyner was barely twenty; Alfred was only eighteen. Initially, Mary stayed home with the children—they lived with her grandmother—so that Alfred could finish high school and then get a job after graduation. With four children, though, and limited education, their lives were a constant struggle. Joyner's father eventually worked for a number of years as an assemblyman with McDonnell Douglas, helping to assemble airplanes. But when he was laid off during the economic downturn of the late 1970s, the Joyner dinners became even smaller. Odd jobs and part-time manufacturing work for Alfred and Mary's job as a nurse's aide kept the family going until Alfred eventually found a job with a railroad company over in Springfield. Even though the Joyners lived on the margin, they were more fortunate than some. They lived in a house rather than the projects, and they always managed to have food on the table.[5]

Despite the limited means and meager lifestyle, Joyner's parents refused to let their children feel downtrodden or think of themselves as victims. They taught them to be grateful for what they had while at the same time encouraged them to work toward a better life. Alfred Joyner was a quick-tempered man who permitted absolutely no backtalk from his children, although he occasionally revealed a tender side. For the future track and field great, however, her mother was her friend, her mainstay, her rock. Mary Joyner gave her children a religious upbringing and became their champion when they needed one. When she discovered that her eldest daughter's fifth-grade teacher was whipping her with a ruler when she performed poorly on math tests, Mary Joyner marched to the school and told the teacher to stop. At home, she established a strict code of conduct. Her complete set of rules, Joyner remembered years later, would fill a book. But she was determined to instill in them the discipline they needed to strive for a better life as well as give them a stronghold against the rough neighborhood that lay just outside their front door.

East St. Louis, Illinois, where Joyner spent the first eighteen years of her life, was a rough place to grow up. Situated just across the Mississippi River from St. Louis, Missouri, twenty miles into the state of Illinois, Joyner later described it as a "rowdy, ghetto city," especially the south end of town, the location of their house on Piggott Avenue. The house sat across from a liquor store, down the street from a pool hall, and just around the corner from a couple of local taverns. "The entire one-block radius around our house was a magnet for assorted winos, pimps, gangsters, ex-cons and hustlers," she wrote in her autobiography.[6] But the men who hung out in the neighborhood, though disreputable, also adhered to a code that kept them from engaging in their illegal habits in front of the neighborhood children. When parents weren't around, these men even served as protectors for the kids. This rough setting was far from idyllic. "Remember that time," Al Joyner mentioned to his sister during one of their later interviews, "when that guy was shot in front of our house? He got shot seven times, and Mom wouldn't let you look."[7] Years later, coming up from the ghetto would be a theme of the many feature articles that sportswriters wrote about the Joyner siblings.

Despite the difficult environment, there were positives to growing up in East St. Louis. In 1969, the Mary E. Brown Community Center opened its doors to the neighborhood where Joyner lived. Now the children and adults of the community had access to a recreation area, library, and rooms for arts and crafts, dancing, and lectures. The young Jackie Joyner practically lived at the Community Center. On Saturday mornings, she was there even before the recreation directors. Once they arrived, she helped set up the ping-pong tables and put out the balls and paddles. Eventually, the directors began paying her to help set up in the mornings and clean up in the evenings. Joyner also used the center to its

A JACKIE OF ALL TRADES

fullest. She took classes like dance and cheerleading, was a regular participant in the daily story time, made arts and crafts, and attended many of the lectures that the center hosted. It was, she remembered, the closest thing to a cultural life they had in East St. Louis.

It was through the Community Center that Joyner found her entrance into track and field. When she was ten, she noticed a sign-up sheet for girls interested in starting track and field. Unfortunately, not enough of the girls who signed up stayed with the sport to form a team, so the coach at the center introduced Joyner to George Ward, who coached girls' track at Franklin Elementary School. Since Joyner attended John Robinson Elementary, Coach Ward would pick her up in the spring afternoons after school and drive her to practice the 440-yard dash with his team. She was happy to be with the team, but the 440-dash was not her favorite race. While she enjoyed the challenge of trying to improve her time, she really longed to try the long jump. Her legs were strong from dance and the cheerleading class she had taken up after dance stopped, and she thought she might be good at that field activity. So Joyner created a sand pit in her front yard and practiced jumping off her front porch. When she tried the long jump on her own one day after practice was over, Coach Ward, amazed at the strength in her legs and a certain natural ability, began having her workout with the team's regular long jumper.

Joyner's entry into athletics could not have come at a better time. While she was signing up to try out track and field at the Community Center in 1972, Congress was passing the Title IX legislation that required federally funded schools to offer similar programs for girls and boys. No longer could public schools host a boys' sport team without also providing a similar opportunity for girls. Coach Ward and Nino Fennoy, who had started a girls' team at another elementary school, were using the law to develop programs in East St. Louis that were new to that community. Eventually, the two coaches decided to combine the talent on their two squads and compete against other elementary schools as a joint Franklin-Freeman Elementary team. Based in part on the success of that early venture, Ward and Fennoy decided to begin a combined squad during the summer of 1974 from all the area elementary schools. There would be both boys' and girls' teams, and these East St. Louis Railers would compete at AAU track meets held during the summer. Joyner was twelve at the time.

Her participation with the Railers would set her on a course that would eventually develop her into a world-class athlete.

Joyner had natural talent and considerable determination but she needed someone to develop her athletic skill. She found someone with the talent for coaching and athletic development initially in the person of Nino Fennoy. Ward and Fennoy had decided to divide the coaching duties by having Ward work with the boys and Fennoy coach the girls. Fennoy had been an average athlete, competing for historically black Lincoln University. After graduation, he decided his future lay in coaching, and he devoted his life to using athletics to help children growing up in the tough neighborhoods of East St. Louis. He preached a sermon roughly similar to the one Ed Temple had been preaching for years at Tennessee State. Sport could be these kids' gateway to college, but to truly succeed, to find that life beyond East St. Louis, they needed a college education. He was a constant presence in Joyner's life during her elementary and junior high years, and by the time she reached high school, he was the head track coach there. He inspired her to work hard so she could make the most of the talent she already had, and encouraged her to stand up to peer pressure and avoid the trouble and pitfalls that kids of those neighborhoods often fell into. Beginning in junior high school, he encouraged his athletes to keep a journal of how they performed at their daily practices, what they thought, and what they ate. Each week, he would review with the girls what they had written in their journals. He knew his athletes almost as well as their parents, perhaps even better. Along with her parents, Fennoy was instrumental in shaping Joyner's attitudes and her outlook on life during her adolescent and teen years.

Joyner was particularly adept at translating Fennoy's coaching tips into results. Even at an early age, there was this driving force that made her want to be the best that she could be, to do whatever it took to continually run faster and leap farther. Nothing beat the feeling of extending her leaps, and watching as her coach extended the tape measure to keep up with her. When she first started practicing the long jump, her jumps routinely measured fifteen feet. But with Joyner's hard work at practices and Fennoy's coaching, she gained approximately a foot each year. Fennoy also found ways to continue the team's running drills during the cold, winter months. The hallways inside the school were roughly 110 feet, so it was easy to fashion a route through the school halls that gave the athletes their 440 drills. These workouts paid off as well. While Joyner had been the slowest runner on the team when she first started training, she entered tenth grade with the fastest 440 time. She was not the only strong athlete on her high school team, however. The Lincoln High girls' track team won the state championship in 1978, Joyner's sophomore year. It was the first girls' sports title for the school, and the team went on to defend the championship for the next two years.

The talented athlete's entry in the multi-event competition that she would become synonymous with was more by happenstance than some grand design. Since Fennoy already had her competing in a number of individual events—sprints and middle distances, hurdles, and the long jump—he felt that it made sense for her to try the pentathlon, the competition that put them all together and included the 100-meter hurdles, high jump, long jump, shot put, and 800 meters. In the spring of 1981, track authorities added two events, the 200-meter sprint and the javelin toss to the pentathlon, making it a seven-event heptathlon. These multi-event competitions are scored by having the athletes compile points for each individual event based upon their performance versus an arbitrary standard. The athlete that accumulates the highest point total wins the competition. At the age of fourteen, Joyner began competing in an event that wasn't even contested at high school meets in the state of Illinois. It was, however, contested at the AAU meets that the team competed in during the summer. The training for her individual events during the season served as her training for the pentathlon. For the additional segments, such as the high jump, she used whatever technique worked to get her over the bar, something as simple as taking a short run-up, planting one foot, and hurling herself in the fetal position up and over. Even with this rudimentary approach and her skill in the other events, Joyner's improvement was rapid. When she was fifteen, just one year after first competing in the pentathlon, she qualified for the Junior Olympics along with her teammate Deborah Thurston, who would be her stiffest competition. At the competition, Thurston should have won the gold. She was the stronger 800-meter runner, which is the last event, and there were not enough points separating the two for Joyner to be able to win the competition without also winning the 800. But Joyner held on, running a personal best to win the 800 meter and setting a national record for her age group. She had won the competition not only through talent and hard work but also, she felt, because she had wanted it more. It was a lesson she held onto for the rest of her athletic career.

While Joyner's success in track and field was more accepted by family and community than her predecessors' had been, there were still instances when she felt the weight of gender stereotypes. Her parents did not overtly object to her running track, but she still sensed their hesitation at the idea that their daughter wanted to be involved in sports. At first reluctant for her to join the Railers track team, they gave their permission when they learned that men they trusted, Ward and Fennoy, would be in charge. For some, however, there remained a concern that girls' participation in sport posed some sort of threat to boys. The male long jumpers at Joyner's school followed her progress carefully. They accepted the fact that other boys might beat them, but their pride and budding masculinity would not tolerate being defeated by a girl. Even Alfred Joyner drew the line when his daughter's athletic prowess "showed up" the opposite sex, particularly her brother. Tired of hearing from her older brother that, despite her success against girls, he could easily beat her, Joyner finally agreed to a neighborhood race. When their father found out she had beaten him by several steps, he had some thoughts about the outcome. As angry at Jackie for winning as he was at Al for losing, Alfred Joyner reminded his children that things like this didn't happen in nice families. "You're not supposed to beat no boy, beat no brother," Joyner reminded his daughter.[8] Despite the inroads of the 1970s, some still thought that girls' track and field was fine only within the context of their gender.

If Joyner's parents were accepting, albeit a bit reluctantly, of track and field, they had deeper concerns about their daughter's request to join the basketball team. In fact, they initially said no. Her parents' more positive attitude toward track stemmed from several factors. The sport was a favorite in the Joyner household since Alfred Joyner had been something of a track star while he was in high school. Mary and Al Joyner also knew Ward and Fennoy personally and appreciated and trusted their oversight as coaches. Finally, their acceptance was also a result of black women athletes' long relationship with the sport and its improved status since the days of Alice Coachman. The basketball team Joyner wanted to join, however, was a different story. It was not a school team and her parents were worried about oversight. Moreover, despite the passage of Title IX and the advances black women athletes had made during the previous half century, there were still those who worried about the negative effects that sport, especially some sports, might have on females. Joyner's parents still associated basketball with men and didn't think women had any business playing it. Their real concern, Joyner eventually discovered, was that they feared she would become a lesbian if she started playing basketball. Such anxieties were not new. Lesbianism had been "linked" to women's sports since the early 1930s. African American women athletes, raised with the notion that deviation from heterosexuality would not be tolerated, generally encountered little suspicion within the black community. By the 1950s, however, all female athletes lived under a certain "cloud of sexual suspicion," particularly those who played on team sports like softball and basketball where the opportunity for lesbianism was more accessible.[9] The Joyners were not alone in their concern. Unlike other areas of the country, East St. Louis had never offered competitive basketball for girls and some parents kept their daughters away from it or made them drop out. Because of her own parents' concern, Joyner did not play basketball until she was in junior high, when the school started sanctioning competitive play for girls and the Joyners felt better about the level of supervision.

Despite her parents' hesitancy about the sport, it was the basketball coaches who came calling when it was time for college recruiters to pay visits to East St. Louis. Joyner's Lincoln High team had gone all the way to the state playoffs in her junior year but lost the final, championship game. They were determined to return in their senior year and win the state trophy, which they did, defeating the rival Chicago Marshall team 64–47. Joyner's leadership as co-captain of the Lincoln team and her own prowess on the court made her one of the top recruiting prospects in the country. She considered the Universities of Illinois and Wisconsin, enough that she made visits to both campuses. But the winters reminded her too much of home. UCLA had always been at the top of Joyner's list and certainly provided a warmer climate. The sports administrators there also allowed her to play two sports. Some colleges had been struck from her list when she discovered they would make her choose between basketball and track and field. She also admired their head basketball coach, Billie Moore, whom Joyner had followed since 1976. Moore coached the U.S. women's Olympic team in 1976; two years later, she brought a national championship home to UCLA. Moreover, the coach seemed to want Joyner, having made several recruiting trips to East St. Louis to convince the young basketball star to become a UCLA bruin.

Eight years under Title IX had altered the organizational and recruiting landscape of college sport for women. Convinced as the decade neared its end that Title IX was here to stay, the NCAA switched its efforts from attempting to derail the legislation to working to take over the leadership of collegiate women's athletics. Many colleges with women's sport programs already belonged to the female-led Association of Intercollegiate Athletics for Women (AIAW), the sole organizational body and supporter of inter-collegiate women's sport competition during most of the 1970s. Yet their position on "sex-separate" sport for women, inherited from the philosophy of women physical educators of the 1930s, seemed outdated in the after-math of Title IX. "Playing nice" and "girls' rules" flew in the face of the message of equality espoused during this era of civil rights and feminism. Moreover, as the male-led NCAA worked to extend their control over U.S. amateur sport, they came armed with powerful incentives. Not only did the NCAA promise to pay teams' travel expenses to championship meets, but it also pledged to add women's sports to its multi-million-dollar tele-vision packages, ensuring increased exposure. Most large colleges chose to belong to both organizations for a time. But when the NCAA announced that it would add women to its national collegiate championship in 1982, most colleges gave over their sole allegiance to the NCAA. The "commer-cial model" of sport had won out over the AIAW's "educational model."[10]

The NCAA's nascent interest in women's collegiate sport precipitated changes to recruiting as well. The progression, so long in coming, had suddenly taken dramatic turns. Since the 1940s, Tuskegee's Cleve Abbott and Tennessee State's Ed Temple had toured the black high schools of the Southeast searching for young talent for their programs with nothing to offer in terms of incentive except work-study programs and the oppor-tunity to acquire a college education. After the passage of Title IX, the AIAW had been cautious about allowing colleges to offer full-ride schol-arships; they finally began permitting them in 1976. By the time Joyner began looking at colleges, however, recruiting had become so important in attracting talent that coaches were beginning to rely on scouting serv-ices to identify the top athletes in the country. At the same time, the NCAA published its own recruiting rules for women, placing restrictions on the process that were more stringent than those for male athletes. All contact until an athlete's final year had to be made through the high school coach. Once she reached her senior year, college coaches could make direct contact through the telephone, but there were strict limitations on visiting with an athlete in her home and watching her play. And the special, "coincidental" meetings male recruiters held with top male prospects, known as "bumps," were off limits for female athletes. By 1981, Grace Lichtenstein's extensive article on recruiting women athletes suggested that "big money" was at stake now that large universities had women's teams and the scholarship money to attract the talent.[11]

But if the NCAA's takeover was all but assured and college recruiting had become the accepted, new way to attract top female high school athletes, something else had altered the collegiate landscape for black women athletes. Even as UCLA became a formidable track and field presence, Tennessee State's preeminence in the sport slowly faded. The balance of power for collegiate women athletes, in general, and track and field, more specifically, had shifted. Title IX had leveled the playing field for women in colleges and universities throughout the country, and Ed Temple simply did not have the budget dollars to compete with universities like Illinois, Wisconsin, and UCLA that could finance recruiting trips for their coaches. The long-held power center in women's track and field of historically black colleges like Tuskegee Institute and Tennessee State would diminish as more and more top African American athletes chose white universities. Joyner's recruiting experience was symbolic of the shift; there is no evidence that she seriously considered attending a historically black college or university.

A trip to visit UCLA during her senior year confirmed the decision for Joyner. She returned home and signed her letter of intent almost immediately, along with her good friend Deborah Thurston, in what was a media event. Joyner was headed west, in part, because a top women's collegiate basketball coach had recruited her. Track and field was still her first love, however, and she looked forward to continuing to grow and improve at the collegiate level in both the heptathlon and the long jump. Joyner's initial transition to UCLA was typical of the freshman experience. She felt like she had chosen the right college for her, but she was homesick, particularly being so far away from East St. Louis. She settled in well with the basketball team, however. By the beginning of the second semester of her freshmen year, she felt like she was beginning to make a real contribution to the team, scoring nineteen points in the Bruin victory over California State–Long Beach in January.

Her experience during this second semester was to be anything but typical, however. The morning after the Cal State–Long Beach game, she received a call from her mother's sister telling her that her mother was in the hospital, brain dead and on life support, having contracted a deadly bacterial infection that led to a rare condition called Waterhouse-Friderichsen syndrome. As if the situation were not bad enough, Joyner's mother and father were in the process of divorcing and therefore the children were the ones faced with the decision to remove their mother from life support. The Joyner children decided it was time to let their mother go and gave the doctors permission to end life support. Mary Joyner died thirty minutes later, at the age of thirty-seven. Though Jackie was only eighteen, she felt she needed to stay strong for her younger sisters, neither of whom was yet out of high school. While her basketball coach tried to convince her to take the semester off to grieve, she flung herself back into life, classes, and sport at UCLA. It was not until toward the end of the first semester of her sophomore year, almost a year after her mother's death, that she finally let go and grieved for the loss of her mother, confidante, and best friend.

While Joyner would normally be comforted when track season started, there was little to cheer her up there. First, there was a stark difference in privileges accorded the two teams. "Going from basketball season to track season was like going from the penthouse to the outhouse," Joyner later remembered.[12] Whereas the basketball team stayed at Marriotts and Hyatts when they traveled, the track team lodged at Days Inns and Motel 6s. The basketball team dined in restaurants where players were told to order whatever they wanted; the track team ate most of their meals at fast-food restaurants. Second, she was under the tutelage of a coach that apparently did not believe in her abilities and did little to train or encourage her. From comments such as "you'll never beat her" to "work on what you want to," Joyner had lost a necessary factor in her success—someone who believed in her and was interested in helping her improve. Finally, she was struggling to adapt to the change from the pentathlon to the heptathlon and the addition of two new events, which happened the spring of her freshman year. The entire situation began to affect her attitude, and it showed in her performances. She did not win any long jump or heptathlon competitions the entire season. For the National Collegiate Championships, she did not even qualify for the long jump finals, and she finished what she considered to be a dismal third in the heptathlon competition. The last competition of the season was the U.S. Championships in Sacramento, California. When Joyner's coach told her she would have to attend the heptathlon competition, which was taking place separately in Spokane, Washington, by herself and then join the team in Sacramento for the long jump competition, it felt like the end of the road for the gifted yet frustrated athlete. She told her roommate that she would not be on the team the following year; she had decided to give up track and field. Just as Althea Gibson needed someone to help her make adjustments to her erratic tennis game, Joyner needed someone who believed in her abilities and was willing to help her make the adjustments she needed to breathe new life into what looked like might be a very short track career. She found that someone in the person of Robert Kersee.

Bobby Kersee had come on board as an assistant track coach at UCLA the same spring that Joyner was struggling. He had come over from California State–Northridge, and several of his athletes had followed him. But he was not assigned to coach Jackie Joyner, much to her regret. As she watched his athletes working out, it looked like Kersee was working just as hard as they were to help them improve. He had also gone out of his way to express his condolences over her mother's death, saying that he had lost his own mother when he was just fourteen. When the news reached Kersee that Joyner would be attending the heptathlon competition by herself without the benefit of a coach, he was livid. He told the heptathlete that he was going to the athletic director to inform her that he was accompanying Joyner to the U.S. Championships in Spokane, even if he had to pay for the trip out of his own pocket. He found it unacceptable that a UCLA athlete was competing somewhere without the benefit of a coach. Kersee did have to pay his own way, but the experience changed Joyner's life. After the first day of competition, Joyner was in fourth place. The long jump, her signature event, kicked off the competition the following day. In what reminded her of her high school coach's tactics, Kersee worked with his new student in the hallway of the hotel that evening to improve her run-up to the board and establish more consistency in her jumps. He also told her that trying to be the best in the long jump portion of the competition was making her tighten up and affecting her performance. It was, he pointed out, just one event out of seven. Joyner felt like she finally had met a coach in college that knew her and was as excited as she was about improving. With Kersee's coaching, she finished second at the U.S. Championships, her best performance all season. She amassed 5,827 points for the competition, a point total that was the best of any UCLA athlete and would have won the college championships earlier that year. When they returned to UCLA, Kersee requested and received permission to begin coaching Joyner full time. It was a partnership that would not only change both of their lives but also help put UCLA and the West Coast on the map as the premier place for women track and field athletes to train.

With a track coach who understood her strengths and weaknesses and most of the grieving over her mother's death behind her, Joyner recaptured her joy for track and field and began her climb to the top. She won the heptathlon competition at both the 1982 and 1983 NCAA Championships, setting new records each year in the multi-event competition for total points. With the 1984 Olympics a little over a year away, she and Kersee turned their attention to preparing for international competition.

While the 1984 Olympics would be Joyner's first attempt at a medal as a top collegiate athlete, it was not her first experience with the anticipation of facing national competitors. Three years earlier, she had been extended an invitation to compete in the long jump competition at the Olympic track and field trials that would determine the U.S. team for the 1980 Olympics to be held in Moscow. This was the first Olympiad to be celebrated under the new organizational structure established by the Amateur Sports Act of 1978. Looking for a way to help the United States remain competitive against the Soviet Union, the act established the United States Olympic Committee (USOC) as the organization authorized to oversee the development of amateur sport in the country. The Act also stripped the Amateur Athletic Association of its governance over international competition, authorizing the USOC to establish national governing bodies for each sport. The AAU's fifty-five-year control of U.S. women's amateur track and field came to an end when it sponsored its last national championship in 1979.[13] The Athletic Congress, or TAC, the newly chartered national governing body for ama-

A JACKIE OF ALL TRADES

teur track and field, hosted its first Senior Men's and Women's Track and Field Championships in June 1980. One week later, TAC hosted the Olympic trials that Joyner had been asked to compete in. A high school senior at the time, she faced her first national competition against world-class track athletes. Joyner was devastated when her fifth-place finish in the long jump kept her out of the top three that earned places on the team. However, the 1980 U.S. team never got a chance to participate in Olympic competition. Cold War tensions between the United States and the Soviet Union continued throughout the 1970s, as each superpower remained distrustful of the intentions of its adversary. When the Soviet Union invaded Afghanistan in December 1979, President Jimmy Carter demanded the withdrawal of Soviet troops from the Middle Eastern nation by 20 February, suggesting that the United States would boycott the Moscow Olympics unless the other superpower complied. When Russian troops remained in Afghanistan, Carter, true to his word, announced his "irreversible decision" that the United States team would not be attending the Olympic games. In April, the USOC bowed to the political pressure and supported the presidential announcement.[14] Joyner had been crushed when she didn't make the Olympic team, yet that paled in comparison to the athletes who had made the team and never enjoyed the experience of facing Olympic competition.

The celebration of another Olympiad was now on the horizon, however, and Joyner decided to take the 1983–84 academic year off to prepare for Olympic competition. Kersee developed a strategy for the heptathlon competition that astounded his young athlete. He felt that she still had incredible potential that she had not reached. Most of her accomplishments thus far had centered on hard work and talent, but her coach could see errors in her technique in every event. As he trained her in the proper technique for jumping, clearing hurdles, and throwing the javelin and shot put, she began shaving seconds off her track times and adding feet to her field events. Her first-place performance at the Olympic trials, which set a new American record, left no doubt that she was the top heptathlete in the country. Yet when she also made the Olympic team for the long jump, Joyner was quickly acquiring a reputation as a generalist who could specialize.

The 1984 Olympics in Los Angeles were a spectacle of American athletic supremacy—the 174 medals the U.S. team won dwarfed West

Germany's 59, the country that stood behind the United States in the final medal count—but they were marred again by political boycott. With the 1980 Olympics in the Soviet Union and the 1984 Olympics in the United States, rumblings of a possible boycott by the Soviet Union emerged in early 1984. On 3 May, a little over two months before the games were scheduled to begin, the Soviet Union announced that they would not send a team to the games because of certain dangers that threatened their athletes' safety—presumably plots to kidnap and mislead young Soviet athletes into defection. In truth, the Soviet boycott probably stemmed as much from Cold War politics as anything, as they considered staying home the most effective means of disrupting the 1984 presidential election cycle and Ronald Reagan's bid for reelection. Despite the underlying reasons, most athletes interpreted the boycott as the Soviet Union repaying the United States for its boycott of the Moscow games four years earlier.[15]

With the East German athletes boycotting as part of the Soviet bloc, the heptathlon competition was wide open. Joyner's chief competition, as it turned out, was not an athlete from the Soviet bloc as she would have expected months before. It was not even Glynis Nunn of Australia who was having the performance of her career. The main competitor Joyner had to overcome was herself and her mental preparedness, particularly in the face of something that plagues athletes throughout their careers—the fear of injury. Joyner had experienced shin splints as early as high school but had been spared any significant injury until the 1983 World Championships when a pulled hamstring during the second day of the heptathlon required her to withdraw from the competition. With that painful experience still fresh in her memory, she became completely inconsolable when a similar though less severe pain occurred during training just two weeks before the games were scheduled to begin. Immediate treatment and rest healed the inflamed hamstring, but the possibility of a re-injury dominated her thoughts. Joyner was certainly among those vying for a gold medal. But with injury concerns affecting her mental preparation and Nunn matching her event for event, she could not convince herself of it. The two athletes were virtually tied going into the 800 meters, the final event of the two-day competition. Nunn crossed the finish line about three seconds ahead of her American competitor; Joyner had won her first Olympic medal, but it was silver rather than the gold she had hoped and trained for. Five points separated her from Nunn's gold-medal performance.

When she finished fifth in the long jump competition two days later, Joyner realized she would have to train for four more years for another opportunity at Olympic gold. Now that she had tasted world-class competition and had a coach who was willing to drive her to new heights, she looked forward to the challenge. Despite the fact that she only had one more year of college, something that certainly would have deterred her predecessors, she was determined to find a way to continue competing in the sport that she loved. Indeed, Jackie Joyner was about to enter the most productive period of her long career.

World Records, Olympic Glory, and "The First Family of Track"

The two years following the 1984 Olympics were full of changes for Jackie Joyner and Bobby Kersee. Joyner, now in her senior year, resumed her studies at UCLA. The five athletes that Kersee coached in the Olympics had won ten medals, including a gold in the triple jump for Joyner's brother, Al. Fresh off Kersee's Olympic success, UCLA appointed him head track and field coach. He also found a way to help athletes, many of whom were just hitting their peak as their college careers ended, to continue training and competing after graduation. Track and field was going through yet another transition in the wake of the collapse of the professional track circuit that Wyomia Tyus had competed in. In 1981, following lengthy discussion regarding open Olympic competition that would include both amateur and professional athletes, the IOC had decided to permit the international governing bodies for each sport to set their own rules for Olympic eligibility, in concert with the IOC. One of the very issues that Wyomia Tyus had addressed during her career was finally evolving. Track and field's governing body still limited Olympic competition to amateurs, but it now permitted athletes to receive payments and retain amateur status as long as the money was used for their athletic training. European meets often paid top stars to compete and offered better prize money than the professional track circuit had.[16] Acquiring sponsors and endorsement contracts on one's own or through an agent was also on the rise, but track and field athletes generally had to win Olympic gold medals before a company thought they were famous enough to sell its products. By establishing his World Class Track Club, Kersee found a way for athletes who had yet to make it big to continue training without going deeply into debt. With a pool of sponsorship money from Adidas, the club paid for training and travel expenses for its members—Al and Jackie Joyner, Florence Griffith, Jeanette Bolden, Valerie Brisco-Hooks, and Greg Foster—all of whom had graduated from college or were close to it. In return, athletes and coach advertised for the company by wearing Adidas shoes and apparel.

In addition to transitions in their athletic lives, there were personal changes for Joyner and Kersee that occurred in the aftermath of the Los Angeles Olympics. Following graduation from college, coach and athlete discovered that their feelings for each other had changed and deepened; they married in a simple ceremony in January 1986. There would be adjustments ahead as the couple learned how to be both coach/athlete and husband/wife. Their fiery relationship at competitions would characterize the remainder of the career of the athlete who would now be known as Jackie Joyner-Kersee.

During the two-year period leading up to the 1988 Olympics, Joyner-Kersee entered the most prosperous period of her long career, the period during which sportswriters hailed her as "superwoman." She dominated the heptathlon and long jump at both the national and international levels. She won the Sullivan Award in 1986, recognizing her as the best U.S. amateur athlete for the year that she twice established a new world record for the heptathlon, set a new American indoor record for the long jump, and became the first heptathlete to exceed 7,000 points. In 1987, she added two more world records to her growing accomplishments and was named "Female Athlete of the Year" by the Associated Press and "Athlete of the Year" by *Track and Field News*. She also received the Jesse Owens Award, recognizing her as the athlete whose performance over the year best personified excellence, and whose relationships with competitors promoted cooperation among nations of the world.[17]

Given this two-year run-up to the Olympics, Joyner-Kersee came into the Seoul games an entirely different athlete than she had in Los Angeles four years earlier. She was now seasoned at international competition, understanding the importance of physical *and* mental preparation. She had also won both the heptathlon and long jump competitions at the U.S.

Olympic trials, setting another world record for the overall event, as well as one world and two American records in individual events. She was not only confident but also had learned to fight through the pain of the minor injuries that invariably occur during a heptathlon competition. The training, expert coaching, mental preparation, and athleticism came together in a spectacular Olympics. She won the gold medal for the heptathlon, setting her fourth world record for the multi-event competition. She also won the gold medal for the long jump, setting a new Olympic record for that event. She had captured the gold medals that had eluded her four years earlier in Los Angeles not once, but twice.

As Joyner-Kersee electrified the world with her world records and gold medals, her presence in the sporting news exploded. Title IX was by this time ten years old and women athletes from any number of sports were becoming more and more accepted in American society. In ways that differed considerably from her predecessors, sportswriters gave considerable space to Joyner-Kersee's athleticism as they began to acquaint the sporting public with this new international sports star. The concern over the femininity of women track and field athletes remained, but on the track and in the field, Joyner-Kersee was all athlete, focused on the competition and her own performance. She found that by separating her on- and off-the-field images reporters seemed content to let her be an athlete on the field and a woman off it. During competition, she was track and field's "wonder woman," "superwoman," and "the world's best female athlete." She was focused and competitive, and sportswriters wrote of her demanding training schedule, dedication to the sport, and athletic ability. Dressed up for classes or an interview, however, she could be seen "wearing lipstick to match her fire-engine red sweat suit." "Her perm gave way at the ears to the sparkle of stud earrings," noticed Phil Hersh of the *Chicago Tribune* when he interviewed Joyner as a senior back at UCLA after the 1984 Olympics. She easily fit into the glamour that was "taken for granted" in Hollywood's hometown. Even women sportswriters, more prominent now in this post–Title IX age, seemed to like the separate on/off-field personas. "Joyner-Kersee looks like a million dollars these days," observed Barbara Lloyd of the *New York Times*. "Her hair is long and thick, and her clothes are model chic."[18] She was, both male and female reporters agreed, an attractive woman—all woman—which seemed an important thing to keep reminding readers.

At times, however, reporters could have a difficult time keeping the two "Jackies" separate. Coming off her successful 1986 track year when she won the Sullivan Award, some sportswriters began suggesting that Joyner-Kersee was the world's greatest athlete. But it was a title that came couched in pretty feminine terms: "Don't bet the world's greatest athlete is a great hulk with a beard that positively needs shaving every day. The world's greatest athlete may very well look good in high heels and mesh stockings, lipstick and bracelets." Making a very good case that Joyner-Kersee may indeed be "the greatest" rather than some big hunk of a man, she was, the article continued, "just 5–10 and 155," a young woman "who can cook, has brown eyes and a nice smile and a figure that could make a chorus line." A little over twenty-five years earlier, another sportswriter had quoted Wilma Rudolph's "vital statistics" and remarked that she had "the legs of a showgirl."[19] Rudolph was Joyner's athletic idol, but showgirls and chorus lines were the connections that the American press made. Black women athletes may have transitioned to the West Coast and to white colleges, but they continued to have to find ways to push back against stereotypes that arose from an American public who needed to be reassured that these athletes were feminine, even glamour women.

While Joyner-Kersee had just capped an incredible three-year run of world records and medals, her sister-in-law, Florence Griffith Joyner, seemed to come out of nowhere to capture sprint titles, medals, and newspaper headlines. A sprinter in the tradition of Wilma Rudolph and Wyomia Tyus, Florence Griffith had been one of the athletes Bobby Kersee coached at California State–Northridge who transferred with him to UCLA. She had graduated from UCLA and become part of Bobby Kersee's World Class Track Club in order to continue training and competing. At the 1984 Olympics in Los Angeles, she won a silver medal in the 200 meters. There she had shown the nation that she had a style all her own when she accepted her medal with four-inch long, curved, elaborately painted fingernails. In 1987, she married Al Joyner, making the foursome of Jackie Joyner-Kersee, Bobby Kersee, Al Joyner, and Florence Griffith Joyner, the "first family" of American track and field. Just as Joyner-Kersee's best days lay ahead of the Los Angeles Olympics, there was also much more to come from her new sister-in-law.[20]

Primarily a 200-meter sprinter who had dabbled in the 400 meters due to a dearth in the field, Kersee worked with Griffith Joyner to become a 100- and 200-meter sprint specialist in preparation for the 1988 Olympic trials. She had recently come out of retirement, shed fifteen pounds, and was committed to stunning the world in Seoul and earning the gold that had eluded her four years earlier. She did not wait until arriving in Seoul to capture the attention of the American public, however. At the Olympic trials in Indianapolis, she set a new record of 10.49 seconds in one of the semifinals of the 100-meter sprint, slashing .27 second off of Evelyn Ashford's previous record of 10.76 seconds. In a sport where hundredths of a second normally distinguished new from old records, Griffith Joyner's performance was on the order of unbelievable. She also caught attention when, spurning the traditional track attire of the day, she displayed a wardrobe of flashy bodysuits of her own creation in a variety of colors and styles.[21] Even as descriptions of her track suits filled the sports pages, her 100-meter record also came under scrutiny.

The difficulty with Griffith Joyner's record was two-fold. First was the issue of her previous best 100-meter time, which had been 10.89 seconds. If trumping a world-record mark by close to .3 of a second was unbelievable, shaving .4 of a second off of a personal record in a single race was unheard of. This incredible improvement in time made people question the reliability of the wind gauge, the second issue. National and international track and field rules state that aiding winds cannot be more than 2 meters, or 4.47 miles, per second in order for a time to be considered a record. Therefore wind recordings are taken at official meets, measuring the average wind speed over ten seconds. For Griffith Joyner's 100-meter heat, the Omega wind gauge registered 0.0, which is rare. Moreover, the gauge also recorded 0.0 on the following race, an occurrence veteran track officials reported they had never heard of. Crosswinds can record calm readings, but that had not been the experience for most of the meet. Indeed, the issue of the legitimacy of the record was so acute because it occurred on a day when strong winds had consistently aided sprinters and jumpers. In the men's triple jump competition that was being contested concurrently with the women's 100 meter, only three of the forty-seven jumps registered legal winds. The readings for the two jumps taken just before Griffith Joyner's historic run indicated winds of 9.62 and 6.48 mph. Omega wind gauge officials announced that they tested the gauge after the race and did not determine any problems. They declared the gauge in working order. There was, they noted, a crosswind during the race in question that would not invalidate the record since crosswinds do not aid runners. Perhaps Griffith Joyner lent credence to her performance with her other heat times—a wind-aided 10.60 seconds in an earlier heat, and 10.70 and 10.61 seconds in the semifinal and final—all under the world mark of 10.76. While there would be more discussion of Griffith Joyner's record in Seoul, the Omega officials stood by their equipment, and national and international track governing bodies later ratified it.[22]

Griffith Joyner gave reporters more to talk about than her record, however. She had designed her own running attire, and it was unconventional to say the least. There were dramatic colors—purple, golden yellow, lime, blue, and pink. Many of her track suits had one leg cut out, an experiment with scissors she told reporters. And then there was the white lace bodysuit, the one she referred to as an "athletic negligee." Her hair was long and flowing, and her nails were still four inches in length, painted exotic colors. She had, no doubt, a style all her own, and she used it to push back against the stereotypes of masculinity and natural athlete that had followed black women athletes for most of the century. Rather than shying away from such displays of power and femininity on the track, she combined overt expressions of sexuality and speed in ways that seemed to indicate she was unconcerned with stereotypes of the past.[23] Perhaps Griffith Joyner was employing the same technique that black sportswriters had used during Alice Coachman's career when they had refuted the myth of masculinization with a sensual, erotic image using peanut oil. All she ever said about the subject was that she liked having her own style; it had been important to her since she was young. Why her style took the form it did will remain, at least on some level, clothed in mystery. What is clear, however, is that Griffith Joyner embraced one of the very images that had surrounded black women athletes for almost fifty years. In doing so, however, she successfully employed the image for own her purposes and to her own advantage.

While it was inevitable that Griffith Joyner's appearance would attract attention, the language that reporters used to describe her indicated that they *were* still concerned with stereotypes. There were multiple references to her "stripping" off her warm-up suit to reveal the latest color. To create excitement over her white lace "athletic negligee," the *Wall Street Journal* engaged in a virtual literary strip tease, observing "off came her top." Elsewhere she was the "glamourpuss," and her one-leggers, the experiment with scissors, were "designed with one leg stretching to the ankle and the other cut off at the crotch." When reporting their conversations with her about the athletic negligee, her voice was "appropriately sultry." And as she prepared to run what became her world-record 100-meter heat, one sportswriter gave readers the following description:

> As she settled into the blocks before the second round of the 100 meters at the U.S. Olympic Track and Field Trials in Indianapolis on Saturday, Florence Griffith Joyner's electric-plum bodysuit caressed her from neck to ankle. Over it she wore a turquoise bikini brief. Yet her left leg was bare; somehow it appeared more naked than any other bare limb in the race.[24]

There were in these descriptions an image from the past—the "rubbing the girls with oil" that Levi Jolley had evoked of Coachman and her teammates and the spectacle nature of "watching Wilma run." But the mere fact that Griffith Joyner could adopt such a style and at the same time have her athletic success recognized by the press showed the extent to which her strategy of manipulating such an image worked to alter stereotypes to her personal advantage.

As sportswriters reported on the sisters-in-law, this first family of track, their news stories highlighted the athletes' contrasting styles and the differing strategies they employed to challenge gender stereotypes. The Seoul games were shaping up to be the "Flo and Jackie show," suggested Fred Klein of the *Wall Street Journal*, "starring two quite different though related gals." Joyner-Kersee was the conservative, hard-working one who planned to spend the lead-up time honing her skills to prepare for her seven-event competition. Griffith Joyner would be taking it easy by working out a couple of times a week and selecting new athletic garb. The press even came up with a nickname for their new glamour athlete, FloJo, which seemed to fit the speedy, flashy track star. When reporter Christine Brennan described how "Flo" had talked "Jackie" into trying one of her one-legged track attire back in April, their different approaches to tackling persistent gender images emerged. Her sister-in-law's creations were not for her, she told reporters, insisting that she preferred the plain old track suits she was used to. "People laughed, and I couldn't keep my mind on my work," she noted. Whereas Griffith Joyner embraced combining her femininity and athleticism on the track, Joyner-Kersee would have none of it, choosing instead to keep the two separate.[25]

Griffith Joyner's success at the Seoul games was every bit as dramatic as her performance at the Olympic trials. She easily won the 100 meter with a wind-aided 10.54 seconds, breaking into a smile well before the finish line. Then she twice set new world records for the 200 meter, the final one of 21.34 seconds coming in the gold medal race. She went on to duplicate Wilma Rudolph's triple-gold performance when the 4x100 relay team won the gold medal. And she added another silver to her collection when she ran the anchor leg with the 4x400-meter relay team. The press observed that her personal fashion was stunted somewhat by Olympic rules that required an athlete to wear the standard Olympic-issue track suits dictated by the U.S. Olympic committee. The shoes, hair, and nails were pure Griffith Joyner, however, as was the white belt she wore around her waist during the race. And there was the smile that split "those cherry-red lipsticked-lips," FloJo's own special "Flo Glow."[26]

Of course, Joyner-Kersee was having the Olympics of her life as well, winning two gold medals and setting her fourth world record, but the glamour and style of "FloJo" seemed to trump the intensive, hardworking, athletic style of her sister-in-law. Even female sportswriter Christine Brennan of the *Washington Post*, acknowledged it:

> In this summer of Joyner-somethings, only the world's greatest sister-in-law could upstage the world's greatest woman athlete. It took just 10.49 seconds and a body suit without a leg for Florence Griffith Joyner to do it. Jackie Joyner-Kersee, who labored across two days to break her own heptathlon world record, probably didn't realize it, and certainly didn't care. But, all of a sudden, her substantial athletic accomplishments were hidden in the blur of the Flo-Jo fashion show.[27]

Joyner-Kersee had become the one who was keeping up with her now more famous sister-in-law as she "matched her gold for gold." The Joyner heptathlete's accomplishments were amazing, but the Joyner sprinter's were even more so. The black press stated the situation bluntly when it observed that, despite another stellar year by Joyner-Kersee, Griffith Joyner had overshadowed her. It took quite a bit, noted another sportswriter, to steal the spotlight from the heptathlete during the trials, but steal it she did.[28] By the end of the Seoul games, the theft was complete. While Brennan's observation that Joyner-Kersee "certainly didn't care" indicated the heptathlete's comfort with her own style, the American public did seem to. For decades, the pure athleticism of black women track athletes had never been more important than questions of their femininity.

If little had changed as black women track athletes still looked for ways to reject or manipulate stereotypes, much had changed for them in retirement. The 1980s were a period of sheer explosion of endorsement contracts for Olympic athletes. Mary Lou Retton, the "darling" U.S. gymnast of the 1984 Olympics, had barely left Los Angeles when the offers started pouring in, eventually bringing in $5 million for the young gold medalist. Athletes could enter into such agreements and retain their amateur status as long as the money went into a trust fund to support their training expenses. For exceptional athletes, the days of worrying about finding enough money to scrape by or having to retire from competition following college were fading. But success in the Olympic world did not always equate to success in the marketplace, at least not on the order of what professional team athletes were able to garner. "Four gold medals don't mean as much as 60 home runs," noted one account executive assessing contract material from the Seoul games.[29] One thing was certain, however. Whereas Althea Gibson, Wilma Rudolph, and Wyomia Tyus had, in different ways, all struggled to make their college degrees and athletic success pay off in retirement, Joyner-Kersee and Griffith Joyner were part of a new world when it came to turning their athletic careers into money.

When it came to endorsement money, it became clear that Griffith Joyner once again had a leg up on her sister-in-law. In the aftermath of winning the Sullivan Award in early 1987, the lack of follow-up by corporate America surprised the world-class heptathlete. Though she recognized that the sprinters, the "glamour" athletes of track and field, would attract more endorsement income over the heptathletes that went from one event to the next often in obscurity, she felt that the prestige of the Sullivan Award might compensate. Both the white and black press speculated that race was the key factor in the dearth of Joyner-Kersee's endorsement success. "The silence," observed George Vecsey of the *New York Times*, "speaks volumes about the low marketability of the finest black athletes in America." As late as 1992, black sportswriter Howie Evans continued the theme, suggesting that the heptathlete who had just defended her Olympic gold would not be on the receiving end of many phone calls from corporate executives asking her to advertise their products: "If Jackie Joyner-Kersee were a blue-eyed blond, the world would split down the middle for her. ... But the complexion of her skin will deny her the megabucks she so richly deserves." Race, though certainly bound up in the issue, was not a complete explanation, however. Evans himself suggested as much when he cited the endorsement fame of black athletes like Michael Jordan, Magic Johnson, and Bo Jackson. Joyner-Kersee's method of separating her two selves contrasted with the image of black women track athletes that Americans had come to accept during the twentieth century. When looking for who might be an appropriate company spokesperson, the style and fashion of "FloJo" attracted more attention than the athleticism of "Jackie." While Joyner Kersee acquired several contracts, Griffith Joyner was expected to make "even more of a splash," thanks as much to her flowing hair, elaborately painted nails, and one-legged track suits as her blazing speed. Sweating and panting for the camera was all right for the men, but companies felt that the public didn't want to see their women athletes selling products in this manner. Gordon Baskin, Griffith Joyner's agent, understood this image completely. He would, he told the black press, be looking for contracts that fit her personality and character of "athletic excellence and beauty." By February 1989, just four months after the games, Baskin had already secured $3 million in contract deals. Florence Griffith Joyner had become, by far, the most commercially successful black woman athlete of the day.[30]

Griffith Joyner's financial success in the aftermath of the Seoul games seemed to indicate a turning point for black women athletes in American society. *New York Times* reporter Michael Janofsky called her new relationship with so many of America's corporations something of a "sociological breakthrough." She was, recognized several sportswriters, the first black female athlete to be in such a position. She had connected with such a broad audience, noted *Sports Illustrated*'s Kenny Moore, that she had become something of a cultural phenomenon. The lesson, he surmised, was that it took more than athletic achievement to make a black woman a star. Calling her a crossover triumph, Griffith Joyner's real success was that "she is able to dress like Madonna and run as fast as O. J. Simpson and nobody will laugh." Her fandom was nothing new. Americans had been fascinated with black women athletic superstars since they had been lining up to "watch Wilma run," admiring those long, slender legs that could have belonged to a showgirl. What was new was Griffith Joyner's willingness to embrace the image to her own advantage. If her post-athletic career was a sociological breakthrough, it was because one black woman had finally joined the rest of the athletic community in turning her sport stardom into endorsement millions. She was not just any black woman athlete, however, but one whom Americans could recognize as the "provocative, sensuous" speedster they had become accustomed to. Not even her "equally well-known sister-in-law," observed Janofsky, had generated the same level of interest.[31]

Even as Joyner-Kersee tried to move the discussion of black women athletes forward to a language of athleticism, American society insisted in latching onto the glamour and style of "FloJo." The "world's greatest female athlete" referred to her own style and strategy in her autobiography and the ways the press tried to pit the two sisters-in-law against each other. Her conservative dress and business-like approach on the track and field were only one side to her personality, she wrote. Off the track, she enjoyed dressing up, styling her hair, and polishing her nails as much as other women. But when she was competing, she was engaged in a battle, and she had more important things to worry about than whether every hair was in place or a fingernail was chipped. "I can't help it," she wrote, "if after running 800 meters in 118-degree heat, I don't look like I just stepped out of a beauty salon."[32] She was not, in other words, interested in adhering to Ed Temple's femininity program in a post–Title IX America. At first, her insistence in being perceived as all athlete during competition seemed to take hold. Sportswriters spent more time showcasing her athletic accomplishments than they had her predecessors'. She had competed not in the more glamorous sprint events like Rudolph, Tyus, and Griffith Joyner, but in the grueling, seven-event heptathlon and had won praise and admiration for it. She had won the title of "world's greatest" and "superwoman." But something seemed to fade in the face of her stylish sister-in-law. Suddenly, the "world's greatest female athlete" was no longer the best female athlete of the year.[33] Hard work, grueling competition, and a post–Title IX athletic style could not stand up to what had become the staple perception of black women track athletes—a flashy sprinter on display, who "stripped" off warm-up suits to show off a bodysuit that "caressed" her skin and revealed one very naked leg.

Indeed, the way in which sportswriters reacted to Joyner-Kersee's post-Seoul career attests to the fact that the American public was still not ready for a black woman athlete who spurned on-the-field femininity and glamour for pure athletic grace. "The world's greatest female athlete" continued to compete for another ten years. During that time, she defended her gold in the heptathlon at the Barcelona games in 1992 and won a bronze in the long jump. Four years later in Atlanta, she was forced to pull out of the heptathlon competition due to injury, ending her attempt to make it three in a row. But five days later, she faced the long jump competition in her characteristically tough, competitive way, battling the pain of a still tender hamstring. She entered the last jump in sixth place, seemingly out of the competition. But her last jump of 22′11¾″ shot her into third place, where she remained to earn her second bronze medal in that event. Despite her continued success in the sport, she was never again able to surpass her own world record, something the press would not let the world forget. As she competed in the world championships in the wake of her Seoul success, she "squandered her chance," and her performances were "disappointing" when time and again she fell off record pace. The progression she had been on in the two years leading up to Seoul had ended, noted Janofsky, "leaving not so much as a hint of better to come." During the 1990 season, he observed that despite her number-one world ranking in the heptathlon and number-seven ranking in the long jump, she had not looked particularly imposing in any event, and some of her best efforts in the long jump and hurdles were merely "ordinary." Winning in and of itself was no longer good enough; if track and field's "wonder woman" was going to remain in the sport chasing her own record, then anything short of passing herself was a disappointment. Thomas Boswell of the *Washington Post* seemed to best sense the public mood when he observed after her second gold in the heptathlon in Barcelona: "Perhaps this XXV Olympiad will be the stage that brings Joyner-Kersee the world attention that has brushed past her without truly sticking."[34]

Sportswriters occasionally offered reasons why Joyner-Kersee should not be excoriated for failing to best her own record, although none of these seemed to truly satisfy. There were the injuries that went with competing so intensely, and these became more prevalent as she remained in the sport and became an "old-timer." She also suffered from exercise-induced asthma. While she had medications to control the condition, she approached taking them with a laissez-faire attitude, which sometimes precipitated life-threatening asthma attacks. It also did not help that both she and her husband/coach were constantly pushing her to the next level, stretching sideways as she toyed with competing in hurdles competition as well as the heptathlon and long jump. Moreover, after the Seoul games, other things such as honoring endorsement contracts and delving into nonprofit work competed with athletic training for her attention. Finally, Kersee was constantly making predictions to the press regarding his wife's ability to break her own record, offering a point total as high as 7,400 at one point.[35] Keeping these increasingly intense possibilities for higher marks in the mind of the public and the press certainly helped focus them in on the record. Kersee admitted as much himself, confessing he had been too hard on his wife during the 1990 and 1991 seasons, pushing for her to break the record. But bound up in these myriad reasons was also the fact that Americans were most satisfied when they had a black woman athlete that fit the image they were accustomed to. A heptathlete that didn't mind letting people see her sweat on the track and field would not hold public attention when they were used to a sprinter that combined her sexuality and speed.

It seemed that little could topple this sexual perception of black women athletes that reached back decades. Yet in the midst of the Olympic success of the Joyner sisters-in-law, something profound shook the world of track and field. There was proof that performance-enhancing drugs were part of the training regime that helped at least one high-profile athlete win a gold medal in Seoul. Suddenly, everyone was under suspicion, and "Jackie" and "Flo" were certainly not immune. As they became central targets, the two athletes discovered that the issues of race and racism were never far away.

The Price of Fame in a Performance-Enhanced Sport

The high-profile athlete that was involved in the Olympic drug scandal was competing for the title of "world's fastest human." The men's 100-meter sprint to be contested in Seoul was to be the latest "race of the century." Carl Lewis was from the United States; Ben Johnson was Canadian. Lewis was the reigning Olympic champion and had won the latest match-up between the two, whereas Johnson had taken the world championships in Rome, setting a new world record. Johnson was faster out of the blocks but Lewis had the kick, all of which seemed almost pointless for a race that lasted less than ten seconds. On top of all of the analysis, one other factor made this an anticipated match-up. Lewis and Johnson made no secret about the fact that they did not like each other. On 23 September 1988, Ben Johnson laid the matter to rest. He became the new gold medalist and the fastest man alive in a world-record time of 9.79 seconds. But three days later, the gold medal was in the hands of Carl Lewis and Johnson had flown back to Canada in disgrace. Having tested positive for a banned substance, the International Amateur Athletics Foundation, the governing body for track and field, stripped him of the gold medal and world record, and suspended him from competition for two years.[36]

The IOC had been testing athletes for twenty years, but this was the first time in Olympic history that a gold-medal track and field athlete had been disqualified for the use of performance-enhancing drugs. Sadly, the Olympic games had entered a new era:

> Johnson hasn't robbed us of our innocence, because athletic innocence was lost many years ago. But to see it happen on this stage, in what we've always believed was the purest form of athletic competition, to see a spectacular athlete, a giant of the earth, cheat at the Olympics is the athletic equivalent of The Day the Music Died.[37]

The memory and illusion of a more innocent age were suddenly gone. The race that had been one of the highlights of the games, "one of the greatest races and rivalries of amateur track and field," was now a lost memory. So too was the illusion that all the money and politics of sport fell away when one athlete met another on the track and competed to their own natural physical limits. It was inevitable, therefore, that rumors would begin to circulate about other track and field athletes. Everyone who had won a gold medal was instantly suspect. Those athletes who had exhibited sudden and dramatic improvement were clearly getting some illegal help, according to the rabid accusations. An unnamed coach from the Soviet Union put numbers to the problem when he was quoted in *Newsweek* saying that perhaps 90 percent of the track athletes— including those from the Soviet Union—used performance-enhancing drugs. "Ben Johnson's mistake," he added, "was getting caught."[38] Overnight, it was a different sport indeed.

In addition to global accusations, some athletes confessed that they knew about the drug habits of other athletes and either identified them through association and implication, or named names. Given their success at the games, Joyner-Kersee and Griffith Joyner immediately came under suspicion. "By all odds," wrote Frank Deford, "Flo-Jo and her sister-in-law, Jackie Joyner-Kersee, should have come away from Seoul as prom queens to the world." But because of "the ugly shadow of drugs," such was not the case. "Their achievements were held up to suspicion, and our affections wavered," he lamented.[39]

The "shadow of drugs" that Deford referred to was not only ugly but also completely familiar, at least in the way the suspicions of the two black women athletes played out, for they centered in their appearance as opposed to their recent athletic successes. The most prominent and scathing attack was leveled by a middle distance Brazilian runner, Joaquim Cruz, winner of the silver medal in the 800-meter competition. Drawing attention to what he described as physical changes in the two athletes, Cruz insinuated that performance-enhancing drugs must be the cause of the changes:

> Florence, in 1984, you could see an extremely feminine person, but today she looks more like a man than a woman. ... And [Jackie] Joyner [Kersee] herself, she looks like a gorilla, so these people, they must be doing something that isn't normal to gain all these muscles.[40]

Something had brought about clear physical changes, insisted Cruz, and all one had to do was look at Griffith Joyner and Joyner-Kersee to see that this was true. In language strikingly similar to what Alice Coachman might have been subjected to fifty years earlier, something was threatening to turn FloJo into a man, although now the culprit was performance-enhancing drugs as opposed to the sport of track and field itself. And while Cruz's attack on Joyner-Kersee also seemed to center in her musculature, it was also clearly and harshly grounded in a long-held racial stereotype that focused attention on her appearance. "FloJo" may be turning into a man, but "Jackie" was devolving into a gorilla, Cruz implied. The specter of race and persistence of racial stereotypes was never more obvious.

Joyner-Kersee and Griffith Joyner, along with their coach/husbands, denied ever taking steroids, but in the aftermath of the Olympics, the accusations did not go away. Cruz eventually claimed he was misquoted and called Joyner-Kersee to apologize. However, he had spoken the words on Brazilian television, and the tape made it clear that he had not been "misquoted" at all. Others leveled accusations, either directly or through innuendo, that centered both around FloJo's physique, her recently acquired muscles, and the "quantum leap" in her sprint performances. Either by association or directly, many of the attacks implicated Bob Kersee. Carl Lewis, thinking he was speaking off-the-record, told University of Pennsylvania students that he thought Kersee should be put out of the sport since Lewis thought the coach tried "to put everyone he knows on drugs." Both sisters-in-law continued to deny ever ingesting drugs. Joyner-Kersee was especially adamant in her insistence, claiming that her childhood memories of the destructive nature of drugs and alcohol in her own family made her particularly loath to put anything foreign into her body. Griffith Joyner continued to insist that her recent track success—and by inference, her musculature—was due to the weight training program that Kersee had put her on. Kersee insisted that the two athletes were ripe for attacks because they had not only won gold medals but also set world records. With the accusations continuing well into 1989, Joyner-Kersee returned to training and competing while Griffith Joyner, overwhelmed with her new life as a celebrity, surprised the sporting world by retiring from competition.[41]

Even as one sister-in-law continued her track and field career and the other made millions in endorsement money, the issue of steroid use in the sport would not go away, as two fellow U.S. track athletes and one coach implicated the first family of track. The first allegation occurred in April 1989 when Olympic medalist and coach Patricia Connolly and Olympic gold medalist Evelyn Ashford testified before a Senate investigation into the use of steroids in sport. Connolly had been involved in women's sport since her competition days alongside Wilma Rudolph in the early 1960s. Ashford was the black athlete whose 100-meter world record of 10.76 seconds Griffith Joyner had so soundly eclipsed. Without naming names during testimony, Ashford insisted that two gold medalists from the 1988 women's track and field team had used steroids. During her testimony, Connolly introduced two pictures of an athlete from a recent issue of the West German magazine *Stern*, one photo from 1984 and one from 1988. Chairman Joseph Biden thought that the pictures depicted two different athletes, but Connolly insisted that they were photographs of the same person, depicting the "before" and "after" physical effects of steroid use. While the testimony only revealed the athlete as one that Ashford had trained and performed baton passes with in relays, the *Washington Post* identified the photos as Griffith Joyner. The second and more damning accusation came from former U.S. sprinter Darrell Robinson. In September 1989, Robinson told the press that Griffith Joyner had purchased a banned substance from him several months before the Seoul games. According to Robinson, the female sprinter paid him $2,000 for some human growth hormones in early 1988, remarking that "when you want to make a million dollars, you have to invest a couple of thousand." He also told the media that Bobby Kersee had asked him what anabolic steroids he was on, noting that "his people" took the same thing. Twice, Robinson said, Kersee gave him a bottle of pills while he was dining with the Kersees in their home. Given all their success, the Kersee/Joyner foursome was clearly a ripe target in a sport now rife with finger pointing and suspicion.[42]

Amid the accusations, innuendo, comments, and testimony, there was never any evidence to confirm one way or the other whether the Kersees or Joyners ever took or distributed anabolic steroids. On the one hand, Joyner-Kersee, along with other athletes, was subjected to random testing throughout the remainder of her career and never failed a drug test. On the other, there was no drug test in the direct aftermath of the 1988 Olympics that could detect the presence of human growth hormones. Moreover, there was at least one case in which an athlete taking anabolic steroids was not caught by testing. It remains the insistence of some athletes that the sisters-in-law did, against their own fervent denials.[43]

Regardless of whether Joyner-Kersee or Griffith Joyner's gold medals and world records were drug-aided or not, the more important issue remains the form the accusations against them took. It is an issue that is at once complicated and disturbing. In the Senate committee's investigation into the drug culture of sport, black female athlete Diane Williams, who admitted to taking anabolic steroids, discussed the changes her body underwent while doping—increased muscle mass, lowered voice, absence of a menstrual period, and increased facial hair—that more resembled those of a man than a woman.[44] Clearly the presence of performance-enhancing drugs in the sport, in general, and among black women athletes, in particular, made it a certainty that accusers would call attention to appearance and the alleged changes to bodies. The simple presence of the attention to perceived bodily contrasts, then, was at once troubling yet unavoidable, it would seem, given the nature of anabolic steroids. However, Joaquim's Cruz's specific allusions—calling Griffith Joyner more man than woman and Joyner-Kersee a gorilla—*were* avoidable. What was indeed disturbing was the manner in which his comments manifested themselves, calling American society back to stereotypes of black women athletes grounded in race and gender.

Conclusion

After Joyner-Kersee's disappointing withdrawal from Olympic heptathlon competition at the 1996 Atlanta games and her come-from-behind win of a bronze medal in the long jump competition, she made it clear that this was her last Olympics. But retirement from sport did not come easily. A little over a month following completion of the Olympic games, she signed a contract to play at least twenty-eight games of basketball with the Richmond Rage in the newly formed women's professional American Basketball League. The switch gave her an opportunity to lend her name and support to the new women's sport venture. It also gave her a much-needed break from the solo world of track and field competition and the enjoyment of once again competing as part of a team. She "struggled" through part of the season, discovering that the game had "passed her by." By February 1997, she was back on the track, running the 55-yard hurdles at the Chase Millrose games at Madison Square Garden. Even while playing basketball, she had kept her eye on the sport, still thinking she had it in her to break the world record for the long jump. By 1998, it was clear that another world record was not in the cards for the athlete who had competed at the world-class level for fourteen years. She did, however, manage one final moment of glory in July of that year when she won her final heptathlon at the Goodwill Games.[45] Her final long jump competition just three days later yielded only sixth place, but she was finally, at the age of thirty-six, retired. She now planned to work as a sports agent and marketing expert. She also wanted to head a charitable foundation aimed at helping children in East St. Louis, a cause she had been involved in since her athletic success at the 1988 Olympics.[46]

A JACKIE OF ALL TRADES

Her sister-in-law had gone on to make millions through endorsement contracts while also dealing with the many fan letters she received in the aftermath of her historic performance at the Seoul games. She did some acting, appearing in several TV series. There was talk of a film contract in which she would portray a female James Bond-style character. LIN toys came out with a FloJo doll, complete with press-on decal nails, hair that could be styled and, of course, a one-legged sprint suit. A dozen Griffith Joyner-designed outfits could be purchased separately. She also went on to design uniforms for the NBA's Indiana Pacers and serve as co-chair to the President's Council on Physical Fitness. In 1990, she and her husband, Al Joyner, had a daughter, whom they named Mary after Al and Jackie's mother. But two months after Joyner-Kersee retired in July 1998, the sports world was rocked by other news. Griffith-Joyner, who had suffered sporadically from grand-mal seizures, had died in her sleep when she suffocated from an epileptic seizure. She was thirty-eight years old, just a year older than Mary Joyner had been when she died.[47]

As Americans who had watched Griffith Joyner seemingly defy the odds in Seoul struggled to come to terms with her death, issues of her special style, wind-aided records, and performance-enhancing drugs all resurfaced. "To some," wrote Jere Longman of the *New York Times*, "Griffith Joyner has come more to symbolize Roger Maris than Babe Ruth, and her accomplishments carry both literal and figurative asterisks."[48] The specter of performance-enhancing drugs had continued to haunt her over the years as some people questioned whether steroid use contributed to her stunning performances in Seoul. "I think, for Florence," remarked Evelyn Ashford upon her teammate and competitor's death, "the drug issue will always come up, whether she did it or not." Others were more caught up with whether the world record she set for the 100-meter sprint at the Olympic trials had been the result of an unrecorded trailing wind that should have, in reality, invalidated the record. The literal asterisk that Longman referred to in his article was a recognition by the International Amateur Athletics Foundation, the world governing body for the sport, that the controversy would not die—their statistics manual eventually appended an asterisk to Griffith Joyner's record with the remarks, "probably strongly wind assisted." Her records in both the 100- and 200-meter sprints remain unbroken. The majority of the obituaries and appreciation feature articles, however, remembered the sensation that "FloJo" had created with her colorful, one-legged track suits; long, painted nails; and flowing hair.[49]

That so much of the focus on Griffith Joyner, both in life and death, centered around her image was probably inevitable given her own flamboyant personal style. It was a style that combined strength, speed, and sexuality. It was a style that controlled and deployed a stereotype for her own purposes. It was a style that captured the popular imagination because it was embedded in the history of black women athletes' place and presence in American society. The result was, despite the public's adoration of their beloved "FloJo," that it did not matter whether the press was discussing steroids or fashion. The talk placed more emphasis on her body and the way she *looked* when she ran than on athletic issues. And as the specter of performance-enhancing drugs loomed large, more comments centered on her increasing bulk than on her decreasing times. It seemed more important to the American public and athletes alike that she looked "more like a man" than that her times were so much more unbelievably fast. For those who refused to believe the rumors, their language articulates the way she used old stereotypes to forge an image all her own:

> Close your eyes and speak her stage name: Flo-Jo. An image forms in the mind. She's running impossibly fast, drawing clear from others in the race while wearing a uniform that's the child of Nike and Victoria's Secret. Her long nails rake the air in abrupt, efficient strokes, and her raven hair trails behind her. At the finish, an expressionless face suddenly beams. It's a picture of speed and beauty and joy, and, once witnessed, it's unforgettable.[50]

When Jere Longman wrote in his obituary of the sprint star that she had "*revolutionized* women's sprinting with her searing speed and flamboyant fashion," he was clearly not thinking of the sensation created when Wilma Rudolph ran with her "long gams" and "blazing speed." But in truth, Griffith Joyner's image was not only unforgettable but also grounded in the past.

The athlete who became known as "wonder woman," "superwoman," and "the world's greatest female athlete" had her own strategy for handling society's continued concern with the masculinity of its women track athletes. The superlatives for Joyner-Kersee's career extended out almost indefinitely, and, for a while, it seemed that Americans would accept her on these terms. Perhaps it would work for her to be "all athlete" on the track and field as long as she reassured the public that she was all woman, with "a figure that would make a chorus line," off of it. Upon her retirement, sportswriters lauded Joyner-Kersee's path-breaking career, noting that she had "helped make it cool for girls to play boys' games and play them hard." Her "greatest achievement," wrote Longman, "was that she helped make it O.K. for women to sweat."[51] Controversy could quickly raise the specter of not only gender but also race, reminding people that "the world's greatest female athlete" was, indeed, a *black* woman athlete. And when Griffith Joyner began her rapid ascent to the top, it became clear that African American woman still lived in a society that preferred that, at least for its athletes, the two personas not be separate. For Americans, a glamorous sprinter was still much more enticing than a "wonder woman" who thought it was all right for people to watch her sweat on the field, even if she was willing to put on her lipstick off of it. Regardless of the stereotypes that sportswriters or Brazilian track athletes continued to invoke, however, Joyner-Kersee found her own way to become the "world's greatest female athlete."

Performance-Enhanced Athletes and "Ghetto Cinderellas"

Black Women Athletes Enter the Twenty-First Century

By the time Jackie Joyner-Kersee approached her fourth Olympic games in 1996, black women athletes had been involved in athletic competition in some form or another for close to eighty years. During that time, they had pushed back against stereotypes that suggested they should not compete, and they had embraced images and opportunities created for them so they could. They had been aided by an expansive black community, and coaches and mentors who dedicated their lives to making it possible for black women to train and compete in tennis, basketball, and track and field. Sometimes the community expected things of these women that they were hesitant, even unwilling, to give, particularly as they determined their place in an increasingly active civil rights movement. For many years they had to find ways to integrate themselves into a white sporting world that, for the most part, did not want them. But at times they found unexpected help in that world that meant the continuation of a career. They had, in short, found it necessary for many of those years to come to terms with what it meant to be *black* women athletes both in the African American community and white society, negotiating issues of race, gender, and class in both places.

As black women approached the twenty-first century, their stories reflected change, but also some strikingly familiar concerns. The world of track and field and its athletes continued to grapple with the over-whelming presence of performance-enhancing drugs. In a sport where accusation as much as testing continued to link athletes' names with steroids, black women track athletes, particularly Gail Devers, Gwen Torrence, and Marion Jones, continued to be front and center. Stereotypes continued to plague the athletes and they discovered new methods to battle them. Yet the ways that their intersection with drugs and innuendo manifested itself and went public differed prominently from their predecessors. After forty years of waiting for another African American woman to take up where Althea Gibson left off, Venus and Serena Williams produced not one but two black women champions. Their race and working-class background combined to indicate that these categories were still very much a part of the world in which they operated, in ways both similar to and different from Washington and Gibson. In short, the record on the changes that have occurred to black women in sport in the aftermath of Joyner-Kersee's career is, to say the least, mixed.

Running Clean?—"The Specter of Illicit Drug Use" and Black Women Athletes

As Joyner-Kersee was battling for her second consecutive Olympic gold in the heptathlon at the 1992 Barcelona games, another drama was play-ing out in the 100-meter sprint. Gwen Torrence, an Atlanta native who competed at the University of Georgia in the 1980s on full scholarship, had won the Olympic trials and was expected to take the gold in Barcelona. But Gail Devers, another Bob Kersee product, could not be ruled out. She had come in second at the trials, and while she had not been particularly close to Torrence's first-place finish, over a month had elapsed. With Kersee breathing down Devers's neck to get in as much training as possible before the games, the race was far from a given.

Gail Devers's story had already been a dramatic one. In June 1988, Devers was a senior at UCLA under Kersee's tutelage. She had qualified for the Olympic trials in four events—the 100- and 200-meter sprints, 100-meter hurdles, and long jump. She chose to concentrate on the 100-meter events and made the Olympic team in both the sprint and hurdles. But in Seoul, she completely fell apart. Not only did she not medal in either of her events, she failed to make the finals. Following numerous tests to account for the seemingly inexplicable decline, doctors finally diagnosed her with Graves' disease, a hyperthyroid condition that had resulted in wild weight fluctuations, the loss of vision in her left eye, uncontrollable shaking and heavy, almost constant menstrual cycles. Fortunately, the condition could be controlled with medication; unfortunately, Devers refused to take it because it was on the IOC's banned substances list. Instead, she chose an alterative regimen, radiation. Slowly, those treatments started to eat away at other tissue in her body. Her feet began to swell and ooze a yellow fluid, and her skin developed small holes. Eventually, her feet could not bear her weight. Once again it took doctors considerable time to diagnose the cause. Finally, in March 1991, they told her that she had experienced a violent reaction to the radiation. Her condition was so severe that the attending physician told Devers that if she had continued to try walking on her feet for two more days, he would have had to amputate. The doctor changed her Graves' therapy, and in about a month she was able to walk painfully in socks around the track at UCLA. She referred to it as her first workout in over two years. Not surprisingly, Kersee had her hurdling in May of that year, just two months after she found out what the radiation was doing to her body. She went on to win the 1991 national championship for the 100-meter hurdles and the silver medal at the world championships. Kersee then began retraining her for the 100-meter sprint, and she qualified for the 1992 Barcelona games in both sprint and hurdle events. Before she prepared to run the sprint final in Barcelona, Jackie Joyner-Kersee remarked to her friend: "You worked hard for this. ... You better get it." When she crossed the finish line 10.82 seconds later, she had gotten it, but by the slimmest of margins. The finish was so close that officials had to examine the replay of the race to determine that Devers had indeed won. The woman who had nearly had to have her feet amputated had just won Olympic gold.[1]

It did not take long for the accusations to begin and when they did, they came from Torrence. Two of the top three finishers, she claimed, were not clean. But the story seemed to change almost hourly. Sprinter Juliet Cuthbert, the race's silver medalist, said Torrence had named names to her. Torrence denied having done so. In one version of the story, Torrence said she was not implicating Devers; in others she apparently was. On one day, Torrence talked as if she was in Devers's corner, insisting that her competitor had won the medal fairly and that she hoped Devers "comes back and whips their butts in the hurdles." Five days later, she was quoted as saying that she and Devers had "never been friends" and she could not help it if Devers was angry over her comments. Torrence eventually apologized for her "unproven allegation." The damage had been done though. Was there reason to suspect someone like Gail Devers, queried the *Wall Street Journal*? "There is reason to suspect every athlete," responded a veteran track fan. "That pervasive suspicion," concluded reporter Roger Lowenstein, "may be as vexing a problem as actual cheating. How, after all, does one prove innocence?"[2] Black women track athletes were once again in the thick of the innuendo and suspicion created by this performance-enhanced sport, but two important things had changed. There was no insinuation that Devers was taking steroids because she looked a certain way. And instead of just being on the receiving end of the accusations, black women athletes were also making them. There was no evidence that Devers had done anything wrong, and she had never failed a drug test. It was all just suspicion on Torrence's part, and probably a case of the disappointment of losing.

In the end, it was Torrence whose image suffered most in the media, particularly in the black press, as her hometown African American paper took her to task. Sportswriter Mark Gray of the *Atlanta Daily World* chose Torrence's "moment of glory" to hold her accountable for the remarks against her teammate. After she went on to win the 200 meter, Gray congratulated the Atlanta sprinter on her gold medal. But he felt that her win had been tainted by the "crude and callous remarks" she had made after her disappointing second-place finish in the 100-meter final. Torrence had come in the favorite to repeat Rudolph and Griffith Joyner's doubles in the sprints. But the nature of sport was, Gray noted, that on any given day and in any given race, anyone could take the victory. Failing to accept this in a display of "sour grapes" had diminished her stature as a champion. "Don't," Gray concluded, "look for her on the cover of a cereal box."[3] Similar to its relationship with Althea Gibson, the black press continued to guide black women athletes, reprimanding them when sportswriters felt the athletes' mouths got the better of them. The difference was that Torrence seemed to have brought the scolding on herself. The black press may not have thought Torrence the right athlete to represent black America. Yet the fact that she and Devers could have their disagreement publicly speaks to the changes that had occurred since the days when black women track athletes worried about how they presented themselves to the public.

Both Devers and Torrence went on to compete in the 1996 Atlanta games. Torrence was hoping to finally capture a gold in the 100 meters, especially at home in Atlanta. But it was not to be. Devers defended her title in another photo finish, duplicating Tyus's back-to-back wins from the 1960s. Torrence came into the race as the reigning world champion, so once again there was disappointment when she took home the bronze medal. She had suffered an injury at the Olympic trials, so perhaps she was just happy to have medaled. Devers had her own disappointment as well, failing to ever medal in the event she had been expected to win all along, the 100-meter hurdles. For whatever reason, though, Torrence had finally left the theatrics and finger pointing behind. "The much anticipated feud between Devers and Torrence didn't occur as both women hugged and took a lap around the track together, all the while laughing, smiling, and shedding tears of happiness," observed the *Atlanta Daily World*. The black press seemed pleased that African American women were, once again, "sisters" on the track.[4]

While track and field still languished in its performance-enhanced state, it seemed that a new, young, African American talent with the right image might help "rescue" the sport from itself. In 2000, Marion Jones showed promise. She broke onto the scene even before Joyner-Kersee exited, but it wasn't until the 2000 Sydney games that she showed the maturity and speed to possibly duplicate the multiple-medal haul that Rudolph, Joyner-Kersee, and Griffith Joyner had taken in a single Olympics. She was not shy about her talents. In the lead-up to the Olympic trials, she let it be known that she intended on competing in five events in Sydney, and she intended on bringing home five gold medals. Just as importantly for trying to repair the sport's tarnished image, she had the looks that American sportswriters and the public liked when it came to women track athletes. She was lovely and wholesome looking, "with golden-brown skin, long eyelashes," and a fetching smile. She had, noted Thomas Hackett of the *New York Times*, burst onto the scene as not only a "radiant diva" but also "the wholesome redeemer of a sport tainted by performance-enhancing drugs." She was, thought sportswriters in the lead-up to the trials, the real deal.[5]

The feminine stereotype that Temple concocted for his athletes had persisted. Yet Jones also had a way of rejecting it that empowered her own image. Her self-assuredness, even cockiness, embodied strength while her smile took off the harsh edges, endearing her to the public and to reporters that covered her sport. It even seemed as if Americans were finally "getting" that this was a new day. As Hackett watched her during her warm-ups in May 2000, he observed that Jones was working to take over top billing in the sport—"not as an adorably cute pixie desperate to please her bearish coach but as an athlete with as much swagger in her step as any man." Before the article concluded, however, it was clear that sportswriters were still working to present such bravado as something more akin to the sexualized image of a previous period. As Jones began her workout, she passed several male athletes that were finishing up their training on the track. She good-naturedly taunted them that the workout was just beginning and they had to pay their dues. The exchange struck Hackett as somehow "symbolic"—"the unattainable woman, cheekily goading tired men in mad pursuit."[6] To the reporter, the moment may have seemed symbolic, but the allusion was not. It was, given the history of black women athletes, not so much a turning point as a familiar image in want of the right athlete.

Jones entered the Olympic trials and the Olympic games as the golden girl of women's track and field, full of confidence and promise; however, the dream quickly unraveled. At the trials, she qualified for all three individual events she told reporters she would—the 100- and 200-meter sprints and the long jump—and she was running a fast-enough 400-meter time to indicate that she would probably be part of both the 4x400- and 4x100-meter relay teams. Once in Sydney, she easily won her first event, the 100-meter sprint. But just two days later her shot-putter husband, C. J. Hunter, tested positive for steroids. As Jones appeared with Hunter at his press conferences, Hunter denied the charges. Though reporters observed that she had "stood by her man," some felt her radiant image was now tainted by inference: "How does anyone who saw in Jones the quintessential American star and our savior of these Games when she won the 100 meters last Saturday night take a second look when she returns to the track tomorrow without noticing a little bloom off the rose?" At the same time, though, they cautioned the sporting world to remember that she was innocent until proven guilty.

Even as whispers continued around the track world, fellow Olympians, reporters, and the public had treated her far less stridently than they had the Joyner sisters-in-law under circumstances that were not as close to home as Jones's.[7]

In the midst of the sport's latest steroid drama, Jones continued her quest for five gold medals with her own feminine brand of self-confidence. Competing in her remaining four events, she medaled in each. While two of the medals turned out to be bronze rather than the gold she had predicted, she returned home from the Sydney games still very much the "darling of the games." Oprah Winfrey welcomed her as a guest on her daytime television show, one of Jones's many appearances. When she appeared on the cover of *Vogue* in a strapless white dress, it transformed her "hard edges," noted reporter Juliet Macur, into glamour. She seemed to have combined the images of "Jackie" and "FloJo" into one. Like Joyner-Kersee, she had two personas. She was all seriousness on the track and field but allowed her feminine side to show off it. And like Griffith Joyner, she had "transcended sports," becoming more than just an athlete.[8]

However, accusations and innuendo regarding performance-enhancing drugs continued to hound her, and she spent much of 2003 and 2004 repeatedly denying that she was using steroids. When ex-husband Hunter told reporters that Jones had used drugs back in 2000, her attorney suggested that Hunter was merely vindictive over their divorce. Amid all the drug controversy, she continued her career. But despite the fact that she had never been proven guilty of using, the bloom was truly now off the rose. She was no longer the favorite she had been at the dawn of the new century. In the summer of the 2004 games, she came into the Olympic trials to compete in both sprints. When she failed to qualify in the 100 meters, she withdrew from the 200.[9]

In October 2007, the careful edifice she had erected over the years finally came tumbling down when she entered a guilty plea for lying to federal investigators in 2003. She acknowledged that she had unwittingly taken THG, an "undetectable designer steroid" also known as "the clear," beginning in 1999 in the lead-up to the 2000 Olympics. She said she lied to protect herself and her coach, Trevor Graham, who had given her the substance, telling her that it was flaxseed oil. After she stopped training with him in 2001, she realized it had been a performance-enhancing drug. The consequences were swift and strident. The IOC stripped her of her medals and struck her name from the Olympic record. The public reaction, however, was less harsh. More than anything, reporters seemed sad, mostly because they believed that she could have won her medals without the drugs. She had dominated in the sprint and been competitive in the long jump long before her admitted drug use. She had seemed the perfect image to transform the sport, sportswriters had thought, with an athletic talent that came in "such an appealing package." Her "luminescent smile" and "charming personality" had contributed into turning her into "a mainstream star."[10] Yet it had also helped soften what may have otherwise been interpreted as just plain showmanship and boastfulness, a strategy that enabled her to push back against the feminine stereotype still in play at the dawn of the new century. Moreover, Jones had fallen far, but despite that, the public still wanted to adore her. Almost twenty years after the accusations against Joyner-Kersee and Griffith Joyner in Seoul, Jones would make it through seven years of drug accusations and an eventual confession without being likened to a gorilla. Black women track athletes at the turn of the millennium continued battling some stereotypes while others seemed to be mercifully abating. In the midst of the Marion Jones's drug revelations, however, the experience of two black women tennis players reflected the experiences of their predecessors in familiar and changing ways.

"Ghetto Cinderellas"— Venus and Serena Williams

While Althea Gibson's breaking of the USLTA color barrier in 1950 was hailed as a historic opening for African Americans, few women have followed in her footsteps. By the 1990s, Leslie Allen had retired, while Zina Garrison, Katrina Adams, and Lori McNeil were still on the tour. Though competing at the top level, none of these players had won a major Grand Slam tournament. Then in 1997, Venus Williams entered the professional tour; one year later, her sister Serena joined her. They quite literally burst onto the tennis scene. By 1998, they were each winning mixed doubles Grand Slam titles. Their first women's doubles Grand Slam titles came the following year, in both the French and U.S. Open. The same year, Serena won the singles title at the U.S. Open. Following directly in Gibson's path, Venus won back-to-back Wimbledon and U.S. Open titles in 2000 and

2001. In 2002, it was her sister's turn to win both championships; in 2003, Serena followed it up by defending in the U.S. Open. Since joining the circuit, their Grand Slam championships to date include twenty-two singles and twelve doubles titles. They have each won four Olympic gold medals—one for singles competition and three for doubles. It is as if they have been bent on making up for lost time since Gibson retired.[11]

Growing up in the poor African American neighborhood of Compton, California, the two sisters' background closely paralleled that of Althea Gibson's. Whereas the black community worked to gentrify Gibson, however, the Williams sisters have embraced their working-class background. In their early years on the circuit, Richard Williams, their father and coach, perpetuated the image of their working-class roots. Williams chose to raise his daughters in Compton because he felt they would grow up learning to handle responsibility. But he also liked the comparisons with certain "great champions" of sport—Larry Bird, Michael Jordan, and Magic Johnson—who had all come from poor beginnings. From the time the older Venus was ten, he began proudly referring to her as a "ghetto Cinderella." When she left the junior field for the professional women's tour, sportswriters picked up on the connection. Their feature articles routinely referred to the "gang-infested public courts" where she learned the game. Even as Richard Williams had thought growing up in the ghetto would teach his daughters responsibility, John Gardner of the *Daily Record* thought it would help quell the fears of Venus's first Wimbledon tournament. She had, after all, been brought up in a world of "drugs and violence in one of California's meanest ghettos," having to dodge bullets even as she tried to train. In the more than fifty years since Gibson had broken the color barrier in white tennis, there was a striking evolution in the acceptability of acknowledging one's humble, even violent background. Billie Jean King had already broken down some of the barriers related to entering the sport with a working-class label. Yet the Williamses embraced and flaunted the image as a badge of honor in ways markedly different from either Gibson or King. However, at times this image has cut another way, sounding remarkably similar to comments competitors made about both Gibson and her predecessor Ora Washington. Competitor Jana Novotna, referring to Venus in 1997, told reporters that "somebody should be there to tell you how to behave, who to say hello to, manners." Regardless of Novotna and other players' denials that their comments contained any racial meaning, most sportswriters and commentators argued that there were cultural roots embedded in them. Indeed, her reference to manners and knowing how to behave suggested, if not racism as she refuted, then the notion that being from a working-class background made a difference, at least in the high-class world of tennis.[12]

While Novotna denied that her comments had anything to do with race, racism was indeed lurking. As Venus Williams came onto the circuit and became successful, it surfaced. Darrell Fry of the *St. Petersburg* [Florida] *Times* argued that WTA officials and players as well as the media were handling the presence of an African American player on the tour about as well as "an elephant being led through a china shop." Early on, the criticisms of Williams included that she was unfriendly, did not speak to her opponents, and did not fraternize with them; in short, she had an "attitude." These were accusations that were reminiscent of those the black press leveled at Gibson, but this time they came from white competitors. While the players who leveled the accusations at her insisted that there was no racism behind their comments, the other African American players observed that they had no trouble getting along with the newest member on the tour. Fry defended Williams by suggesting that she seemed strange or aloof to the other players because they expected her to fit comfortably in a world she was unaccustomed to. She had, he asked tour members to remember, grown up in Compton, "a predominantly black and widely impoverished area outside Los Angeles." Once again, the image of "ghetto Cinderella" that Richard Williams had embraced for his daughters had cut a different way than he intended.[13]

No invectives against the Williamses have been infused with as much racism, however, as the incident at the 2001 Masters Tournament at Indian Wells, California. The two sisters were scheduled to play each other in the semifinal match, and their match-ups were always greeted with much interest and hype by tennis fans. While news reports indicated that Venus pulled out of the match at the last minute with an injury, Serena provided a different account in her autobiography. The elder Williams sister was experiencing tendonitis in her knee the afternoon before the match, but chose to see how she was feeling the following day. When she arrived the next morning for the match, it was clear to her that she could not play, and she told officials so. However, tournament officials, not wanting to cancel the match-up and disappoint the fans, kept deferring an announcement, hoping that she would change her mind. Finally, they announced the match's cancellation just minutes before it was scheduled to begin, infuriating the crowd. The following day, eighteen-year-old Serena played Kim Clijsters, another relative newcomer to the tour, in the tournament final. When Williams entered the court, the vast majority of the crowd greeted her with resounding boos, including the racial epithet, "Nigger," and told her to go back to Compton. Her father and sister received the same treatment when they entered the stands, and Richard Williams indicated that he heard some people yell that they wished it were 1975 so that they could "skin him alive." Most of the crowd, which Serena characterized as "rich, white and old," felt that their father had pulled Venus out because he routinely chose which sister would make it to the finals, or win. The crowd's treatment of the Williams family continued throughout the match—which Williams won in three sets—although things did subside a little toward the end. While tournament director Charles Pasarell told reporters that he was cringing during the incident, his own comments cast doubt on some of the more vituperative remarks by the crowd: "If Richard says someone yelled something, maybe they did," Pasarell told reporters, "but I know that's not Indian Wells people." Tournament officials did nothing to halt the crowd's derisive treatment of the Williamses nor correct the view that Venus had pulled out of the semifinal just moments before the match was set to begin. The two sisters have refused to return to the tournament in the intervening years.[14]

What caused the overwhelmingly strong reaction against the Williamses at Indian Wells? Was this an undercurrent of racism run amok? Perhaps, but what the Williamses experienced at the 2001 tournament also echoes back to what it meant to be a *black* woman athlete through much of the twentieth century. Race had made their experience of sport different from white women athletes. It continued to be a factor in the new century. And when African American women's race was combined with an open embrace of a rough background, it seemed to be especially unsettling. A *Newsweek* article published the year following the Indian Wells tournament abounded with the stereotypes that had followed black women athletes out of the African American community, images that sometimes stood in stark contrast to one another. The Williams sisters had grabbed the attention of both fanatics and casual fans, the authors noted, "with their muscular, superconfident style and their peculiar path to success." Of course, they could not help but stand out as "two strong African-American women in a country-club sport. But what sets them apart goes deeper than race, raw talent or even their multicolor hair beads." They were raised on the "mean streets" of Compton and have shaken off the conventional, elite tennis protocol by "skipping tournaments, picking fights and wrapping themselves in the cocoon of their protective family." But their power and expertise on the courts were not to be denied. Venus had served faster than any other woman in the history of the game, even faster than many men. As for Serena, she was "so muscular that the crowd sometimes whistles when she takes off her warm-up jacket to reveal her sculpted shoulders." Tennis fans, in ways similar to track fans, may have whistled at and adored her. Her competition's remarks were not so "flattering," however. American tennis legend Chris Evert noted that both sisters' athletic ability and raw aggression made it hard for "the women who aren't 'Amazons' to compete with them."[15]

Women athletes had developed strategies to confront notions of aggression and power as they competed in sport through much of the twentieth century. In the twenty-first, Americans continue to seem unsure as to whether they find such attributes acceptable. The crowd may whistle at Serena Williams's muscular shoulders and warm to Marion Jones's male-like swagger, but there have also been claims of unfair Amazonian advantage. When images of masculine athletic strength are conflated with race, the vitriol thrown at African American women athletes has been particularly biting. Even before Don Imus's now infamous remarks about the Rutgers's women's basketball team, the outspoken, though popular, talk-show radio host was taking on the Williamses. Confessing to Josh Young of the *Washington Times* that he didn't like Venus Williams, "I'm just sick of her and her father," he elaborated to the reporter. "It's not a race [thing]. She just needs to lighten up." Not a race thing? His comments on the Rutgers's basketball team in April 2007 would seem to suggest otherwise: "That's some rough girls from Rutgers. Man, they got tattoos," Imus remarked to his executive producer, Bernard McGuirk. "Some hardcore ho's," McGuirk agreed, taking the image a step farther. Not only did Imus not disagree, he took the image even further when he responded, "That's some nappy-headed ho's there, I'm going to tell you that." Strong, powerful, black women athletes were not just Amazons or muscular beauties now; in the hard-biting, traditionally working-class sport of basketball, they became "nappy-headed ho's."[16] The confluence of race, class, and gender that surrounded black women in sport during much of the twentieth century remains, invoking similar and revised images on the athletes in today's mainstream society.

Beyond the personal enjoyment and affirmation of participating and winning in competition, the central reason that African American women had entered competitive sport in the first place during the twentieth century was for a personal form of betterment. Beginning in the late 1930s, sport became a new avenue to competition and athletic glory, yes, but more important, to a college education and the possibility of a life better than many women would otherwise have known. African American women athletes had understood this; their mentors had known it as well. Cleve Abbott had arranged for Coachman to come to Tuskegee High School and Institute probably in the single manner she ever would have attended—through their work-study program, the only type of athletic "scholarship" that existed at that time. Hubert Eaton and Robert Johnson had repeatedly urged Gibson not to let anything derail the completion of her college education, even opportunities to compete in USLTA and international tennis tournaments. Ed Temple was every bit as proud of his athletes' college degrees as he was of their Olympic and national championships. And Nino Fennoy counseled Joyner-Kersee that a college education was vastly more important than winning long jump competitions.

As they focused on bettering their individual lives, they found ways to challenge existing stereotypes and forge a place in American society for African American women interested in competitive sport. In the case of Washington, Coachman, and Gibson, they boldly rejected the stereotypes, playing the sports they chose, how they wanted, despite how the press or public—black or white—might perceive their participation. Other athletes, like Rudolph and Tyus, embraced stereotypes related to their femininity in order to push back against those who grounded them in masculinity. Still others like Joyner-Kersee and Griffith Joyner manipulated these same gender stereotypes to their advantage. When black women athletes confronted segregation and efforts to end it, they negotiated their positions in the civil rights movement. In the process, they sometimes came head-to-head with those in the black community who had supported and sustained their careers, or found a voice that was appropriate to their particular place, time, and history.

Black women athletes have entered the twenty-first century accompanied by a complicated history. On the one hand, they found ways to overcome the boundaries of gender, race, and class to do what they loved—compete in sport. During the last part of the twentieth century up to the present, new opportunities have continued to present themselves. Anita DeFrantz, an Olympic rower with the 1976 U.S. Olympic team, currently serves as a member of the International Olympic Committee. Debi Thomas was the U.S. National Figure Skating Champion in 1986 and 1988, and in 1986 became the first African American woman to win a world championship in singles competition. Dominique Dawes competed in three Olympic games from 1992 through 2000, winning a total of five medals. She became the first African American woman to win Olympic gold in gymnastics when she was part of the gold-medal-winning U.S. team in 1996. And at the London Olympics in 2012, Gabby Douglas became the first African American to become the individual all-around gold medal champion in gymnastics. Despite these isolated breakthroughs, African American women still flock largely to track and field and basketball, sports whose access make them more practical for most black women without the resources to train in more expensive sports. Fortunately, with the WNBA remaining a viable entity, both of these sports now provide career opportunities for exceptional athletes after college. On the other hand, even as the athletes overcame boundaries of gender, race, and class, American conceptions of these categories meant that stereotypes have continued to surface. Some of these stereotypes have abated since the performance-enhancing drug era in track has shifted away from trying to "prove," by how they look, that the athletes are taking steroids. But others, built around longstanding racism, live on. In the wake of Gabby Douglas's gold-medal performance at the 2012 Olympics, the topic of her hair erupted over social media and talk shows. As the Twitter universe asked in a huff, "Why hasn't anyone tried to fix Gabby Douglas' hair?" bloggers questioned whether the public really wanted her to spend the night before the final competition with "a hot comb and some lye."[17] Clearly, appearances remain important.

Yet these athletes continue to successfully employ strategies to subvert such images. Venus and Serena Williams are classic examples of this, exhibiting the strength and ownership black women exert in relationship to athletic endeavors. Their economic success on and off the tennis court has ensured that, once they retire from the sport, they will not encounter the financial difficulties of many of their predecessors. Moreover, their strategy of conflating fashion and power, so like that of Florence Griffith Joyner, has allowed them to move beyond the more critical tennis establishment and establish a fan base with the general public. When they first came onto the tour, they brought with them a fashion all their own with hair beads and brightly colored tennis outfits, attracting attention from sportswriters and fans alike. Over the years, outfits like Serena's black catsuit and Venus's knee-length black tennis "boots," denim miniskirt, and black crop-top made headlines even as the sisters ruled the Grand Slam circuit, indicating they would reject dominant stereotypes and craft an image for themselves that was all their own. Then in 2007, Venus opened her own clothing line, EleVen, featuring both on- and off-the-court apparel. Since that time, she has designed all of her own tennis attire, ranging from purple/turquoise tie-dye and white open-back lace-up tennis dresses, to a black-lace corset tennis dress with red piping and skin-colored shorts.[18] Her and her sister's ability to push against bounds of the traditional white tennis dress coupled with their power on the court clearly reflect the strong legacy of their twentieth-century predecessors. African American women athletes of the twenty-first century refuse to be defined or limited by the stereotypes that have accompanied them into this century. It is in this regard that they most resemble the women who came before them.

INTRODUCTION

1. The African American *Pittsburgh Courier* provided the description of Coachman's 1941 high jump victory. "Tuskegee Lassie Goes Up and Over to Retain Title," *Pittsburgh Courier*, 29 July 1941, 16.

2. Coachman's married name is Davis. Alice Coachman Davis, Interview by author, tape recording, Tuskegee, Alabama, 10 February 2003.

3. Many scholars have already explored women athletes' navigation of such stereotypes. Susan K. Cahn, *Coming on Strong: Gender and Sexuality in Twentieth-Century Women's Sport* (New York: Free Press, 1994), is the seminal book-length study into femininity/sexuality, class, and women in sport, and its insights remain extremely relevant. Other important works include Gwendolyn Captain, "Enter Ladies and Gentlemen of Color: Gender, Sport, and the Ideal of the African American Manhood and Womanhood During the Late Nineteenth Centuries," *Journal of Sport History* 18 (Spring 1991): 81–102; Mary Jo Festle, *Playing Nice: Politics and Apologies in Women's Sports* (New York: Columbia University Press, 1996); Cindy Himes Gissendanner, "African-American Women in Competitive Sport, 1920–1960," in *Women, Sport, and Culture*, ed. Susan Birrell and Cheryl L. Cole (Champaign, IL: Human Kinetics, 1994); Gissendanner, "African American Women Olympians: The Impact of Race, Gender, and Class Ideologies, 1932–1968," *Research Quarterly for Exercise and Sport* 67 (June 1996): 172–82; Patricia Vertinsky and Gwendolyn Captain, "More Myth Than History: American Culture and Representations of the Black Female's Athletic Ability," *Journal of Sport History* 25 (Fall 1998): 532–61; Rita Liberti, "'We Were Ladies, We Just Played Basketball Like Boys': African American Womanhood and Competitive Basketball at Bennett College, 1928–1942," *Journal of Sport History* 26 (Fall 1999): 567–84; Pamela Grundy and Susan Shackelford, "Black Women Embrace the Game," in *Shattering the Glass: The Remarkable History of Women's Basketball* (Chapel Hill: University of North Carolina Press, 2005); Martha Verbrugge, *Active Bodies: A History of Women's Physical Education in Twentieth-Century America* (Oxford: Oxford University Press, 2012).

4. While the work of many theoretical scholars has been transformed by what Kimberlé Crenshaw called the intersectionality of race, class, and gender, my own approach is grounded less in theory and more in historical analysis and narrative. Kimberlé Crenshaw, "Mapping the Margins: Intersectionality, Identity Politics, and Violence against Women of Color," *Stanford Law Review* 14 (1991): 1241–99. For a recent overview of the theory, see Michele Tracy Berger and Kathleen Guidroz, ed., *The Intersectional Approach: Transforming the Academy through Race, Class, and Gender* (Chapel Hill: University of North Carolina Press, 2009).

5. This narrative approach addresses the problem of limited sources, especially for the athletes who competed during the first half of the century. The black press began following women athletes within the black community as early as the 1920s, and, by mid-century, the white press was writing about them as well. However, the details that can be gleaned from the sports pages—scores, descriptions of games, matches, and track meets, and the names of players—often generate more questions than they answer. Where possible, interviews, personal papers, and autobiographies supplement the press accounts, yet oral and archival information are not abundant for "famous" athletes and virtually nonexistent for many women who competed against and alongside them.

6. Jacqueline Jones's monograph remains a valued overview of the work lives of black women. See Jacqueline Jones, *Labor of Love, Labor of Sorrow: Black Women, Work and the Family, From Slavery to the Present* (New York: Vintage Books, 1986).

ONE

1. Randy Dixon, "Ora Washington, E. Brown Cop Net Crowns," *Philadelphia Tribune*, 29 August 1929, 10. For Washington's strengths on the court, see Sam Lacy, "Althea Gibson Vs. Ora Washington for Women's All-Time," *Baltimore Afro-American*, 17 September 1953, 13.

2. Pamela Grundy argues Washington was the "first black female athletic star" in the African American community and, while I have paraphrased the title, I certainly concur. See Pamela Grundy, "Ora Washington: The First Black Female Athletic Star," in *Out of the Shadows: A Biographical History of African American Athletes*, ed. David K. Wiggins (Fayetteville: University of Arkansas Press, 2006), 78–92; "Bennett Cage Team Facing Two Games," *Greensboro Daily News*, 9 March 1934, 12.

3. For the preeminent work on the changing perceptions of gender and sexuality within women's sport, see Susan Cahn, *Coming on Strong: Gender and Sexuality in Twentieth-Century Women's Sport* (Cambridge, MA: Harvard University Press, 1994).

4. I am indebted to Pamela Grundy for sharing with me her interview of Washington's nephew, J. Bernard Childs, and for her previous research into Washington's background. See Grundy, "Ora Washington: The First Black Female Athletic Star," 78–92.

5. Because Virginia, still recovering from the financial setbacks of the Civil War, did not issue birth certificates from 1896 to 1912, the exact date of Washington's birth is unknown. Grundy, "Ora Washington: The First Black Female Athletic Star," 81. The age I use for the introductory paragraph is calculated from an age reference Washington makes to a sportswriter late in her career. See "Injury Forces Ora Out of Singles Play," *Baltimore Afro-American*, 9 August 1941, 20, in which Washington says she is forty.

6. Grundy, "Ora Washington: The First Black Female Athletic Star," 80–81; J. Bernard Childs, Interview by Pamela Grundy, Bowling Green, Virginia, 4 October 2003.

7. Grundy, "Ora Washington: The First Black Female Athletic Star," 81–82.

8. Literature on the Great Migration is vast, particularly in terms of the conflation of problems driving blacks north and the emergence of black communities in northern cities. Some important works include Peter Gottlieb, *Making Their Own*

Way: Southern Blacks' Migration to Pittsburgh, 1916–1930 (Urbana: University of Illinois Press, 1987); James R. Grossman, *Land of Hope: Chicago, Black Southerners, and the Great Migration* (Chicago: University of Chicago Press, 1989); Milton C. Sernett, *Bound for the Promised Land: African American Religion and the Great Migration* (Durham, NC: Duke University Press, 1997); Victoria W. Wolcott, *Remaking Respectability: African American Women in Interwar Detroit* (Chapel Hill: University of North Carolina Press, 2001); James N. Gregory, *The Southern Diaspora: How the Great Migration of Black and White Southerners Transformed America* (Chapel Hill: University of North Carolina Press, 2005); Davarian L. Baldwin, *Chicago's New Negroes: Modernity, the Great Migration, and Black Urban Life* (Chapel Hill: University of North Carolina Press, 2007); Lisa Krissoff Boehm, *Making a Way Out of No Way* (Jackson: University Press of Mississippi, 2009); and Isabel Wilkerson, *The Warmth of Other Suns: The Epic Story of America's Great Migration* (New York: Random House, 2010). In contrast to the more traditional narratives on the causes of black migration during this period, Steven Hahn places the movement into a long-standing African American social and political framework. See Steven Hahn, *A Nation Under Our Feet: Black Political Struggles in the Rural South from Slavery to the Great Migration* (Cambridge, MA: Belknap Press of Harvard University Press, 2003), 465–76.

9. The many artistic facets of the Harlem Renaissance have resulted in an extensive literature on the subject. For example, see Nathan Irvin Huggins, *Harlem Renaissance* (London: Oxford University Press, 1971); David Lewis Lettering, *When Harlem Was in Vogue* (New York: Alfred A. Knopf, 1981); Cary D. Wintz, *Black Culture and the Harlem Renaissance* (Houston: Rice University Press, 1988); George Hutchinson, *The Harlem Renaissance in Black and White* (Cambridge, MA: Belknap Press of Harvard University Press, 1995); Cheryl A. Wall, *Women of the Harlem Renaissance* (Bloomington: University of Indiana Press, 1995); J. Martin Favor, *Authentic Blackness: The Folk in the New Negro Renaissance* (Durham, NC: Duke University Press, 1999); and James F. Wilson, *Bulldaggers, Pansies, and Chocolate Babies: Performance, Race and Sexuality in the Harlem Renaissance* (Ann Arbor: University of Michigan Press, 2010).

10. Allen Guttmann, *Women's Sports: A History* (New York: Columbia University Press, 1991), 106, 112; Vassar Catalogue; quoted in Guttmann, *Women's Sports*, 113.

11. Guttmann, *Women's Sports*, 113–16. For more on the emergence of women's sports in the United States, also see Ellen W. Gerber et al., *The American Woman in Sport* (Reading, MA: Addison-Wesley Publishing Company, 1974).

12. Gerber et al., *The American Woman in Sport*, 124–25; Cahn, *Coming on Strong*, 14.

13. Cahn, *Coming on Strong*, 15–16.

14. Ibid., 17–18; Grundy, "Ora Washington: The First Black Female Athletic Star," 83.

15. Judith Weisenfeld, *African American Women and Christian Activism: New York's Black YWCA, 1905–1945* (Cambridge, MA: Harvard University Press, 1997), 3, 33–34, 157, 172–78.

16. Weisenfeld, *African American Women and Christian Activism*, 1, 89; Nancy Robertson, *Christian Sisterhood, Race Relations, and the YWCA, 1906–1946* (Urbana: University of Illinois Press, 2007), 2.

17. Stephanie Y. Felix, "Committed to Their Own: African American Women

Leaders in the YWCA. The YWCA of Germantown, Philadelphia, Pennsylvania, 1870–1970" (Ph.D. diss., Temple University, 1999), 66, 77, 82–85, 128–29.

18. Grundy, "Ora Washington: The First Black Female Athletic Star," 83; Childs interview, 4 October 2003.

19. While tennis has antecedents dating back to the Middle Ages, the version of tennis played today, modern lawn tennis, arose during the second half of the nineteenth century in England. Its migration to the United States, which occurred sometime in the 1870s, remains disputed, with at least four people having been credited with bringing the sport to American soil. Grace Lichtenstein, "Net Profits," in *Nike Is a Goddess: The History of Women in Sports*, ed. Lissa Smith (New York: Atlantic Monthly Press, 1998), 58–59; Sundiata Djata, *Blacks at the Net: Black Achievement in the History of Tennis*, Sports and Entertainment, ed. Steven A. Riess (Syracuse, NY: Syracuse University Press, 2006), 2–3. For more on the origins of modern lawn tennis and its history in Anglo-American societies, see E. Digby Baltzell, *Sporting Gentlemen: Men's Tennis from the Age of Honor to the Cult of the Superstar* (New York: Free Press, 1995).

20. Delegates at the organizing meeting determined that ATA membership could be acquired in one of three ways. First, local tennis associations, comprised of five or more clubs within a single state, could join as an association. Second, for those clubs without a local association, sectional tennis associations could be formed with five or more clubs in a geographical area of more than one state, as defined by the ATA. Finally, in a state or area where no local or sectional associations existed, individual tennis clubs with five or more members could be admitted as ATA members. The initial membership of the association comprised one local tennis association, New York, and twelve individual clubs. In 1928, the membership consisted of eleven associations, representing ninety-eight clubs, and an additional fifteen individual club memberships. American Tennis Association Revised Constitution, August 1951; American Tennis Association Executive Bulletin, No. 20, July 1957; and 1952 ATA National Interscholastic Championship program, Eaton papers, UNCW; "To Hold Big Tennis Games in Baltimore," *New York Age*, 28 June 1917, 6. For more on African Americans in tennis, and the early years of the ATA, see Djata, *Blacks at the Net*.

21. Jules Tygiel, *Past Time: Baseball as History* (Oxford: Oxford University Press, 2000), 72–73, 77–79; Cahn, *Coming on Strong*, 31–36. For more on saloon culture, see Madelon Powers, *Faces Along the Bar: Lore and Order in the Workingman's Saloon, 1870–1920* (Chicago: University of Chicago Press, 1998). For the emergence of popular culture, see Lawrence W. Levine, *Highbrow/Lowbrow: The Emergence of Cultural Hierarchy in America* (Cambridge, MA: Harvard University Press, 1986). For the rise of leisure among the working class, see Roy Rosenzweig, *Eight Hours for What We Will: Workers & Leisure in an Industrial City, 1870–1920* (Cambridge: Cambridge University Press, 1983); Kathy Piess, *Cheap Amusements: Working Women and Leisure in Turn-of-the-Century New York* (Philadelphia: Temple University Press, 1986); and John F. Kasson, *Amusing the Million: Coney Island at the Turn of the Century* (New York: Hill & Wang, 1978).

22. Grundy, "Ora Washington: The First Black Female Athletic Star," 84; Edgar Brown, "'Izzy' Channels Loses to Quaker Girl; Big Upset," *Chicago Defender*, 22 August 1925, 8; "Thompson Beats Brown for Net Crown," *Chicago Defender*, 5 September 1925, 8; "American Tennis Assn. 1925 Ratings, *Chicago Defender*, 24 April 1926, 8.

23. Frank A. Young, "Saitch Wins National Net Crown," *Chicago Defender*,

28 August 1926, 10; "Sylvester Smith Comes from Behind to Win Penn Tennis Open Championship," *Chicago Defender*, 6 August 1927, 8; "Thompson Beats Saitch for Title," *Chicago Defender*, 27 August 1927, 9; "Ted Thompson and Miss Ballard Lead American Tennis Assn. 1927 Ratings," *Chicago Defender*, 3 March 1928, 8; "National Tennis Title Play August 20 at Bordentown," *Chicago Defender*, 29 July 1929, 8.

24. Edgar G. Brown, "National Women's Champion Could Hold Own with Suzanne Lenglen, Says Edgar Brown," *Pittsburgh Courier*, 2 June 1923, 7. The one exception to the scarcity of information on earlier players and contemporaries of Washington is Lucy Diggs Slowe, who went on to become Dean of Women at Howard University after her tennis career.

25. Vassar and other elite and upper-middle-class schools began offering tennis with the transition from calisthenics to sports during the final quarter of the nineteenth century. Those wealthy enough to belong to clubs or resorts continued to play through these avenues once they left school. When organization came to the sport in the 1880s, it did not take long for the men who ran the association to include women's titles. With the formation of the United States Lawn Tennis Association (USLTA) in 1881, leaders within the organization established a women's singles title before the new decade, in 1889. Guttmann, *Women's Sports*, 113, 124; Mary Jo Festle, *Playing Nice: Politics and Apologies in Women's Sports* (New York: Columbia University Press, 1996), 55.

26. Festle, *Playing Nice*, 54–56, 70–71. Festle also explores how society noticed women tennis players who employed the opposite tactic, choosing to highlight their femininity in obvious ways, as did Gussie Moran during the 1950s by wearing lace panties under her tennis skirts. Still other women tennis players chose to employ what Festle terms "apology" tactics, downplaying their athleticism in order to "prove" they were still feminine. Still, women tennis players fared much better than their counterparts in sports like basketball and track and field.

27. Norman, "Big Tennis Games in Baltimore," *New York Age*, 28 June 1917, 6; Norman, "The American Tennis Association," *Crisis* 29, no. 1 (November 1924): 22; Cahn, *Coming on Strong*, 117–18. For more on black womanhood, see Jacqueline Jones, *Labor of Love, Labor of Sorrow: Black Women, Work, and the Family from Slavery to the Present* (New York: Basic Books, 1985). For descriptions of women's play, see Edgar G. Brown, "National Women's Champion Could Hold Own with Suzanne Leglen, Says Edgar Brown," *Pittsburgh Courier*, 2 June 1923, 7; and Edgar G. Brown, "East Outclassed As West Again Cops Tennis Honors," *Pittsburgh Courier*, 8 September 1923, 7.

28. Pamela Grundy suggests, appropriately, I think, that Washington made the move also to get out from under the shadow of fellow Germantown star, Lula Ballard. Grundy, "Ora Washington: The First Black Female Athletic Star," 84–85.

29. "National Net Championship Play Aug. 19," *Chicago Defender*, 10 August 1929, 8; David W. Kellum, "Saitch Wins New York Net Crown," *Chicago Defender*, 24 August 1929, 9.

30. Sam Lacy, "Althea Gibson vs. Ora Washington for Women's All-Time Net Title," *Baltimore Afro-American*, 12 September 1953, 13.

31. Cahn, *Coming on Strong*, 36–40.

32. Basketball was a newly developed sport. In the fall of 1891, James Naismith had been asked to create an indoor game that would help tame a class of rowdy boys at the International Training School of the Young Men's Christian Association. His

goal was to develop a game that would emphasize teamwork and discipline over brute strength. The timing of its birth fit in perfectly with the transition from exercise to sports underway in many women's colleges. See Pamela Grundy and Susan Shackelford, *Shattering the Glass: The Remarkable History of Women's Basketball* (Chapel Hill: University of North Carolina Press, 2005), 12.

33. For this section on women's basketball, I have used Pamela Grundy's and Susan Shackelford's pioneering work into the early history of sport. For more information, see Grundy and Shackelford, *Shattering the Glass,* 10–83.

34. These rules, with the court divided into three sections and the roughly nine-member team assigned to sections, remained the official rules until the 1930s, when they were replaced by the two-section, six-player girls' rules.

35. Cahn, *Coming on Strong,* 39–43. For working-class women, sport was in competition with other emerging forms of leisure such as dance halls, amusement parks, and movie theaters. See Kathy Piess, *Cheap Amusements: Working Women and Leisure in Turn-of-the-Century New York* (Philadelphia: Temple University Press, 1986).

36. For more on women's basketball during this period, see Pamela Grundy, "From Amazons to Glamazons: The Rise and Fall of North Carolina Women's Basketball, 1920–1960," *Journal of American History* 87 (June 2000): 112–46.

37. For more on collegiate basketball for African American women, see Rita Liberti, "'We Were Ladies, We Just Played Basketball Like Boys': African American Womanhood and Competitive Basketball at Bennett College, 1928–1942," *Journal of Sport History* 26 (Fall 1999): 567–84. For issues regarding African American women athletes and historically black colleges, see Gwendolyn Captain, "Enter Ladies and Gentlemen of Color: Gender, Sport, and the Ideal of African American Manhood and Womanhood during the Late Nineteenth and Early Twentieth Centuries," *Journal of Sport History* 18 (Spring 1991): 81–102. For a good study on the growth of basketball in an African American community, see Gerald R. Gems, "Blocked Shot: The Development of Basketball in the African American Community of Chicago," *Journal of Sport History* 22 (Summer 1995): 135–48.

38. Cahn, *Coming on Strong,* 23–25; 33–36. Martha Verbrugge's history of female physical education in America and the professionalization and growth of women's physical education as a vocation both in white and black America is an important addition to the scholarship. See Martha Verbrugge, *Active Bodies: A History of Women's Physical Education in Twentieth-Century America* (Oxford: Oxford University Press, 2012). For more on the early twentieth century and the threat of the "new woman," see Marybeth Hamilton, *When I'm Bad, I'm Better: Mae West, Sex, and American Entertainment* (Berkeley: University of California Press, 1995).

39. High school women's basketball was so organized in the state of Iowa that they had, by 1920, begun a state tournament. Although Iowa retained girls' rules until the early 1990s, Iowa women's basketball was a competitive brand of the sport that contrasted sharply with the moderated form insisted upon by women P.E. instructors. See Max McElwain, *The Only Dance in Iowa: A History of Six-Player Girls' Basketball* (Lincoln: University of Nebraska Press, 2004).

40. Verbrugge argues that despite the insistence of physical educators, even women in middle- and upper-class collegiate programs pushed back against the concept of moderation. Verbrugge, *Active Bodies,* 109–13.

41. "Philly Girls Win Again," *Pittsburgh Courier,* 14 March 1931, A4; "Victory

Gives Local Lassies Basketball Crown," *Philadelphia Tribune*, 9 April 1931, 11; "Germantown 'Y' Girls Defeat Rankin," *Pittsburgh Courier*, 11 April 1931, A5.

42. Some accounts refer to Briggs as the "retired" circulation director; however, most references seem to indicate that he was still active.

43. Grundy, "Ora Washington: The First Black Female Athletic Star," 86. For information on Otto Briggs, see "Dan Burley's Confidentially Yours," *New York Amsterdam News*, 13 November 1943, 6B.

44. "Hornets Top Darts' Quint to Cop 27th," *Philadelphia Tribune*, 24 December 1931, 11; "Hornets Given Big Scare … Keep Winning Streak Unsmirched," *Philadelphia Tribune*, 14 January 1932, 11; "In Liberty Bell Town," *Baltimore Afro-American*, 13 February 1932, 20; Randy Dixon, "Tribune to Present First Section of All-Philly Fives Next Week," *Philadelphia Tribune*, 10 March 1932, 10; Dick Sun, "Hornets and Newsgirls Play for National Title," *Philadelphia Tribune*, 4 February 1932, 10.

45. Randy Dixon, "Fans in Pandemonium as Hornets Lace Newsgirls in Thrill Saturated Clash," *Philadelphia Tribune*, 11 February 1932, 11.

46. Dick Sun, "Hornets and Newsgirls Play for National Title," *Philadelphia Tribune*, 4 February 1932, 10; Randy Dixon, "Fans in Pandemonium as Hornets Lace Newsgirls in Thrill Saturated Clash," *Philadelphia Tribune*, 11 February 1932, 11; "Tribune Girls Stop Hornets," *Baltimore Afro-American*, 27 February 1932, 15; "Ora Washington Is Stopped as Aces Lose First Go," *Atlanta Daily World*, 26 February 1932, 7; Dick Sun, "Tribune Girls Coast to Easy Victory over the Hornets," *Philadelphia Tribune*, 25 February 1932, 11. Articles also appeared in the *New York Amsterdam News* and the *Chicago Defender*.

47. Randy Dixon, "Newsgirls Top Hornets for National Title," *Philadelphia Tribune*, 7 April 1932, 10.

48. The following articles cover the final three games of the series: "Hornets Crush Newsgirl's Bid in Great Game," *Philadelphia Tribune*, 10 March 1932, 10; "Inez Patterson on Rampage as Tribune Girls Subdue Hornets," *Philadelphia Tribune*, 17 March 1932, 11; Randy Dixon, "Newsgirls Top Hornets for National Title," *Philadelphia Tribune*, 7 April 1932, 10; Bill Gibson, "Rens Nose Out Celtics," *Baltimore Afro-American*, 31 December 1932, 16.

49. "Tribune Girls Practicing," *New York Amsterdam News*, 12 October 1932, 9; "Greatest Girl Court Ace Now with Tribune," *Philadelphia Tribune*, 3 November 1932, 10; "Phila. Girl Champs Open Court Season," *New York Amsterdam News*, 30 November 1932, 9; "Can't Stop Ora," *Baltimore Afro-American*, 14 January 1933, 15; "Philly Tribune's Girls Lost When Score Is Counted," *Chicago Defender*, 25 February 1933, 8.

50. Randy Dixon, "Sports," *Philadelphia Tribune*, 17 March 1932, 10; "Tribgirls Thwart Title Threat of Seashore Dames," *Philadelphia Tribunes*, 13 January 1938, 13; "Tribgirls Grab Thriller in Tuneup for 4000-Mile Tour," *Philadelphia Tribune*, 10 February 1938, 12; "Champion Tribune Girls Here Again Thursday," *Atlanta Daily World*, 27 February 1938, 5; "And Over Here," *Norfolk Journal and Guide*, 3 February 1934, 12.

51. Verbrugge, *Active Bodies*, 127–37. Also see Patrick B. Miller, "To 'Bring the Race along Rapidly': Sport, Student Culture, and Educational Mission at Historically Black Colleges during the Interwar Years," *History of Education Quarterly* 35 (1995): 111–33.

52. "Inez Patterson on Rampage as Tribune Girls Subdue Hornets," *Philadelphia Tribune*, 17 March 1932, 11. Most of the *Philadelphia Tribune* article, including the reprimand, appeared in other black papers under the title, "Ora Washington Loses, Honored Just Same," *Atlanta Daily World*, 20 March 1932, 5.

53. Randy Dixon, "Sports," *Philadelphia Tribune*, 17 March 1932, 10.

54. "Philly Girls Win 97 Out of 109 Games," *Pittsburgh Courier*, 3 March 1934, A5. See also "Tribune Girls Win 97 of 109 Games to Tour Southland," *Baltimore Afro-American*, 3 March 1934, 18. The tour schedule was laid out in "Philly Girls are Ready to Meet Teams in Dixie," *New York Amsterdam News*, 10 March 1934, 10, as well as in "Tribune Girls Map out Southern Tour," *Philadelphia Tribune*, 8 March 1934, 10.

55. Liberti, "'We Were Ladies, We Just Played Basketball Like Boys,'" 575–76; Ivora King, "Feminine Yet Athletic," *Baltimore Afro-American*, 19 September 1931, 13. For a differentiation between colleges such as Fisk, Hampton, and Howard and other historically black normal and industrial colleges, see Verbrugge, *Active Bodies*, 87–152; and Cahn, *Coming on Strong*, 69–70.

56. This description of the impending match comes from the white *Greensboro Daily News*, an almost unheard of occurrence in the Jim Crow South given that both teams were African American. See "Bennett Cage Team Facing Two Games," *Greensboro Daily News*, 9 March 1934, 12. The article made a mistake with the number, however. There were three games scheduled and played, not two.

57. "Tribune Girls Defend Record on Cage Tour through South," *Norfolk Journal and Guide*, 31 March 1934, A12; "Tribune Girls Settle Fuss on Court with Bennett's 5," *Chicago Defender*, 24 March 1934, A4; Dick Sun, "Tribgirls Dazzle Down Home Fans in Victorious Tour," *Philadelphia Tribune*, 22 March 1934, 10. The Tribunes went on to win their other two games of that southern tour, against the State Normal School women in Fayetteville, North Carolina, and the YWCA team in Lynchburg, Virginia. They did not fair so well on the "western" part of their tour, stops in five different cities in Ohio. Their record in Ohio was 2–3, which reporters mostly attributed to travel fatigue. See "Tribune Girls Win and Lose in West," *Philadelphia Tribune*, 29 March 1934, 10.

58. Dick Sun, "Tribgirls Dazzle Down Home Fans in Victorious Tour," *Philadelphia Tribune*, 22 March 1934, 10; As quoted in Liberti, "'We Were Ladies, We Just Played Basketball Like Boys," 573–74.

59. Bennett continued to sponsor a basketball team through the 1941–42 season, but its commitment began to wane in the late 1930s when it joined the Women's Sports Day Association, which espoused noncompetitive sporting activities. Liberti, "'We Were Ladies, We Just Played Basketball Like Boys," 577–78.

60. Ric Roberts, "Tribune Girls Should Give Fans an Unusual Treat," *Atlanta Daily World*, 21 February 1938, 5.

61. Lucius Jones, "Tribune Girls Realized Dream When They Defeated White Quintette By 21–19," *Atlanta Daily World*, 25 February 1938, 5; Edgar T Rouzeau, "Nation's Net Stars Vying for Titles at Lincoln," *Pittsburgh Courier*, 20 August 1938, 17; Harry Webber, "Ora Beats Flora in Tennis Feud," *Baltimore Afro-American*, 5 August 1939, 21.

62. Harry Webber, "Ora Beats Flora in Tennis Feud," *Baltimore Afro-American*, 5 August 1939, 21; "A Negro Helen Wills," *Philadelphia Tribune*, 10 March 1932, 11;

Llewellyn Harris, "Harris Looks to the Tennis Battlefronts," *Atlanta Daily World*, 4 September 1935, 5.

63. Webber, "Ora Beats Flora in Tennis Feud," 21. Randy Dixon, "The Sports Bugle," *Pittsburgh Courier*, 21 January 1939, 17. Pamela Grundy argues that Washington's uneasy relationship with the public stemmed more from gender than class issues. While she gives a nod to the "uneasy fit" between Washington's working-class background and the tennis circles comprising the nation's African American elite, she writes far more prolifically about the ways in which Washington's style of tennis and demeanor flouted contemporary conceptions of womanhood and femininity. While no doubt gender issues played a part in explaining Washington's position within and to the African American communities, I believe the evidence speaks much more directly to the class issues at hand, particularly in light of evidence that supports similar problems encountered by Gibson. See Grundy, "Ora Washington: The First Black Female Athletic Star," 90–91.

64. "Injury Forces Ora Out of Singles Play," *Baltimore Afro-American*, 9 August 1941, 20; "Philly Cagers to Play Nurses," *Baltimore Afro-American*, 25 October 1941, 23. Washington mentioned being forty in this 9 August article, although, as I mentioned earlier, there is uncertainty surrounding it since the state of Virginia was not issuing birth certificates during the time period she was born.

65. Fay Young, "George Stewart, Panama, and Althea Gibson Win Nat'l Net Titles," *Chicago Defender*, 30 August 1947, 11.

66. Childs interview, 4 October 2003; "Basketball of Sorts Premier Philadelphia Sport 55 Years Ago," *Philadelphia Tribune*, 1 January 1963, 17; "Ora Washington, Inez Patterson and Sadie Dixon Hailed," *Philadelphia Tribune*, 1 January 1963, 18; Claude Harrison Jr., "Sports Roundup," *Philadelphia Tribune*, 3 August 1963, 13; "Born Too Soon," *Philadelphia Tribune*, 11 May 1965, 14; "'Superwoman' of Tennis, Ora Washington, Dies," *Philadelphia Tribune*, 5 June 1971, 2. There are discrepancies between some information in the obituary and previous articles. The age listed in the obituary would put her birth year a couple of years earlier than Washington admitted to being in 1941. Also, the number of trophies listed here, at 104, was considerably less than the 155 Washington claimed in the same 1941 article. See "Injury Forces Ora Out of Singles Play," *Baltimore Afro-American*, 9 August 1941, 20. Finally, the obituary credits her for fourteen years as the women's black tennis champion rather than the eight years she actually held the crown.

TWO

1. Earlier versions of this chapter appear in Jennifer H. Lansbury, "'The Tuskegee Flash' and 'The Slender Harlem Stroker': Black Women Athletes on the Margin," *Journal of Sport History* 28, no. 2 (Summer 2001): 233–52, and Jennifer H. Lansbury, "Alice Coachman: Quiet Champion of the 1940s," in *Out of the Shadows: A Biographical History of African American Athletes*, ed. David K. Wiggins (Fayetteville: University of Arkansas Press, 2006), 144–61.

2. Alice Coachman Davis, Interview by author, tape recording, Tuskegee, Alabama, 10 February 2003.

3. The extent to which Coachman was forgotten within the black community is apparent through comments Rudolph made in her autobiography about her

predecessor. Rudolph began the last chapter of the book remembering and paying tribute to Coachman. Yet even she failed to remember Coachman's accomplishment correctly. "Alice Coachman was a sprinter," Rudolph wrote, "and she goes way back; she was the first black woman ever to represent the United States in the Olympic Games." Rudolph credits another high jumper from Tuskegee, Mildred McDaniel, with the distinction of being the first African American to win Olympic gold. McDaniel did win a gold medal—in 1956 at the Melbourne Games—breaking Coachman's Olympic record and setting a new world record in the process. But the fact that Coachman was first was lost even on Rudolph. Wilma Rudolph, *Wilma: The Story of Wilma Rudolph* (New York, New American Library, 1977), 167; Louise Mead Tricard, *American Women's Track and Field: A History, 1895 through 1980* (Jefferson, NC: McFarland & Company, 1996), 327, 358. Tidye Pickett and Louise Stokes were the first African American women to represent the United States in the Olympic games, in 1932 at Los Angeles. See Tricard, *American Women's Track and Field*, 183. Moreover, Rudolph's own teammates—Barbara Jones and Mae Faggs—as well as Catherine Hardy of Fort Valley State College, won Olympic gold medals before McDaniel as part of the 400-meter relay team in 1952. McDaniel was actually the fifth African American woman to win an Olympic gold medal.

4. Except where otherwise supplemented and noted, biographical information on Coachman comes from Alice Coachman Davis, Interview by author, tape recording, Tuskegee, Alabama, 10 February 2003.

5. Dave Kindred, "Little Girl Who Liked to Jump Grows Up to Make History," *Atlanta Constitution*, 17 September 1995, sec. F, 4; Coachman interview, 10 February 2003.

6. Ross C. Owens, "Record of Tuskegee Women Track and Field Team, 1929– 1949," in *History of Athletics at Tuskegee*, n.p., n.d., 1–4; Capt. R. S. Darnaby, "Women in Sports: Jean Lane Wins 3 Firsts in Tuskegee Women's Meet," *Chicago Defender*, 16 May 1942, 20; "Nat'l Women's Meet at Tuskegee on May 8," *Chicago Defender*, 2 May 1942, 19. Other black colleges hosting relay carnivals during this period were Prairie View State in Texas and Alabama State in Montgomery. Prairie View added women's events to their annual relays in 1936, with Alabama State follow- ing. See Susan K. Cahn, *Coming on Strong: Gender and Sexuality in Twentieth-Century Women's Sport* (Cambridge, MA: Harvard University Press, 1994), 118–19.

7. Owens, "Record of Tuskegee Women Track and Field Team," 6. Field events included, at the time, the broad and high jumps, the shot put, and the baseball, javelin, and discus throws.

8. Coachman interview, 10 February, 2003.

9. "Tuskegee Girls Keep AAU Track Championships," *Baltimore Afro-American*, 9 September 1939, 21; "Wilberforce Lass Stars; Tuskegee Girls Retain National AAU Track Title," *New York Age*, 13 July 1940, 5.

10. Tricard, *American Women's Track and Field*, 5–6.

11. Ibid., 7–10.

12. Cahn, *Coming on Strong*, 112–17. Also see Tricard, *American Women's Track and Field*, 17–31, 72–78.

13. Tricard, *American Women's Track and Field*, 60–68.

14. While the meet that took place in May at the Oaksmere School in Mamaroneck, New York, was the first and best known, other qualifying meets were

held in the Midwest and in Los Angeles and the results compared. See Tricard, *American Women's Track and Field*, 72.

15. Ibid., 72–78; "American Girls Are Second in Olympics," *New York Times*, 21 August 1922, 14. The *Chicago Tribune, Boston Globe,* and *Washington Post* all followed the competition as well.

16. Tricard, *American Women's Track and Field*, 82; Cahn, *Coming on Strong*, 59–60.

17. Cahn, *Coming on Strong*, 60–64, 81–82. The contrast between track and field and swimming further illustrates the race, class, and femininity issues at play here. The AAU had brought women's swimming under its control a decade earlier, but P.E. instructors continued to support that sport, which was largely populated by white, middle-class women. See Cahn, *Coming on Strong*, 129–30.

18. Cahn, *Coming on Strong*, 113–17; Tricard, *American Women's Track and Field*, 37.

19. Tricard, *American Women's Track and Field*, 152, 219, 249–98; Cahn, *Coming on Strong*, 117. For more on women's track and field of the period, and African American women's entrance into the sport, see Susan Cahn, "'Cinderellas' of Sport: Black Women in Track and Field," in *Coming on Strong*, 110–39.

20. Pickett fell in the semifinal heat and therefore did not qualify for the finals. Tricard, *American Women's Track and Field*, 177, 183, 224.

21. Martha Verbrugge, *Active Bodies: A History of Women's Physical Education in Twentieth-Century America* (Oxford: Oxford University Press, 2012), 93–96, 125–52.

22. For more on the development of male coaches of women's teams during the early twentieth century, see Cahn, *Coming on Strong*, 64–68, 117; and Pamela Grundy and Susan Shackelford, "Black Women Embrace the Game," in *Shattering the Glass: The Remarkable History of Women's Basketball* (Chapel Hill: University of North Carolina Press, 2005), 47–49. Indeed, many of the team photographs of the period include a male coach.

23. Tuskegee had a high school as well as the more famous trade school. While the high school members of the team competed for the junior titles at the Tuskegee Relays, those who accompanied the team to national championships competed along with the senior girls for the national titles.

24. Louis R. Harlan, "Booker T. Washington and the Politics of Accommodation," in *Black Leaders of the Twentieth Century*, ed. John Hope Franklin and August Meier (Urbana: University of Illinois Press, 1982), 2–3. Washington's quote is from his Atlanta Exposition address in 1895. Booker T. Washington, *Up from Slavery*, One Hundred Great Masterpieces of American Literature Series (Franklin Center, PA: Franklin Library, 1977), 148.

25. When Washington secured enough money to erect the first building, students did the work, a pattern that lasted for many years. By the turn of the century, nineteen years into the school's existence, the campus consisted of forty buildings, all but four of which were constructed using student labor. Harlan, "Booker T. Washington and the Politics of Accommodation," in Franklin and Meier, *Black Leaders of the Twentieth Century*, 3–4.

26. Ibid., 4. When the track team traveled north to compete in the nationals, this network of alumni proved quite beneficial. Even above the Mason-Dixon line, African Americans were not welcomed at many hotels. Moreover, providing hotel

accommodations for the team could prove to be expensive. Prior to departure, Coachman remembered how Coach Abbott would handle the arrangements: "We stayed in private, what you might call boarding houses. Coach would call [ahead]— we had so many Tuskegeeans all over the United States … we didn't have any problems finding a place. 'Cause Coach wanted all of us to be together." No doubt staying together was logistically simpler for Abbott, but it also helped continue molding them as a team, contributing to their success on the cinderpath. The broad, Tuskegee community consisting of alumni throughout the country, particularly the Northeast, helped make such accommodations possible. Coachman interview, 10 February 2003.

27. John Lake, "Tuskegee Girls' Team Wins National A.A.U. Championship," *Chicago Defender*, 2 October 1937, 1; Tricard, *American Women's Track and Field*, 241–42.

28. Owens, "Record of Tuskegee Women Track and Field Team," 3–4; "Tuskegee Girl Steals Track Show by Wins," *Chicago Defender*, 15 May 1937, 14; Coachman interview, 10 February 2003; "Tuskegee Girls in Nat'l A.A.U. Meet April 12," *Chicago Defender*, 12 April 1941, 23; and Tricard, *American Women's Track and Field*, 241–53.

29. Owens, "Record of Tuskegee Women Track and Field Team," 6–8; "Tuskegee Girls Defend National Title July 6," *Chicago Defender*, 29 June 1940, 22; Fay Young, "The Stuff Is Here," *Chicago Defender*, 19 April 1941, 23.

30. Owens, "Record of Tuskegee Women Track and Field Team," 1–4; Coachman interview, 10 February 2003. By the time Abbott started the women's track team, he already had established his credibility with a thirteen-year, win-loss record of 107–13 as coach of Tuskegee's football squad. Cleveland Leigh Abbott bio, Athletic Department, Tuskegee University, Tuskegee, Alabama.

31. Coachman interview, 10 February 2003; Frank A. Young, "Tuskegee's 11th Annual Women's Track Meet," *Chicago Defender*, 13 May 1939, 8.

32. Coachman interview, 10 February 2003. In all likelihood, the *Chicago Defender* picked up on this tradition when it reviewed the team in an article prior to the 1940 nationals, referring to young Rowena Harrison as "the baby of the team." Harrison may have been the youngest, but she was only one of the "babies." "Tuskegee Girls Defend National Title July 6," *Chicago Defender*, 29 June 1940, 22.

33. Coachman Interview, 10 February 2003; "Alice Coachman Gets Second Individual Award," *Baltimore Afro-American*, 11 July 1942, 23; "3 Negro Track Girls Named All-American," *Chicago Defender*, 18 December 1943, 11. The SIAC was the athletic conference established by African American colleges that were shut out of competition with white colleges in team sports such as football, baseball, and basketball. The Tuskegee women's basketball team played schools such as Clark, Morris Brown, Alabama State, Arkansas A&M, Florida A&M, Grambling, and Tennessee State. Coachman remembers that the conference was competitive, and the Tuskegee team had to play well to win. Roulhac, *Jumping over the Moon*, 63–71.

34. Tricard, *American Women's Track and Field*, 251–84. The twenty-three titles were for Coachman's individual and relay events. In addition, she won ten team titles as a Tigerette.

35. Cahn, *Coming on Strong*, 122–28; Patricia Vertinsky and Gwendolyn Captain, "More Myth than History: American Culture and Representations of the Black Female's Athletic Ability," *Journal of Sport History* 25 (Fall 1998): 544–45. For more on the controversy between women educators and the AAU during the 1920s, see chapter 1.

36. Leila Perry Glover, Interview by Susan K. Cahn, Atlanta, Georgia, 8 May 1992; quoted in Cahn, *Coming on Strong*, 122.

37. Sportswriter Paul Gallico pinned Babe Didrickson with the term "muscle Moll" in an article published by *Vanity Fair* in 1932. Impressed with Didrickson's athletic feats, he had trouble reconciling such athleticism with traditional norms of femininity. Didrickson's focus on her own strength bewildered and fascinated the sportswriter, but in ways that he likened to a circus act. The "peculiar and mysterious fascination" that she exercised over others, Gallico suggested, "may be the same thing that keeps me lingering in front of the bearded lady and the Airy Fairy Lillian, the Albino girl, or Mirzah, the snake charmer." Paul Gallico, "The Texas Babe," *Vanity Fair*, October 1932, 36, quoted in Grundy and Shackelford, *Shattering the Glass*, 58.

38. Coachman thought that talking with either teammates or competitors during meets would rob her of the energy she needed to perform her best and retain her titles and help Tuskegee win the team title. "I would talk to you all you wanted after the meet, but I knew what it was doing to my body," she recalled in later years. Whereas we might refer to this as an athlete's *focus* today, at the time Coachman was considered a bit peculiar. In truth, however, Coachman needed to save her energy. At her peak, she competed in the high jump, the 50 and 100 meters, and served as anchor on Tuskegee's 400-meter relay team. Coachman interview, 10 February 2003.

39. Coachman interview, 10 February 2003; Sam Lacy, "'Coachman Best' Says Walsh," *Baltimore Afro-American*, 15 July 1944, 18. During the year or so Coachman found herself distinctly in the minority as a member of the All-American teams selected to compete against the Canadians, she felt only community and teamwork with her fellow athletes: "We were there to do a job. … Any trouble at all came from outside, not the team." Butch Moore, "Alice Coachman Modest Despite Awards, Honors," *Albany Herald*, 13 March 1974, sec. B, 1, Alice Coachman Davis papers, Special Collections, John Hope and Aurelia Elizabeth Franklin Library, Fisk University, Nashville, Tennessee.

40. Leila Perry Glover, Interview by Susan K. Cahn, Atlanta, Georgia, 8 May 1992; quoted in Cahn, *Coming on Strong*, 134.

41. Glover Interview by Cahn, 8 May 1992; quoted in Cahn, *Coming on Strong*, 123. Interestingly, Alice Coachman made the same comment in *Jumping over the Moon*.

42. "Tuskegee University, webpage: Choir History." http://www.tuskegee.edu/Global/story.asp?S=1131717 (accessed 10 July 2007). While at Tuskegee, Coachman, as a student on an athletic work-study scholarship, also spent time during the week working jobs for the athletic department in locations such as the tennis court, track field, gymnasium, locker rooms, and swimming pool. Women athletes on this program also mended uniforms for the football team.

43. "Tuskegee Girls Retain Nat'l Track Crown; Lula Hymes Is Star of Meet," *Pittsburgh Courier*, 13 August 1938, 17; "Tuskegee Girls Successfully Defend National Track Title," *New York Age*, 9 September 1939, 8; "Tuskegee Lassies to Defend Track Honors," *Chicago Defender*, 5 August 1939, 9; "Tuskegee Girls' Team Rules Women's Track World," *Pittsburgh Courier*, 7 July 1945, 18.

44. "Tuskegee Lassie Goes Up and Over to Retain Title," *Pittsburgh Courier*, 29 July 1941, 16; "Tuskegee Takes 6th Straight," *Baltimore Afro-American*, 11 July 1942, 23; "Alice Coachman Crowned National Sprint Queen," *Baltimore*

Afro-American, 7 July 1945, 18; Sam Lacy, "'Coachman Best' Says Walsh," *Baltimore Afro-American*, 15 July 1944, 18.

45. For examples of white press coverage of Coachman in which race became a factor, see "Miss Walsh Wins Easily," *New York Times*, 1 July 1945, sec. III, 3; and "Tuskegee's Women Gain Track Title," *New York Times*, 5 August 1946, 27. I have argued previously that the white press's treatment of Coachman stems from white sportswriters' tendency to construct her public identity based primarily upon gender, with race playing a secondary role, hence the similar treatment of Coachman to white women track athletes. Athleticism was a distant third resulting in her loss in the public memory. See Jennifer H. Lansbury, "'The Tuskegee Flash' and 'the Slender Harlem Stroker': Black Women Athletes on the Margin," *Journal of Sport History* 28, no. 2 (Summer 2001): 233–52.

46. A modiste is a female maker of or dealer in women's clothing, hats, etc., that is, in women's fashion; a dressmaker.

47. Levi Jolley, "Coed Cinder Champs Carry High Hopes: Glory Gals Look to Bright Future in Many Fields after Graduation," *Baltimore Afro-American*, 12 July 1941, 19. Susan Cahn explores efforts on the part of coaches and journalists to help cultivate a feminine image. See Cahn, *Coming on Strong*, 133–34.

48. Coach Petty, often lauded in other articles that reported the team's national success, was also cast in a different light in the peanut oil story. Characterized here as youthful and attractive, she also comes across as cagey, as the reporter hinted that she was holding something back—attempting to "hide" the team's secret from the press. Levi Jolley, "Tigerettes Owe Success to Dr. Carver's Peanut Oil," *Baltimore Afro-American*, 13 July 1940, 19.

49. News of the special "powers" of the peanut oil resurfaced during Coachman's trip to London for the Olympics in 1948. The U.S. Olympic women's track and field team was a day out of New York bound for London when Coachman realized the oil was not in her suitcase. For Coachman and the other three athletes from Tuskegee, it was a disappointment. The article, however, suggested that the absence of the oil did not portend well for the Olympic team, given its longtime use by the successful Tigerettes. The Olympic coaches cabled Cleve Abbott, who promised to send the oil ahead to London by air. Russ J. Cowans, "Rush Carver Peanut Oil to Olympic Team Gals," *Chicago Defender*, 31 July 1948, 11.

50. Roulhac, *Jumping over the Moon*, 71; Leila Perry Glover, Interview by Susan K. Cahn, Atlanta, Georgia, 8 May 1992; quoted in Cahn, *Coming on Strong*, 122; Lansbury, "'Tuskegee Flash," 234.

51. "Miss Walsh Gains 3 A.A.U. Crowns," *New York Times*, 7 July 1948, 28; "Alice Coachman, Albany Negro Star, Betters Record, Makes Olympic Team," *Albany Herald*, 13 July 1948, 9. Coachman's jump in the Olympic trials did not establish a new record, however, because the meet was not an AAU championship event. "Women's Olympic Track and Field Team Sails for London," *Baltimore Afro-American*, 24 July 1948, 7. Of the twelve-member team, nine were African American. Tuskegee claimed three of the athletes, and one alumnae in Coachman.

52. Roulhac, *Jumping over the Moon*, 112; "Women in Sports: Finnish Girl Invites Lula Hymes as Guest During 1940 Olympics," *Chicago Defender*, 1 July 1939, 8. These earlier Tuskegee women track athletes were denied first one, and then a second, Olympic opportunity when the 1944 games were canceled as well. The *Chicago*

Defender reported on the effect of the 1940 cancellation on the women track athletes. See "Women Track Stars Are Hit by European Warfare," *Chicago Defender*, 20 July 1949, 24.

53. In later years, Coachman remembered qualifying for the 50-meter dash as well, but choosing not to compete in order to focus all her energy and preparation on the high jump competition. Moreover, she had been experiencing back pain on the trip over. According to Coachman, Coach Catherine Meyer was angry with her for choosing not to compete. However, the 50-meter dash was not contested at the Olympics, and Coachman is not listed as qualifying for the 100 meter, the other sprint she usually competed in. Tricard, *American Women's Track and Field*, 295.

54. Typical of coverage that sought to feminize women track and field athletes, the white press routinely referred to Blankers-Koen as "the Dutch housewife," and the "blond, slender, 30-year-old mother of two." See "American Athletes Sweep the Olympics," *Life*, 23 August 1948, 28; *New York Times*, 15 August 1948, sec. V, 1.

55. Coachman interview, 10 February 2003. The closest any of the other athletes got to the medal stand was Dorothy Dodson, who placed fourth in the javelin competition. Tricard, *American Women's Track and Field*, 290. Both the women's coach Catherine Meyer, who predicted the U.S. team would come away with at least three gold medals, and the black press expressed high hopes for the U.S. women track and field athletes prior to the start of the competition. See Edwin B. Henderson, "Bronze Athletes Hold Margin on Olympics," *Baltimore Afro-American*, 24 July 1948, 7.

56. Wilfred Smith, "U.S. Relay Sprinters Win; Ruled Out," *Chicago Tribune*, 8 August 1948, Pt. 2, 1. Coachman remembers employing a strategy against the two Europeans that Coach Chris Roulhac had given her. She was consistently hitting her jumps while Tyler and Ostermeyer would miss periodically. Approaching the bar from opposite sides, she remembered how her two competitors began coming to the left to see if they could improve their performance. Before getting to the takeoff point where she would leap over the bar, Roulhac told Coachman to take a lot of steps during her run. In trying to imitate her and reduce their number of missed jumps, the two Europeans threw off their own rhythm and ended up with even more missed attempts. "I got 'um," Coachman recalled, at least in part to a good coach. Coachman interview, 10 February 2003.

57. *New York Times*, 15 August 1948, sec. V, 1; Bert Prather, "Alice Coachman Wins High Jump: Albany Negress Is Olympic Champ," *Atlanta Constitution*, 8 August 1948, sec. B, 11; *Chicago Tribune*, 8 August 1948, sec. 2, 1.

58. "Tuskegee Negro Wins 3 National Track Crowns, *Albany Herald*, 1 July 1945, 12; "Albany Negro Star Wins Three Titles in AAU Track Meet," *Albany Herald*, 5 August 1946, 8; and "Alice Coachman Stars in AAU Track Meet," *Albany Herald*, 30 June 1947, 8, are good examples.

59. The two photographs consist of Mell Patton, a U.S. hopeful for the men's track team, and swimmer Ann Ross whose picture includes the following caption: "Olympic Beauty: Ann Ross, one of the U.S. Olympic swimming hopefuls, strikes a pretty pose as she climbs the ladder to the diving board. She should be a winner in a beauty contest if not in the water." Clearly, women swimmers were dealing with their own set of gender issues at the time. See "Alice Coachman, Albany Negro Star, Betters Record, Makes Olympic Team," *Albany Herald*, 13 July 1948, 9.

60. Harley Bowers, "Alice Coachman, Albany Track Star, to Seek Olympic Crown This Week," *Albany Herald*, 25 July 1948.

61. Forrest "Spec" Towns was the other Georgian who had won Olympic gold up to that point, in 1936 for the 110-meter hurdles. See *Atlanta Constitution*, 8 August 1948, sec. B, 11. For the front-page article of Coachman's win, see "Albanian Cops High Jump Title at Olympics, Sets New Record," *Albany Herald*, 8 August 1948, 1.

62. Joseph M. Sheehan, "Olympians Return to Noisy Welcome," *New York Times*, 28 August 1948, 17; Ed Decker, "Alice Coachman," in *Contemporary Black Biography: Profiles from the International Black Community*, 32 vols., ed. Shirelle Phelps (Detroit: Gale Research, 1992), 18: 30.

63. Alice Coachman Davis papers, Special Collections, John Hope and Aurelia Elizabeth Franklin Library, Fisk University, Nashville, Tennessee; Roger Bond, "Big Welcome Given Olympic Champ Here," *Albany Herald*, 2 September 1948, 1. Coachman interview, 10 February 2003.

64. For Coachman's Olympic coverage by the *Herald*, see "Albanian Cops High Jump Title at Olympics, Sets New Record," *Albany Herald*, 8 August 1948, 1; "Alice Coachman to Receive Big 'Welcome Home,'" *Albany Herald*, 10 August 1948, 1; "Mammoth Parade Planned for Alice Coachman's Return," *Albany Herald*, 26 August 1948,1; "Coachman Day Planned; Wide Coverage Set," *Albany Herald*, 30 August 1948; 1; "Olympic Ace Will Arrive Home Today," *Albany Herald*, 1 September 1948, 1; and Roger Bond, "Big Welcome Given Olympic Champ Here," *Albany Herald*, 2 September 1948, 1.

65. Helen Nash, "Fw: Alice Coachman Ads for Coca-Cola," 23 September 2004, personal e-mail (24 September 2004). Interestingly, Coachman's ability to endorse the soft drink was genuine. Years later she remembered how a nice, cold Coca-Cola was one of the few things she wanted after winning the gold medal in London. Coachman interview, 10 February 2003.

66. Alice Coachman Davis papers, Special Collections, John Hope and Aurelia Elizabeth Franklin Library, Fisk University, Nashville, Tennessee.

THREE

1. Althea Gibson, *I Always Wanted to Be Somebody* (New York: Harper & Brothers, 1958), 36.

2. Gibson's titles actually came at the U.S. Championships at Forest Hills, the forerunner to the U.S. Tennis Open.

3. Mary Jo Festle has expertly dealt with the gender, race, and class issues that surrounded Gibson as she broke into 1950s white women's tennis. See Mary Jo Festle, "Members Only: Class, Race, and Amateur Tennis for Women in the 1950s," in *Playing Nice: Politics and Apologies in Women's Sports* (New York: Columbia University Press, 1996); and Festle, "'Jackie Robinson without the Charm': The Challenges of Being Althea Gibson," in *Out of the Shadows: A Biographical History of African American Athletes*, ed. David K. Wiggins (Fayetteville: University of Arkansas Press, 2006), 187–205. Festle's chapter in *Playing Nice* situates Gibson in the culture of 1950s women's tennis, examining the class and gender issues common to all women players and the unique racial obstacles that Gibson confronts. My previous research on Gibson concerned the press's construction of Gibson's public identity, exposing how

sportswriters' focus on her race and gender overshadowed their discussion of her athleticism. See Jennifer H. Lansbury, "'The Tuskegee Flash' and 'the Slender Harlem Stroker': Black Women Athletes on the Margin," *Journal of Sport History* 28, no. 2 (Summer 2001): 233–52.

4. Ted Poston, "The Story of Althea Gibson," reprinted in the *Pittsburgh Courier*, magazine section, 26 October 1957, 3.

5. For important works that explore class tension among African American women, see Darlene Clark Hine, *Black Women in White: Racial Conflict and Cooperation in the Nursing Profession, 1890–1950* (Bloomington: Indiana University Press, 1989); Evelyn Brooks Higginbotham, *Righteous Discontent: The Women's Movement in the Black Baptist Church: 1880–1920* (Cambridge, MA: Harvard University Press, 1993); and, more recently, Victoria Wolcott, *Remaking Respectability: African American Women in Interwar Detroit* (Chapel Hill: University of North Carolina Press, 2001). Each of these studies addresses class conflict within a group of either working or activist African American women, whereas Gibson's situation cut across the African American community and involved predominately male, African American sportswriters.

6. Except where otherwise supplemented and noted, early biographical information on Althea Gibson comes from her autobiography, *I Always Wanted to Be Somebody*. The small family lived for several years with Gibson's aunt until they could afford an apartment of their own. Gibson is not specific regarding when the family moved to their apartment on 143rd Street, but she was at least nine or ten since she mentions first living for a while when she was seven or eight with another aunt in Philadelphia.

7. Gibson, *I Always Wanted to Be Somebody*, 8–10. Mary Jo Festle suggests that Gibson's home was an abusive one, using these early childhood stories from her autobiography as well as her later relationship and comments about the Eaton family as evidence. While it is clear that Gibson's father did not shy away from corporeal punishment, even bordering on abuse, Gibson also comes across as someone who knew how to work the system, exaggerating the circumstances to get what she wanted. See Festle, "Jackie Robinson without the Charm," 189–90.

8. While this chapter argues that class, gender, and race issues became most obvious with Gibson's emergence as a champion of the white tennis world, it is worth noting that the notion of "a better class of people" was important to those helping her even at this point in her life.

9. Sundiata Djata, *Blacks at the Net: Black Achievement in the History of Tennis*, Sports and Entertainment, ed. Steven A. Riess (Syracuse, NY: Syracuse University Press, 2006), 10; Gibson, *I Always Wanted to Be Somebody*, 28.

10. Others within the African American community supported Gibson during her Harlem years. "One of the people who did a lot for me in those early days at the Cosmopolitan [Tennis Club] was Mrs. Rhoda Smith," Gibson remembered in her autobiography. "Rhoda is a well-off society woman . . . and she practically adopted me. She bought me my first tennis costume and did everything she could to give me a boost." Gibson also became good friends with Edna and Sugar Ray Robinson following an introduction by a mutual friend. Through the years, she often turned to them when she was faced with tough decisions, as when she was trying to decide whether to accept Eaton's and Johnson's offer. Gibson, *I Always Wanted to Be Somebody*, 32, 39.

11. The phrase is borrowed from the dedication to Gibson's 1958 autobiography, *I Always Wanted to Be Somebody*, which reads, "to my two doctors."

12. Thomas W. Young to Hubert A. Eaton Sr., 26 July 1957, Eaton papers, UNCW.

13. Gibson also recognized and acknowledged Eaton's and Johnson's role in her tennis success. After leaving the Eatons' to begin classes at Florida A&M, her letters to Eaton expressed her gratitude: "I also wish to thank you and Mrs. Eaton for the way you have opened your heart and your home to me during the years gone by. I shall never forget. I hope that you will always think me worthy of your generosity and kindness." And upon capturing her first Wimbledon singles title in 1957, she sent telegrams to each that read: "This victory belongs also to you. Thank you so much. Love, Althea." Althea Gibson to Hubert A. Eaton Sr., 22 September 1952, and Telegram from Althea Gibson to Hubert A. Eaton Sr., 8 July 1957, Eaton papers, UNCW.

14. Alice Shaw to Hubert A. Eaton Sr., 20 September 1958, Eaton papers, UNCW.

15. Eaton's son and oldest child, Hubert Eaton Jr., reflected years later that "tennis was the love of my dad's life." Hubert A. Eaton Jr., M.D., Interview by author, tape recording, Wilmington, North Carolina, 14 July 2005.

16. Hubert A. Eaton, *Every Man Should Try* (Wilmington, NC: Bonaparte Press, 1984), xi–25; Smith, *Whirlwind*, 10–39; Gibson, *I Always Wanted to Be Somebody*, 52. African American doctors in the South often ran clinics that provided medical *and* surgical care to blacks since they were denied entry into white hospitals. Reflecting on the years of sharing his court with others, Eaton reminisced years later in his autobiography: "The balls were white, the courts were green, and the color of the players varied." Eaton, *Every Man Should Try*, 25.

17. Gibson, *I Always Wanted to Be Somebody*, 52.

18. Johnson picked up his nickname while playing football at Lincoln University. Wearing a helmet in those days was optional, recalled one of his teammates. "He had let his hair grow long, slicked it back and wouldn't wear a helmet. And there he'd go running down the field with his hair flowing back, streaking and looking like a whirlwind. I guess that's why they started calling him that." Hildrus A. Poindexter, Interview by Doug Smith, quoted in Doug Smith, *Whirlwind, The Godfather of Black Tennis: The Life and Times of Dr. Robert Walter Johnson* (Washington, DC: Blue Eagle Publishing Co., 2004), 21.

19. Gibson, *I Always Wanted to Be Somebody*, 37–38; Eaton, *Every Man Should Try*, 27–28; Smith, *Whirlwind*, 55–56; Eaton Jr. interview, 14 July 2005. Areas of difference in the various accounts include which of the two doctors proposed the specific plan; whether they knew Gibson was a high school dropout before talking with her; whether Gibson agreed to the plan immediately or took some time to think it over; and when she left New York to move south to Wilmington.

20. Gibson, *I Always Wanted to Be Somebody*, 37–38.

21. Ibid., 46.

22. Festle, *Playing Nice*, 56–57, 144.

23. Gibson, *I Always Wanted to Be Somebody*, 28–29.

24. Gibson, I Always *Wanted to Be Somebody*, 8; Fay Young, "Althea Gibson Not As Talkative Now As She Was on the 1951 Net Tour," *Chicago Defender*, 7 July 1956, 17; Bruce Schoenfeld, *The Match: Althea Gibson and Angela Buxton: How Two*

Outsiders—One Black, the Other Jewish—Forged a Friendship and Made Sports History (New York: HarperCollins Publishers, 2004), 69, 85, 185.

25. Eaton Jr., interview, 14 July 2005.

26. Eaton papers, UNCW. Also see Gibson's chapter entitled, "Look Away, Dixie Land," in her autobiography, *I Always Wanted to Be Somebody*, 44–57; Eaton Jr. interview, 14 July 2005; Gibson, *I Always Wanted to Be Somebody*, 29.

27. Ibid., 42.

28. Eaton Jr. interview, 14 July 2005.

29. Ibid.; William H. Wiggins to Dr. Hubert A. Eaton, 9 May 1949, and Walter M. Austin to Dr. Hubert A. Eaton, 9 May 1949, Eaton papers, UNCW.

30. Gibson, *I Always Wanted to Be Somebody*, 44; Eaton Jr. interview, 14 July 2005. Althea Gibson to Hubert A. Eaton, 29 April 1950 and 9 November 1953; and Hubert A. Eaton to Althea Gibson, 11 April 1951, 22 January 1953, and 3 December 1953, Eaton papers, UNCW, provide good examples of the Eaton/Gibson relationship. Eaton Jr. remembers that, similar to a typical father/daughter relationship, Gibson would call or write his father seeking his advice about a particular matter, he would give her various recommendations, and then she would end up doing what she wanted to do in the first place.

31. Althea Gibson to Hubert Eaton, 6 January 1951, Eaton papers, UNCW, in which Gibson writes Eaton that she is back at school at the start of a new year, after having gone to New York over Christmas for a family reunion. Gibson, *So Much to Live For*, 66–70; Eaton Jr. interview, 14 July 2005.

32. Kevin G. Gaines, *Uplifting the Race: Black Leadership, Politics and Culture in the Twentieth Century* (Chapel Hill: University of North Carolina Press, 1996), 1–4; Eaton, *Every Man Should Try*, 27.

33. 1952 ATA National Interscholastic Championship program, Eaton papers, UNCW; Gerald F. Norman, "The American Tennis Association," *Opportunity* 5, no. 8 (August 1927): 245.

34. "Finance a Big Problem for Most Tennis Players," *Chicago Defender*, 11 May 1940, 22. Financial problems were also common at the national level, as the ATA sought to subsidize local educational programs and junior tournaments, provide financial help to individual players, finance demonstration tours, and purchase insurance for national tournaments against bad weather, or other reasons, that might result in cancellation. "American Tennis Ass'n Does a Great Big Job," *Chicago Defender*, 20 April 1940, 23.

35. Festle, *Playing Nice*, 55. There were a few exceptions to this phenomenon, Festle notes, such as the state of California, which developed a notable system of largely outdoor public courts.

36. "Problems Confront Those Who Seek to Promote Tennis," *Chicago Defender*, 27 April 1940, 23.

37. "Players and Officials Clash on Removal of Title Tennis from College Atmosphere," *Baltimore Afro-American*, 30 August 1947, 12.

38. For example, see "Prairie View's Tennis Team One of Greatest," *Chicago Defender*, 13 April 1935, 16; "Tuskegee Announces Relay Carnival Date," *Chicago Defender*, 22 January 1938, 9; and "Kathryn Jones, Minnis Win S.I. [Southern Intercollegiate] Tennis Crowns," *Chicago Defender*, 16 May 1942, 19. Also see Captain, "Enter Ladies and Gentlemen of Color," 81–102.

39. "Problems Confront Those Who Seek to Promote Tennis," *Chicago Defender*,

27 April 1940, 23. Also see "Schools Aided the A.T.A.," *Chicago Defender*, 6 April 1940, 22, and "South May Rival Pacific Coast in U.S. Tennis World," *Chicago Defender*, 20 July 1940, 23. "Hampton to Celebrate Third Annual Women's Day, May 7," *Chicago Defender*, 7 May 1938, 7. Black colleges did reach some working-class African Americans by extending athletic scholarships or work-study programs to those who displayed athletic prowess, as in the case of Althea Gibson. In truth, however, these fortunate few comprised a small segment of the population.

40. Walter M. Austin to Dr. Hubert A. Eaton, 9 May 1949, Eaton papers, UNCW; Gibson, *I Always Wanted to Be Somebody*, 60.

41. Eaton, *Every Man Should Try*, 34.

42. Gibson, *I Always Wanted to Be Somebody*, 54–55; "Reggie Weir Wins N.Y. Net Singles Title," *Chicago Defender*, 16 August 1930, 8; *Chicago Defender*, 29 August 1931, 9; *Chicago Defender*, 27 August 1932, 9; "'Who'll Succeed Weir?' Is Question Net Fans Ask," *Chicago Defender*, 11 August 1934, 16.

43. Arthur E. Francis to Hubert Eaton, 12 June 1950; Arthur E. Francis to Maplewood Country Club, Maplewood, New Jersey, 14 June 1950; Arthur E. Francis to Robert Clark, Chairman of the Tournament Committee, Cherry Valley Club, Long Island, New York, 14 June 1950; Bertram L. Baker to Hubert Eaton, 7 July 1950, Eaton papers, UNCW.

44. Sarah Palfrey Cooke also spoke out on Gibson's behalf. After Gibson received the invitation to play at Forest Hills, Cooke took her to play some practice rounds there at the West Side Tennis Club. Gibson, *I Always Wanted to Be Somebody*, 68–69.

45. Schoenfeld, *The Match*, 55. For comparison of Gibson's tennis to Marble's, see *New York Times*, 7 July 1957, sec. V, 4.

46. Alice Marble, "A Vital Issue," *American Lawn Tennis*, July 1950, 14, Eaton papers, UNCW. Years later, Hubert Eaton Jr. remembered that letter as "one hell of an indictment" against the white tennis establishment. Eaton Jr. interview.

47. Marble's letter was preceded by the following introduction by the magazine: "*American Lawn Tennis* is privileged to turn over its editorial columns to Miss Alice Marble. Miss Marble's column this month deals with an issue of such importance to the game that we felt that its rightful position was on a page specifically devoted to opinion. We hope on future occasions to carry editorials by other outstanding tennis personalities. At times we may disagree with their opinions, but in this case *American Lawn Tennis* wishes to go on record as wholeheartedly supporting the sentiments and opinions expressed by Miss Marble in the following editorial." *American Lawn Tennis*, July 1950, 14.

48. "ATA Sidelights," *Baltimore Afro-American*, 1 September 1951, 16; Gibson, *I Always Wanted to Be Somebody*, 52. The conflict between Forest Hills and the ATA nationals was often a matter of timing since both came at the end of the season. Regarding the instance when Eaton tried to intercede on Gibson's behalf, certain unnamed ATA officials had objected to her "deserting" the ATA, threatening to "fix it" so that Gibson would not be able to play at Forest Hills again if she didn't participate in the ATA nationals that year. Rather than playing the women's doubles at Forest Hills as Eaton had lobbied for, Gibson entered and walked away with the ATA women's national title.

49. A&M administrators took issue with not being invited to the meeting when Baker later wrote them, requesting that the college fund part of the trip. Bertram L.

Baker to A. S. Gaither, 29 March 1951; and A. S. Gaither to Bertram Baker, 7 April 1951, Eaton papers, UNCW.

50. Bertram L. Baker to A. S. Gaither, 29 March 1951, and Robert W. Johnson to Bertram Baker, 15 April 1951; 1951 Minutes and Proceedings of the American Tennis Association, Eaton papers, UNCW. For Florida A&M administrators' position, see A. S. Gaither to Bertram Baker, 7 April 1951, Eaton papers, UNCW. There is no direct evidence as to why Eaton, Johnson, and the college administrators were not invited to the New York meeting. The inference in the letters form Johnson and Florida A&M athletic director A. S. Gaither, however, is that ATA executive secretary Bertram Baker purposely orchestrated the meeting without inviting them so as to direct the meeting, and this aspect of Gibson's career, as he saw fit.

51. Robert W. Johnson to Bertram Baker, 15 April 1951, Eaton papers, UNCW.

52. Hubert A. Eaton Sr. to Althea Gibson, 19 April 1951, Eaton papers, UNCW.

53. Ibid. The following year, Gibson opted to skip the tour altogether so she could remain in school. Bertram L. Baker to H. V. S. Smith, 24 May 1952, Eaton papers, UNCW.

54. R. Walter Johnson to Bertram L. Baker, 21 January 1954; R. Walter Johnson to Bertram L. Baker, 21 December 1955; and Bertram L. Baker to R. Walter Johnson, 9 January 1956, Eaton papers, UNCW. Also, see R. Walter Johnson to Dr. Alphonso Elder, 29 August 1957, and R. Walter Johnson to Dr. Sylvester B. Smith, 18 September 1958, Eaton papers, UNCW.

55. Bertram L. Baker to R. Walter Johnson, 9 January 1956, Eaton papers, UNCW.

56. Gibson was an interesting mix of passivity and bravado. In certain situations, such as the ATA issue regarding the European tour, the evidence suggests that she initially sided with Baker and the ATA officials who wanted her to make the tour and worry about school later. However, in the end, she listened to the advice of her mentors and sought compromise. Later, her seeming passivity over being a racial hero, in truth, can also be seen in terms of the significant independence it took to stand against those within the black community who wanted her to be a civil rights champion. Rather than try to enter the murky waters of psychoanalysis, I endeavor in this chapter to show the ways in which Gibson's personality complicated both her own trajectory and her relationship with the communities that helped her.

57. Armistead S. Pride and Clint C. Wilson II, *A History of the Black Press* (Washington, DC: Howard University Press, 1997), 133. Also see Roland E. Wolseley, *The Black Press, U.S.A.*, 2d ed. (Ames: Iowa State University Press, 1990).

58. "Vivacious Althea Gibson to Defend Her National Women's Title This Week," *Pittsburgh Courier*, 21 August 1948, 11; Sam Lacy, "A to Z with Sam Lacy," 30 August 1947, 12; Jackie Reemes, "Althea Will Be Back," *New York Amsterdam News*, 9 September 1950, 27; *Pittsburgh Courier*, 12 August 1950, 23; Fay Young, "Through the Years," *Chicago Defender*, 30 August 1947, 11.

59. Gibson, *I Always Wanted to Be Somebody*, 88–89. For more on the Cold War and its relationship to the African American civil rights movement, see Mary L. Dudziak, *Cold War, Civil Rights: Race and the Image of American Democracy* (Princeton, NJ: Princeton University Press, 2000), especially the introduction, 3–17. For more on the goodwill tours and other aspects to the "cultural cold war," see Penny von Eschen, *Satchmo Blows Up the World: Jazz Ambassadors Play the Cold War* (Cambridge, MA: Harvard University Press, 2004); and Damion Thomas, "'The

Good Negroes': African-American Athletes and the Cultural Cold War, 1945–1968" (Ph.D. diss., University of California, Los Angeles, 2002).

60. Schoenfeld, *The Match*, 140–41; Fay Young, "Fay Says," *Chicago Defender*, 14 July 1956, 17.

61. African Americans continued to play baseball, of course, as the Negro Leagues became the black counterpart to the Major Leagues and an important part of black culture during the Jim Crow era.

62. When Rickey signed Robinson to the Dodger organization to start the 1946 season with his top farm team in Montreal, the *Afro-American* dispatched Lacy to follow Robinson for his first three years in professional baseball in order to bring Robinson's story to their African American readership. Mark W. Schraf, *"Wendell Smith,"* in *Twentieth-Century American Sportswriters*, ed. Richard Orodenker, vol. 171; *Dictionary of Literary Biography* (Detroit: Gale Research, 1996), 319–22; J. Douglas English, "Sam Lacy," in *Twentieth-Century American Sportswriters*, ed. Richard Orodenker, vol. 171; *Dictionary of Literary Biography* (Detroit: Gale Research, 1996), 176–77.

63. Jules Tygiel, *Baseball's Great Experiment: Jackie Robinson and His Legacy*, 2nd ed. (New York: Oxford University Press, 1997), 15–17, 64–67, 196.

64. Hubert A. Eaton Sr. to Althea Gibson, 6 April 1950, Eaton papers, UNCW.

65. Fay Young, "Fay Says," *Chicago Defender*, 14 July 1956, 17; Young, "Althea Gibson Not As Talkative," *Chicago Defender*, 7 July 1956, 17.

66. Gibson, *I Always Wanted to Be Somebody*, 158.

67. For a more comprehensive treatment of the Chicago incident, Gibson's falling out with the black press, and their tendency to view her accomplishments through the lens of race, see my article, "'The Tuskegee Flash' and 'the Slender Harlem Stroker,'" *Journal of Sport History* 28, no. 2 (Summer 2001): 233–52. In that article, I argued that Gibson's problems with the black press were a result of their tendency to view the careers of black women athletes predominately through the lens of race. While race remains central to the explanation of African American sports journalists' treatment of Gibson, another look at the sources suggests that a more dynamic understanding of Gibson's place in African American and American society is necessary.

68. Russ Cowans, "Sports Writers Sour on Althea," *Chicago Defender*, 27 July 1957, 1; Cowans, "She Should Be Told," *Chicago Defender*, 27 July 1957, 24; Wendell Smith, "Has Net Queen Althea Gibson Gone High Hat?" *Pittsburgh Courier*, 27 July 1957, 24; Fay Young, "Fay Says," *Chicago Defender*, 14 July 1956, 17.

69. Russ Cowans, "Sports Writers Sour on Althea," *Chicago Defender*, 27 July 1957, 1; Cowans, "She Should Be Told," *Chicago Defender*, 27 July 1957, 24; Wendell Smith, "Has Net Queen Althea Gibson Gone High Hat?" *Pittsburgh Courier*, 27 July 1957, 24; *Chicago Defender*, 14 September 1957, 24; Sam Lacy, "From A to Z," *Baltimore Afro-American*, 22 June 1957, 16. Eaton's son thought Gibson's trouble with the black press had a class element to it: "Middle-class Afro Americans can be wishy-washy sometimes. You would think that they would be proud to see her come up in the world. But at the same time, in the other breath, they would kind of put her down, as to what she was, you know." Eaton Jr. interview, 14 July 2005.

70. As I have shown, many of the black press papers blame the incident on Gibson's rudeness to news reporters, making no mention of the Jim Crow episode at the hotel and restaurant. In her autobiography, Gibson does not specifically mention

the incident, but it is clear she is referring to it when she discusses becoming "Public Enemy No. 1" with some black newspapers because she won't turn her "tennis achievements into a rousing crusade for racial equality" (see Gibson, *I Always Wanted to Be Somebody*, 158–59). A *Time* magazine article that appeared shortly after Gibson won the River Forest Tournament in Chicago connects Gibson's sentiments about the black press with the episode in Chicago. The exchange involved, in part, the Oak Park Hotel, which would not allow Gibson a reservation. "Officials and newsmen burned with rage," observed the *Time* article, "but Althea hardly noticed it" (see "That Gibson Girl," *Time*, 26 August 1957, 48).

71. Ted Poston, "The Story of Althea Gibson," reprinted in the *Pittsburgh Courier*, magazine section, 26 October 1957, 3.

72. Gibson, *I Always Wanted to Be Somebody*, 151–52.

73. The title of the John Wayne movie is *The Horse Soldiers*, a Civil War film in which Gibson plays a house slave at a plantation that Wayne and his union soldiers use as a rest stop between battles. This synopsis of Gibson's life in the ten years following her retirement from tennis is taken from her second autobiography. See Althea Gibson, with Richard Curtis, *So Much to Live For* (New York: G. P. Putnam's Sons, 1968).

74. Gibson and Darben eventually renewed their relationship and, although they maintained separate apartments and never remarried, remained together until his death in the late 1990s. Frances Clayton Gray and Yanick Rick Lamb, *Born to Win: The Authorized Biography of Althea Gibson* (Hoboken, NJ: John Wiley & Sons, 2004), 165–71; Eaton Jr. interview, 14 July 2005; The Southeastern Regional Black Archives Research Center and Museum, Florida A&M University, Tallahassee, Florida.

75. Schoenfeld, *The Match*, 2–7.

76. Gibson, *So Much to Live For*, 68, 17.

77. Eaton Jr. interview, 14 July 2005.

78. Gibson, *I Always Wanted to Be Somebody*, 2.

79. Zina Garrison showed promise during the 1980s, turning professional in 1982. She had success as a doubles partner, winning a number of women's and mixed doubles championships, but was never able to capture the women's singles title at Wimbledon or the U.S. Open. In 1990, she overcame some stiff competition, knocking out Monica Seles and Steffi Graf, to make it to the final, but lost to Martina Navratilova.

FOUR

1. The members of the 1960 Olympic women's 400-meter relay team were Martha Hudson (Pee Wee), Barbara Jones (B. J.), Lucinda Williams (Little Dancer), and Wilma Rudolph (Skeeter). The nicknames for the athletes are pulled from Ed Temple, with B'Lou Carter, *Only the Pure in Heart Survive* (Nashville: Broadman Press, 1980), 61–67. Rudolph wrote that her nickname of Skeeter got started because, with her long arms and legs, she looked like a mosquito. Wilma Rudolph, *Wilma: The Story of Wilma Rudolph* (New York: New American Library, 1977), 83.

2. Jerry Footlick, "Wilma Reserves Hurrying for the Cinders Only," The Ed Temple Collection, Special Collections and Archives, Brown-Daniel Library, Tennessee State University, Nashville, Tennessee.

3. First awarded in 1930, Rudolph was the third woman to win the Sullivan Award. Swimmer Ann Curtis won the award in 1944 and diver Patricia Keller McCormick won in 1956. "Wilma Voted Amateur of Year Award," *Chicago Tribune*, 3 January 1962, sec. B, 2.

4. See L. J. "Brock" Brockenbury, "Storming the Citadel," *Time*, 10 February 1961, Temple Collection, TSU.

5. Tennessee State, organized as a black normal school in 1912, underwent several name changes during its first sixty years. When it gained full land-grant university status in 1958, it became Tennessee State Agricultural and Industrial State University, also known in shorthand as Tennessee A&I. It did not become Tennessee State University, its name today, until 1968. To avoid confusion, I refer to the university throughout this chapter and the next as either Tennessee State University, or, more often, just Tennessee State.

6. In his biographical essay in *Out of the Shadows*, Wayne Wilson has ably recapped the various discrepancies in the accounts of Rudolph's life. The most frequent differences include the number of children in her family and Rudolph's birth order, her birthplace, the childhood illnesses that necessitated the brace on her leg, the afflicted leg, the age at which she was able to walk without the brace, the summer she first attended Ed Temple's summer track program at Tennessee State, and some details of her track career. See Wayne Wilson, "Wilma Rudolph: The Making of an Olympic Icon," in *Out of the Shadows: A Biographical History of African American Athletes*, ed. David K. Wiggins (Fayetteville: University of Arkansas Press, 2006), 403.

7. Despite certain inaccuracies within Rudolph's autobiography itself as noted in note 6, I use it as the source for this portion of the chapter unless other primary sources provide compelling contrary evidence. Rudolph, *Wilma*, 5–13.

8. Ibid., 29.

9. Ibid., 41.

10. Ed Temple, Interview by author, tape recording, Nashville, Tennessee, 17 July 2007. The rule regarding the cars was designed to prevent the young women athletes from hooking up with young men.

11. Temple, *Pure in Heart*, 182–83; Temple interview, 17 July 2007. In 1978, Tennessee State dedicated its new 400-meter, all-weather track to Ed Temple. By that time, thirty-two of his Tigerbelles had participated in Olympic games. Thirty-one of them returned to Nashville for the dedication ceremony, including Rudolph. See "Tennessee State Honors Coach with a New Track," *New York Times*, 9 April 1978, sec. S, 4.

12. Rudolph, *Wilma*, 59.

13. The year that Rudolph first attended Temple's summer program at Tennessee State is one of the items that is in dispute in the different accounts of her life. Although Rudolph puts the year at 1956, other accounts show her competing for Tennessee State in the junior division at the AAU Nationals at Ponca City, Oklahoma, in 1955. See Louise Mead Tricard, *American Women's Track and Field: A History, 1895 through 1980* (Jefferson, NC: MacFarland & Company, 1985), 352. Regardless of the specific year she began, she attended the summer track program for several years while a high school student and, during this time, built a strong bond with Temple and Tennessee State.

14. Ibid., 69–70; Temple interview, 17 July 2007.

15. "Chicago Comet Girls Take 2d in A.A.U. Track," *Chicago Tribune*, 19 June

1955, A4; Ralph Bernstein, "Six Records Fall in Girls AAU Meet," *Washington Post and Times Herald*, 18 August 1956, 8; "Tigerbelles Capture 5th AAU Title in Row," *Chicago Defender*, 18 July 1959, 24.

16. The AAU first held junior championships for women in 1946 in conjunction with the senior women's indoor championship meet. For the next several years, the junior championships were contested sporadically. When contested, they were held in conjunction with the senior outdoor nationals. The first year that Rudolph joined the Tigerbelles at the nationals in Ponca City, Oklahoma (1955), was the year that the AAU had established the "girls" division of the meet. Tricard, *American Women's Track and Field*, 281–351.

17. Temple interview, 17 July 2007.

18. Ibid. The recorded times for both runners were 24.2 seconds. Tricard, *American Women's Track and Field*, 362. Mae Faggs was Temple's first recruit to the program he began in 1952. He didn't consider her the best or fastest on the team, but without her, he suggested, the TSU women's track program "might not have been on the map." Temple, *Pure in Heart*, 61.

19. Blankers-Koen had also won gold in 1948 in the 80-meter hurdles.

20. Third- and fourth-place finishes were so close in the 100 meters that originally Daniels was brought to the victory stand for the bronze. Scrutiny of the photo finish, however, revealed that she had taken fourth place. Tricard, *American Women's Track and Field*, 360.

21. Tricard, *American Women's Track and Field*, 358–60; Rudolph, *Wilma*, 97.

22. Rudolph's autobiography does not indicate which was the case. Although there is no direct evidence to indicate why Temple made the decision he did, evidence does suggest that, recognizing her innate athletic ability, Temple bent the rules for Rudolph. He could be quite strict with his athletes once they were part of his program, even kicking them off the team for infractions of the rules. Of course, Temple may have been less strict in his application of rules before young women came to his program.

23. Rudolph, *Wilma*, 119–24.

24. Sid Ziff, "Wilma Proves They're Not All 'Muscle Molls'"; Lee D. Jenkins, "Barbara Jones, Nation's Fastest Female, Proves Feminine, Too"; and Bob Harding, "Temple Leads the Girls," all from the Temple Collection, TSU.

25. Arthur Daley, "Sports of *The Times*: In Praise of the Greeks," *New York Times*, 9 September 1960, 20.

26. Ibid.

27. Ibid.

28. Melvin Durslag, "Fastest Female," Temple Collection, TSU.

29. The focus of physical education classes during WWII to help make men, and women, fit for the war effort may also have helped usher in a return to intercollegiate competition for women, thereby also contributing to increased acceptance for U.S. women's track and field. See Ying Wushanley, *Playing Nice and Losing: The Struggle for Control of Women's Intercollegiate Athletics, 1960–2000* (Syracuse, NY: Syracuse University Press, 2004), 14–15.

30. The two countries also agreed upon dual contests on separate dates in weightlifting and wrestling for men, and basketball for men and women.

31. The dual meets took place every year from 1958 to 1965 except in 1960 and

1964, which were Olympic years. A meet was scheduled for 1966, but the Soviet Union withdrew in protest over United States' policies in Vietnam. "U.S., Russia Agree on Dates for Meets," *New York Times*, 16 March 1958, sec. S, 1; "Who Won Meet? Russians Hedge," *New York Times*, 17 July 1961, 15; "U.S.-Soviet Event Start in 1958," *New York Times*, 12 July 1966, 16. For more on these dual meets, see Joseph M. Turrini, "It Was Communism Versus the Free World: The USA-USSR Dual Track Meet Series and the Development of Track and Field in the United States, 1958–1985," *Journal of Sport History* 28 (Fall 2001): 427–71.

32. Temple Collection, TSU.

33. There were others within the world of track and field who desired a new image. Bobby Murray, coach of the men's track team at Buffalo State University in New York, wanted to begin a women's track program. But although women made up over half of the student body numbering 2,700, he couldn't convince school officials to let him start one. The real problem preventing the sport's growth in the United States was in trying to "break some of the barriers" regarding social acceptance. See Frances Lewine, "Women Track Stars Cite Extra Benefits," *Nashville Tennessean*, 26 January 1959, 11, Temple Collection, TSU.

34. Bob Harding, "Temple Leads the Girls," Temple Collection, TSU; Temple interview, 17 July 2007.

35. Lee D. Jenkins, "Barbara Jones, Nation's Fastest Female, Proves Feminine, Too," Temple Collection, TSU.

36. Frances Lewine, "Women Track Stars Cite Extra Benefits," *Nashville Tennessean*, 26 January 1959, 11. Suggesting that women should take up track and field for their figure was a common theme during this period. In a second article that appeared in spring 1961, the reporter recommended, "Make tracks, girls! You may never win a medal but the waistline's worth it." See Mary Phyllis Ridley, "Be Slim— Run with Women," Temple Collection, TSU.

37. Temple interview, 17 July 2007. Rudolph's story and her embodiment of Temple's feminine image to advance women's track and field exposes the way in which 1950s American society circumscribed the concept of femininity, including the focus toward heterosexuality to combat fears over a lesbian presence in sport. Many other scholars have already explored issues of gender and sport, as indicated in note 2 in the Introduction. In particular, Susan Cahn does a masterful job addressing gender, sport, and sexuality, including fears of lesbianism, in *Coming on Strong*. More specific to African American women, Ramona Bell's dissertation, which includes a chapter on Wilma Rudolph, exposes how representations of the bodies of black women athletes reflected conflict over the ways whites and African Americans constructed and under-stood race and gender during the last forty years of the twentieth century. See R. J. Bell, "Competing Identities: Representations of Black Female Sporting Body from 1960 to the Present" (Ph.D. diss., Bowling Green State University, 2008). My own focus is more on race and racism, and the ways they changed black women athletes experience from those of white women. Where gender does inevitability enter their narrative, I am concerned primarily with the various strategies that black women ath-letes used to counter stereotypes in order to navigate their own complicated place at the intersection of white and black society—in short, to delve further into the issues Cahn introduces in her chapter on women's track and field. See Cahn, "'Cinderellas' of Sport: Black Women in Track and Field," in *Coming on Strong*, 110–39.

38. Jack Clowser, "National AAU Winners: Track Stars Train Here to Meet Reds," *Cleveland Plain Dealer*, 29 June 1959, 34; Stan Hochman, "Coach Called It: Red Gals Too Much"; and Brad Wilson, "Wants U.S. Help in A.A.U. Fight," 15 August 1962, all from Temple Collection, TSU.

39. For more on the concept of the Russian women athlete as "other," see Cahn, *Coming on Strong*, 132–33.

40. "'We Don't Want Amazons,'" *Detroit News*, Sec. B, 1, Temple Collection, TSU.

41. Stan Hochman, "Coach Called It: Red Gals Too Much"; "Temple Bemoans Few Meets; A&I Girls Win 10th AAU"; and Frances Lewine, "Women Track Stars Cite Extra Benefits," *Nashville Tennessean*, 26 January 1959, 11, all from Temple Collection, TSU.

42. "Boys: Your (Duty?) Not to Date Olympic Girls," 26 July 1964, Temple Collection, TSU.

43. "Double Sprint Champion Didn't Walk until She Was 8," *Philadelphia Inquirer*, 10 September 1960, 12; Jerry Footlick, "Price of Fame Heavy on Wilma's Head," 11 September 1960, Temple Collection, TSU; Temple interview, 17 July 2007. Rudolph relates in her autobiography that the fame and attention coming her way caused jealousy on the part of some of her teammates, especially during their European travels after the Olympics. Some of the other athletes stopped speaking to her in Rome, which was fairly mild compared to what happened in London. While there for the British Empire Games, they hid her curlers so that she had to appear at the banquet with her hair still wet from running in the rain at the meet, and they purposely "dogged it" on the 400-meter relay to try to lose the race. According to Rudolph, she came forty meters from behind in the anchor leg to win the race, and the British fans went wild, further cementing her relationship with the European crowds. Coach Temple does not remember such difficulties, but suggests that all the athletes were a bit cross on the tour because they wanted to go home. Regardless of whose memory was more "accurate," Rudolph's track success in Europe following the Olympic games served to solidify her celebrity status with the European fans. See Rudolph, *Wilma*, 138–40; Temple interview, 17 July 2007.

44. Sid Ziff, "Wilma Proves They're Not All 'Muscle Molls'"; "Double Sprint Champion Didn't Walk until She Was 8," *Philadelphia Inquirer*, 10 September 1960, 12; and "A&I Star Sets '200' Record," *Nashville Banner*, 3 September 1960, 9, all from Temple Collection, TSU.

45. Robert L. Teague, "Wilma Rudolph Kept on the Run," Temple Collection, TSU.

46. I am taking issue here with Susan Cahn's interpretation that "the few athletes who attained a visible presence" during this period, of which Rudolph was the most notable, were considered exceptional in relation to their femininity and acceptability. The evidence indicates a clear transition from Coachman's career, helped particularly by the Cold War, Ed Temple's success, and Rudolph's popularity and prominence in the sport. The majority of Cahn's evidence is during the mid-1950s, prior to the time I argue the change had fully taken hold. See Cahn, *Coming on Strong*, 133–37.

47. Temple interview, 17 July 2007. Althea Gibson also remembered the difficulty of dealing with her hair—and Karol Fagero's surprise at the time and trouble—when she traveled on the State Department goodwill tour. See Gibson, *I Always Wanted to Be Somebody*, 91–94.

48. Jack Disney, "Wilma Overcomes Ills," Temple Collection, TSU. It is interesting

how Rudolph's unwed pregnancy, even to this day, generally remains absent from American public memory.

49. Jesse Owens, "Wilma Rudolph: Gazelle of the Track," *Saturday Evening Post*, October 1976, 44 (Temple Collection); Wilson, "Wilma Rudolph," in *Out of the Shadows*, 214–15. Wilson argues that use of the nicknames in context with their European origins enabled sportswriters to suggest Rudolph's race without explicit mention of it, allowing them to avoid the race issue. The contrast with athletes like Coachman, her teammates, and even Gibson remains striking, however. The European nicknames, while meant to be flattering, were still grounded in racial images that linked African American sporting ability to their nature, a nature that was comparable to, the image would have us believe, the nature of animals known for speed.

50. In her autobiography, Rudolph imbues considerable racial significance to the events surrounding her homecoming following the 1960 Olympics. She asserts that the parade, as the first integrated event in the history of the town, broke the color barrier. She also relates remarks made by Judge Hudson, a white judge of the city, at the evening banquet: "Ladies and gentlemen, you play a piano. You can play very nice music on a piano by playing only the black keys on it, and you can play very nice music on the same piano by playing only the white keys on it. But ladies and gentlemen, the absolute best music comes out of that piano when you play both the black keys and the white keys together." Everyone applauded after the speech, the track star remembered. Rudolph, *Wilma*, 144–45.

51. The Millrose Athletic Association began as a recreation club for the employees of the John Wanamaker Department Store in 1908, and the first games were held the same year at a local armory. In 1914, having outgrown the armory, the association moved the games to Madison Square Garden where they now enjoy the distinction of being the oldest continuous sporting event held there. Originally the Wanamaker 1-½ Mile race, the Wanamaker Mile was born in 1926 when the length was shortened. It is a highlight of the meet and often run at 10:00 p.m., a holdover from the days when Ted Husing, a legendary sports announcer, would broadcast the race live on his radio show. "Millrose Games, webpage: History." http://www.millrose-games.com/2008/history/ (accessed 22 February 2008).

52. The Drake Relays also had a "queen." In 1961, it was Miss Lynn Auld of the University of South Dakota, who had the opportunity to meet and "chat with" the "queen of women's track," Wilma Rudolph. See "Track Queens," *Washington Post*, 29 April 1961, sec. A, 14. Ralph Alexander, "Wilma's Speed Wows 13, 622," Temple Collection, TSU; "Millrose Games, webpage: History." http://www.millrose-games.com/2008/history/ (accessed 5 February 2008); "Drake Relays, webpage: Archive-History." http://www.drakerelays.org/archive.htm (accessed 5 February 2008); "The Penn Relays, webpage: History of the Penn Relays." http://www.pennathletics.com/ViewArticle.dbml?DB_OEM_ID=1700&KEY=&ATCLID=236852&SPID=559&SPSID=10779 (accessed 5 February 2008); "Millrose Games, webpage: Millrose Decade by Decade, 1927–1938." http://www.millrose-games.com/2008/history/decade1928–1937.htm (accessed 5 February 2008); "Storming the Citadel," *Time*, 10 February 1961, Temple Collection, TSU. "Track Queen," *Los Angeles Times*, 17 January 1961, sec. C, 2.

53. Sam Balter, "One for the Book," *Los Angeles Mirror*, 18 January 1961; Harley Tinkham, "Full House Looms for Wilma," *Los Angeles Mirror*, 21 January 1961, 6;

Ralph Alexander, "Wilma's Speed Wows 13,622"; L. J. "Brock" Brockenbury, "Tying the Score," all from Temple Collection, TSU.

54. Jesse Abramson, "Miss Rudolph Breaks Millrose's Barrier Against Distaff Side," Temple Collection, TSU. Admiral John J. Bergen, Rear Admiral, of the Navy Reserves, was the chairman of the Graham-Paige investment firm that bought control of Madison Square Garden in 1959. In November 1960, the firm announced plans for a new $38,000,000 sports and entertainment complex to include the fourth and existing Madison Square Garden arena. Robert M. Lipsyte, "Bergen, Quesada Near Agreement," *New York Times*, 14 November 1960, 45.

55. "Storming the Citadel," *Time*, 10 February 1961; Thomas Reynolds, "Where There's a Wilma ... 9,295 Desert Home and TV Set for Track," 19 February 1961; "Sellout Crowd Will See Cal Relays," 26 May 1961; and Bud Collins, "Admirers Storm Wilma Rudolph," *Boston Herald*, 7 May 1961, 63, all from Temple Collection, TSU. Other indoor meets that Rudolph participated in that season include the Mason-Dixon Games in Louisville, Kentucky, the Cal Relays in Modesto, California, and the prestigious Drake Relays at Drake University in Des Moines, Iowa.

56. Robert K. Barney, Stephen R. Wenn, and Scott G. Martyn, *Selling the Five Rings: The International Olympic Committee and the Rise of Olympic Commercialism*, rev. ed. (Salt Lake City: University of Utah Press, 2004), 75.

57. Temple interview, 17 July 2007.

58. "Storming the Citadel," *Time*, 10 February 1961, Temple Collection, TSU.

59. "Where There's a Wilma ... 9,295 Desert Home and TV Set for Track," 19 February 1961; Ralph Alexander, "Wilma's Speed Wows 13,622"; L. J. "Brock" Brockenbury, "Tying the Score"; "Storming the Citadel," *Time*, 10 February 1961, all from Temple Collection, TSU; "3 Olympic Stars Eclipsed at Drake," *New York Times*, 30 April 1961, sec. S, 1; "Track Queens," *Washington Post*, 29 April 1961, sec. A, 14.

60. Mary Phyllis Ridley, "Be Slim—Run with Women," Temple Collection, TSU; Sid Ziff, "Wilma Proves They're Not All 'Muscle Molls,'" Temple Collection, TSU; "Millrose Track Chief Predicts Meet Records Here on Friday," *New York Times*, 1 February 1961, 44. The image of women athletes as "beauty queen" had been applied to women in other sports, but not track and field athletes. See Cahn, *Coming on Strong*, 47.

61. Jeane Hoffman, "Speedy Wilma Rudolph Not Interested in Racing Men," *Los Angeles Times*, 19 January 1961, sec. C, 1; "Storming the Citadel," *Time*, 10 February 1961, Temple Collection, TSU.

62. "The Penn Relays, webpage: History of the Penn Relays." http://www.pennathletics.com/ViewArticle.dbml?DB_OEM_ID=1700&KEY=&ATCLID=236852&SPID=559&SPSID=10779 (accessed 7 February 2008).

63. Tom C. Brody, "At Last the Girls Are Ours," 68, *Sports Illustrated*, Temple Collection, TSU.

64. Rudolph's autobiography does not mention when she and Eldridge began dating again, but it could not have been for more than a year, probably less. Eldridge was, in reality, Rudolph's second husband. In 1961, she had married William Ward, a fellow student at Tennessee State. They divorced the following year, sometime in 1962. She and Eldridge married sometime during the summer of 1963. They remained married for seventeen years; Rudolph filed for divorce in 1980, indicating that the marriage had never really worked. See Smith, *Wilma Rudolph*, 90–91.

65. Although she doesn't mention it in her autobiography, Rudolph gave birth to one more child several years later, in 1971. See Maureen M. Smith, *Wilma Rudolph: A Biography* (Westport, CT: Greenwood Press, 2006), 89.

66. Rudolph, *Wilma*, 161, 163. Some of the jobs that Rudolph mentions in the ten or so years following leaving her teaching job in Clarkesville include various positions with the Job Corps program; a program called "Operation Champ," through a special request of Vice President Hubert Humphrey, that sent star athletes into the ghettos to teach their sports to the kids; various jobs out in California, including an administrator position at UCLA's Afro-American Studies program; and Mayor Daley's Youth Foundation program in Chicago. Rudolph discusses only some of her positions and moves in her autobiography. For a more comprehensive accounting of these years, see Smith, *Wilma Rudolph*, 86–90.

67. Jesse Owens, "Wilma Rudolph: Gazelle of the Track," *Saturday Evening Post*, October 1976, 44, Temple Collection, TSU.

68. Temple, *Pure in Heart*, 64.

FIVE

1. Paul Zimmerman, "Briton Zips 48.1 for Hurdles Mark," *Los Angeles Times*, 16 October 1968, G1; "Oerter, Miss Tyus Retain Crowns," *Washington Post*, 16 October 1968, D1.

2. Tyus achieved her eighth world record before she retired as a member of the U.S. women's 4x100-meter Olympic gold-medal relay team.

3. Jim Cour, "Fleet Ex-Olympian Wyomia Likes Motherhood and Track," *Baltimore Afro-American*, 5 April 1968, 9. The next sprinter to repeat as Olympic champion in the 100 meter was Carl Lewis, although one of his victories came in a boycotted Olympics and the other came when gold medalist Ben Johnson tested positive for steroids and was stripped of his gold medal and world record (1984 and 1988, 1984 being the year the Soviet Union boycotted the Los Angeles Olympics). The only other track athlete to win back-to-back Olympic gold in the 100 meter has been Gail Devers, another African American woman, in 1992 and 1996.

4. George Strickler, "U.S. Wins 10 Olympic Gold Medals," *Chicago Tribune*, 21 October 1968, C1. The "year of awakening" is borrowed from David Wiggins's description of the athletic protests of that year in David K. Wiggins, "'The Year of Awakening': Black Athletes, Racial Unrest, and the Civil Rights Movement of 1968," in *Glory Bound: Black Athletes in a White America*, Sports and Entertainment, ed. Steven A. Riess (Syracuse, NY: Syracuse University Press, 1997), 104–22.

5. Ed Temple, with B'Lou Carter, *Only the Pure in Heart Survive* (Nashville: Broadman Press, 1980), 64, 68.

6. "Wyomia Tyus, Track and Field," Top 100 Sports Illustrated Women, http://sportsillustrated.cnn.com/siforwomen/top_100/43/ (accessed 27 February 2012); Emily Wilkens, "Diet, Exercise Yield Athlete's Trim Body," *Hartford Courant*, 26 September 1976, 10E.

7. Wyomia Tyus, *Inside Jogging for Women: A Comprehensive Guide to Running for Fun and Fitness* (Chicago: Contemporary Books, 1978), x–xi; John C. Walter and Malina Iida, eds., *Better than the Best: Black Athletes Speak, 1920–2007* (Seattle: University of Washington Press, 2010), 134–36; Anne Janette Johnson, *Great Women*

in Sports (Detroit: Visible Ink Press, 1996), 480; "Wyomia Tyus—Early Training," Wyomia Tyus Biography, http://sports.jrank.org/pages/4979/Tyus-Wyomia-Early-Training.html (accessed 1 July 2011).

8. Tyus, *Inside Jogging*, x.

9. From 1955 through 1969, Tennessee State won the national outdoor champi- onship every year but 1964, when they came in second, losing by one point. Tricard, *American Women's Track and Field*, 353–526.

10. "Sports & Recreation: Wyomia Tyus," The New Georgia Encyclopedia, http://www.georgiaencyclopedia.org/nge/Article.jsp?id=h=836 (accessed 8 March 2012); Tyus, *Inside Jogging*, x; Temple, *Only the Pure in Heart*, 65.

11. Tyus, *Inside Jogging*, x; Walter and Iida, *Better than the Best*, 137; Tricard, *American Women's Track and Field*, 432, 442–43.

12. Tricard, *American Women's Track and Field*, 456; "U.S. Girls Trounced by West Germans in Track," *Washington Post*, 31 July 1963, B10; Earl Clanton III, "Two Records Set by Tenn. Track Belles," *Baltimore Afro-American*, 22 February 1964, 10; Bill Anderson, "Tenn. State's Wyomia Tyus Seen as Wilma's Successor," *Norfolk Journal and Guide*, 13 June 1964, 23.

13. Wilfrid Smith, "U.S. Track Team Piles Up Wide Lead," *Chicago Tribune*, 26 July 1964, B1; "Edith McGuire Wins 2 Titles," *Chicago Tribune*, 8 August 1964, B1; Frank Litsky, "Miss McGuire Excels in Track," *New York Times*, 9 August 1964, S1; Bill Anderson, "Tenn. State's Wyomia Tyus Seen as Wilma's Successor," *Norfolk Journal and Guide*, 13 June 1964, 23; "Americans Win Two Olympic Gold Medals in Track and Two in Swimming," *New York Times*, 17 October 1964, 20.

14. Tom C. Brody, "At Last the Girls Are Ours," 68, *Sports Illustrated*, Temple Collection, TSU.

15. James Oliver Horton and Lois E. Horton, *Hard Road to Freedom: The Story of African America*, vol. 2 (New Brunswick, NJ: Rutgers University Press, 2002), 156.

16. Lyndon B. Johnson, "The Voting Rights Act Should be Passed," in Raymond D'Angelo, *American Civil Rights Movement: Readings and Interpretations* (New York: McGraw Hill/Dushkin, 2001), 349–50.

17. "Soviet Men Lead U.S. Track Stars, 58 to 57," *Chicago Tribune*, 1 August 1965, B1.

18. "Polish Fans in a Tizzy, Irena Runs Rivals Dizzy," *Los Angeles Times*, 24 March 1966, B5; David Halberstam, "Irena Kirszenstein People's Choice in Warsaw," *New York Times*, 8 August 1965, S4; Jerry Shnay, "Grandstand," *Chicago Tribune*, 13 April 1967, Ind12; "Polish Sprinter, Who Failed Sex Test, to Lose Victories, Medals," *Los Angeles Times*, 26 February 1968, B4. The issue of "proof of sex" first surfaced in Olympic competition twenty years earlier, just a few days after Alice Coachman won her gold medal. The International Amateur Athletic Federation, governing body for track and field, ruled in August 1948 that women track athletes would have to prove they were women before competing in the Olympic games and any time a world record was set. Doctor-signed medical certificates would be acceptable for establishing proof. "Women Must Prove Sex to Run in Olympics," *Atlanta Constitution*, 11 August 1948, 8.

19. David Halberstam, "Warsaw Toasting Its Girl Runners," *New York Times*, 7 August 1965, 17.

20. "Foul Costs Pennel New U.S. Record," *Washington Post*, 16 January 1966, C5;

"Pennel Vaults to World Mark, But … ," *Chicago Tribune*, 15 January 1966, B1; "2 Women Set Indoor Records," *Chicago Tribune*, 26 February 1966, F1; "Women Set 3 Records in AAU Meet," *Chicago Tribune*, 6 March 1966, B4; "Miss Tyus 1st in N.A.A.U. Meet 100-Yard Dash," *Chicago Tribune*, 3 July 1966, B4.

21. Darlene Clark Hine, William C. Hine, and Stanley Harrold, *African Americans: A Concise History*, Volume Two: Since 1865 (Upper Saddle River, NJ: Prentice Hall, 2004), 434.

22. For an interesting perspective on Harry Edwards, see Tommie Smith with David Steele, *Silent Gesture: The Autobiography of Tommie Smith* (Philadelphia: Temple University Press, 2007), 114–25.

23. Wiggins, "'Year of Awakening,'" 110–11.

24. Both Amy Bass and Douglas Hartmann have examined and articulated this transition from *Negro* to *black* athlete that occurred during 1968 and was centered around the Olympic protest. See Amy Bass, *Not the Triumph but the Struggle: The 1968 Olympics and the Making of the Black Athlete* (Minneapolis: University of Minnesota Press, 2002) and Douglas Hartmann, *Race, Culture, and the Revolt of the Black Athlete: The 1968 Olympic Protests and Their Aftermath* (Chicago: University of Chicago Press, 2003).

25. Tricard, *American Women's Track and Field*, 501–7; Frank Litsky, "Matthews and Beamon Score Victories in Meet at Montreal," *New York Times*, 10 August 1967, 30.

26. Wiggins, "'Year of Awakening,'" 108. Muhammad Ali had been stripped of his heavyweight boxing title when his stance as a conscientious objector to the Vietnam War was denied and he was found guilty of draft evasion.

27. Neil Amdur, "Negro Hopes to Pin Down Medal," *New York Times*, 12 October 1968, 45; Steven Stern, *Fists of Freedom: The Story of the '68 Summer Games*, VHS. Directed by George Roy (HBO Sports, 1999).

28. Al Stilley, "Temple Wants Negro Voice on Olympic Committee," *Nashville Banner*, 19 October 1968, The Ed Temple Collection, Special Collections and Archives, Brown-Daniel Library, Tennessee State University, Nashville, Tennessee.

29. Bob Cohn and Steve Ball Jr., "The Elucidation of Wyomia," *Los Angeles Times*, 14 September 1969, M25; Walter and Iida, eds., *Better than the Best*, 145; Kenny Moore, "The Eye of the Storm," *Sports Illustrated*, 12 August 1991, 71, 130–31.

30. Pete Axthlem, "The Angry Black Athlete," *Newsweek*, 15 July 1968, 57D, quoted in Hartmann, *Race, Culture, and the Revolt of the Black Athlete*, 142.

31. Hartmann, *Race, Culture, and the Revolt of the Black Athlete*, 85–87; Bass, *Not the Triumph*, 189–91. Bass calls the shift from *Negro* to *black* athlete paradigmatic, arguing that this most important, redefining work of the OPHR and its boycott discussions was not only political and racial but also *masculine*. For more on the black power movement and its masculine focus, see Joseph Peniel, ed., *The Black Power Movement: Rethinking the Civil Rights–Black Power Era* (New York: Routledge, 2006); and Rolland Murray, *Our Living Manhood: Literature, Black Power, and Masculine Ideology* (Philadelphia: University of Philadelphia Press, 2007).

32. Al Stilley, "Temple Wants Negro Voice on Olympic Committee," *Nashville Banner*, 19 October 1968, Temple Collection, TSU.

33. Martin Luther King's assassination in April had briefly united the athletes behind the boycott question. Even long jumper Ralph Boston who had long been against boycotting went on record to say he was considering joining forces with Smith, Evans, and

even Edwards. But as the months wore on, the unity evaporated. Even though a possible boycott had dwindled from all African American athletes to the black track and field athletes, the elimination of blacks from the U.S. Olympic track squad was still projected to make a significant impact. Of the approximately sixty spots available on the track and field team, African Americans were expected to win roughly twenty-five of them and to dominate in the sprints. John Wiebusch, "King's Death May Cause Boston to Join Olympic Boycott," *Los Angeles Times*, 9 April 1968, B1; "Edwards Sees 'Total' Negro Olympic Boycott," *Los Angeles Times*, 12 April 1968, B11.

34. Richard Stone, "Revolt in Sports," *Wall Street Journal*, 19 June 1968, 1; William Gildea, "Negro Boycott Vote Set for Weekend," *Washington Post*, 26 June 1968, D4. The OPHR was active during the opening months of 1968 as black athletes continued to struggle with whether to boycott the Olympic games. In February 1968, all but nine track and field athletes boycotted the New York Athletic Club (NYAC) Games and a crowd of six hundred outside the games protested the club's exclusion of blacks and Jews. An end to the NYAC's discrimination had been one of the demands set forth by the OPHR during its organization. Frank Litsky, "Young Sets 2-Mile New York A.C. Meet Mark," *New York Times*, 17 February 1968, 19. In April, the athletes also realized one of the goals of the OPHR platform when the IOC voted to rescind its invitation to South Africa and Rhodesia to participate in the Mexico City games. Despite IOC president Avery Brundage's insistence that racial politics did not play a role in their decision, world opinion leaned the other way. Most people felt that the boycott threats of nations around the world in response to South Africa and Rhodesia's apartheid policies influenced the IOC. "32 African Nations Vote to Boycott '68 Olympics," *Los Angeles Times*, 27 February 1968, B2; "Athletes Petition for U.S. Boycott of Olympics if South Africa Stays," *Washington Post*, 12 April 1968, D4; "Olympic Committee Votes to Bar South Africa from Mexico Games," *New York Times*, 24 April 1968, 35.

35. The USOC had decided to separate the track and field trials for the Mexico City games into two stages. Those who passed the first stage would go on to high-altitude training to prepare for racing in the challenge of the high altitude that Mexico City would present. While this was billed as "training" by the USOC, Tommie Smith argues that the first set of trials was really a "diversion" by the USOC to ensure that the official trials were not marked by controversy or protest. See Smith, *Silent Gesture*, 165.

36. "Track Mark Tied by Miss Ferrell," *New York Times*, 3 July 1967, 23; Lynn Lilliston, "Olympic Hopefuls to Toe the Mark," *Los Angeles Times*, 9 August 1968, E1; Shav Glick, "Margaret Bailes May Be the First to Run 11 Seconds Flat," *Los Angeles Times*, 23 August 1968, E8; Bill Becker, "Miss Tyus, Mrs. Bailes Offer Fast 1, 2," *New York Times*, 27 August 1968, 50; Tricard, *American Women's Track and Field*, 516.

37. Bob Ottum, "Dolls on the Move to Mexico," *Sports Illustrated*, 2 September 1968, 16–18.

38. "Blacks Delay Boycott Plan," *Chicago Tribune*, 2 July 1968, C1.

39. "Why Boycott Failed Told by Edwards," *Chicago Tribune*, 1 September 1968, B1; Smith, *Silent Gesture*, 166. A 4 September article by the *Chicago Defender* indicated that Smith and other black Olympic athletes concurred with Edwards's paper at the Philadelphia Black Power conference that indicated that athletes would not boycott the games. This would seem to contradict Smith's autobiography, in which he

indicated that the final decision on a boycott was not reached until the Denver meeting at the end of September. There may have been an issue of not wanting to contradict Edwards, publicly, however, in order to preserve the illusion of unity as much as possible. See "U.S. 'Olympians' Show Strength in Canada," *Chicago Defender*, 4 September 1968, 26.

40. "Games Must Go On—U.S. Olympians," *Los Angeles Times*, 4 October 1968, F9. Also see Gary Kale, "'We'll Win Our Share of Medals' Predicts Olympian Wyomia Tyus," *Norfolk Journal and Guide*, 12 October 1968, 14.

41. "Olympic Win Would Put Wyomia in Special Class," *Baltimore Afro-American*, 12 October 1968, 24; Goerge Strickler, "Oerter Wins 4th Discus Title in Row," *Chicago Tribune*, 16 October 1968, D1; Tyus, *Inside Jogging*, ix; George Strickler, "U.S. Sweeps 400; Beamon Jumps 29–2½!," *Chicago Tribune*, 19 October 1968, F1; Strickler, "U.S. Wins 10 Olympic Gold Medals," *Chicago Tribune*, 21 October 1968, C1.

42. Smith, *Silent Gesture*, 1.

43. The use of the term "Black Power" was standard throughout the black and white press. Cal Jacox of the African American newspaper, *Norfolk Journal and Guide*, observed that there were "numerous demonstrations of 'black power'" in Mexico City, specifically citing the "black power" gesture of Smith and Carlos. Cal Jacox, "From the Press Box: 'Black Power' in Mexico," *Norfolk Journal and Guide*, 26 October 1968, B25. The caption under a photo in a *New York Times* article was entitled, "Black Power Gesture." See "Some Negroes Threaten to 'Go Home' with Smith and Carlos," *New York Times*, 19 October 1968, 45. For other examples, see "Suspend 2 Negro Olympians: Black Power Show Causes Banishment," *Chicago Tribune*, 19 October 1968, 1; "Reaction to Expulsion Runs Gamut," *Washington Post*, 19 October 1968, C2; and "Black Stars Dominate Olympic Track Races," *Cleveland Call and Post*, 26 October 1968, 1A.

44. Smith, *Silent Gesture*, 22, 173.

45. George Strickler, "Oerter Wins 4th Discus Title in Row," *Chicago Tribune*, 16 October 1968, D1; Joseph M. Sheehan, "2 Black Power Advocates Ousted from Olympics," *New York Times*, 19 October 1968, 1. Smith and Carlos were not actually banished from the Olympic village. Having completed their race and not scheduled to run in either of the relays, they had already left the village to join their wives at the El Diplomatico Hotel. Smith, *Silent Gesture*, 172.

46. Sam Lacy, "Lacy 'Hits' Protest at Olympics," *Baltimore Afro-American*, 19 October 1968, 1; Smith, *Silent Gesture*, 169; Al Stilley, "Temple Wants Negro Voice on Olympic Committee," *Nashville Banner*, 19 October 1968, Temple Collection, TSU.

47. When asked about the meaning of their clenched fists on the victory stand, Evans replied that it was merely a salute and that "different people have different ways of saluting." Despite the fact that black berets were often worn by those associated with the black power movement, Evans told reporters they wore the berets because it was raining. "Evans Won His Medal for Blacks and Others," *Washington Post*, 19 October 1968, C1. Years later, he recalled thinking that he smiled so broadly on the victory stand because he thought those who disagreed with what he was doing would have a hard time shooting someone who was smiling. Steven Stern, *Fists of Freedom* (HBO Sports, 1999).

48. "Confusion, Shock Grip U.S. Squad after Pair Ousted," *Los Angeles Times*,

19 October 1968, A1; "Some Negro Athletes Threaten to 'Go Home' with Smith and Carlos," *New York Times*, 19 October 1968, 45; "Suspend 2 Negro Olympians," *Chicago Tribune*, 19 October 1968, 1. Some white Olympic athletes also expressed their shock at Smith and Carlos's treatment. Harold Connolly, four-time U.S. Olympic hammer-thrower who had long expressed support for the OPHR's agenda, thought there would be white athletes who also might choose to go home. And the all-white Harvard rowing team that had read a statement in support of the black athletic cause felt an obligation to their teammates to compete although disagreeing with the ouster of two track athletes.

49. Charles Maher, "A Czech Dilemma," *Los Angeles Times*, 24 October 1968, E2; Charles Maher, "Olympic Politics," *Los Angeles Times*, 22 October 1968, E2.

50. Kathleen Light, "Champ 'Had to Be First,'" *Atlanta Constitution*, 1 November 1968, 17, Temple Collection, TSU; Shirley Povich, "This Morning ... with Shirley Povich," 19 October 1968, C1.

51. Light, "Champ 'Had to Be First,'" Temple Collection, TSU.

52. "Maddox and Georgia Honor Wyomia Tyus," *New York Times*, 25 January 1969, 34; "Ga.'s Maddox Salutes Wyomia," *Baltimore Afro-American*, 1 February 1969, 8.

53. Bob Cohn and Steve Ball Jr., "The Elucidation of Wyomia," *Los Angeles Times*, 14 September 1969, M25; "Stork Set to Overtake Former Female Sprinter," *Baltimore Afro-American*, 10 July 1971, 8; "Names in the News," *Los Angeles Times*, 15 January 1972, E2.

54. In light of previous unsuccessful attempts at a pro track circuit, the real issue was whether the ITA could break even, let alone make money. Most sportswriters felt that the key to success was the money to be made through possible television rights. Neil Amdur, "Ryun and Seagren Among Stars Signed for 48-Meet Track Circuit," 15 November 1972, 55; Shirley Povich, "Watch Out for Cinders," *Washington Post*, 16 November 1972, D1; John Husar, "Pro Track's Road Show Rehearses in Pocatello," *Chicago Tribune*, 4 March 1973, B1.

55. "O'Neal Captures Pro's $500 Dash," *Washington Post*, 25 March 1973, D6; Neil Amdur, "Pro Track Draws 15,501 to Garden," *New York Times*, 7 June 1973, 59; "Jipcho Runs Fastest Pro Mile—3:56.6," *Los Angeles Times*, 30 May 1974, D1; "Milburn, Oldfield Triumph," *New York Times*, 28 March 1976, 170.

56. Neil Amdur, "Jipcho Mile Gives I.T.A. Some Hope," *New York Times*, 31 May 1974, 13.

57. Ron Reid, "Three for the Money," *Sports Illustrated*, 3 March 1975, 58; Howie Evans, "Fun and Games at Pro Track; Thrills, Too," *New York Amsterdam News*, 16 June 1973, D11; John Hall, "Two to Grow On," *Los Angeles Times*, 19 June 1974, C3; Walter and Iida, *Better than the Best*, 148.

58. Robert K. Barney, Stephen R. Wenn, and Scott G. Martyn, *Selling the Five Rings: The International Olympic Committee and the Rise of Olympic Commercialism* (Salt Lake City: University of Utah Press, 2004), 75, 104; Gary Deeb, "TV Sports' Legitimacy Is Waning," *Chicago Tribune*, 13 January 1976, C3.

59. Cahn, *Coming on Strong*, 250. The major "defeat" of the decade was the Equal Rights Amendment (ERA). When it passed both houses of Congress in 1972, the women's movement hoped that ratification by the required number of states would finally ensure an amendment to the U.S. Constitution that prevented discrimination

based upon gender. While thirty-four states quickly ratified the amendment, it fell three states short of the required three-fourths majority before the final, 30 June 1982 deadline.

60. Paula Giddings, *When and Where I Enter: The Impact of Black Women on Race and Sex in America* (New York: William and Morrow Co., 1984), 307–9.

61. In some events contested on "The Challenge of the Sexes," the women were given a handicap. For example, the woman golfer hit from different tees than the man, and the female swimmer swam freestyle while the male swam an individual medley. "Ryun Does 4:00.4 in Mile as Keino Fades to Third," *New York Times*, 229; Dave Distel, "Challenge of the Sexes: A Sports Smorgasbord," *Los Angeles Times*, 28 October 1975, D16A; Amdur, "Pro Track Draws 15,501 to Garden," 59.

62. Olga Connolly, "Destroying a Myth," *Los Angeles Times*, 25 September 1973, B1; John O'Connor, "TV Review," *New York Times*, 21 September 1973, 83. For articles playing up Riggs's age, see Mike Royko, "Even Silly Old Men Have Their Rights," *Los Angeles Times*, 22 September 1973, part III, 1; "For Love or Money," *New York Times*, 22 September 1973, 30.

63. For more on the evolution of the professional women's tour, see Festle, *Playing Nice*, 145–49.

64. Marilynn Preston, "Women in Sports: A 'Fad' Gains Big Yardage," *Chicago Tribune*, 27 January 1975, C5.

65. Jim Cour, "Fleet Ex-Olympian Wyomia Likes Motherhood and Track," *Baltimore Afro-American*, 5 April 1975, 9; Jerry Soifer, "Mother Runs Best … Some of the Time," *Los Angeles Times*, 9 May 1975, D1.

66. Cour, "Fleet Ex-Olympian Wyomia Likes Motherhood and Track," 9; George Solomon, "Clothed Streaker Decries Bare Press," *Washington Post*, 17 March 1974, D4; "Sprint Champ—5 Years Off and as Fast as Ever," *Christian Science Monitor*, 28 June 1974, F3; Kenneth Denlinger, "Now It Takes a Sermon," *Washington Post*, 27 June 1976, 39.

67. Paul H. Heyse, "An Historical Study of the Rise and Fall of the International Track Association" (M.A. thesis, Bowling Green State University, 1993), 53–58.

68. Gary Deeb, "Real 'Stars' in TV Booth," *Chicago Tribune*, 11 July 1976, K5; Margaret Roach, "A Women's Sports Unit Seeks an Increased Role," *New York Times*, 21 November 1976, 185; "The Olympics: Should We or Shouldn't We," *Los Angeles Times*, 29 April 1978, C2; Linda Kay, "Former Olympians Have New Challenge," *Chicago Tribune*, 15 July 1982, F3; "Opening to Stir Memory," *New York Times*, 24 July 1984, B11; "Sports People," *New York Times*, 10 April 1985, B14.

69. Connie Aitcheson, "Wyomia Tyus," *Sports Illustrated*, 14 July 2008. http://sportsillustrated.cnn.com/vault/article/magzine/MAG1141780/index.htm (accessed 30 August 2011).

70. Temple interview, 17 July 2007.

SIX

1. Jackie Joyner-Kersee, with Sonja Steptoe, *A Kind of Grace: The Autobiography of the World's Greatest Female Athlete* (New York: Warner Books, 1997), 223–25.

2. The other two athletes are Larisa Turchinskaya, who scored 7007 points in 1989, and Carolina Kluft, who scored 7001 in 2003 and 7032 in 2009. "Heptathlon

All-Time," IAAF.org: Home of World Athletics, http://www.iaaf.org/statistics/toplists/inout=o/age=n/season=0/sex=W/all=y/legal=A/disc=HEP/detail.html (accessed 9 March 2012).

3. Michael Janofsky, "America's Seventh Wonder of Games," *New York Times*, 3 August 1992, C1.

4. Jim Murray, "Could It Be That She Really Is the Finest Athlete in the World?" *Los Angeles Times*, 6 January 1987, OCB1.

5. Except where otherwise supplemented and noted, biographical information for Joyner-Kersee comes from her autobiography, *A Kind of Grace.*

6. Mike DiGoivanna, ""Joyner's Year of Happy Living," *Los Angeles Times*, 12 February 1985, D1; Joyner-Kersee, *A Kind of Grace*, 15.

7. Tony Kornheiser, "The Joyners: Long Before the Medals Came the Ties that Bind," *Washington Post*, 26 February 1987, D1.

8. Phil Hersh, "Joyners' Family Ties Help Olympic Push," *Chicago Tribune*, 18 June 1984, E17.

9. Cahn, *Coming on Strong*, 177–81.

10. Ibid., 248–49, 254–57; Wushanley, *Playing Nice and Losing*, 154–59. For a women's sport program that continued to flourish using "girls' rules" long past the passage of Title IX, see Max McElwain, *The Only Dance in Iowa: A History of Six-Player Girls' Basketball* (Lincoln: University of Nebraska Press, 2004).

11. Fred Mitchell, "Colleges Discover Prep Wonder Women," *Chicago Tribune*, 30 June 1980, D3; Grace Lichtenstein, *New York Times*, 8 February 1981, SM 7.

12. Joyner-Kersee, *A Kind of Grace*, 134.

13. The AAU had been the governing body for men's track and field since the late nineteenth century. It continues to promote mostly youth sport programs as a voluntary organization. For more on the Amateur Sports Act of 1978, see "The Amateur Sports Act of 1978," in *Law and Amateur Sports,* ed. Ronald J. Waicukauski (Bloomington: Indiana University Press, 1982), 114–60.

14. Alfred E. Senn, *Power, Politics, and the Olympic Games: A History of the Power Brokers, Events, and Controversies that Shaped the Games* (Champaign, IL: Human Kinetics, 1999), 176–81.

15. Senn, *Power, Politics, and the Olympic Games*, 197–98; Joyner-Kersee, *A Kind of Grace*, 170.

16. In the aftermath of her Olympic success, meet promoters in Europe were offering Griffith Joyner $30,000 just to compete. Michael Janofsky, "Griffith Joyner Runs at a Different Level," *New York Times*, 1 February 1989, 23; Senn, *Power, Politics, and the Olympic Games*, 192; Herb Schmertz, "Swan Song for U.S. Track and Field?," *New York Times*, 10 July 1988, S7; Thomas George, "Conspicuous Absences Revive a Debate," *New York Times*, 29 July 1989, C5.

17. For an explanation of the Jesse Owens Award, see "Florence Griffith-Joyner Wins 1989 Jesse Owens Award," *Los Angeles Sentinel*, 16 March 1989, A4.

18. Phil Hersh, "East St. Louis Roots Keep Joyner Growing," *Chicago Tribune*, 24 January 1985, C1; Barbara Lloyd, "Joyner-Kersee Is on Course for Even Greater Conquests," *New York Times*, 22 February 1988, C1.

19. Jim Murray, "Could It Be that She Really Is the Finest Athlete in the World?" *Los Angeles Times,* 6 January 1987, OCB1; Jerry Footlick, "Wilma Reserves Hurrying for the Cinders Only," Temple Collection, TSU.

20. Frank Litsky, "A Sprinter's Form Overtakes Fashion," *New York Times*, 18 July 1988, C3.

21. Phil Hersh, "Griffith-Joyner Nails 100-Meter Dash Final," *Chicago Tribune*, 18 July 1988, C1.

22. Phil Hersh, "2 World Marks Wear Joyner Name," *Chicago Tribune*, 17 July 1988, C1; Phil Hersh, "Griffith-Joyner Nails 100-Meter Dash Final," *Chicago Tribune*, 18 July 1988, C1; Frank Litsky, "Griffith Joyner Keeps Going," *New York Times*, 18 July 1988, A1; Christine Brennan, "With Her Speed, Scissors, She Cuts a Unique Figure," *Washington Post*, 22 July 1988, F1.

23. See Patricia Vertinsky and Gwendolyn Captain, "More Myth than History: American Culture and Representations of the Black Female's Athletic Ability," *Journal of Sport History* 25 (Fall 1998): 532–61. Vertinsky and Captain argue that Griffith Joyner's flaunting of a fashion steeped in hypersexuality was, indeed, her attempt to dismantle the dominant society's employment of race and Amazonian stereotypes. "Dressed in flamboyant, 'sexy' fashions," they write, "she uses the sports media to profile her power, beauty, and superb athletic skills and to demonstrate forms of resistance to old charges of masculinity." They note, however, that such a strategy edges dangerously close to exchanging a stereotype grounded in masculinity for one—the intensely alluring black female—steeped in sexuality (p. 553).

24. Kenny Moore, "On Top of the Worlds," *Sports Illustrated*, 14 September 1987, 18; Frederick C. Klein, "The Flo and Jackie Show," *Wall Street Journal*, 25 July 1988, 15; Phil Hersh, "Griffith-Joyner Nails 100-Meter Dash Final," *Chicago Tribune*, 18 July 1988, C1; Kenny Moore, "Heart and Seoul," *Sports Illustrated*, 1 August 1988, 22; Kenny Moore, "Get Up and Go," *Sports Illustrated*, 25 July 1988, 14.

25. Klein, "Flo and Jackie Show," 15; see also, Christine Brennan, "With Her Speed, Scissors, She Cuts a Unique Figure," *Washington Post*, 22 July 1988, F1.

26. Phil Hersh, "Olympics," *Chicago Tribune*, 30 September 1988, D3; Ken Denlinger, "Even in Uniform, Expect to See FloJo's Special Style," *Washington Post*, 18 September 1988, 103; Mike Downey, "Joyner Pulls a Fast One in Winning 100," *Los Angeles Times*, 25 September 1988, C1.

27. Christine Brennan, "The Relative Power of Griffith Joyner," *Washington Post*, 16 September 1988, E1.

28. Christine Brennan, "There are Sprinters, Then There's Griffith Joyner," 30 September 1988, D1; Joe Illuzzi, "Flo-Jo Propelled Track into 21st Century: Year in Review," *New Pittsburgh Courier*, 14 January 1989, 8.

29. Paula Span, "The Real Olympic Gold," *Washington Post*, 14 September 1988, C1.

30. George Vecsey, "Silence Was Not Golden," *New York Times*, 10 August 1987, C6; Howie Evans, "Jackie Joyner-Kersee Deserves $2M Bonus," *New York Amsterdam News*, 8 August 1992, 52; "Griffith Joyner Already Reaping Golden Benefits," *Los Angeles Sentinel*, 22 September 1988, B4; Michael Janofsky, "Griffith Joyner Runs at a Different Level," *New York Times*, 1 February 1989, A23.

31. Michael Janofsky, "Griffith Joyner Runs at a Different Level," *New York Times*, 1 February 1989, A23; Kenny Moore, "The Spoils of Victory," *Sports Illustrated*, 10 April 1989, 50; "Griffith Joyner Already Reaping Golden Benefits," *Los Angeles Sentinel*, 22 September 1988, B4.

32. Joyner-Kersee, *A Kind of Grace*, 220.

33. Diana Nyad argued that Griffith Joyner was the best female athlete of the year, over her sister-in-law and tennis player Steffi Graf. Diana Nyad, "This Year's Top Female Athlete Is …" *New York Times*, 2 October 1988, S15.

34. Christine Brennan, "Joyner-Kersee Has Slow Start in Heptathlon," *Washington Post*, 23 July 1990, B3; "Joyner-Kersee Off Her Record Pace," *New York Times*, 23 July 1990, C5; Michael Janofsky, "Still Racing with the Wind," *New York Times*, 9 June 1991, S1; Thomas Boswell, "Joyner-Kersee Alone Atop Olympus," *Washington Post*, 3 August 1992, A1.

35. For some examples of Kersee's predictions and his confession of pushing his wife toward the record, see "Record Start by Joyner-Kersee," *New York Times*, 23 September 1988, D24; John Geis, "Joyner-Kersee's Long Jump Is 2nd Best in World This Year," *Washington Post*, 17 June 1990, B3A; Thomas Boswell, "Joyner-Kersee Alone Atop Olympus," *Washington Post*, 3 August 1992, A1.

36. Sally Jenkins, "Lewis and Johnson, 1 on 1 with History," *Washington Post*, 16 September 1988, E1; Randy Harvey, "9.79 in 100 of Century, Johnson Smashes Lewis and Record," *Los Angeles Times*, 24 September 1988, B1; Phil Hersh, "IOC Strips Johnson of medal in 100," *Chicago Tribune*, 27 September 1988, D1.

37. Tony Kornheiser, "Johnson's Dramatics Stole the Olympic Show and Spirit," *Washington Post*, 3 October 1988, B1.

38. Fred Hiatt, "U.S., Soviets Pledge Combined Efforts to Rout Drugs," *Washington Post*, 3 October 1988, B13.

39. Frank Deford, "Olympian Changes," *Sports Illustrated*, 10 October 1988, 126.

40. Phil Hersh, "Olympics," *Chicago Tribune*, 30 September 1988, D3.

41. Tony Kornheiser, "Johnson's Dramatics Stole the Olympic Show and Spirit," *Washington Post*, 3 October 1988, B1; Kenny Moore, "The Spoils of Victory," *Sports Illustrated*, 10 April 1989, 50; Fred Hiatt, "U.S., Soviets Pledge Combined Efforts to Rout Drugs," *Washington Post*, 3 October 1988, B13.

42. Congress, Senate, Committee on Foreign Relations, *Steroids in Amateur and Professional Sports—The Medical and Social Costs of Steroid Abuse*, 101st Cong., 1st sess., 3 April 1989, 8; Christine Brennan, "Ashford: 2 Women Gold Medalists Used Steroids," *Washington Post*, 4 April 1989, D1; Christine Brennan, "Drug Claims Denied by Griffith Joyner," *Washington Post*, 22 September 1989, D1.

43. Christine Brennan, "Drug Claims Denied by Griffith Joyner," *Washington Post*, 22 September 1989, D1.

44. Congress, Senate, Committee on Foreign Relations, *Steroids in Amateur and Professional Sports—The Medical and Social Costs of Steroid Abuse*, 101st Cong., 1st sess., 3 April 1989, 12, 15.

45. Sports and media mogul Ted Turner began the Goodwill Games in 1986 as a way to try to ease tensions during latter years of the Cold War period. They initially occurred every four years on an in-between cycle to the Olympic games. Following the end of the Cold War era, the focus of the games shifted toward youth initiatives. The final Goodwill Games took place in Brisbane, Australia, in 2001. "Where the World's Best Athletes Prove It," http://www.goodwillgames.com/ (accessed 6 April 2012).

46. Joyner-Kersee did attempt a comeback in the long jump when she trained and competed at the 2000 Olympic trials. But her best jump was almost three feet short of her own American record and left her in sixth place. See Bob Baum, "Track and Field Ending Painful for Jackie Joyner-Kersee," *New Pittsburgh Courier*, 19 August 2000, 7.

Ross Atkin, "Jackie Joyner-Kersee Makes Tracks to Basketball," *Christian Science Monitor*, 28 October 1996, 12; Jere Longman, "For Joyner-Kersee, the Longest Jump," *New York Times*, 17 October 1996, B15; Jere Longman, "A Queen Retires the Way She Ruled, With Class," *New York Times*, 21 July 1998, C5; Jere Longman, "Johnson Leads Record 4x400; Joyner-Kersee Triumphs," *New York Times*, 23 July 1998, C1; William C. Rhoden, "Taking One Last Leap on Two Steady Feet," *New York Times*, 26 July 1998, SP10. On Joyner-Kersee's passion for working with children, see Paul Simon, "Athlete Honors Her Heritage," *New Pittsburgh Courier*, 19 November 1988, 5; Howie Evans, "Joyner-Kersee Mobbed at Games," *New York Amsterdam News*, 11 February 1989, 60; and Chico Renfroe, "Sports of the World: Jackie Joyner-Kersee Tells Eastlake Meadows Girls 'Always Try Your Best,'" *Atlanta Daily World*, 25 May 1990, 5.

47. Kenny Moore, "The Spoils of Victory," *Sports Illustrated*, 10 April 1989, 50; Joe Illuzzi, "Flojo Says Goodbye," *New Pittsburgh Courier*, 11 March 1989, 6; Jere Longman, "Florence Griffith Joyner, 38, Champion Sprinter, Is Dead," *New York Times*, 22 September 1998, C23; Jim Slater, "Flo-Jo Seeks a Dynamic NBA Uniform," *New Pittsburgh Courier*, 15 July 1989, 5; "Griffith Joyner Retires from Track and Field," *Los Angeles Sentinel*, 2 March 1989, B2.

48. The comment regarding Roger Maris refers to the urban legend baseball commissioner Ford Frick created when he suggested that an asterisk would be placed next to Maris's name if he needed more than 154 games to pass Babe Ruth's single season homerun record during the 1961 season. Major League Baseball had played 154 games during Ruth's career, as opposed to the 162 that they began playing in 1961 with the addition of two new teams. While it took Maris 162 to break the record, an asterisk was never placed next to his record.

49. Jere Longman, "Florence Griffith Joyner, 38, Champion Sprinter, Is Dead," *New York Times*, 22 September 1998, C23.

50. Tim Layden, "Florence Griffith Joyner (1959–98)," *Sports Illustrated*, 28 September 1998, 6.

51. Tim Layden, "Farewell to Jjk," *Sports Illustrated*, 3 August 1998, 29; Jere Longman, "A Queen Retires the Way She Ruled: With Class," *New York Times*, 21 July 1998, C5.

EPILOGUE

1. Andre Higgs, "Crystal Ball Proves Accurate for Devers-Roberts," *Los Angeles Sentinel*, 15 September 1988, B2; Kenny Moore, "Dash to Glory," *Sports Illustrated*, 10 August 1992, 18, 19.

2. William Gildea, "'Happy Games' Produce More Controversy than Contentment," *Washington Post*, 6 August 1992, B9; Michael Janofsky, "U.S. Sprinter Said to Have Named Drug Users," *New York Times*, 4 August 1992, B10; Kenny Moore, "Dash to Glory," *Sports Illustrated*, 10 August 1992, 18, 19; Christine Brennan, "Devers, Christie Dash to Olympic Gold in 100," *Washington Post*, 2 August 1992, D1; William Drozdiak, "Olympics Battle Chemical Imbalance," *Washington Post*, 7 August 1992, A1; Roger Lowenstein, "Earvin Wasn't the Only Magic at Games," *Wall Street Journal*, 10 August 1992, A7.

3. Mark Gray, "Sports of the World: Torrence's Brilliance Overshadowed by Her Mouth," *Atlanta Daily World*, 9 August 1992, 8.

4. Jere Longman, "Bailey Sets 100 Mark; Devers in Photo Finish," *New York Times*, 28 July 1996, S1; Darryl D. Lassiter, "Gail Devers Takes Gold in Women's 100 Meters," *Atlanta Daily World*, 8 August 1996, 5.

5. Thomas Hackett, "Speed Demon," *New York Times*, 14 May 2000, SM162.

6. Ibid.

7. Harvey Araton, "Marion Jones Needs a Quiet Understanding," *New York Times*, 24 September 2000, S1.

8. Juliet Macur, "After Tribulations Come the Trials," *New York Times*, 9 July 2004, D1.

9. Liz Robbins, "Jones Is Said to Have Used Banned Drugs in Sydney," *New York Times*, 23 July 2004, D1.

10. Duff Wilson and Michael S. Schmidt, "In Plea, Track Star Will Admit to Using Steroids, Lawyers Say," *New York Times*, 5 October 2007, A1; Lynn Zinser and Michael Schmidt, "Jones Admits to Doping and Enters Guilty Plea," *New York Times*, 6 October 2007, D1; Lynn Zinser, "Jones's Soaring Career Has Turned into Cautionary Tale," *New York Times*, 11 January 2008, D5.

11. For more on Venus and Serena Williams, including racism they have encountered on the tour, see R. Pierre Rodgers and Ellen B. Drogin Rodgers, "'Ghetto Cinderellas': Venus and Serena Williams and the Discourse of Racism," in *Out of the Shadows: A Biographical History of African American Athletes,* ed., David K. Wiggins (Fayetteville: University of Arkansas Press, 2006), 353–71.

12. Robin Finn, "Defying Her Sport's Logic, A Tennis Prodigy Emerges," *New York Times*, 7 September 1997, http://www.lexisnexis.com.mutex.gmu.edu/hottopics/inacademic (accessed 2 April 2012); David Kelly, "Tennis: Father of the Ghetto Queens," *Belfast Telegraph*, 30 June 2006, http://www.lexisnexis.com.mutex.gmu.edu/hottopics/inacademic/ (accessed 2 April 2012); John Gardner, "Ghetto Blaster," *Daily Record*, 20 June 1997, http://www.lexisnexis.com.mutex.gmu.edu/hottopics/inacademic/ (accessed 2 April 2012); Josh Young, "Sport Takes Its Bumps in High-Pressure Match," *Washington Times*, 6 September 1997, http://www.lexisnexis.com.mutex.gmu.edu/hottopics/inacademic (accessed 2 April 2012); Filip Bondy, "It's Advantage Venus, Says Once & Future Coach," *New York Daily News*, 7 September 1997, http://www.lexisncxis.com.mutex.gmu.edu/hottopics/inacademic (accessed 2 April 2012).

13. Filip Bondy, "It's Advantage Venus, Says Once & Future Coach," *New York Daily News*, 7 September 1997, http://www.lexisnexis.com.mutex.gmu.edu/hottopics/inacademic (accessed 2 April 2012); Darrell Fry, "Women's Tour Must Deal with Its Prejudices," *St. Petersburg Times*, 8 September 1997, http://www.lexisnexis.com.mutex.gmu.edu/hottopics/inacademic (accessed 2 April 2012).

14. Serena Williams, with Daniel Paisner, *On the Line* (New York: Grand Central Publishing, 2009), 65–82. For news coverage on the Indian Wells incident, see "Unpopular: Williams Booed after Indian Wells Win," *Sports Illustrated*, http://sportsillustrated.cmm.com/tennis/news/2001/03/17/williams_win_ap/ (accessed 29 March 2012); "Avoiding the Issue: Sisters Venus, Serena Are Reluctant Rivals on the Court," *Sports Illustrated*, 24 March 2001, http://sportsillustrated.cmm.com/tennis/news/2001/03/17/williams_rivalry_ap (accessed 29 March 2012); "Williams's Dad Alleges Racism," *Washington Post,* 27 March 2001, D2; Saeed Shabazz, "Race and Sports: Father of Serena and Venus Williams Denounces Racial Epithets," *Final Call*, 10 April 2001, http://www.finalcall.com/nationalwilliams04–10–2001.htm (accessed

29 March 2012); Allison Samuels, "Life with Father," *Newsweek*, 2 July 2001, http://www.lexisnexis.com.mutex.gmu.edu/hottopics/inacademic/ (accessed 29 March 2012); Richard Williams Laments His Tennis Star Daughters Are Subjected to Racial Slurs; Denies Rigging Their Matches," *Jet*, 9 April 2001, http://www.lexisnexis.com.mutex.gmu.edu/hottopics/inacademic/ (accessed 29 March 2012).

15. Marc Peyser and Allison Samuels, "Venus and Serena against the World," *Newsweek*, 24 August 1998, http://www.lexisnexis.com.mutex.gmu.edu/hottopics/inacademic (accessed 2 April 2012).

16. David Carr, "Network Condemns Remarks by Imus," *New York Times*, 7 April 2007, B7; Lisa Olson, "Imus' Remarks Deserve a Harsher Penalty," *New York Times*, 11 April 2007, F2.

17. Vanessa Williams, "Tied Up in Knots over Golden Girl's Tresses," *Washington Post*, 3 August 2012, C1.

18. Helen Chandler, "The highs and lows of the Williams sisters' wardrobe," CNN, 26 May 2010, http://www.cnn.com/2010/SPORT/tennis/05/25/tennis.venus.serena.fashion/index.html (accessed 21 June 2013).

SELECTED BIBLIOGRAPHY

PRIMARY SOURCES

Manuscript Collections

Dr. Hubert A. Eaton Sr. Private Papers, 1938–1991, Manuscript Collection, William Madison Randall Library, The University of North Carolina at Wilmington, Wilmington, NC.

Althea Gibson Collection, The Southeastern Regional Black Archives Research Center and Museum, Florida A&M University, Tallahassee, FL.

The Ed Temple Collection, Special Collections and Archives, Brown-Daniel Library, Tennessee State University, Nashville, TN.

Alice Coachman Davis Papers, Special Collections, John Hope and Aurelia Elizabeth Franklin Library, Fisk University, Nashville, TN.

Autobiographies

Carlos, John, with Dave Zirin. *The John Carlos Story*. Chicago: Haymarket Books, 2011.

Eaton, Hubert A. *Every Man Should Try*. Wilmington, NC: Bonaparte Press, 1984.

Gibson, Althea. *I Always Wanted to Be Somebody*. New York: Harper & Brothers, 1958.

Gibson, Althea, with Richard Curtis. *So Much to Live For*. New York: G. P. Putnam's Sons, 1968.

Joyner-Kersee, Jackie, with Sonja Steptoe. *A Kind of Grace: The Autobiography of the World's Greatest Female Athlete*. New York: Warner Books, 1997.

Rudolph, Wilma. *Wilma: The Story of Wilma Rudolph*. New York: New American Library, 1977.

Smith, Tommie, with David Steele. *Silent Gesture: The Autobiography of Tommie Smith*. Philadelphia: Temple University Press, 2007.

Temple, Ed, with B'Lou Carter. *Only the Pure in Heart Survive: Glimpses into the Life of a World Famous Olympic Coach*. Nashville: Broadman Press, 1980.

Washington, Booker T. *Up from Slavery, One Hundred Great Masterpieces of American Literature*. Franklin Center, PA: The Franklin Library, 1977.

Williams, Serena, with Daniel Paisner, *On the Line*. New York: Grand Central Publishing, 2009.

Books

Owens, Ross C. *History of Athletics at Tuskegee.* n. p., n.d.

Tyus, Wyomia. *Inside Jogging for Women: A Comprehensive Guide to Running for Fun and Fitness.* Chicago: Contemporary Books, 1978.

Interviews

Childs, J. Bernard. Interview by Pamela Grundy of Bowling Green, Virginia, 4 October 2003.

Davis, Alice Coachman. Interview by author, 10 February 2003, Tuskegee, Alabama. Tape recording.

Eaton, Hubert A., Jr., M.D. Interview by author, 14 July 2005, Wilmington, North Carolina. Tape recording.

Temple, Ed. Interview by author, 17 July 2007, Nashville, Tennessee. Tape recording.

Periodicals

Albany Herald, 1945–1948.

American Lawn Tennis, 1950.

Atlanta Constitution, 1948–1995.

Atlanta Daily World, 1932–1996.

Baltimore Afro-American, 1931–1975.

Boston Globe, 1939–1958.

California Eagle, 1940–1961.

Chicago Defender, 1924–1968.

Chicago Tribune, 1939–1988.

Christian Science Monitor, 1974–1996.

Cleveland Call and Post, 1968–1974.

Crisis, 1920–1928.

Ebony, 1957–1958.

Greensboro Daily News, 1934.

Hartford Courant, 1970–1976.

Jet, 1957–1958, 2001.

Life, 1948–1958.

Los Angeles Sentinel, 1988–1989.

Los Angeles Times, 1960–1988.

New Pittsburgh Courier, 1988–2000.

New York Age, 1917–1958.

New York Amsterdam News, 1932–1992.

New York Times, 1922–2008.

Norfolk Journal and Guide, 1934–1968.

Opportunity, 1920–1928.

Philadelphia Tribune, 1925–1971.

Pittsburgh Courier, 1923–1966.

Sports Illustrated, 1957–2008.

Time, 1957–1958.

Wall Street Journal, 1968–1992.

Washington Post, 1940–2012.

SECONDARY SOURCES

Books and Journal Articles

Baker, William J. *Jesse Owens: An American Life*. New York: Free Press, 1986.

Baldwin, Davarian L. *Chicago's New Negroes: Modernity, the Great Migration, and Black Urban Life*. Chapel Hill: University of North Carolina Press, 2007.

Baltzell, E. Digby. *Sporting Gentlemen: Men's Tennis from the Age of Honor to the Cult of the Superstar*. New York: Free Press, 1995.

Barney, Robert K., Stephen R. Wenn, and Scott G. Martyn. *Selling the Five Rings: The International Olympic Committee and the Rise of Olympic Commercialism*, revised edition. Salt Lake City: University of Utah Press, 2004.

Bass, Amy. *Not the Triumph but the Struggle: The 1968 Olympics and the Making of the Black Athlete*. Minneapolis: University of Minnesota Press, 2002.

Bell, R. J. "Competing Identities: Representations of Black Female Sporting Body from 1960 to the Present." Ph.D. diss., Bowling Green State University, 2008.

Berger, Michele Tracy, and Kathleen Guidroz, eds. *The Intersectional Approach: Transforming the Academy through Race, Class, and Gender*. Chapel Hill: University of North Carolina Press, 2009.

Boehm, Lisa Krissoff. *Making a Way Out of No Way*. Jackson: University Press of Mississippi, 2009.

Cahn, Susan K. *Coming on Strong: Gender and Sexuality in Twentieth-Century Women's Sport*. Cambridge, MA: Harvard University Press, 1994.

Capeci, Dominic J., Jr., and Martha Wilkerson. "Multifarious Hero." *Journal of Sport History* 10 (Winter 1983): 5–25.

Captain, Gwendolyn. "'Enter Ladies and Gentlemen of Color': Gender, Sport, and the Ideal of the African American Manhood and Womanhood during the Late Nineteenth and Early Twentieth Centuries." *Journal of Sport History* 18 (Spring 1991): 81–102.

Carroll, John M. *Fritz Pollard: Pioneer in Racial Advancement*. Urbana: University of Illinois Press, 1998.

Cohen, Greta L, ed. *Women in Sport: Issues and Controversies*. Newbury Park, CA: Sage Publications, 1993.

Crenshaw, Kimberlé. "Mapping the Margins: Intersectionality, Identity Politics, and Violence against Women of Color." *Stanford Law Review* 14 (1991): 1241–99.

Davis, Laurel R. "The Articulation of Difference: White Preoccupation with the Question of Racially Linked Genetic Differences among Athletes." *Sociology of Sport Journal* 7 (1990): 179–87.

Davis, Michael B. *Black American Women in Olympic Track and Field: A Complete Illustrated Reference*. Jefferson, NC: MacFarland, 1992.

Decker, Ed. "Alice Coachman." In *Contemporary Black Biography: Profiles from the International Black Community*, 32 vols., edited by Shirelle Phelps. Detroit: Gale Research, 1992.

Djata, Sundiata. *Blacks at the Net: Black Achievement in the History of Tennis. Sports and Entertainment*. Syracuse, NY: Syracuse University Press, 2006.

Dorinson, Joseph, and Joram Warmund, eds. *Jackie Robinson: Race, Sports, and the American Dream*. Armonk, NY: M. E. Sharpe, 2002.

Dudziak, Mary L. *Cold War, Civil Rights: Race and the Image of American Democracy*. Princeton, NJ: Princeton University Press, 2000.

Edmonds, Anthony O. *Joe Louis*. Grand Rapids: Eerdmans, 1973.

English, Douglas. "Sam Lacy." In *Twentieth-Century American Sportswriters*, edited by Richard Orodenker. Detroit: Gale Research, 1996.

Favor, J. Martin. *Authentic Blackness: The Folk in the New Negro Renaissance*. Durham, NC: Duke University Press, 1999.

Felix, Stephanie Y. "Committed to Their Own: African American Women Leaders in the YWCA. The YWCA of Germantown, Philadelphia, Pennsylvania, 1870–1970." Ph.D. diss., Temple University, 1999.

Festle, Mary Jo. *Playing Nice: Politics and Apologies in Women's Sports*. New York: Columbia University Press, 1996.

———. "'Jackie Robinson without the Charm': The Challenges of Being Althea Gibson." In *Out of the Shadows: A Biographical History of African American Athletes*, edited by David K. Wiggins. Fayetteville: University of Arkansas Press.

Fligstein, Neil. *Going North: Migration of Blacks and Whites from the South, 1900–1950*. New York: Academic Press, 1981.

Fredrickson, George M. *The Black Image in the White Mind: The Debate on Afro-American Character and Destiny, 1817–1914*. New York: Harper and Row, 1971.

Gaines, Kevin G. *Uplifting the Race: Black Leadership, Politics and Culture in the Twentieth Century*. Chapel Hill: University of North Carolina Press, 1996.

Gems, Gerald R. "Blocked Shot: The Development of Basketball in the African American Community of Chicago." *Journal of Sport History* 22 (Summer 1995): 135–48.

Gerber, Ellen, Jan Felshin, Pearl Berlin, and Waneen Wyrick. *The American Woman in Sport*. Reading, MA: Addison-Wesley Publishing Company, 1974.

Giddings, Paula. *When and Where I Enter: The Impact of Black Women on Race and Sex in America*. New York: William Morrow and Company, 1984.

Gilmore, Al-Tony. "The Myth, Legend, and Folklore of Joe Louis: The Impressions of Sport on Society." *South Atlantic Quarterly* 82 (Summer 1983): 256–68.

Gissendanner, Cindy Himes. "African-American Women in Competitive Sport, 1920–1960." In *Women, Sport, and Culture*, edited by Susan Birrell and Cheryl L. Cole. Champaign, IL: Human Kinetics, 1994.

———. "African American Women Olympians: The Impact of Race, Gender, and Class Ideologies, 1932–1968." *Research Quarterly for Exercise and Sport* 67 (June 1996): 172–82.

Gottlieb, Peter. *Making Their Own Way: Southern Blacks' Migration to Pittsburgh, 1916–1930*. Urbana: University of Illinois Press, 1987.

Gray, Clayton, and Yanick Rick Lamb. *Born to Win: The Authorized Biography of Althea Gibson*. Hoboken, NJ: John Wiley & Sons, 2004.

Gregory, James N. *The Southern Diaspora: How the Great Migration of Black and White Southerners Transformed America*. Chapel Hill: University of North Carolina Press, 2005.

Grossman, James R. *Land of Hope: Chicago, Black Southerners, and the Great Migration*. Chicago: University of Chicago Press, 1989.

Grundy, Pamela. "Ora Washington: The First Black Female Athletic Star." In *Out of the Shadows: A Biographical History of African American Athletes*, edited by David K. Wiggins. Fayetteville: University of Arkansas Press, 2006.

———. "From Amazons to Glamazons: The Rise and Fall of North Carolina Women's Basketball, 1920–1960." *Journal of American History* 87 (June 2000): 112–46.

Grundy, Pamela, and Susan Shackelford. *Shattering the Glass: The Remarkable History of Women's Basketball*. Chapel Hill: University of North Carolina Press, 2005.

Guttmann, Allen. *Women's Sports: A History*. New York: Columbia University Press, 1991.

———. *From Ritual to Record: The Nature of Modern Sports*. New York: Columbia University Press, 1978.

Guy-Sheftall, Beverly. *Daughters of Sorrow: Attitudes toward Black Women, 1880–1920, Black Women in United States History*. Brooklyn: Carlson Publishing, 1990.

Hahn, Steven. *A Nation under Our Feet: Black Political Struggles in the Rural South from Slavery to the Great Migration*. Cambridge, MA: Belknap Press of Harvard University Press, 2003.

Hale, Grace Elizabeth. *Making Whiteness: The Culture of Segregation in the South, 1890–1940*. New York: Vintage Books, 1998.

Hall, M. Ann. *Feminism and Sporting Bodies: Essays on Theory and Practice*. Champaign, IL: Human Kinetics, 1996.

Hamilton, Marybeth. *When I'm Bad, I'm Better: Mae West, Sex, and American Entertainment*. Berkeley: University of California Press, 1995.

Hargreaves, Jennifer. *Sporting Females: Critical Issues in the History and Sociology of Women's Sports*. London: Routledge, 1994.

Harlan, Louis R. "Booker T. Washington and the Politics of Accommodation." In *Black Leaders of the Twentieth Century*, edited by John Hope Franklin and August Meier. Urbana: University of Illinois Press, 1982.

Harley, Sharon, and Rosalyn Terborg-Penn, eds. *The Afro-American Woman: Struggles and Images, Series in American Studies*. Port Washington, NY: Kennikat Press, 1978.

Hartmann, Douglas. *Race, Culture, and the Revolt of the Black Athlete: The 1968 Olympic Protests and Their Aftermath*. Chicago: University of Chicago Press, 2003.

Heyse, Paul H. "An Historical Study of the Rise and Fall of the International Track Association." M.A. thesis., Bowling Green State University, 1993.

Higginbotham, Evelyn Brooks. *Righteous Discontent: The Women's Movement in the Black Baptist Church: 1880–1920*. Cambridge, MA: Harvard University Press, 1993.

Hine, Darlene Clark. *Black Women in White: Racial Conflict and Cooperation in the Nursing Profession, 1890–1950*. Bloomington: Indiana University Press, 1989.

———. *Culture, Consciousness, and Community: The Making of an African American Women's History*. Greenville, NC: East Carolina University, 1994.

———. *Hine Sight: Black Women and the Re-Construction of American History*. Brooklyn: Carlson Publishing, 1994.

Hine, Darlene Clark, William C. Hine, and Stanley Harrold. *African Americans: A Concise History*, Volume Two: Since 1865. Upper Saddle River, NJ: Prentice Hall, 2004.

Hine, Darlene Clark, and Kathleen Thompson. *A Shining Thread of Hope: The History of Black Women in America*. New York: Broadway Books, 1998.

Hine, Darlene Clark, Wilma King, and Linda Reed, eds. *"We Specialize in the Wholly Impossible": A Reader in Black Women's History*. Brooklyn: Carlson Publishing, 1995.

Hoberman, John. *Darwin's Athletes: How Sport Has Damaged Black America and Preserved the Myth of Race*. Boston: Houghton Mifflin Company, 1997.

Howell, Reet, ed. *Her Story in Sport: A Historical Anthology of Women in Sports*. West Point, NY: Leisure Press, 1982.

Huggins, Nathan Irvin. *Harlem Renaissance*. London: Oxford University Press, 1971.

Hull, Gloria T., Patricia Bell Scott, and Barbara Smith, eds. *All the Women Are White, All the Blacks Are Men, but Some of Us Are Brave*. New York: City University of New York, 1982.

Hutchinson, George. *The Harlem Renaissance in Black and White*. Cambridge, MA: Belknap Press of Harvard University Press, 1995.

Jones, Jacqueline. *Labor of Love, Labor of Sorrow: Black Women, Work, and the Family, from Slavery to the Present*. New York: BasicBooks, 1985.

Kane, Mary Jo, and Susan L. Greendorfer. "The Media's Role in Accommodating and Resisting Stereotyped Images of Women in Sport." In *Women, Media and Sport: Challenging Gender Values*, edited by Pamela J. Creedon, 28–44. Thousand Oaks, CA: Sage, 1994.

Kasson, John F. *Amusing the Million: Coney Island at the Turn of the Century*. New York: Hill & Wang, 1978.

Kelley, Robin D. G. "'We Are Not What We Seem': Rethinking Black Working-Class Opposition in the Jim Crow South." *Journal of American History* 80 (June 1993): 75–112.

Lansbury, Jennifer H. "'The Tuskegee Flash' and 'the Slender Harlem Stroker': Black Women Athletes on the Margin." *Journal of Sport History* 28 (Summer 2001): 233–52.

———. "Alice Coachman: Quiet Champion of the 1940s." In *Out of the Shadows: A Biographical History of African American Athletes*, edited by David K. Wiggins, 146–61. Fayetteville: University of Arkansas Press, 2006.

Lenskyj, Helen Jefferson. *Out on the Field: Gender, Sport, and Sexualities*. Toronto: Women's Press, 2003.

Lettering, David Lewis. *When Harlem Was in Vogue*. New York: Alfred A. Knopf, 1981.

Levine, Lawrence W. *Highbrow/Lowbrow: The Emergence of Cultural Hierarchy in America*. Cambridge, MA: Harvard University Press, 1986.

———. *Black Culture and Black Consciousness: Afro-American Thought from Slavery to Freedom*. New York: Oxford University Press, 1977.

Liberti, Rita. "'We Were Ladies, We Just Played Basketball Like Boys': African American Womanhood and Competitive Basketball at Bennett College, 1928–1942." *Journal of Sport History* 26 (Fall 1999): 567–84.

Lichtenstein, Grace. "Net Profits." In *Nike Is a Goddess: The History of Women in Sports*, edited by Lissa Smith. New York: Atlantic Monthly Press, 1998.

Lomax, Michael E. "Black Baseball's First Rivalry: The Cuban Giants versus the Gorhams of New York and the Birth of the Colored Championship." *Sport History Review* 28 (November 1997): 134–45.

McElwain, Max. *The Only Dance in Iowa: A History of Six-Player Girls' Basketball*. Lincoln: University of Nebraska Press, 2004.

Mead, Chris. *Champion: Joe Louis, Black Hero in White America*. New York: Scribner's, 1985.

Miller, Patrick B. "To 'Bring the Race along Rapidly': Sport, Student Culture, and Educational Mission at Historically Black Colleges during the Interwar Years." *History of Education Quarterly* 35 (1995): 111–33.

Miller, Patrick B., and David K. Wiggins, ed. *Sport and the Color Line: Black Athletes and Race Relations in Twentieth-Century America*. New York: Routledge, 2004.

Morton, Patricia. *Disfigured Images: The Historical Assault on Afro-American Women, Contributions in Afro-American and African Studies*. New York: Greenwood Press, 1991.

Oglesby, Carole A., ed. *Women and Sport: From Myth to Reality*. Philadelphia: Lea & Febiger, 1978.

Piess, Kathy. *Cheap Amusements: Working Women and Leisure in Turn-of-the-Century New York*. Philadelphia: Temple University Press, 1986.

Plowden, Martha Ward. *Olympic Black Women*. Gretna, LA: Pelican Publishing Co., 1996.

Powers, Madelon. *Faces Along the Bar: Lore and Order in the Workingman's Saloon, 1870–1920*. Chicago: University of Chicago Press, 1998.

Pride, Armistead S., and Clint C. Wilson II. *A History of the Black Press*. Washington, DC: Howard University Press, 1997.

Rader, Benjamin G. *American Sports: From the Age of Folk Games to the Age of Televised Sports*. Englewood Cliffs, NJ: Simon & Schuster, 1983.

Rampersad, Arnold. *Jackie Robinson: A Biography*. New York: Alfred A. Knopf, 1997.

Robertson, Nancy. *Christian Sisterhood, Race Relations, and the YWCA, 1906–1946*. Urbana: University of Illinois Press, 2007.

Robnett, Belinda. *How Long? How Long?: African American Women and the Struggle for Civil Rights*. New York: Oxford University Press, 1997.

Rosenzweig, Roy. *Eight Hours for What We Will: Workers and Leisure in an Industrial City, 1870–1920*. Cambridge: Cambridge University Press, 1983.

Roulhac, Nellie Gordon. *Jumping over the Moon: A Biography of Alice Coachman Davis*. Philadelphia: the author, 1993.

Sailes, Gary A. "The Myth of Black Sports Supremacy." *Journal of Black Studies* 21 (June 1991): 480–87.

Sammons, Jeffrey T. *Beyond the Ring: The Role of Boxing in American Society*. Urbana: University of Illinois Press, 1988.

———. "'Race' and Sport: A Critical Examination." *Journal of Sport History* 21 (Fall 1994): 203–78.

Schoenfeld, Bruce. *The Match: Althea Gibson and Angela Buxton: How Two Outsiders—One Black, the Other Jewish—Forged a Friendship and Made Sports History*. New York: HarperCollins Publishers, 2004.

Schraf, Mark W. "Wendell Smith." In *Twentieth-Century American Sportswriters*, edited by Richard Orodenker. Detroit: Gale Research, 1996.

Sernett, Milton C. *Bound for the Promised Land: African American Religion and the Great Migration*. Durham, NC: Duke University Press, 1997.

Shapiro, Joseph P. *No Pity: People with Disabilities Forging a New Civil Rights Movement*. New York: Random House, 1993.

Simons, William. "Jackie Robinson and the American Mind: Journalistic Perceptions of the Re-Integration of Baseball." *Journal of Sport History* 12 (Spring 1985): 39–64.

Smith, Doug. *Whirlwind, the Godfather of Black Tennis: The Life and Times of Dr. Robert Walter Johnson*. Washington, DC: Blue Eagle Publishing Co., 2004.

Smith, Lissa, ed. *Nike Is a Goddess: The History of Women in Sports*. New York: Atlantic Monthly Press, 1998.

Smith, Maureen M. *Wilma Rudolph: A Biography*. Westport, CT: Greenwood Press, 2006.

Smith, Suzanne E. *Dancing in the Street: Motown and the Cultural Politics of Detroit.* Cambridge, MA: Harvard University Press, 1999.

Smith, Yvonne. "Women of Color in Society and Sport." *Quest* 44 (Summer 1992): 228–50.

Stanley, Gregory Kent. *The Rise and Fall of the Sportswoman: Women's Health, Fitness, and Athletics, 1860–1940.* New York: Peter Lang, 1996.

Suggs, Welch. *A Place on the Team: The Triumph and Tragedy of Title IX.* Princeton, NJ: Princeton University Press, 2005.

Thomas, Damion. "'The Good Negroes': African-American Athletes and the Cultural Cold War, 1945–1968." Ph.D. diss, University of California, 2002.

Tricard, Louise Mead. *American Women's Track and Field: A History, 1895 through 1980.* Jefferson, NC: McFarland & Company, 1996.

Tuck, Stephen G. N. *Beyond Atlanta: The Struggle for Racial Equality in Georgia, 1940–1980.* Athens: University of Georgia Press, 2001.

Tucker, Sherrie. *Swing Shift: "All-Girl" Bands of the 1940s.* Durham, NC: Duke University Press, 2000.

Turrini, Joseph M. "It Was Communism versus the Free World: The USA-USSR Dual Track Meet Series and the Development of Track and Field in the United States, 1958–1985." *Journal of Sport History* 28 (Fall 2001): 427–71.

Tygiel, Jules. *Baseball's Great Experiment: Jackie Robinson and His Legacy, Expanded ed.* New York: Oxford University Press, 1997.

———. *Extra Bases: Reflections on Jackie Robinson, Race, and Baseball History.* Lincoln: University of Nebraska Press, 2002.

Verbrugge, Martha. *Active Bodies: A History of Women's Physical Education in Twentieth-Century America.* Oxford: Oxford University Press, 2012.

Vertinsky, Patricia, and Gwendolyn Captain. "More Myth Than History: American Culture and Representations of the Black Female's Athletic Ability." *Journal of Sport History* 25 (Fall 1998): 532–61.

von Eschen, Penny. *Satchmo Blows up the World: Jazz Ambassadors Play the Cold War.* Cambridge, MA: Harvard University Press, 2004.

Wall, Cheryl A. *Women of the Harlem Renaissance.* Bloomington: University of Indiana Press, 1995.

Walter, John C., and Malina Iida, eds. *Better than the Best: Black Athletes Speak, 1920–2007.* Seattle: University of Washington Press, 2010.

Ward, Brian. *Radio and the Struggle for Civil Rights in the South.* Gainesville: University Press of Florida, 2004.

Weisenfeld, Judith. *African American Women and Christian Activism: New York's Black YWCA, 1905–1945.* Cambridge, MA: Harvard University Press, 1997.

White, Deborah Gray. *Too Heavy a Load: Black Women in Defense of Themselves.* New York: W. W. Norton & Company, 1999.

Wieisbrot, Robert. *Freedom Bound: A History of America's Civil Rights Movement.* New York: Norton, 1990.

Wiggins, David K. "Wendell Smith, the Pittsburgh Courier-Journal, and the Campaign to Include Blacks in Organized Baseball, 1933–1945." *Journal of Sport History* 10 (Summer 1983): 5–29.

———. *Glory Bound: Black Athletes in a White America.* Syracuse, NY: Syracuse University Press, 1997.

Wiggins, David K., ed. *Out of the Shadows: A Biographical History of African American Athletes.* Fayetteville: University of Arkansas Press, 2006.

Wiggins, David K., ed. *Sport in America: From Wicked Amusement to National Obsession.* Champaign, IL: Human Kinetics, 1995.

Wiggins, David K., and Patrick B. Miller. *The Unlevel Playing Field: A Documentary History of the African American Experience in Sport.* Urbana: University of Illinois Press, 2003.

Wigginton, Russell T. *The Strange Career of the Black Athlete: African Americans and Sports.* Westport, CT: Praeger Publishers, 2006.

Wilkerson, Isabel. *The Warmth of Other Suns: The Epic Story of America's Great Migration.* New York: Random House, 2010.

Williams, Linda D. "Sportswomen in Black and White: Sports History from an Afro-American Perspective." In *Women, Media and Sport: Challenging Gender Values,* edited by Pamela J. Creedon, 45–66. Thousand Oaks, CA: Sage, 1994.

Wilson, James F. *Bulldaggers, Pansies, and Chocolate Babies: Performance, Race and Sexuality in the Harlem Renaissance.* Ann Arbor: University of Michigan Press, 2010.

Wintz, Cary D. *Black Culture and the Harlem Renaissance.* Houston: Rice University Press, 1988.

Wolcott, Victoria. *Remaking Respectability: African American Women in Interwar Detroit.* Chapel Hill: University of North Carolina Press, 2001.

Wolseley, Roland E. *The Black Press, U.S.A., 2d ed.* Ames: Iowa State University Press, 1990.

Woodward, C. Vann. *The Strange Career of Jim Crow, 3d rev. ed.* New York: Oxford University Press, 1974.

Wushanley, Ying. *Playing Nice and Losing: The Struggle for Control of Women's Intercollegiate Athletics, 1960–2000.* Syracuse, NY: Syracuse University Press, 2004.

Films

Stern, Steven. *Fists of Freedom.* HBO Sports, 1999.

Websites

CNN. Chandler, Helen. "The highs and lows of the Williams sisters' wardrobe," 26 May 2010. Accessed 21 June 2013. http://www.cnn.com/2010/SPORT/tennis/05/25/tennis.venus.serena.fashion/index.html.

Drake Relays. "Drake Relays: Archive-History." Accessed 5 February 2008. http://www.drakerelays.org/archive.htm.

Final Call. Shabazz, Saeed. "Race and Sports: Father of Serena and Venus Williams Denounces Racial Epithets," *Final Call*, 10 April 2001. Accessed 29 March 2012. http://www.finalcall.com/nationalwilliams04–10–2001.htm.

Goodwill Games. "Where the World's Best Athletes Prove It." Accessed 6 April 2012. http://www.goodwillgames.com/.

IAAF.org: Home of World Athletics. "Heptathlon All-Time." Accessed 9 March 2012. http://www.iaaf.org/statistics/toplists/inout=o/age=n/season=0/sex=W/all=y/legal=A/disc=HEP/detail.html.

LexisNexis. Bondy, Filip. "It's Advantage Venus, Says Once & Future Coach," *New York Daily News*, 7 September 1997. Accessed 2 April 2012. http://www.lexisnexis.com.mutex.gmu.edu/hottopics/inacademic.

———. Finn, Robin. "Defying Her Sport's Logic, A Tennis Prodigy Emerges," *New York Times*, 7 September 1997. Accessed 2 April 2012. http://www.lexisnexis.com.mutex.gmu.edu/hottopics/inacademic.

———. Fry, Darrell. "Women's Tour Must Deal with Its Prejudices," *St. Petersburg Times*, 8 September 1997. Accessed 2 April 2012. http://www.lexisnexis.com.mutex.gmu.edu/hottopics/inacademic.

———. Gardner, John. "Ghetto Blaster," *Daily Record*, 20 June 1997. Accessed 2 April 2012. http://www.lexisnexis.com.mutex.gmu.edu/hottopics/inacademic/.

———. Kelly, David. "Tennis: Father of the Ghetto Queens," *Belfast Telegraph*, 30 June 2006. Accessed 2 April 2012. http://www.lexisnexis.com.mutex.gmu.edu/hottopics/inacademic/.

———. Peyser, Marc, and Allison Samuels. "Venus and Serena against the World," *Newsweek*, 24 August 1998. Accessed 2 April 2012. http://www.lexisnexis.com.mutex.gmu.edu/hottopics/inacademic.

———. "Richard Williams Laments His Tennis Star Daughters Are Subjected to Racial Slurs; Denies Rigging Their Matches," *Jet*, 9 April 2001. Accessed 29 March 2012. http://www.lexisnexis.com.mutex.gmu.edu/hottopics/inacademic/.

———. Samuels, Allison. "Life with Father," *Newsweek*, 2 July 2001. Accessed 29 March 2012. http: //www.lexisnexis.com.mutex.gmu.edu/hottopics/inacademic/.

———. Young, Josh. "Sport Takes Its Bumps in High-Pressure Match," *Washington Times*, 6 September 1997. Accessed 2 April 2012. http://www.lexisnexis.com.mutex.gmu.edu/hottopics/inacademic.

Millrose Games. "Millrose Games: Millrose Decade by Decade, 1927–1938." Accessed 5 February 2008. http://www.millrose-games.com/2008/history/decade1928–1937.htm.

———. "Millrose Games: History." Accessed 22 February 2008. http://www.millrose-games.com/2008/history/.

The New Georgia Encyclopedia. "Sports & Recreation: Wyomia Tyus." Accessed 8 March 2012. http://www.georgiaencyclopedia.org/nge/Article.jsp?id=h-836.

Sports Illustrated. "Unpopular: Williams Booed after Indian Wells Win," *Sports Illustrated*. Accessed 29 March 2012. http://sportsillustrated.cmm.com/tennis/news/2001/03/17/williams_win_ap/.

———. "Avoiding the Issue: Sisters Venus, Serena Are Reluctant Rivals on the Court," *Sports Illustrated*, 24 March 2001. Accessed 29 March 2012. http://sportsillustrated.cmm.com/tennis/news/2001/03/17/williams_rivalry_ap.

Sports Illustrated Vault. Aitcheson, Connie. "Wyomia Tyus," *Sports Illustrated*, 14 July 2008. Accessed 30 August 2011. http://sportsillustrated.cnn.com/vault/article/magzine/MAG1141780/index.htm.

The Penn Relays. "The Penn Relays: History of the Penn Relays." Accessed 5, 7 February 2008. http://www.pennathletics.com/ViewArticle.dbml?DB_OEM_ID=1700&KEY=&ATCLID=236852&SPID=559&SPSID=10779.

Top 100 Sports Illustrated Women. "Wyomia Tyus, Track and Field." Accessed 27 February 2012. http://sportsillustrated.cnn.com/siforwomen/top_100/43/.

Tuskegee University. "Tuskegee University: Choir History." Accessed 10 July 2007. http://www.tuskegee.edu/Global/story.asp?S=1131717.

Wyomia Tyus Biography. "Wyomia Tyus—Early Training." Accessed 1 July 2011. http://sports.jrank.org/pages/4979/Tyus-Wyomia-Early-Training.html.

INDEX

Abbott, Cleve, 47–48, 53–59, 113, 121, 202, 243
Abbott, Jessica, 54, 56, 57, 59, 60, 74
ABC, 180, 187
Adams, Katrina, 238
Adidas, 210
affirmative action, 181
Afghanistan invasion, 207
African American community: black athlete protests, 162–71, 173–77, 188; civil rights movement, 6, 104–5, 112, 152–53, 157–60, 162–64, 174, 177, 188; competitive sport appropriateness and respectability, 12, 34–38, 53, 65; Great Migration, 15–16, 78; integration impacts, 98–99; outdoor exercise and sport opportunities, 12–13, 18; racial pride and assimilation, 34–35, 42, 44; social expectations, 12–13, 231–32; sports associations, 12–13, 74, 75, 76–80, 85; supportive environments, 4–7, 231–32; tennis clubs, 21, 22, 23, 24, 40, 41; women's basketball, 27–42; women's tennis, 76, 80–87, 112; Young Women's Christian Association (YWCA), 18–20, 23. *See also* specific athlete; track and field
African American Cosmopolitan Tennis Club, 79–80, 85
African American Ideal and Turf Tennis Clubs of New York, 21
African American Interstate Tournament, 21
Afro-American Studies Center, 178
agriculture: African American farmers, 14–15, 78; pest infestations, 14, 15
Alabama, 159

Albany, Georgia, 3, 43, 47, 66, 69, 70–71, 140
Albany Herald, 43–44, 69–70, 71, 132
Albany State Teacher's College, 66, 70, 71
Albany State University, 72
Alice Coachman Day, 43–44, 70, 71
Alice Coachman Foundation, 72
Ali, Muhammad, 163, 165
All-American Women's Track and Field Team, 3, 59, 63
Allen, Leslie, 238
All-Philly Girls' Basketball Team (1932), 35
Althea Gibson Sings , 109
amateur athletics, 24, 192–93, 202–3, 206–7, 209–10, 217
Amateur Athletic Union (AAU): loss of governance, 206; Sullivan Award, 116; summer track meets, 197–98; women's basketball, 28; women's track and field events, 48, 49, 50–52, 56, 123, 126, 140, 156, 162, 164
Amateur Sports Act (1978), 206
Amazon analogy, 242
American Basketball League, 226
American Lawn Tennis, 94
American Physical Education Review, 49
American Tennis Association (ATA): Althea Gibson, 74, 75, 76, 77–78, 80, 89–101, 103, 111; association growth, 89–90; collegiate players, 92; Cosmopolitan Tennis Club, 80; future directions, 95–96, 99; Hubert Eaton, 82, 89; importance, 92; integration impacts, 98–99; internal conflicts, 90–91, 98–99; leadership roles, 24; national championships, 22–23, 41; Ora Washington, 22–23,

40, 41; origins, 21; player develop-
ment programs, 98–99; Robert
Johnson, 82, 89
anabolic steroids, 225–26. *See also*
performance-enhancing drug use
apartheid policies, 165
Arkansas, 104
Ashe, Arthur, 76, 112
Ashford, Evelyn, 213, 224–25, 227
Associated Press, 210
Association of Intercollegiate Athletics
for Women (AIAW), 202
Athlete of the Year, 210
athletic clubs, 17
athletic negligee, 214–15
Atlanta Constitution, 68–69, 176
Atlanta Daily World, 38, 234, 235
Atlanta, Georgia, 38, 56, 140, 158
Atlanta Olympics (1996), 220, 226, 235
Austin, Walter, 92
Australia, 172

Bailes, Margaret, 169, 172
Bailey, Cora, 47
Baker, Bertram, 93, 96–97, 98–99, 103
Baker, Beverly, 95
Ballard, Lula, 23, 25, 41
Balter, Sam, 141
Baltimore Afro-American: Alice
Coachman, 63–64, 71; Althea
Gibson, 96, 100; black athlete
protests, 174; and major league base-
ball, 102–3; Ora Washington, 39,
40; Philadelphia Tribunes, 32, 33;
Wyomia Tyus, 172, 185
Baltimore, Maryland, 23
banned substances. *See* performance-
enhancing drug use
Barcelona Olympics (1992), 220, 232,
233
Barnes, Margaret, 57
baseball, 22
Basie, William James "Count", 70
basketball: Alice Coachman, 59–60;
Althea Gibson, 79; competitive sport
appropriateness and respectability,
34–38; feminine image stereotype,

26–28, 36–38; girls' rules, 29;
Hornets–Tribunes championship
series, 31–32; Jackie Joyner-Kersee,
200–204, 226; Ora Washington,
11–13, 25–26, 29–39; rough
play/dirty tactics, 35; rules
of the game, 26–27, 37; Wilma
Rudolph, 119–20, 122, 125; women
athletes, 26–29; Wyomia Tyus, 154
Basket Ball for Women, 27
Baskin, Gordon, 218
Battle of the Sexes (television broadcast),
183
Beamon, Bob, 165, 175, 179
Belafonte, Harry, 140
Bennett College, 36–38, 53
Berlin Olympics (1936), 72
Beverly Hills High School, 188
bicycle face, 18
bicycling, 17–18
Biden, Joseph, 224
Biloxi, Mississippi, 38
Bird, Larry, 239
Birmingham, Alabama, 158
B. J. *See* Jones, Barbara
black athlete protests, 162–71, 173–77,
188
black colleges and universities: competitive sport programs, 5, 34–38, 45,
47, 56–61, 92; recruitment efforts,
202, 203; sport scholarships, 9, 45;
tennis teams, 90–92; women's track
and field events, 53
black community: black athlete protests,
162–71, 173–77, 188; civil rights
movement, 6, 104–5, 112, 152–53,
157–60, 162–64, 174, 177, 188;
competitive sport appropriateness
and respectability, 12, 34–38, 53,
65; Great Migration, 15–16, 78;
integration impacts, 98–99; outdoor
exercise and sport opportunities, 12–
13, 18; racial pride and assimilation,
34–35, 42, 44; social expectations,
12–13, 231–32; sports associations,
12–13, 74, 75, 76–80, 85; supportive environments, 4–7, 231–32; ten-

National Collegiate Athletic Association (NCAA), 202–3
National Collegiate Championships, 205
National Football League (NFL), 6
National Guard, 104
National Indoor Championships, 93, 99, 140, 164
National Intercollegiate Championships, 91
National Organization for Women (NOW), 181
National Outdoor Championships, 162, 164, 169
National Track and Field Hall of Fame, 72, 148, 188
National Women's Track and Field Committee, 50
NBC, 180
Negro athlete versus *black* athlete, 163–64, 175
Netter, Mildrette, 172
network television coverage, 180, 182–83, 187
New Broadway Athletic Club, 32
Newell, Lucy, 57
New Jersey Athletic Association, 109
New Orleans, Louisiana, 38
Newsgirls. *See* Lady Tribunes
Newsweek, 222, 241
New York Age, 62
New York Amsterdam News, 100–101
New York Athletic Club, 165
New York, New York, 16, 62, 70, 140
New York State Open tennis tournament, 80
New York Times: Alice Coachman, 68; Edith McGuire, 157; Florence Griffith Joyner, 218, 227; Jackie Joyner-Kersee, 211, 217; Marion Jones, 235; Olympic Games, 128–29, 148, 157; Soviet female athletes, 161; Wilma Rudolph, 138, 148; women's track and field coverage, 50, 68, 128–29, 138, 148, 157; Wyomia Tyus, 157
New York University, 52
Nicklaus, Jack, 184

Nineteenth Amendment (U.S. Constitution), 19, 182
Noel, Ken, 165
nonviolent resistance, 152, 158, 162
Norfolk Journal and Guide, 81
Norman, Peter, 172, 173
Novotna, Jana, 239–40
Nunn, Glynis, 191, 208–9

O'Brien, Parry, 142
Ocean City, New Jersey, 48
Ogilvie, Bruce, 186
O'Hara, Michael, 179, 180, 187
Oldfield, Brian, 180, 183
Olympic Games: Alice Coachman, 45, 65–71, 130; black athlete protests, 165–66, 173–77, 188; black women athletes, 244; boycotts, 207–8; eligibility requirements, 209; Florence Griffith Joyner, 212–13, 215–16, 227; Gail Devers, 232–33, 235; Gwen Torrance, 233–35; Jackie Joyner-Kersee, 191–92, 193, 210–11, 215–16, 220, 226; Jesse Owens, 4, 71–72; Marion Jones, 235–38; medal count, 207–8; performance-enhancing drug use, 221–22, 225, 236–38; political aspect, 177; television coverage, 143, 180; Tennessee State University women's track program, 121, 124, 126; Venus and Serena Williams, 239; Wilma Rudolph, 4, 115–16, 124–25, 127, 130, 136–37; women's track and field events, 3, 50, 52, 115–16, 124–27, 130, 135–37, 156–57, 207–9; Wyomia Tyus, 151, 156–57, 171–72, 176–77
Olympic Hall of Fame, 188
Olympic Project for Human Rights (OPHR), 165–68, 170, 172–73, 189
Omega wind gauge, 213–14
O'Neal, Lacey, 179, 183, 186
Onteora Club, 52
Orangeburg, South Carolina, 38
Oregon Track Club, 169
Ottum, Bob, 170

outdoor exercise and sport opportunities, 9, 12–13, 17–18, 22, 184
Owens, Jesse, 4, 71–72, 163, 174–75

paddle tennis, 79
Palo Alto, California, 147
Pan-American games, 164
Paris, France, 50
Parks, Rosa, 104, 157
Pasarell, Charles, 241
Patterson, Audrey, 67
Patterson, Inez, 30, 32, 33, 35
peanut oil, 64, 117, 214
Penn Relays, 141, 146
Pennsylvania Tennis Open, 23
performance-enhancing drug use, 194, 221–28, 232–34, 236–38
Perkins, Mildred, 35
Perry, Bob, 102
Perry, Leila, 57, 61, 62, 72
pest infestations, 14, 15
Peters, Roumania, 75, 80, 82
Petty, Christine Evans, 57, 58, 64, 65, 130
Philadelphia Inquirer, 136
Philadelphia, Pennsylvania, 15, 16, 19–21, 29–35, 41–42, 123, 140
Philadelphia Tribune, 30, 31, 35, 41
Philadelphia Tribunes, 12, 30, 31–33, 35–38, 40
physical educators, 27–29, 45, 51–52, 60, 127–28, 202
Pickett, Tidye, 52, 56
Pittsburgh Courier, 30, 36, 40, 62, 63, 100, 102
play days, 27, 29, 38, 51
Playground Association of America, 18
Police Athletic League, 76, 79, 81
Polish track stars, 161
Ponca City, Oklahoma, 123
Poston, Ted, 76
Povich, Shirley, 176–77
Prairie View College, 91
President's Council on Physical Fitness, 227
press. *See* black newspapers; sportswriters; white newspapers

Press, Irina, 161
Press, Tamara, 134–35, 161
Primatene, 192
Princeton University, 163
professional track circuit, 152, 178–80, 182–87, 192–93, 209
professional women's basketball, 226
Providence, Rhode Island, 66
Purifoy, Lillie, 57

Quicksteppers (basketball team), 30–31

race/racism: Alice Coachman, 71; black athletes, 6–7, 34–35, 162–64, 175; black women athletes, 5–7, 12–13, 44, 45, 60, 73, 188–89, 244; Joyner sisters-in-law, 221; Martin Luther King, Jr., 158; northern racism, 16; performance-enhancing drug use, 194, 221–28, 232–34, 236–38; racial pride and assimilation, 34–35, 42, 44; tennis, 74, 94; track and field, 132; United States Lawn Tennis Association (USLTA), 93–94; Venus and Serena Williams, 239–42; women's movement, 181–82; Wyomia Tyus, 188–89
racial advocacy. *See* Gibson, Althea
racial barriers: Alice Coachman, 44, 61; Althea Gibson, 44, 74, 75–76, 93–96, 103, 105, 239; black athletes, 6–7, 12; black women athletes, 231–39; Wilma Rudolph, 140; women's tennis, 238; women's track and field, 130–32
racial stereotypes. *See* gender and racial stereotypes
racial uplift, 88–89
radiation treatments, 233
radical activism, 152–53, 162–65
radio broadcasts, 22
Radio City Music Hall, 62
Rainey, Joe, 29, 32
Randolph-Macon Women's College, 49
Rankin Club, 30
Reagan, Ronald, 208
Reemes, Jackie, 100–101

56, 57–58; United States–Soviet Union dual track meets, 131–32, 134–35, 147, 156, 160–61; women athletes, 47–52, 116–17, 146. *See also* Coachman, Alice; Griffith Joyner, Florence; Joyner-Kersee, Jackie; Rudolph, Wilma; Tyus, Wyomia

Track and Field News, 210

Tribunes, 12, 30, 31–33, 35–38, 40

Trickett, Vicki, 141

triple jump, 175, 209, 213

Truman, Harry S, 70, 104

Tuskegee Concert Choir, 62

Tuskegee flash. *See* Coachman, Alice

Tuskegee Institute: Alice Coachman, 43, 44–45, 47–48, 54–62; basic philosophies, 54–55; competitive sport programs, 34, 45, 47, 53–54, 56–65, 203; educational and cultural focus, 54–56, 61–62; male–female athlete camaraderie, 65; Philadelphia Tribunes team tour, 38; Roumania Peters, 75; sport scholarships and programs, 9; tennis teams, 91; track and field events, 47, 56, 57–58, 120

Tuskegee Relays, 47, 56, 57–58, 120

Tuskegee Tigerettes, 43, 46, 48, 52, 56–65, 73, 130

Tygiel, Jules, 103

Tyler, Dorothy, 3, 68

Tyus, Willie and Marie, 154

Tyus, Wyomia: awards, 161–62, 188; basketball teams, 154; black athlete protests, 176–77; celebrity status, 177, 185, 186; childhood, 154–55; civil rights movement impacts, 166–68, 176–77, 189; earnings gaps, 184; gender and racial stereotypes, 243; invitational track and field meets, 162, 186; marriage and family, 178, 185, 188; national championships, 156; Olympic Games, 151, 156–57, 171–72, 176–77; Olympic medals, 151, 157, 172; Olympic trials, 169; outdoor exercise and sport opportunities, 154–55;

personality, 189; post-track career years, 178, 187–88; professional track circuit, 152, 178–80, 182–87, 209; retirement, 151–52, 177–78; Sullivan Award, 161; at Tennessee State University, 155–56; track and field career, 150–57, 160, 161–62, 164–65, 169; as track coach, 188; world records, 156, 160, 161–62, 172, 179

Ullyot, Joan, 185

United States–British Commonwealth track meet, 164

United States Lawn Tennis Association (USLTA), 75, 78, 93–95, 96, 98–99, 101, 112, 238

United States–Soviet Union dual track meets, 131, 134–35, 147, 156, 160–61

University of California at Berkeley, 26, 163

University of California at Los Angeles, 9, 178, 201–6, 209, 212, 232

University of California at San Francisco, 185

University of Georgia, 232

University of Illinois, 201, 203

University of Michigan, 82

University of North Carolina, 166

University of Pennsylvania, 141

University of Wisconsin, 201, 203

upper-class African Americans, 12, 20–21, 76–77, 80–81, 83, 87, 90, 111. *See also* American Tennis Association (ATA); Eaton, Hubert A.; Johnson, Robert W. (Whirlwind)

upper-class women: basketball, 29; sport appropriateness, 28–29, 51; sport opportunities, 17–18, 26; white feminine image stereotype, 51, 112

U.S. National Championships, 93–95, 96, 100–101, 102, 108, 156, 205–6

U.S. National Figure Skating Champions, 244

U.S. Olympic Committee, 47, 137, 165, 173–75, 206, 207

U.S. Olympic Hall of Fame, 72, 148
U.S. Open Tennis, 75, 76, 238–39
U.S. State Department, 101–2, 130

Vassar College, 17, 49, 52
Vecsey, George, 217
Vogue, 237
voting rights, 159–60
Voting Rights Act (1965), 104, 160, 182

Walker, Art, 175
Walker, Buddy, 79, 81
Walker, Mabel, 66
walking competitions, 48
Wall Street Journal, 214–15, 234
Walsh, Stella, 51, 52, 60, 63, 141
Wanamaker Mile, 141
Ward Baking Company, 109
Ward, George, 197–98, 200
war industries, 16
Washington, Booker T., 54–55, 88
Washington, D.C., 62, 123, 140
Washington, James Thomas (Tommy),
    14–15
Washington, Kenny, 6
Washington, Laura Young, 14
Washington, Ora: athletic career, 11–
    13, 41–42; basketball career, 11–13,
    25–26, 29–39; biographical back-
    ground, 13–16; celebrity status, 13,
    74; gender and racial stereotypes,
    243; outdoor exercise and sport
    opportunities, 8, 18; post-retirement
    years, 41; retirement announcement,
    39, 40–41; tennis championships,
    11, 22–23, 25, 33–34, 39–41
Washington Post, 176–77, 216, 220, 225
Washington Times, 242
Waterbury, Connecticut, 43, 48
Waterhouse-Friderichsen syndrome, 204
Wayne, John, 109
Webber, Harry, 39
Weir, Reginald, 93, 99
Wellesley College, 17, 49
Wembley Stadium, 3
West Virginia State College, 91
White House, 62

white middle-class femininity, 134, 138,
    146, 149
white newspapers: Alice Coachman,
    67, 68–70, 131–32; black athlete
    protests, 176–77; black women ath-
    letes, 7; Florence Griffith Joyner,
    215–16, 225; Jackie Joyner-Kersee,
    193, 210, 217, 220–21; Ora
    Washington, 12; sexism, 117, 128–
    29, 149, 212; track and field cover-
    age, 43–44, 63, 68–70, 71, 74,
    116–17, 130, 131–32, 135–37,
    142–46; Wilma Rudolph, 137–39,
    142–46, 149; Wyomia Tyus, 176–77
white racist groups, 159
white women: feminine image stereo-
    type, 17, 24, 26, 34, 42, 45, 51,
    107; gender stereotypes, 5–6, 61;
    team sports, 12, 26, 30; tennis, 12,
    25, 241; track and field athletes, 44,
    60–61, 73, 116, 132; women's
    movement, 153, 180–85; Young
    Women's Christian Association
    (YWCA), 20
Whitworth, Kathy, 184
Wilberforce College, 75
Wilkins, Roy, 140
Williams, Diane, 225
Williams, Lucinda, 127, 132, 153
Williams, Richard, 239, 240, 241
Williams, Venus and Serena, 76, 112,
    232, 238–42, 244–45
Williston Industrial High School, 87
Wills, Helen, 22, 24, 25
Wilma Rudolph Foundation, 148
Wilmington, Delaware, 22
Wilmington, North Carolina, 82, 83,
    87, 88
Wilson, Diana, 164
Wimbledon: amateur events, 24; Helen
    Wills, 22; Louise Brough, 95; Venus
    Williams, 238–39. *See also* Gibson,
    Althea
wind-aided records, 127, 213–14, 216,
    227
Winfrey, Oprah, 237
Winter, Bud, 163